Praise for *The Road to Khartoum*:

"Mr. Chenevix Trench's biography is very efficient." —*New York Review of Books*

"The author offers the firm authority that comes from a careful and common-sense analysis of all available evidence. He manages to make General Charles Gordon's eccentric behavior understandable in rational terms. To do so is surely no small achievement." —*Newsweek*

THE ROAD TO
KHARTOUM
A Life of
General Charles Gordon

CHARLES CHENEVIX TRENCH

Carroll & Graf Publishers, Inc.
New York

CONTENTS

PREFACE

General Gordon has been portrayed, or caricatured, as hero, martyr, evangelist, rebel, imperial pro-consul and anti-imperialist. He chain-smoked, he was at times a poseur, and a heavy drinker. He may have had homosexual tendencies, sternly suppressed. Lord Cromer described him as 'mad or half-mad', Gladstone was warned that he had 'a small bee in his bonnet'. He changed his opinions so flagrantly and so often that, whatever views are held of him, evidence for them can be found in his voluminous correspondence. The British press and public believed him to be the greatest living expert on the Sudan; but he knew no Arabic, was ignorant of civil administration, and was out of his depth as Governor-General. On his last mission to Khartoum he wholly misjudged the situation, military and political – a misunderstanding which contributed as much as Gladstone's procrastination to the final tragedy.

With all his imperfections, he was (as Gladstone conceded) a hero of heroes; a magnificent fighting soldier; a man inspired by a deep, if highly idiosyncratic, religious faith, of extraordinary energy and fertility of mind, who delighted always in being at variance with conventional opinion; a much loved, infuriating eccentric.

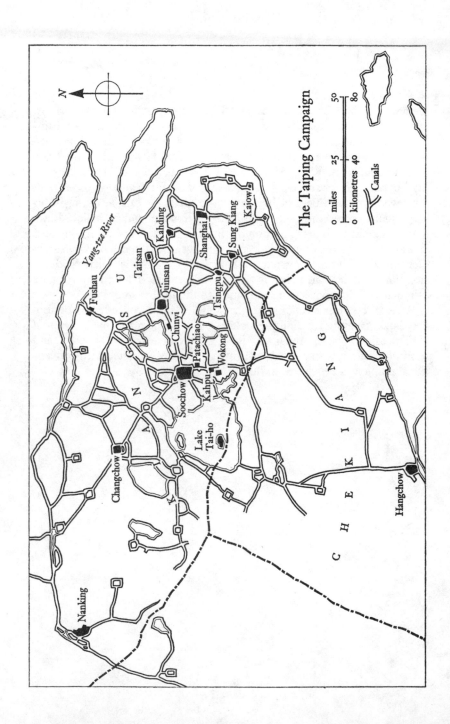

The Taiping Campaign

Canals

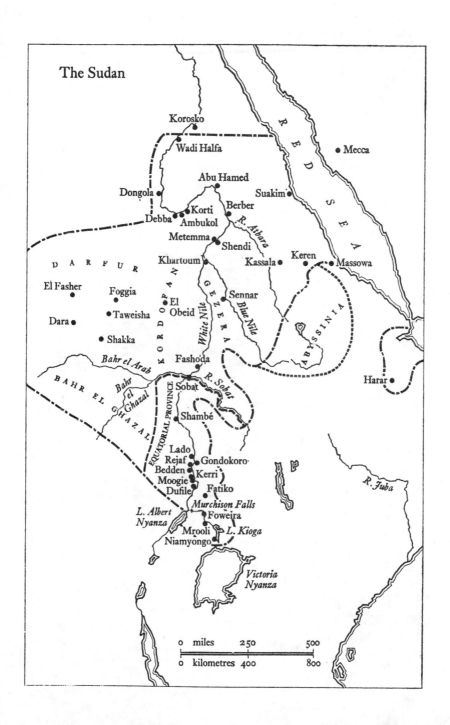

The Sudan

Korosko
Wadi Halfa
Mecca
Abu Hamed
Dongola
Suakim
Korti
Berber
Debba
Ambukol
R. Atbara
Metemma
Shendi
Khartoum
Kassala
Keren
Massowa
D A R F U R
El Fasher
Foggia
El
Obeid
Sennar
GEZERA
White Nile
Blue Nile
Dara
Taweisha
KORDOFAN
ABYSSINIA
Shakka
Harar
Bahr el Arab
Fashoda
Bahr
el
Ghazal
R. Sobat
BAHR EL
GHAZAL
Sobat
EQUATORIAL PROVINCE
Shambé
Lado
Rejaf
Gondokoro
R. Juba
Bedden
Kerri
Moogie
Dufile
Fatiko
Murchison Falls
L. Albert
Nyanza
Foweira
Mrooli
L. Kioga
Niamyongo
Victoria
Nyanza

R E D   S E A

o   miles   250   500
o   kilometres 400   800

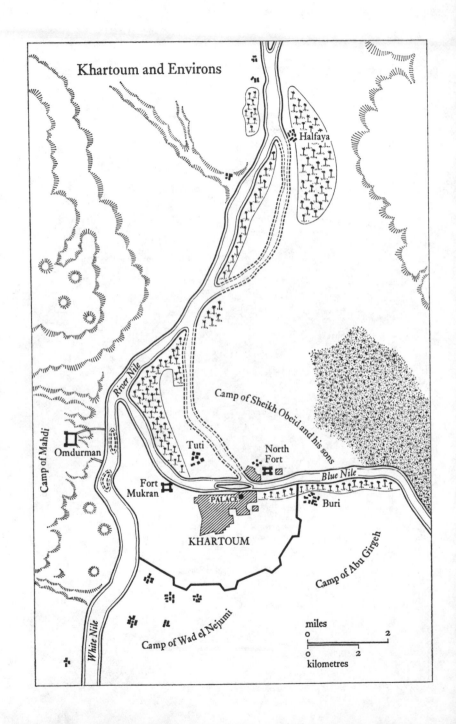

Khartoum and Environs

Halfaya

River Nile

Camp of Sheikh Obeïd and his sons

Camp of Mahdi

Omdurman

Tuti

North Fort

Blue Nile

Fort Mukran

PALACE

Buri

KHARTOUM

Camp of Abu Girgeh

White Nile

Camp of Wad el Nejumi

miles
0   2

0   2
kilometres

1

♠ CHARLEY GORDON

The boy was born at Woolwich on 28 January 1833, fourth son of Henry William Gordon, Royal Artillery, who rose to be a lieutenant-general, and fathered eleven children on Elizabeth, daughter of Samuel Enderby, a London merchant with a stake in Antarctic exploration.

The family followed the flag to Dublin, Leith Fort, Corfu and back to Woolwich. At the age of ten Charley went to Taunton School, spending his holidays at Woolwich. His upbringing was typical of those families, allied to, but not of, the landed gentry, with neither great wealth nor great influence, whose clever sons found careers in the Church, the Civil Service and the Law, while the not so clever sons entered the Army, the Navy or the service of the East India Company.

He was a naughty boy, ruthless and resourceful. It was no fun being at enmity with Charley Gordon. The Commandant of the Military Academy found his house overrun with mice which had been transferred from the Gordon residence. Any visitor so imprudent as to leave his top-hat in the Gordons' front hall would be well advised, before putting it on, to make sure that the little fellow had not used it as a cuspidor. With powerful water squirts and crossbows (made by friendly Arsenal workmen) he and his brothers waged aggressive guerilla war against the Royal Military Academy. There was in him something of a bully, and an unpredictability which disconcerted even his nearest and dearest. His father confessed that in the very bosom of his family he often felt as though he were sitting on a powder-keg.

Gordon made no great mark at Taunton School, except for an unusual skill at map-making. At the age of sixteen he entered the Military Academy.

He shone at field-sketching and fortifications, but in other respects his conduct was unsatisfactory. He had a hot temper, little self-control and a keen eye for the injustice which results from unimaginative discipline. Enraged by some petty restriction about leaving the dining-hall, he butted a cadet corporal in the stomach, sending him reeling down a flight of stairs and through a glass door. Admonished and told he would never make an officer, he confirmed that opinion by ripping off his epaulettes and hurling them at his company commander's feet.

There was at the Academy a tradition of toughness, defiance of authority, sit-down strikes, beating-up of civilians and bullying. An official inquiry found that Officer-Cadet Gordon had hit a junior on the head with a hairbrush. The circumstances of the assault must have been discreditable, for he thereby lost six months' seniority and the chance of following brothers Henry and Enderby into the Royal Artillery. Instead, he was commissioned in June 1852, at the age of nineteen, into the Royal Engineers.

The Royal Engineers was to become a *corps d'élite* in the latter half of the nineteenth century, not socially – officers were drawn from the same social class as those of the Line – but professionally. The rank-and-file* were described as 'very fine, intelligent fellows – a contrast to the Line'. There was no purchase in the corps. The officers were reputed to be brainy and well versed in the recondite sciences which were encroaching on straightforward fighting. Moreover they had perhaps more opportunities of distinguishing themselves than others. It was engineer officers who placed the ladders for the storming parties, exploded powder-bags against the gates of enemy forts, blew up magazines to prevent them falling into enemy hands, stayed behind till the rearguard had passed to demolish the bridges. Anywhere in the rapidly growing empire, doing an infinite variety of semi-military jobs – surveying the Rockies, commanding native irregulars, making roads through the Himalayas, exploring jungles, building railways in Canada and forts in the Khyber – could be found junior officers of the Royal Engineers, engaged in work of far more responsibility and interest than their contemporaries of the Line.

After nineteen months' technical training, Gordon was sent to Pembroke to construct fortifications, the purpose of which (since Britannia indubitably ruled the waves) escaped his comprehension.

It was perhaps in Pembrokeshire that he became keen on shooting, his favourite recreation. One can imagine him taking a normal part in the narrow social life of a small military station, paying his duty calls, filling a gap at a dinner-table, attending an occasional Officers' Mess guest night and no doubt indulging in the horseplay and drinking customary on these occasions. He learned enough about wine to know what was bad. He was, like most subalterns, pressed for money; he developed the habit of frugality in his personal requirements, but when he had money to spare he would give it away to almost anyone who asked for some.

* The Royal Engineers was a corps of officers only. The rank-and-file were the Corps of Sappers and Miners.

At first he was bored at Pembroke, but not for long, for he made two great friends, Captain Drew and his wife, 'a very stylish person'. The Drews were a religious couple who saw in their young friend a brand to be plucked from the burning. Soon after he met them, he told his sister Augusta of the exhilaration of 'turning over a new leaf'.

As a boy he had shown no religious inclinations. Sunday at Woolwich had been purgatory to him, and during the Reverend Capel Molyneux's hour-long sermons he had been perpetually apprehensive of dropping off to sleep. 'You worshipped him,' he told Augusta, a strong-minded spinster twelve years older than himself; but young Gordon was unimpressed by a fashionable parson who spent more time cutting a dash in the Row than visiting the poor.[1] So he had never been confirmed, and took the Sacrament for the first time at Pembroke on Easter Sunday, 1854.

Gordon never joined any church; he preferred services to be 'plain', sermons to be short and to the point. Drew's evangelism was a more rewarding experience, and spinning along in a dog-cart through deep wooded valleys, beside the rocky coast and over the long shoulders of heather and peat was more conducive to reflection than 'the curtained family pew where you could have made your toilet and no one had been any the wiser'. He no longer wondered at Augusta burying herself in 'useful books . . . no novels can come up to the sermons of M'Cheyne or the *Commentaries* of Scott.'*

At this stage in his spiritual development Gordon's letters show little sign of interest in specific doctrine: they are full of his exultation at being changed, a point frequently stressed by M'Cheyne. It was, perhaps, from Scott that he eventually acquired the habit of repeatedly reading and examining every passage of the Bible to discover its true meaning – often with results which to other people seemed most extraordinary.

So one must not think of him, at this stage, as being deeply involved in religious thought, but rather as being happy and excited in a new experience. 'Dearest Augusta, pray for me, I beg of you.' He hoped that his 'dear mother and father think of eternal things: can I do or say anything to either of them to do good?' From his letters it seems that he could not.

In 1854 professional experience, distinction and promotion were to be won only in the Crimea, where he was ordered in the autumn.

---

* Thomas Scott was famous for his *Commentaries*, in which he endeavoured to discover the hidden message and meaning of every section of the Bible. Robert M'Cheyne, a Presbyterian minister, had won a great reputation as a missionary to the Jews in Palestine and in a religious revival in Scotland.

2

THE CRIMEA

The great battles of the Crimea – the Alma, Balaclava and Inkerman – were over. The British and French armies, having failed – or, rather, omitted – to take Sebastopol by a *coup de main*, had settled down to a long siege. Lord Raglan, like more distinguished invaders of Russia, expecting to win the war before Christmas, had omitted to make provision for the winter of 1854–5. It was colder than the War Office had expected. In November a terrible wind had swept down from the steppes over the camps above Balaclava. Dressed still in the ragged remnants of the uniforms they had worn through a scorching summer, with few tents, few greatcoats and at the most two blankets each, the men lay shivering on the frozen ground. Their damp clothes froze solid, their beards and whiskers froze solid. There was no firewood, and when they had burned all the roots they could find, they had to eat their salt-pork raw. There was no tea, and nothing with which to grind the green coffee they were issued instead, nor any means of roasting it. Horses died by the hundred, gnawed each other's tails to bloody stumps and stampeded through the camp in search of food. In Balaclava harbour, six miles down a rough steep track, there were warm clothes, blankets, tents, food and fodder in such abundance that, for want of storage space, much of it was dumped in the sea; but there were no labourers, no tools to repair the track, nor any carts or pack animals to carry up supplies if it had been repaired.

In mid-November the frost changed to five days of torrential rain, followed by a hurricane which sank twenty-one ships off Balaclava together with their precious cargoes. There were comparatively few battle casualties; but through desertion, self-inflicted wounds, gangrene, fever, cholera, dysentery, rheumatism and starvation, the British army in the Crimea was reduced by January to 11,000 effectives with 23,000 sick. *The Times* calculated that by the end of March Lord Raglan and his staff would be the sole survivors.

Those who remained in camp above Balaclava were fortunate compared to the unhappy wretches who were evacuated to the Barrack Hospital at

Scutari. There they found food which healthy, hungry men could hardly have stomached. They found the hospital floors alive with vermin and deep in the ordure of the dysentery and cholera cases for whom there were no bedpans; the few latrines were choked with filth. They lay in their lousy clothes because these could not be washed and there was nothing else to wear. By the end of December the ruthless energy of Miss Nightingale and her nurses had effected some marginal improvement, but the hospital death-rate was still appalling.

None of these horrors was apparent to the newly-arrived Gordon, who wrote on passing through Scutari, 'Our wounded have everything they want, and all comforts.' His strongest strictures were, sapper-like, for the state of the road which was the British army's lifeline: 'bad beyond description, quite a morasse the whole way up'. He saw his brothers, Henry and Enderby, who warned him of officers being killed by the fumes of their charcoal stoves, 'so I shall keep a sharp look-out not to use it'. But two other officers, disdaining the warmth of charcoal, froze to death the same night. One could not win.

He was sadly disillusioned by the lack of offensive spirit: 'No one seems to interest himself in the siege, but all appear to be engaged in foraging expeditions for grub.' It is extraordinary to find in his letters not a trace of complaint, or even consciousness of the malignant fate which, aided by red tape and ineptitude, was destroying the British army. He remarked on the ample rations: Enderby was 'in a capital hut and looks better than I ever saw him . . . of course he is well fed.' He wanted nothing from home. 'I have got a splendid outfit, and two chamois leather vests and drawers. Even Enderby admired my coat.' The mud, he admitted, had been dreadful, but the ground was now frozen under a foot of hard snow, and the walking was 'pretty good'. His mother really must not believe 'all the atrocious fibs which are told in the papers of our misery'. There were really no hardships for the officers: 'The men are the sufferers, and that is partly their own fault, as they are like children thinking everything is to be done for them.'

The British forces were divided into the Right Attack and the Left Attack. Four sapper companies, including Gordon's, were allocated to the Right Attack, the objective of which was the formidable Redan fortress. The Russian positions were extraordinarily strong, covered by a ditch eleven foot deep cut in solid rock, with underground dug-outs and magazines roofed with heavy beams, ships' tanks filled with earth, and sandbags. Gun positions were heavily revetted and protected. Land-mines were buried in front of the ditch. An abattis of felled trees, with intermeshed branches pointing outwards, made an obstacle almost as formidable as barbed wire.

In January and February 1855 the sappers were employed in clearing snow from the trenches, digging drains to carry away flood-water, making revetments, traverses and splinter-proof magazines, sloping and lining embrasures, blasting trenches and battery positions out of solid rock – often under fire and exposed to weather which killed men of sheer cold and exhaustion. They were the expert advisers in all problems of the siege and the trenches, the infantry supplying tools, muscles and protection.

R.E. officers were also specialists in map-making and field-sketching. In an assault they guided the infantry columns; led the parties carrying up assault equipment – ladders, grappling-irons for pulling away the abattais, wool-sacks to give some protection against grape and musketry, gabions (baskets of wicker or hoop iron) which were carried forward empty and filled with earth where cover was quickly needed; they organized the working parties to consolidate a captured position before the counter-attack.

Gordon's first experience of command was on the night of 14 February, when he was detailed to link up the forward British rifle-pits with those of the French on the right so as to form a continuous trench line. His ardent spirit was disappointed at the night's work, which began in muddle and ended in farce:

I got, after some trouble, eight men with picks and shovels, and asked the captain of the advanced trench to give me five double sentries to throw out in advance . . . I led forward the sentries and found the sentries of the advance had not held the caves, so there was just a chance of the Russians being in them. I went on, however, and, though I did not like it, explored the caves almost alone. We then left two sentries on the hill above the caves, and went back to get round and post two sentries below. However, just as soon as we showed ourselves outside the caves and below them, bang! bang! went two rifles, the bullets hitting the ground close to us. The sentries with me retired in a rare state of mind, and my working party bolted, and were stopped with great difficulty. It was not a Russian attack, but two sentries whom I had placed above the caves had fired at us, lost their caps, and bolted to the trench. Nothing after this would induce the sentries to go out, so I got the working party to go forward with me.

Gordon was disgusted at those whose zeal was less than his: 'The line officers are too much disposed to stay in the little huts and holes when the men are working for us, and leave them to do as they like. I am determined to report them next time . . . [the men] do not deserve the praise they get as they grumble and growl dreadfully.'[1] By 21 February the first crocuses appeared, and the worst seemed to be over. As for the press reports, 'If people knew what trash appears in the papers, they would stare. Everyone out here is sick and tired of bygone grievances.'

A general planning an assault required a detailed knowledge of the enemy fortifications, rifle-pits and gun emplacements. In 1855 it could be obtained only by an officer skilled at field-sketching, armed with a telescope, standing or lying in the open to draw the enemy's fire so that he could, from the puffs of smoke, plot their positions. This was Gordon's speciality. He gained a reputation as an expert in front-line geography. He was kept busy sketching enemy positions, making plans of the parallels and taking his turn in the forward trenches. 'I do not think I was ever in better health, and I enjoy the work amazingly.' From time to time there was an armistice to bury the dead. The Russians emerged from their trenches and rifle-pits, which Gordon took the opportunity of sketching, and called for tobacco. Their officers, 'not particularly clean', came up and chatted in bad French while the burial parties were at work.

Religious references in his letters home are no more than one would find in the letters of thousands of Victorian soldiers on active service. 'The siege will not last much longer (D.V.).' A shell burst above so-and-so 'and by what is called chance struck him in the back. I am glad to say he was a serious man.' Someone else had died, 'I am glad to say he was well-prepared.' Once he laments the lack of 'a good working clergyman'; but there is only one reference to Bible-reading, and only once does he record attending a church service. Indeed his letters and diary contain more appreciation of the Crimean countryside in spring – the flowers, the new grass, wolves and deer on the Tchernaya Plain, a small hunting-box in such a pretty place up in the Baidar Valley – than concern for the state of his soul.

Most men are frightened in war but try, more or less successfully, to overcome their fear. A few are excited and stimulated. Gordon was one of the fortunate few. Many years later he wrote: 'I went to the Crimea hoping, without having a hand in it, to be killed. I survived and lived, never fearing death but not wishing to be too closely acquainted with God, nor yet to leave Him.'[2] A gap of thirty years is apt either to blur, or to over-dramatize, recollections of youthful thoughts and feelings. It seems highly unlikely that he wanted to be killed: his letters all indicate that he was thoroughly enjoying himself.

With the warmer weather and the appearance of new grass, hyacinths and crocuses, morale was improving. So was the condition of the horses, enabling the British to plan not, indeed, a mobile campaign against the Russian field army, but a race-meeting. The siege batteries were stocked up with more than 500 rounds a gun. It was learned that new allies, 15,000 Sardinians, were joining the besiegers, and perhaps more welcome was the rapid progress of the light railway and the arrival of a labour corps of 24,000 Croats, to say nothing of some buffaloes.

By April the allies had all the requisites for success except training and good staff work. The seasoned men who had died at the Alma, Balaclava and Inkerman had been replaced by drafts of raw boys and foreign mercenaries. After successive postponements, in June there was an attack which failed, owing to faulty liaison between the allies, incompetent staff work and (Gordon insisted) lack of courage and dash by the British infantry. 'The Russians,' he wrote,

opened with a fire of grape which was terrific. They mowed down our men in dozens. The trenches were crowded with men, who foolishly kept in them, instead of rushing over the parapet in a mass ... Unfortunately our men dribbled out of the ends of the trenches ten and twenty at a time, and as soon as they appeared they were cleared away.

So ended our assault, of the result of which we felt so sure ... I am confident ... that if we had left the trenches in a mass some of us would have survived and reached the Redan.

His family were not to believe one word of the absurd reports in the papers: 'Our troops never once passed the abattis in front of their position and we never spiked a gun of the Russians.'[3]

On 28 June Lord Raglan died, 'of wear and tear and general debility,' wrote Gordon. 'He is universally regretted, as he was so kind, although not a good Commander-in-Chief which one would not expect from his age ... I hope he was prepared, but do not know.'[4]

Gordon's life was dull, tiring, not particularly dangerous. As autumn approached, he longed for a week's partridge-shooting.

On 8 September, after a three-day bombardment, another assault was launched. The Zouaves attacked with great *élan*, and within ten minutes had planted the tricoleur on the summit of their objective, the Malakoff fort, enabling General MacMahon to make good his terse boast, '*J'y suis, j'y reste*.' The British had not fared so well. Owing to their infantry's incurable aversion to digging, their assault had to cover 250 yards of open ground – not, like the French, 25 yards. Gordon, in reserve, watched it all. 'Our men went forward well, losing apparently few, put their ladders in the ditch and mounted the salient of the Redan. But though they stayed there for five minutes or more, they did not advance, and tremendous reserves coming up drove them out ... We should have carried everything before us, if the men had only advanced.'

It was decided to try again next morning, but 'during the night I heard terrible explosions, and going down to the trenches at four a.m. I saw a splendid sight, the whole town in flames, and every now and then a terrific explosion.' The Russians, having lost the Malakoff, had decided that the city was untenable, so they blew up their forts and magazines, scuttled their ships and evacuated it. So Gordon could write on 10 September, 'We are at last in possession of this vile place . . . Is it not glorious?'

He took part in the demolition of the naval base, enjoyed (though it was bitterly cold and snowing) some duck-shooting in the dockyard bay, and practised a new hobby: 'I mean to send you a lot more photographs . . . What a splendid thing photography is! It is so accurate, and tells the truth so much better than any letter.' He expected to be abroad four or five years, 'which *individually* I would sooner spend in war than peace. There is something indescribably exciting in the former.' But the war formally ended in March 1856. He had performed competently the subaltern's primary duty of walking in front of his men to be shot at first, and had acquired a reputation for field-sketching and reconnaissance. The demolitions, with French and British engineers working side by side, had enlarged his professional experience. But he had had no opportunity to earn particular distinction. 'What easily earned C.B.s there have been,' he observed, and no doubt there was, as usual, a good deal of heart-burning on this matter, but not on Gordon's part. '*Remember*,' he wrote, '*I do not think* it is a hard case that we, the subs, do not get anything.' Actually he got a mention in despatches in a list of fifteen sapper subalterns who had done their duty, and, from the French, the *Légion d'Honneur*, a very acceptable consolation prize.

He gained in experience, he gained also in friendship from the war in the Crimea. This is what his contemporaries most remembered of him. Everyone he met not only respected and trusted Gordon: they liked him, he was a popular fellow; his very nickname 'Charley' indicates a friendly, extrovert personality. He was below average height, slight but well-knit in figure. He wore his curly brown hair short, a thin moustache and side-whiskers. His forehead was broad, his nose rather short and broad in the bridge. His rather shy, diffident manner hardly accorded with a firm mouth and a strong, square jaw. He talked at times very fast, with a slight stammer. His most remarkable feature, which so many have remarked, were his extraordinarily clear, compelling eyes – blue according to some, grey to others. But if his friends differed in descriptions of their colour, they were agreed on the effect they had. 'I always declared,' wrote Mrs Freese*, 'that he could see through a millstone, and I certainly think he saw through everybody in the most remarkable way.' W. G. Lilley, a clerk in the Royal Engineers, wrote:

His clear blue eye seemed to possess a magic power over all who came within its influence. It read you through and through, it made it impossible for you to tell him anything but the truth, it invited your confidence, it kindled

* See p. 57 ff.

with compassion at every story of distress and it sparkled with good humour at anything really witty or funny. From its glance you knew at once that at any risk he would keep his promise, that you might trust him with anything and everything, and that he would stand by you if all other friends deserted you.

A small Sudanese boy declared, 'Gordon Pasha could see all through me' and 'could see quite well in the dark because he had the light inside him'. His sapper friend, Gerald Graham, remarked on the 'steadfast, truthful gaze of the grey-blue eyes'; and to Garnet Wolseley* 'his full, clear and bright blue eyes seemed to court something, while at the same time they searched into your inner soul.'[5] Perhaps Gordon's friends exaggerated his discernment, for his penetration was often at fault and he was taken in by many plausible impostors.

He was generally in high spirits, effervescent with humour; and although few of his recorded jokes indicate wit of a high order, his natural gaiety and talkativeness made him an asset at most gatherings. Later he developed a horror of dinner parties, but as a young man he was not anti-social. When he was joking or pulling someone's leg his whole face seemed to smile and his eyes twinkled with fun. He had great charm of manner – not the charm of a polished man of the world, but that of a perfectly truthful and open mind, giving and demanding confidence, sometimes playfully, sometimes earnestly, sometimes with humility. But he was subject to sudden outbursts of temper, usually provoked by some subordinate's idleness or mendacity, and delinquents quailed at his fury. He regarded his temper as characteristic of 'the Gordon tribe', tough, crafty and contumacious, of which he was extremely proud.

Gerald Graham, who won the V.C. at Sebastopol, and Garnet Wolseley were two men whose friendship, dating from the Crimea, Gordon retained to the end of his life.

In May 1856, Gordon was appointed assistant commissioner to an international commission set up under the Peace of Paris to survey the new Russo-Turkish boundary in Bessarabia. Obviously he owed the opportunity to his skill at surveying. He spent three years on boundary delineation, first in Bessarabia, then in Armenia. At first he found the work interesting and rewarding: it was outside the rut of soldiering; it brought him into daily contact with foreign officers, of whom he found the French the most congenial; the boundaries passed through wild, unsettled country offering good rough shooting; the work was sufficient but not arduous, the responsibilities hardly overwhelming; with the camp moving every few days, there was much variety, and he was treated to a sort of leisurely, subsidized safari.

* Later Field Marshal Lord Wolseley.

But three years was too long for a job which was professionally a branch-line leading nowhere. Nor did the social life in the Taurus mountains appeal to him: 'The ladies are very pretty, but have not very cleanly habits in general; they do not hesitate in taking a bone and gnawing it. They live in extremely dirty houses, or rather huts. They are generally all princesses, and the men all princes who, however, do not hesitate to accept small donations.' He was quite sticky from shaking hands with so many princes, but bore these trials with the constancy of a martyr.

He returned home for Christmas 1858, to be posted in May 1859 as adjutant to the Royal Engineers' depot at Chatham. He thought very little of home service – the 'useless trush' he had to read up for the half-yearly inspections, and the flummery of dress uniforms and ceremonial parades. 'You will need,' he warned his friend Charles Harvey with somewhat overweighted irony, 'at least eighteen pairs of spurs as you require them on all occasions. Sleeping in them is a nuisance at first, but you soon get used to them. Steel chain straps are the correct thing, they clank as you walk.'[6]

Having done his twelve months at Chatham, he applied for a posting to China, where a promising little war was in progress.

3
⌂ THE TAIPING REBELLION

⌂ The basic cause of the war was the reluctance of the Chinese Government to allow the import of English manufactured goods and Indian opium, which was a stronger and to addicts more rewarding smoke than the native product. In two 'Opium Wars' the British had extorted from the Emperor the island of Hong Kong, exemption for all foreigners from Chinese jurisdiction, freedom to propagate the Gospel throughout the empire, navigation rights on the Yangtse, and the right to settle, trade and keep military forces in seventeen 'Treaty Ports', including Shanghai.

This was not enough. Her Majesty's Government, assisted by the French, decided that to impress upon the Emperor the eternal verities of Free Trade, nothing less would suffice than a personal visit by the British Commissioner, Lord Elgin. To facilitate this, in August 1860, an Anglo-French squadron captured the Taku Forts at the mouth of the river leading to Pekin. Further chastisement was to be inflicted by land forces accompanying His Lordship.

In the same month the Son of Heaven died. His heir being a child, government of the empire devolved on a Council of Regency presided over by the Dowager Empress, xenophobic and confident that the foreign devils could soon be driven into the sea.

At this juncture, in September 1860, Gordon arrived, 'rather late for the amusement'. He followed the force marching on Pekin, to whose war aims had now been added that of rescuing a number of British officers and Indian cavalry *sowars* who, imprudently approaching the Chinese forces as envoys under a flag of truce, had been carried away. The army halted under the walls of the Imperial capital, and Gordon took the opportunity of visiting the Summer Palace, a complex of elegant buildings crammed with the finest products of Chinese civilization.

The imprisoned envoys were returned, save four who had been tortured to death. Moreover other British and Indian prisoners of war had been beheaded. The worst atrocities had been committed within the Summer Palace, which Lord Elgin decided to pillage and destroy in retribution.

Gordon had his doubts about this demoralizing work with everyone wild for plunder, but did not refuse his share of the prize money. 'We went out and, after pillaging it, burnt the whole place, destroying in a vandal-like manner most valuable property which would not be replaced for four millions. Although I have not as much as many, I have done well.' To the Royal Engineers' Mess at Chatham he presented '*such* a piece of plunder, part of a throne out of the Summer Palace, beautifully carved'. He sent his mother and sisters sables, jade, vases and enamels; and to Henry a curious cup: 'I am afraid to say how much gin has been drunk out of it.'[1]

Six days later the Treaty of Pekin was signed. Gordon was to spend the next eighteen months in peace-time engineering duties with an Anglo-French force which was to remain in the Tientsin area until the Chinese paid a large indemnity. Commanding the British contingent was General Staveley who was Gordon's connection by marriage. Gordon got on quite well with this 'essentially selfish man'.

He viewed the prospect without pleasure:

It will be a black hole and dull enough. You have no idea how dirty I am and how callous one becomes to hands one would be vexed at in a servant ... The 31st and 60th are in a very bad state. The men are most unruly and I feel more and more disgusted at the British soldier. They are much demoralized, drunkenness on duty being common. Grumbling, dirty, idle, helpless to a degree and without the smallest spark of *esprit de corps*, what a brute the ordinary British linesman is. The lash is going constantly, and as usual without avail.

The sappers were hardly better, with his senior sergeant 'so cracked as to render it necessary to remove him', and a colour-sergeant reduced for drunkenness.[2]

Gordon's principal job was to build quarters for the troops, for which he had some 600 Chinese artisans to supervise and administer. With the cold weather matters improved. There was a wonderful supply of pheasants, wild duck and sand-grouse. Theatricals and toboggan-racing were organized, and the skating was first rate: 'We ought to be quite professional by the end of the winter.' He was sent to reconnoitre some 400 miles of the Great Wall, returning through country no European had yet visited. So, eventually, he came to like 'the country, the work and independence'.

He found time to administer a charitable fund for paupers. Assuming that the local mandarins must feel a squirearchical concern for the deserving poor, he invited them to select suitable recipients for his bounty; but the mandarins flatly refused to be involved in anything so preposterous. So Gordon invited applicants for a public distribution of money. Three thousand arrived, of whom eight were trampled to death in the rush. He caught smallpox. It was a light attack and he soon recovered; but sickness and enforced leisure had revived his interest in 'eternal things'. 'I am glad to say,' he wrote to Augusta, 'that this disease has brought me back to my Saviour.' In retrospect he did not regard this as a definite conversion.

Meanwhile Shanghai was threatened by the Taiping rebels, who had already overrun much of the empire, including the great city of Nanking. They were followers of Hung-sen-Tsuen, a peasant born near Canton. He was a man of powerful mind, subject to visions, trances and ecstatic utterances. He had received some instruction from an American missionary named Roberts, from which he evolved an exotic form of Christianity in which the Trinity consisted of God the Father, Jesus the Elder Brother, and himself, the Younger Brother. In 1850, after a forty days' trance, he had proclaimed 'the noble principles of the Heavenly King, the sovereign King Tsuen'. The principles were later summarized in a brief, all-embracing edict: 'The Heavenly Father sits on the throne above. The Heavenly Brother, Christ, is the next honourable, sitting on the right of the Father, excelled by no man. By the grace of the Father and Brother we sit on his left. United as one, we reign. Disobey the Heavenly Will and you will be ground to pieces with a pestle.' The Heavenly King, generally known by his title, Tien Wang, claimed sovereignty over all kingdoms upon earth, and in defiance of the reigning Pure Dynasty inaugurated a new Dynasty of Perpetual Peace by starting a peculiarly bloody civil war.

This could be regarded as a rebellion of Chinese against Manchus, of Christians against heathens, of the oppressed against obscurantist tyranny. The reforms envisaged by the Taiping leaders included the development of the railways and steam shipping; canals, famine- and flood-relief; the establishment of hospitals; the prohibition of infanticide, judicial torture, official corruption, 'lily feet'. They practised, or at least preached, a primitive form of communism, and the distribution of land to the peasants in plots varying according to its fertility and the size of their families.

A programme including the abolition of sin and such complex land reforms would have required an administrative machine which did not exist, so it was never put into effect. But there is abundant evidence of the devastation and collapse of rural society, with hundreds of thousands dying of starvation, beheaded, crucified and buried alive in every province overrun by the Taipings.

Such freedom fighters could hardly fail to secure widespread support in British progressive circles. Several missionaries wrote ecstatic accounts of sober, God-fearing *Wangs* (the title given to Taiping leaders), chaste Taiping women and industrious children.

In Pekin different views prevailed. Li Hung Chang, a provincial governor, put into verse the opinion of the mandarin establishment:

> It is truly the greatest sacred duty
> Of all patriotic sons of the Middle Kingdom,
> To strike to the black heart
> The Long-Haired bandits;
> To pluck out their lying tongues,
> To burn deep the sockets of their eyes,
> To rip open their vile bellies,
> To rub salt into many cuts,
> To trim close their ears,
> To draw forth the nails . . .

He blamed the Christian missionaries for the whole sorry business; and ordered the flaying alive, pressing to death and decapitation of rebel prisoners.

By 1854 the Taiping movement was over-extended. Many of the Wangs, succumbing to worldly temptation, had acquired wealth, palaces and seraglios. The Eastern King proclaimed himself as the Holy Ghost and sentenced the Heavenly King to forty lashes for kicking his pregnant wives. The Heavenly King had the Holy Ghost and hundreds of his adherents executed. The peasants began to view the rebels as terrorists rather than liberators, and even some of the missionaries began to wonder if the Younger Brother was really following in the steps of St Paul. Mr Roberts, the American who had originally 'converted' Tien Wang, now announced, 'He is crazy; nor can I believe any good will arise out of the rule of such a wicked despot.'[3]

However, with the Imperial forces under pressure in the north, the rebellion in the doldrums was blessed with a heavenly wind. The hierarchy was reconstituted by the creation of new Wangs, including one who was to be the most famous of all, Chung Wang, the Faithful King, a commander of great ability. The Heavenly Capital of Nanking was cleansed of its besiegers and within one month Chung Wang captured the great cities of Soochow and Hangchow, overran the rich provinces of Kiangsu and Chekians, and moved on Shanghai. The Shanghai front was a small part of the whole, but for the rebels the capture of the port was a worth-while object. Only sixteen years ago it had been of no importance, but now it was a large commercial city, with as many as 250 ships in its harbour. It was a haven for wealthy Chinese merchants who might be induced to part with their riches. With their coffers thus replenished, the rebels might do business with European merchants perfectly willing to sell them arms. They could recruit gunners and other military 'experts' among the foreign sailors and adventurers who proliferated in the Treaty Ports.

It was the threat to Shanghai that brought the British into the arena. As often in imperial history, humanitarian and commercial motives were mixed. They wished to prevent bloodshed and pillage; they were concerned with Shanghai's position as a flourishing international port and with their country's trading privileges: it was obvious that the Taipings would not consider themselves bound by treaties made by the Imperial government.

In August 1860, the Faithful King himself, Chung Wang, advanced to the very walls of the city, but was repulsed by the British and French contingents. Chung Wang then left the Shanghai front in charge of one of the best Taiping generals, and returned to Nanking.

Meanwhile in February 1861, Sir James Hope, British naval commander in the Far East, had sailed his squadron up the Yangtse to Nanking and invited the Heavenly King to behave himself. Inspired by a vision, Tien Wang was at first obdurate. 'Tut, tut, tut,' said Mr Harry Parkes, the Admiral's political adviser, 'this won't do at all. He must have another vision.' And so he did, promising not to approach within thirty miles of Shanghai for a year.

The Vice-Consul at Ningpo found in official dealings with the Taipings

a rough and blunt sort of honesty, quite unexpected and surprising after years of intercourse with the effete Imperial mandarins. Nevertheless it is undeniable that the latter, bad and corrupt as they are, represent in our eyes a 'principle' entitled to our respect, whereas the Taipings have a fume of blood and a look of carnage about them. Their chief condition for success is to strike terror, first by numbers, and secondly by the tawdry harlequin garb worn by them which . . . has such a strange effect on the minds of all classes of people. Their long, shaggy black hair adds to the wildness of their look, and when this fantastic appearance is accompanied by a certain show of fury and madness, it is really little to be wondered at that the mild Chinese will either take to flight or submit . . . There is nothing in the past records so dark and bad, such abominations committed under the name of religion, such mock-heroic buffoonery, such horrors accompanied by pantaloonery and so much flimsy web worked in the midst of blood. Taipingdom is a huge mass of *Nothingness* . . . there is nothing to lay hold on in it. It is a gigantic bubble, that collapses on being touched – but leaves a mark of blood on the finger.[4]

Sir Frederick Bruce, now British minister in Pekin, advised Her Majesty's Government that trade was what mattered, and the indemnity due to Britain and France under the Treaty of Pekin, to secure which the Imperial customs revenue was to be collected by foreign officials, an arrangement with which the Taipings were unlikely to co-operate. In September 1861, anticipating renewed hostilities, the Shanghai merchants raised and paid for a private army known optimistically as the Ever Victorious Army. Its command was entrusted to two American soldiers-of-fortune, Frederick Ward and Henry Burgevine. Ward was soon killed in action. Burgevine, aged about thirty-five, was a Southerner who, in travels and adventures in four continents, had gathered no moss. He had a way with him; but he drank and was thoroughly untrustworthy. The rank-and-file were Chinese, his officers a mixed bunch of adventurers, mainly Americans who, despite the fact that the war between the states was in full swing, hoped to find more lucrative employment by fighting against – or for that matter, for – the Taipings. It was hardly the most promising officer-material.

Events in Pekin facilitated some sort of common action against the Taipings. The Dowager Empress had connived at a *coup d'état* by her brother-in-law, Prince Kung, who overthrew the anti-foreign party in November 1861, and sent 9,000 Imperialist troops to co-operate with the Ever Victorious Army. As the smoke of burning villages and the stench of unburied corpses approached Shanghai, the case for British intervention was daily strengthened. It was strengthened also by a huge increase in the demand for opium; the 1862 import was almost treble that of 1861.[5]

At this juncture General Staveley assumed command of all the British land forces in China and, with the French and Prince Kung, decided that combined military action must be taken to clear the rebels from within thirty miles of Shanghai. With this Bruce agreed, provided the Imperialists were responsible for the government of the liberated area. The objects of the allies were entirely different: the Imperial authorities wanted to crush the rebellion, the European powers wanted only to safeguard their commercial interests in Shanghai; but within limits they could co-operate.

British reinforcements arrived from Tientsin, two battalions with artillery and a sapper detachment commanded by Gordon. He came ashore at Shanghai on 3 May 1862, just in time for an attack on the rebel stronghold of Tsingpu, some thirty miles to the west. The operation might have been tailor-made for him.

Staveley decided to make a personal reconnaissance, accompanied by his engineer officer. They approached by boat, but not close enough to satisfy Gordon who scrambled ashore. 'To my dismay,' wrote Staveley, 'I saw him gradually going nearer and nearer, by rushes from cover to cover until he got behind a small outlying pagoda within 100 yards of the wall, and here he was quietly making a sketch and taking notes. I, in the meantime, was shouting myself hoarse in trying to get him back, for not only were the rebels firing at him from the walls, but I saw a party stealing round to cut him off.' Gordon got back safely with his sketch and information, and in the attack directed the crossing of the creek and the scaling of the wall.

Unfortunately the Imperialists proved incapable of holding the places secured by their allies, and were driven back to the immediate neighbourhood of Shanghai for the rest of the summer. From the foreign settlement on any day could be seen the smoke of burning villages, of which the survivors poured into the Chinese town until there were 70,000 refugees within the walls. Outside, the roads were lined with corpses and in hot weather the sickly smell of death pervaded even the foreign settlement. The summer climate was trying indeed, damp and sticky, with dense fogs and the air oppressively still: at night there was an incessant croaking of frogs, the singing of mosquitoes, the whirr of bats and big, buzzing beetles; in the morning boots would be found covered with mould, and knives, keys, pistols with rust. European troops were constantly ill with malaria, dysentery, cholera. For officers the cost of living was ruinous, since prices found a level which the wealthy merchants would pay. So Gordon was lucky in being lent, rent-free, a merchant's house which he shared with his second-in-command, a young Irish subaltern named Thomas Lyster. Apart from his generous host, he found Shanghai Europeans 'a dollar-grinding set, rascally and ungrateful ... who pay no taxes and we are here to defend them'.[6] He kept up his interest in photography and managed to wangle some very expensive government photographic apparatus from Hong Kong. Somehow he acquired the best horse in Shanghai; and when the autumn came he had good shooting, for duck, snipe and pheasants abounded and Staveley gave him a well-trained pointer. In Shanghai bachelor society Gordon was a popular figure, sociable and serene. He took a drink or two in company, gin or brandy; but he refused invitations which might bring him into contact with young women: he had, he said, better ways of spending his time than 'spooning'. Lyster found him 'the best fellow in the world', 'the beau ideal of a soldier' and 'a great favourite with the Chinese'.

Gordon was employed, with a strong escort, in surveying the surrounding country. He was a firm believer in the military adage that time spent in reconnaissance is never wasted: 'Knowledge of the country is everything, and I have studied it a great deal.' Soon he was expert on the intricate waterways of East Kiangsu. His written orders to Lyster when the latter had to work on his own betray a preoccupation with detail and a reluctance to delegate authority which in later years became obsessive. Surely an officer of the Royal Engineers, in charge of a survey party of two sappers, did not have to be told that they each must take four blankets and an empty paliasse, how this baggage would be carried from the steamer to the West Gate, or who should carry the theodolite and chain.

A renewed advance by the main Imperialist forces on Nanking compelled the Faithful King to relax pressure on Shanghai. But Chung Wang had unquestionably defeated the British, French, Imperialists and Ever Victorious Army combined. The only towns outside Shanghai which the allies still held were Kajow, twenty-five miles to the south, garrisoned by British troops; and Sunkiang, twenty-five miles to the south-west, held by the E.V.A. now expanded to a strength of 5,000.

Despite setbacks, the E.V.A. had acquired some characteristics of a disciplined force. They were still paid by the Shanghai merchants, but at least they were paid regularly. With Ward's death, command devolved on Burgevine. About the same time Hung Chang* was appointed Futai (Governor) of Kiangsu Province with overall command against the Taipings. His principal commander was a former Taiping rebel who had changed sides, General Ching. Trouble ensued. Ching complained of the bad behaviour of the E.V.A. towards the local inhabitants; the E.V.A.'s financial backers, nervous of their own creation, reduced their subscriptions, and the E.V.A. behaved worse. Burgevine's conduct towards the Chinese was offensive and overbearing.

Li Hung Chang† considered foreigners largely responsible for the rebellion: 'I hate all these foreigners, but it would not be wise to let them know ... Each and every one sings the same song: "I will do this and I will do that: but you must let me have my own way and not interfere with me." And it makes hair grow stiff on my neck to know that we are obliged to put up with it, and say "Yes, Yes," and smile.' On the whole he found the English slightly less objectionable than others, except when drunk. He was also suspicious of the E.V.A., 'lazy and mutinous'. The Futai, therefore, complained to Staveley of the conduct of the E.V.A. in general and Burgevine in particular, and requested that a British officer be appointed in his place. The E.V.A.'s undisciplined looting showed it to be seriously out of control, partly because it had received no pay for two months. Burgevine, accompanied by his bodyguards, visited the mandarin banker who was the E.V.A.'s paymaster, struck him in the face and carried off all the cash he could find. After this there could be no question of him retaining command; to everyone's relief he went quietly; and the

* See p. 27.
† It should be mentioned that the authenticity of his memoirs is not above suspicion.

Futai took over responsibility for paying the E.V.A., which thus became an integral part of the Imperial army.

Bruce disapproved of British officers taking service with the Chinese Government. If there must be one in command of the E.V.A., he should 'be concerned with trading rather than leading men in the field'. General Staveley's observations on this ministerial suggestion are not recorded, but he recommended Gordon for the job, provided Her Majesty's Government agreed. The Futai and Staveley drew up an agreement that the E.V.A. should be under the joint command of a British and a Chinese officer, both with the Chinese rank of colonel, and should come under the orders of the Futai.

It is strange that Staveley should have recommended Gordon, whose qualifications on paper were rather thin, as Gordon himself realized. Staveley had seen that he was brave, cool under fire, professionally competent and particularly good in reconnaissance and field-sketching. Gordon had a friendly, extrovert personality, and would be most unlikely to offend the Chinese by such jolly pranks as tying two together by the pigtails, a practice common among the high-spirited young Britons in Shanghai. But the E.V.A. was basically an infantry brigade with its own artillery component and flotilla of gun- and transport-boats, and Gordon was an engineer with no experience of amphibious operations. It required a commander with plenty of active service experience, and Gordon had little. Its rank-and-file were Chinese, and Gordon could not speak their language. It was an administrator's nightmare, and Gordon's only experience of military administration had been a few months as depot adjutant. He would never have solicited a recommendation from his brother-in-law. But it seems probable that Staveley thought, 'Just the job for Charley.' So it was.

On 24 March 1863, as a thirty-one-year-old brevet-major, he assumed command. His Chinese joint-commander was a tactful nonentity called Li Adong who helped with administration.

4

THE EVER VICTORIOUS ARMY

The Ever Victorious Army when Gordon took it over had a strength varying almost from day to day between 3,000 and 5,000, divided into five or six infantry battalions, four siege- and two field-batteries. It received very high pay, to which was added special compensation for wounds and, in Burgevine's time but not in Gordon's, prize money for every town captured, the exact amount being settled by hard bargaining before the E.V.A. would attack. The officers' pay was calculated to attract deserters from ships and volunteers from British regular forces; Gordon thought, 'There is not the slightest chance of getting any men for less – it is by far the most dangerous service for officers I have ever seen.'

The basic infantry weapon was the percussion–cap model of the old Tower musket, reasonably accurate up to 80 yards; the commander's bodyguard and one battalion were armed with muzzle-loading rifles, accurate up to 400 or 500 yards. The artillery component was very strong, equipped with two 8-inch howitzers, four 32-pounder siege-guns, twenty-two 12-pounder howitzers, fourteen mortars and six rocket-tubes. The artillery for its own protection carried stout elm mantlets, proof against small arms, and 150 foot of pontoon bridge for crossing creeks.

Besides these, the E.V.A. had its own flotilla of fighting and transport ships, consisting of two armed steamers, two large siege-gun boats, and a number of junks; these could carry all the artillery and 2,000 infantry in one lift. Best of the steamers was the *Hyson*, an iron paddle-boat 90 foot long, armoured with stout elm planking and armed with a 32-pounder in the bows and a 12-pounder howitzer in the stern. She drew 3 ft 6 ins, but her bottom being fitted with wheels, she could crawl through even shallower water. The funnel could be lowered to pass under bridges. The steamers had terrific mobile fire-power, and were invaluable as infantry transports or for towing gun-boats and barges.

As for the personnel of the E.V.A., in Gordon's own words, 'you never saw such a rabble'. The rank-and-file were mainly local peasants, not by repute as brave and tough as the Cantonese who formed the hard core of the rebellion. The only foreign other ranks were one sergeant per battery and some corporals and private soldiers in Gordon's body-guard. Properly handled, the Chinese were well behaved and quick to learn. Drunkenness, a perennial problem with British troops, was almost unknown, and so long as the men had an occasional hand-out of prize money, there was very little crime other than mutiny, desertion and looting.

In winter the *élite* bodyguard wore a dark-blue jacket, the other infantry rifle-green, and the artillery light blue – all with scarlet facings and green turbans; in summer all wore khaki. Such, at least, was the intention, but in fact 'we wear anything we can get. The men are mostly in rags.' They were trained in a simple battle-drill, with more stress laid on speed than on dressing and alignment. Apart from talking in the ranks, they drilled well. The artillery was uncommonly good.

The only officers with professional experience were five British regulars whom Gordon brought in for his brigade staff, and a few ex-rankers such as Major Tapp, a former petty officer in the Royal Navy. The remainder were what Burgevine himself described as roughs. Nearly all were good fighters, but few were good soldiers; and the majority were products of the American military doctrine, that soldiering was simply a matter of riding and shooting, which any red-blooded American could do by instinct, especially if he had never been taught. They certainly had no intention of being taught by a Britisher. Moreover there were no articles of war applicable to the E.V.A., no means of disciplining an officer other than dismissal. This, however, was easily effected: the offender would be told to clear out in two hours, and the Provost-Marshal, an old bo'sun of the Royal Navy, directed to expedite his departure. They were compulsive drinkers, gamblers and brawlers, bringing to the E.V.A. the habits of the California gold-mining camps. They were touchy over rank and precedence, apt to become worked up over imaginary grievances, and riddled with jealousies: half of them were generally quarrelling with the other half, a situation not without its advantages for their commander. From these strictures an exception must be made of the steam-boat captains, Americans experienced in river navigation and first-class officers, especially Captain Davidson of the *Hyson*.

By 1863 the Taipings were past their best, but still formidable, and seemed to be braver and tougher than the soldiers of the government. They had modern rifles and artillery, a couple of steamers, and a con-siderable number of foreign volunteers whose military qualifications were at least as high as those of Gordon's officers. The weakness of the Taipings was in training and discipline, which made them slow in tactical movement and easy to out-manoeuvre. But behind the fortifications and water defences of their strongholds, they were extraordinarily hard to defeat.

It is a mark of Gordon's eccentric genius that he turned two of the enemy's advantages – the high morale of the Taipings and the intricate waterways of Kiangsu and Chekiang – into his own assets. Because the Taipings were better fighters than his own troops, he enlisted many prisoners into the E.V.A., trusting them to fight fiercely against their former comrades within a couple of days of their capture. As for the ubiquitous waterways, others had regarded them as obstacles but Gordon, with his intimate surveyor's knowledge of the country, and depth of the canals and the height of the bridges, saw them rather as routes for supply, ways by which he could outflank a somewhat immobile enemy and bring his heavy guns to bear.

Finally there was the problem of the Imperial authorities, personified by the Futai, Li Hung Chang, and General Ching, operational commander of the Imperial troops whom Gordon had no intention of obeying. Foreigners regarded the Chinese as corrupt, cruel and insanitary. Chinese thought that the indifference of the foreign devils to human dignity was the mark of the beast. Li Hung Chang complained of their 'pretended superiority over the Asiatics . . . Some day I will ask them, "Was your country civilized and studying the Seven Arts before ours?" ' Gordon refused any emoluments beyond his British Army pay, a contrast to most foreigners who regarded China as an inexhaustible milch-cow. But Li was suspicious of a gift-horse: 'Can it be that this officer is not worth much?' Nor was he reassured when Gordon insisted on sole operational command: 'The thought is troubling me that this new British colonel and I may not get on well together.'

However, when Gordon reported in person on 27 March 1863, Li took a liking to him:

He is superior in manner and bearing to any of the foreigners I have come in contact with, and does not show that conceit which makes most of them repugnant in my sight. Besides, while he is possessed of a splendid military bearing, he is direct and business-like. Two hours after his arrival he was inspecting troops and giving orders; and I could not but rejoice at the manner in which his commands are obeyed.

A splendid military bearing was not, in fact, one of Gordon's qualities, but on a mandarin with an instinctive dislike of the profession of arms, his modest, unassuming manner made a good impression. Nevertheless, to curb his independence, 'I must arrange, some way, to have General Gordon accept money.' Soon he had nothing but praise. 'It is a direct blessing from Heaven.' He agreed that Gordon should be responsible directly to him, not to General Ching.

Gordon's first care was to reassure his parents, who would be vexed at his entering a dubious foreign service. His mother might 'depend upon my not doing more than I think my duty and that I will risk nothing'. His mother might not have been reassured had she known that he conceived it the duty of a commanding officer not only to direct but personally to lead the critical assaults, smoking a cigar and carrying only a light cane. In his plain Royal Engineer's undress uniform, with neither belt nor sword, while his officers, armed to the teeth, were belted and booted like theatrical banditti, he gave the E.V.A. a unique panache.

The E.V.A. was in rather poor shape when he took over, after defeat and the loss of two 32-pounders in February. Fifty officers had signed a protest at the dismissal of Burgevine, and the troops had been infected with their discontent. Gordon called an officers' meeting, assured them that he did not mean to sack them all, and for the moment won the confidence of these suspicious, resentful men. Within a week he was leading them to capture Fushau, a fortified town north-west of Shanghai, which quickly succumbed to his artillery without the infantry firing a shot. For this operation Gordon was promoted to the rank of *tsung-ping* (brigadier) in the Imperial army. He was in rank equal to Ching, which made their relations no easier.

He returned to find that Burgevine had been up to no good. A plausible rogue, smarting under his dismissal, he had persuaded the American and British Ministers to intercede with Prince Kung on his behalf. It seemed that Gordon's tenure of command would be short. Li Hung Chang, however, insisted on retaining him.

The main Taiping base on this front was the city of Soochow, seventy miles west of Shanghai. It was an important communications centre at the junction of the Grand Canal, running roughly north and south, and four tributary canals. Immediately west of it lay the Tai-ho lake, thirty-five miles square; so by capturing Soochow and gaining command of the lake, the Imperialists would drive a deep wedge between the main Taiping forces at Nanking to the north and Hangchow to the south. This was Li's object for 1866: but two outlying positions had first to be taken – Taitsan, thirty miles north-west of Shanghai, and Quinsan, on the canal joining Taitsan and Soochow.

The theatre of operations was a great alluvial plain, covering some 50,000 square miles, thickly populated, wealthy (before being overrun by the Taiping hordes) with tea plantations and silk factories, dotted with a few isolated hills and intersected in all directions by rivers, creeks and canals. Land-communications consisted only of narrow footpaths, but movement by water was easy. Everything had been laid waste – crops trampled down, pagodas destroyed, villages recognizable only by blackened walls of roofless houses: on the slimy banks of the canals, blocking the willow-pattern bridges, underneath the graceful bamboo clumps, sprawled the ubiquitous corpses, blackened and shining in the sun, grotesquely swollen, pulsating with maggots; each with its attendant swarm of flies settled like a black fur on the corrupt flesh or buzzing round in an angry swarm.

The rebel chief in Taitsan had passed word secretly to Li that he would surrender the place, and an Imperial force marched in. But no sooner was the advance guard inside than the gate was shut and thousands of shaggy-haired Taipings, howling like fiends, swarmed upon the Imperialists who were utterly unprepared. When, after a brief fight, they surrendered, 300 were at once decapitated to encourage the survivors to join the rebels. Among the victims was Li's brother, speared in the rump, which honed the edge of the Futai's hatred of the Long Hairs. He ordered Gordon with 2,600 men to avenge this atrocious treachery.

Like most towns in Kiangsu, Taitsan was walled and surrounded by a canal which was bridged opposite the four gates. Gordon made his approach with a flotilla of gun-boats and barges led by the *Hyson*, and surrounded the town. Having discovered by a personal reconnaissance that the canal skirting the west wall was clear of stakes, and that some ruined houses would give cover for his artillery, he disembarked his guns and gradually pushed them forward, covered by one another's fire and by the elm mantlets, until they were within 100 yards of the wall, a range at which the 32-pounder's fire was devastating. The *Hyson* came steaming up with her own 32-pounder, and soon a long section of the wall had crumbled into a feasible breach. Now the boats were poled forward to bridge the canal and the 4th Battalion advanced with great *élan*, led by Major Bannon with Gordon sauntering along beside him. The enemy in Taitsan numbered about 10,000 of whom 2,000 were picked men, and some of their guns were served by foreigners. Swarming onto the walls, they poured a tremendous fire into the attacking columns. Bannon was killed, and only on a third attempt, led by Gordon himself, was the breach cleared in a rush which carried the column on into the town.

It was Gordon's first experience of leading a storming party, which he did in a highly individual style. Smoking a cigar, carrying only his 'Wand of Victory', he strolled coolly forward, now yanking by the pigtail some private who seemed less than eager for the fray, now taking a nervous subaltern gently by the elbow and guiding him into the breach as though assisting an elderly aunt across the road. E.V.A. losses were heavy, especially in officers. 'It really was a most tremendous fight . . . the rebels fought most desperately.'

As Gordon was scrambling up the breach, he heard a voice call, 'Mr Gordon! Mr Gordon! You won't let me be killed?' It was a wounded deserter from the 31st Foot. 'Take him down to the river and shoot him!' ordered Gordon loudly; then, *sotto voce*, 'Put him in my boat, let the doctor attend him and then send him down to Shanghai.' There he was court-martialled and sentenced to a few months' imprisonment. Other captured foreigners, American, French and Indian, were shot.

No one has understood what made this ramshackle band of brigands follow Gordon with such extraordinary valour. In the eighteen months of his command, out of an officer establishment of about 105, 35 were killed and 54 wounded. Other rank casualties were smaller but still heavy. Of the motives which commonly inspire men to kill and die, religion and politics can be ruled out. Patriotism would have drawn most of the officers to Gettysburg and Chattanooga rather than to Taitsan. The private soldiers were killing men of their own race, and an increasing proportion were fighting against those who a few days earlier had been their friends and comrades. They were well paid, but although money can draw men to the colours, it cannot make them brave.

Probably the Ever Victorious Army was inspired mainly by an *esprit de corps*, almost equally hostile to the Imperialists and to the Taipings; it did not inhibit pillaging; it could lead to mass desertions if officers and men resented innovation; there was the ever-present danger of defection to the enemy. But somehow, by his extraordinary gift of leadership, Gordon held his 'rabble' together, forged them into a hard fighting force and kept them (between mutinies and sit-down strikes) loyal to their paymasters.

If Gordon inspired the E.V.A., what inspired Gordon? It was not militant Christianity, for religion did not then dominate his life. When a forlorn hope wavered, he 'prayed them up the breach', a vivid description of a commander carrying his men forward by his own will power. 'Thank Him if they succeeded, if not, was content, never wanted to know Him any closer, swinging as a pendulum in wide sweeps.'[1] Working it all out, watching his E.V.A. for disaffection, planning and fighting sixteen major actions in as many months, he had little time for speculation on 'eternal things'. He himself considered in retrospect that his real conversion to Christianity was after his return from China. Nor could patriotism have been for him a powerful motive; certainly the safety of the Shanghai merchants and the customs revenues was hardly a cause to stiffen the sinews and summon up the blood. The Imperial authorities were corrupt, obscurantist and almost as cruel as the Taipings.

Gordon was simply a professional soldier eager for experience and promotion, a fighter exhilarated by danger, fascinated by the problems of command, seeing battle as the supreme challenge. He rationalized his actions by explaining that it was his duty to 'rid the neighbourhood of Shanghai of these freebooters' and to show China that British officers were not all 'actuated by greed'; but essentially he acted as he did because when there was a fight on, he could neither keep out of it nor give less than his best.

Although no stickler for the minutiae of close-order drill and cere-monial, he was a strict disciplinarian with a flaring temper and a biting tongue – so much so that he sometimes deputed to another the task of administering an official rebuke, lest he say something which could not be forgiven. His control over the men was the more remarkable because he knew hardly any Chinese.

Often he was reduced to tears by the sufferings of 'his' wounded. Orientals regard tears as the proper expression of a man's grief, proving in this case that their commanding officer really cared for them as human beings, not mere cannon-fodder. As medical officer for the E.V.A. he secured the efficient Dr Moffitt, his personal friend who later married one of his sisters. Any conscientious commanding officer visits his men in hospital, but Gordon's hospital visiting went far beyond the call of duty. In these matters his concern contrasted with his apparent callous-ness in the Crimea.

He had a fondness for children, particularly small boys, and rescued many an orphan of the Taiping tempest. Six became his devoted per-sonal servants. At the height of the Quinsan battle he was seen carrying in his arms a naked urchin who, educated at his protector's expense, grew up to be a senior police officer and head of the Shanghai clan named 'Quincey', all very proud of their origin.

The storming of Taitsan produced a crop of atrocity stories, amply publicized in the press, angrily denied by Gordon. The Futai dealt expeditiously with such matters:

A former *hsien-kwan* [magistrate] of Taitsan brought me complaints that Gordon's men, when they captured the place, stripped it dry as a fishbone of everything valuable, and killed surrendered rebels by the hundreds. He asked if I would not give him an order to Gordon to protect his life and property. The impudence of this rascal, who himself encouraged the Long Hairs! . . . I was wondering whether it would not be well to call some of the guard and have an end made to his troubles in the yard. But I thought better of it, and so sent him back with a letter to Gordon, written in English, asking the commander to please cut the fellow's head off upon its presentation. He went away very gleefully.

In Li's opinion Gordon could do no wrong:

> What a sight for tired eyes and elixir for a heavy heart it is to see this splendid Englishman fight! ... If there is anything I admire nearly as much as the superb scholarship of Tseng Kuo-Fan, it is the military qualities of this fine officer. Fight – move – fight again – move again – landing his men – planning by night and executing by day – planning by day and executing by night! He is a glorious fellow!

It was after the storming of Taitsan that Gordon first enlisted in the E.V.A. large numbers of Taiping prisoners, 700 of them in this one place. He came to rely more on them than on any others. Eventually his own bodyguard, of company strength, was composed mainly of ex-rebels, except for its commander, a gigantic northerner promoted for gallantry to commissioned rank.

Ching now demanded an immediate attack on Quinsan, but Gordon thought the E.V.A. needed training, discipline and new equipment, for which he took them back to Sunkiang. This they resented, as they wanted leisure to dispose of their booty. Moreover the officers loudly protested at a regular British captain, Cooksley, being put in charge of the commissariat, potentially a lucrative appointment with local rank of lieutenant-colonel, so that he might issue orders to battalion commanders who were 'apt to be troublesome when rations were issued'. Gordon, according to one of them, 'flew into a passion, saying he was General and would alone command and do what he liked, and gave us twenty-four hours to reconsider'. At this they all resigned, at the same time assuring him 'as men, if not as gentlemen which I've doubt you consider us', that they had no desire to evade the Quinsan operation. He replied curtly that their resignations would take effect immediately. Next morning they changed their minds and reported for duty.[2]

So it was back to Quinsan, where General Ching urged a direct attack on the east wall. But Gordon, despite his aggressive leadership, was a very prudent tactician. He noted the strong granite walls, the ditch forty yards wide, and an 18-pounder served by an Englishman. He preferred what later military thinkers would call 'the indirect approach'. To this Quinsan was vulnerable, since it could be by-passed to the south by boats moving along a canal some four miles from the walls, and its communications cut where this waterway joined the main Quinsan-Soochow canal.

Brushing aside Ching's objections, he set off next morning in the

Hyson, followed by boats carrying his field artillery, the E.V.A.'s 4th Battalion and 500 men of Ching's. All fell out as he had planned. After the canal had been cleared of a line of stout stakes, the rebel retreat was cut off at Chunyi, nine miles to their rear, where he left a detachment to hold two stockades whence the rebels had fled. With the *Hyson* and several towed gun-boats, he set off on a bloody rampage towards Soochow. Along the bank ran a narrow road, and along the road ran mobs of helpless rebels, confined to it by the canal on one side and the Yansingho lake on the other. Four horsemen tried to run the gauntlet; the leader, at full gallop, was shot off his horse; the others pulled up, one of them hauled him up behind his saddle and galloped on: 'They deserved to get off,' Gordon commented. The creek was jammed with boats filled with fleeing rebels. Here and there were stockades, blasted into splinters by the *Hyson*'s 32-pounder. It was a massacre of helpless men by volleys of musketry and murderous discharges of grapeshot. They steamed to within three-quarters of a mile of Soochow and then back, repeating the slaughter. At Chunyi they found 500 Imperialists Gordon had left there under pressure from the whole Taiping garrison of Quinsan, 7,000 or 8,000 strong, a great mass of men on the north bank in the darkness. To clear the way Gordon resorted to the *Hyson*'s steam-whistle 'which had a singular effect'. Belching smoke and flame, howling like a banshee, invulnerable as a tank to musketry, the *Hyson* moved slowly forward pouring grapeshot and musketry into the screaming mob until suddenly it disintegrated. Gordon pursued to within a mile of Quinsan, then returned to Chunyi. At day-break the town was occupied with no further trouble.

It was a staggering blow to the rebels: 'They never got such a licking before.' With the loss of two killed and five wounded, Gordon had routed an enemy ten times as large as his own, taken 2,000 prisoners, 1,500 boats, a strongly fortified town, a mass of arms and artillery, and killed 4,000 to 5,000 of the enemy. Quinsan, besides being a communications centre and dominating the flat country around it, contained a useful arsenal and foundry capable of manufacturing shells. Henceforth the rebels did not possess 'one foot of ground outside the towns they hold'.

Ching was 'surly as a bear' at this brilliant victory won by ignoring his advice, and Gordon did not handle him with tact. Both complained to the Futai, who was not strong enough to call them both to order. 'Ching is far from being a great military man. Besides, he has a bad temper like Gordon, and they are both quick to say hot words.' He sent his military secretary, a former British Army surgeon called Macartney, to patch up the row and Ching made a sulky apology.

Gordon had decided to transfer the E.V.A. base from Sunkiang to

Quinsan, a junction of five navigable waterways and strategically better placed. Moreover his soldiers there would be removed from the demoralizing influence of their families and merchants who bought their plunder. They well appreciated the point, and when the daily parade was called, the artillery-men proclaimed their intention of blowing to pieces the Chinese officers with their small guns and the foreign officers with their big guns. Believing that the N.C.O.s were at the bottom of the trouble, Gordon called them up and threatened to shoot one in five unless they revealed the writer of this outrageous proclamation. His threat was received with derisive groans. Indicating a corporal who groaned the loudest, he told two of his bodyguard to shoot him, which was promptly done. The remainder were marched into cells and left to reflect for one hour, at the end of which they gave the culprit's name: it was the man who had been shot – or so they said.

There is no more extraordinary episode in Gordon's career. He was an idealist, to be sure, but he was also a realist and a ruthless man of action. As a realist he must have known that the loyalty of the E.V.A. was to its leaders rather than to a cause, and that in the case of the old E.V.A., enlisted by Ward and Burgevine, it would be to their officers, not to him; so he deliberately filled his bodyguard with youthful Taiping prisoners loyal to the man who had saved them from the executioner. No military code could have legally justified this summary execution for what was gross insubordination rather than mutiny. But if Gordon had merely ordered the corporal's arrest, there could have ensued a free-for-all fight in which he and his escort would have been overwhelmed. As it was, the mutiny collapsed. But when one considers his delicate position as a foreign devil under Chinese command, executing without trial a Chinese soldier, one can only marvel at his resolution – and at his confidence that Li Hung Chang would support him.

The sequel was succinctly recorded in Gordon's journal. 'Men then desert, 1,700 only out of 3,900 remain. Very disorderly lot. Ward spoilt them. G recruits rebel prisoners, who are much better men.'

No doubt after this incident the E.V.A.'s slack discipline was tautened by a wholesome element of fear. But there was more in Gordon for his men to admire than courage, resolution and ruthlessness. Physically he was extraordinarily tough and abstemious. He worked day and night, probably because he had to do, or chose to do, much of his officers' work as well as his own; yet he never seemed tired. Smoking too much, he took no interest in food and subsisted largely on raw eggs purloined at night from the larder and sucked a dozen at a time. In the hot weather he carried under his arm a battered pewter tea-pot, refreshing himself occasionally from the spout – a prudent measure in a country where the unboiled water crawled with lethal germs. He never suffered from malaria, though nearly everyone else did. On operations he slept in his clothes and boots, in a sleeping bag sewn from two blankets, yet always looked clean and tidy.

His air of modesty concealed the arrogance of a man who knows he is right and cannot waste time arguing. Without consulting the Futai, on 29 June he wrote to the Taiping chiefs advising them to make peace and offering his good offices with the Imperial authorities. Of mandarins he wrote: 'I like them, but they require a great deal of tact, and getting in a rage with their apathy is detrimental.' But that was exactly what he did. 'Gordon,' wrote Li, 'must control his tongue . . . He demands the respect of those who are inferior to him in rank. Why, then, does he not accord me the honours that are due as head of the military and civil authority?'

Gordon's arrogance was not based on prejudices of colour: in later years he was to treat his British colleagues – and, indeed, superiors – with even less respect than that accorded to General Ching. But when one of his British officers was pelted with earth by Imperialist soldiers, Gordon demanded an immediate apology from the mandarin in command, failing which he would bring up guns and 'knock his stockade about his ears'. He got his apology.

5

THE GREAT GENERAL KO

The hottest weeks of the year Gordon spent at Quinsan, training his troops and replacing eleven of his officers who had died of DTs. The *Hyson* was under repair and it was really too hot to wage war. It was not, however, too hot to quarrel with the Futai, who now began grudging him money. Gordon complained, which the Futai thought unreasonable. 'Gordon thinks of nothing but money these days and demands coins of me as if I were the god of gold and silver. He says the men will not fight any more unless they are paid. I tell him that as soon as Soochow is in our hands there will be funds sufficient to pay all arrears and some good bounty.'

That was the way things were done in China, but it was not the way they were done in the Royal Engineers. Gordon suddenly felt he could stand no more and resigned. However, he would stay on until his resignation was accepted, and in the meanwhile he planned his last operation with the E.V.A.

Li wanted an attack on Soochow before he was ready for it. Again Gordon favoured the indirect approach. 'The great thing in taking stockades from the rebels is to cut off their retreat, and the chances are they will go without trouble; but attack them in front, and leave their rear open, and they will fight most desperately.' Soochow should be pinched out, before it was assaulted, by cutting its communications to north and south along the Grand Canal and then gaining control of the Tai-ho lake immediately to the west of it. This involved the capture first of Kahpu and Wokong, canal junctions south of the city. Kahpu could be reached by boat from Quinsan, and Gordon decided to surprise the enemy by making his thirty-five mile approach along winding waterways in darkness.

But on 26 July 1863, a few hours before they were due to start, there was more trouble, this time from the artillery officers, who, unsettled by strange rumours about Burgevine, sent Gordon an illiterate 'round robin', refusing to move in protest at being placed under command of

Major Tapp. He set off without them. As poker-players they knew their bluff had been called, and they hurried after him to report for duty. The rebels were taken by surprise, Kahpu and Wokong were captured almost without a shot and Gordon returned to Shanghai. Fortunately he left the *Hyson* at Kahpu.

The situation was suddenly changed by Burgevine who on 1 August with a band of ruffians hijacked a small steamer, the *Kajow*, and joined the rebels in Soochow. He was not entirely opportunist, writing to Gordon, 'I am perfectly aware that both sides are equally rotten. But on the Taiping side there is at least innovation. The rebel Mandarins are without exception brave and gallant men, and could you see Chung Wang, who is here now, you would immediately say that such a man deserved to succeed.'

It was a point of view with which Gordon had some sympathy, but there could now be no thought of resignation, for Burgevine's defection might set off a chain-reaction in the E.V.A. and would give fresh heart to the rebels. Gordon's first thought was for his siege-guns, left in Quinsan. He galloped there through the night and sent them to Taitsan, now held by a British garrison. It had been a near thing: during the evening three of Burgevine's warriors actually marched into Gordon's room expecting to find their chief installed there.

His next move was on Patachiaou, another canal junction half-way between Soochow and Kahpu. There was a magnificent bridge, 300 yards long, of fifty-three arches. Unfortunately the demolition of one arch to make way for the *Hyson* brought down twenty-six more 'like a pack of cards . . . the arches falling one after another as fast as a man could run . . . I regret it immensely, as it was unique and very old, in fact a thing to come some distance to see.'

There was another bridge between Patachiaou and Soochow which became a sort of neutral ground where the foreigners on both sides could talk and smoke together. Gordon encouraged fraternization, particularly between Captain Davidson of the *Hyson* and his old pal Captain Jones, skipper of the *Kajow*, hoping to gain from it more than he lost. He wrote secretly to Moh Wang, the Taiping commander in Soochow, a friendly letter, suggesting that if any foreigners wished to leave the Taiping service, it would be politic to let them go. He had a meeting with Burgevine who, affable and plausible as ever, suggested they join forces and march on Pekin. Although refusing Jones the loan of blacksmith's tools to repair the rebel artillery ('I said it was a peculiar request'), Gordon sent them medical supplies and obtained from the authorities an amnesty for any foreigner who now deserted the Taipings. On 14 August, under pretence of trying to capture the *Hyson* by boarding,

Jones and forty others ('a nice lot, all the scum of Shanghai') surrendered.[1]
Burgevine was escorted to Shanghai and allowed to leave the country.

Gordon hoped much from his communication with Moh Wang, but
he was frustrated by the arrival of rebel reinforcements under command
of Chung Wang, the Faithful King himself, whom he admired as the
bravest and most talented of all the Taiping leaders, worth 5,000 men to
them. Clearly the isolation of Soochow must now be pressed forward.
For this it was necessary to block the Grand Canal, running north-west
from Soochow. But before this could be done, Gordon had an unexpected
setback. The *Firefly* had been sent down to Shanghai with wounded. It
was moored for the night off Li Hung Chang's house where it was
boarded by a gang of foreigners who took it off, with its big guns, to join
the rebels.

This transformed the situation. With the *Firefly* possibly on Lake
Tai-ho, Gordon could not count on surrounding Soochow. Besides,
there was the menacing presence of Chung Wang with a large field
army forty miles to the north-west. Gordon had to press on with
preparations for the very thing he wished to avoid, the direct assault on
Soochow.

'To be happy on earth,' ran a proverb, 'one must be born in Soochow.'
It was famed for its marble buildings, elegant gardens, the richness and
variety of its silk products, the intelligence of its men and the expertise
of its courtesans. This splendour had not survived four years of Taiping
occupation, but the walls had been kept in good repair, the wide, deep
moat was as formidable as ever; and beyond it, within range of guns
mounted on the city walls, had been constructed a strong system of
entrenchments and stockades, with shell-proof dug-outs and forests of
needle-sharp bamboo stakes. These, in turn, were covered by a breast-
work, and the breastwork by an encircling creek. Some 40,000 rebels
were in the city and in the Faithful King's field army. While preparing
for an assault, Gordon continued his attempts to make the Wangs see
reason. In the past Li Hung Chang had believed the only good Long
Hair was a dead one: 'They do not repent, the hounds.' But he had
recently modified his views, and the Imperialist camp was full of ex-
rebels, their heads meekly shaved in token of their submission to the
Pure Dynasty. Li still, however, thought that the delicate task of sub-
verting Chinamen should be left to subtle Chinese minds. But Gordon
persisted, presenting Moh Wang with a fine horse. Now nothing would
promote surrender so much as a successful assault.

On 27 November Gordon tried a night-attack, probably a mistake
because the E.V.A.'s training was not up to this most difficult of operations. Two days later another attack was made by daylight. Unfortunately

Chung Wang, the Faithful King, had just arrived in the city with his yellow-robed guard of picked warriors. Along the blood-soaked breast-work, in the battered stockades, there was desperate hand-to-hand fighting. Chung Wang led three counter-attacks; but the stockades, once stormed, were held. The leader of Chung Wang's guard was captured and the Futai would have executed him, but Gordon kept him in his own bodyguard 'as contented as possible'. That night the Faithful King returned to Nanking.

These attacks cost the E.V.A. 18 officers and 341 other ranks, a butcher's bill abhorrent to Gordon. But on 2 December on Ching's boat, he met the second-in-command of the rebels in Soochow, Lar Wang, and immediately took to him. He was a young man dressed simply in silk with a black headcloth, very distinguished looking with an intelligent and pleasing expression. He came straight to the point: 'I want you to help me,' he said, explaining that Moh Wang, whose wife and children were held hostages in Nanking, would fight to the last, but that he and most of the others wished to surrender. Gordon pointed out that the rebellion now had not a chance of success, and that it was no longer Imperialist policy to execute all surrendered rebels. He then left Lar Wang to settle details with Ching. He made no explicit promise of safe-conduct, but that was implicit in the whole course of the negotiations, and he had not 'the very remotest idea but that perfect faith would be kept with the Wangs'.

On 3 December Ching told Gordon that Lar Wang and the other Wangs would definitely surrender. Gordon impressed on the Futai that the Wangs must be well treated, and Li agreed. The Wangs disposed of Moh Wang by stabbing him at a banquet. 'It is glorious news,' Li rejoiced. 'I have issued an order granting pardon to the Wangs and a majority of their followers.'

During the night of 4-5 December Lar Wang's men shaved their heads, chased Moh Wang's men out by the West Gate and withdrew from the East and North Gates. Ching's troops occupied the former; and Gordon, keeping them strictly in hand, halted the E.V.A. outside the North Gate.

The E.V.A. expected much from Soochow, and to compensate them for not looting it, Gordon asked the Futai for a bonus of two months' pay. This, Li protested, was impossible, so Gordon, threatening resig-nation, gave him until three o'clock that afternoon to change his mind. While waiting for an answer, he went into the city to see what was hap-pening.[2] He found the Wangs cheerful and quite satisfied with their treatment. He went to Moh Wang's palace, accompanied by one of his officers who wrote a vivid description of the scene:

Picture to yourselves a large hall with a dark vaulted high wood roof, against the walls a number of gigantic but much disfigured Chinese deities, a table capable of holding about 150 guests, strewn with the débris of a feast, chairs and stools upset, candlesticks with the candles burnt out, and a deathlike silence and gloom. Half-way down this room was the bulky headless body of a man dressed in gorgeously-embroidered silk robes.

In a pocket Gordon found the letters he had written to Moh Wang. Much moved, he ordered the body to be decently buried. Now that it was all over, he was suffering from depression and anti-climax.

At three o'clock Ching informed him that the E.V.A. would receive a bonus of only one month's pay which Gordon accepted under protest, and paraded his men in the knowledge that this was not a matter in which he could expect his officers' support. The men received their commander's announcement with a howl of disapprobation. Early next morning, the 6 December, he marched them back to Quinsan. They passed the Futai's boat, moored in the canal, with angry growls and demonstrations. Gordon himself returned to Soochow. He again found the Wangs quite happy with the situation, and they cheerfully offered him 1,000 recruits for the E.V.A. Afterwards he saw them riding in high spirits, apparently unarmed, to the surrender ceremony and a banquet at the Futai's headquarters.

It was Li Hung Chang's triumph:

High credit will come from the Court for this splendid outcome, and Prince Kung will leap with joy when he receives the news ... but it is a good time that Gordon's services be dispensed with ... the way he speaks of the Wangs one would think that they were brothers of his. Last night, to please the Wangs, I invited them to a council of peace and a banquet. There was much merriment and good-nature, and I enjoyed meeting these men – Long-Haired rebels though they were.

The sequence of events now becomes confused, with various people under stress of emotion giving different accounts. Gordon went with Macartney to the East Gate to see what was happening. There was a crowd at Li's boat, and disorderly bands of Imperialist soldiers running riot into the town and shooting exuberantly into the air. Early in the afternoon Ching arrived, not looking at all himself. When Gordon asked how the surrender ceremony had gone, he first declared that the Wangs had not turned up for it, then that they had demanded authority over half the city and, on this being refused, had gone away. Gordon did not believe a word of it, and asked Macartney to go to Lar Wang's palace and discover the truth, while he accompanied Ching to the South Gate. During their ride Gordon pressed Ching with questions. Where was

Lar Wang? Why was there still so much shooting? Ching, occasionally discharging his own rifle in simulated *joie de vivre*, replied that he had not set eyes that day on Lar Wang. At the South Gate they parted company and Gordon, puzzled, apprehensive and exasperated, asked the interpreter for the true facts. The man replied noncommittally that something bad might have occurred.

The darkening streets were crowded with Imperialist troops looting and ex-rebels armed and alert. A nephew of Lar Wang begged Gordon to escort the females of the family to his own house for safety. But when they got there they found it crammed with Taipings, shaven but turbulent, who made Gordon prisoner. Perhaps they thought they could hold him as hostage for the safety of the Wangs, or that his presence would protect them against rampaging Imperialists; perhaps they did not think at all, but out of instinctive xenophobia grabbed an important foreign devil. His situation was perilous. He was utterly exhausted, his nerves at full stretch; his tough constitution, his cheerful, imperturbable nature had suddenly, after nine months' continual strain, overwork and fighting, reached the point of collapse; and he was distraught by a growing conviction that the Futai had not played fair with the Wangs. There was no one he could consult; he had no communication, save through a frail link of a terrified interpreter, with the truculent armed mob who jostled him in the flickering torch light.

During the long hours of that night he came to a decision which, if implemented, would have been mutiny. He would take his steamers up to the Futai's camp and, at the point of the *Hyson*'s 32-pounder, seize his superior officer as a hostage for the Wangs' safety.

In the morning his gaolers, as inexplicably as they had held him, let him go. He made his way to the East Gate where Ching arrived, blaming the Futai for anything which might be amiss, but Gordon was in no mood for excuses: 'I told him what I thought.' His position had improved, but he still did not know what had happened to the Wangs. The next arrival was an American officer, who said that on the Futai's orders Ching had executed them. He produced a son of Lar Wang, who, pointing across the creek to some objects lying beside the Futai's stockade, said that his father had been beheaded.

Gordon's worst fears were now realized. Li had tricked him, he was dishonoured, no Taiping would ever trust him again! He crossed the creek and found nine corpses beheaded and split down the middle.

Who had killed the Wangs, and why?

The mandarin Pwa, a local landowner attached to the Futai's headquarters, said afterwards that no one but Gordon had the smallest intention of sparing their lives. From numerous conflicting accounts, four provided by the Futai himself, it is pretty clear that it was he who ordered the execution. The official Chinese version says that the Wangs came to his camp armed and still defiant, demanding that Soochow remain in their hands. It is not unlikely that the Wangs' demeanour lacked humility and penitence, and by this alone in Chinese opinion they merited death. Moreover their atrocious treachery in Taitsan, of which his own brother had been a victim, made the Futai disinclined to take chances.

No mitigation of Li Hung Chang's conduct occurred to Gordon as he picked up Lar Wang's head, wrapped it in a silk scarf and went back to await the steamers. Half-demented with rage and shame, convinced that he himself was forever dishonoured, he determined to confront the Futai at his camp and – ? We do not know. Perhaps he hardly knew himself. In his official report he wrote that he meant to compel the Futai to resign the governorship of Kiangsu to him, failing which he would hand back to the Taipings the towns he had captured. In a private letter he wrote, 'If I had come across the Futai, it would have gone hard with him.' Later, when the Futai attempted a reconciliation, Gordon replied that, 'if I caught him, I should be obliged to shoot him.'[3]

Fortunately, when Gordon arrived at his camp, Li was no longer there; so all Gordon could do was to leave a furious letter setting out his ultimatum, return to Quinsan and go to bed.

The Futai asked Macartney to translate the letter. He refused, explaining that it had been written while Gordon was emotionally disturbed. Li then told Macartney, 'Tell Gordon that . . . I accept myself the full and sole responsibility for what has been done. But also tell Gordon that this is China, not Europe . . . They came with their heads unshaved, they used defiant language, and I saw that it would not be safe to show mercy.'

Macartney entered Gordon's room next morning and found him sitting on his bed sobbing. Gordon reached under the bed and brought out an object which he held up in Macartney's face. 'Do you see that? It is the head of Lar Wang, foully murdered.' He then burst into hysterical tears and Macartney, a doctor and an eminently balanced man, realizing that he was in no state for rational discussion, withdrew.

At breakfast Macartney pointed out that if Gordon persisted in his mad scheme, not only would all his good work be undone, but the E.V.A., deprived of pay, would resort to plunder. There might even be war between China and Britain. Gordon angrily retorted, 'I will have none of your tame counsels', and ordered the *Hyson* to prepare to attack the Futai's camp. Macartney galloped ahead to warn Li, but Gordon contented himself with going to Ching and demanding that Lar Wang's body be properly buried.

Having heard of these events General Brown, who had succeeded Staveley, transferred the E.V.A. to his own command, prior to disbanding it, and asked Gordon to keep it from misbehaviour until matters were sorted out. To this Gordon agreed. He also, most injudiciously, sent his account of these events to the Shanghai newspapers.

So the E.V.A. remained in Quinsan, an increasing menace because it had nothing to do. But the rest restored Gordon to a more balanced state of mind. By Christmas he was feeling cheerful enough to invite Lyster over for a few days' sport with teal and pheasants. It was some consolation that Lar Wang's son had not been slaughtered. 'I have him here, a very sharp young fellow and very lively. His poor father was a very good Wang, and far superior to any of the Imperialists.' But Gordon still insisted that, 'if faith had been kept there would have been no more fighting, as every town would have given in . . . I fear all my work has been thrown away.'[4]

On New Year's Day, 1864, there arrived the mandarin Pwa heading a procession bearing congratulations from the Emperor, 10,000 taels and long snake-flags captured from the Taipings. Gordon accepted two flags, but flogged the bullion-carriers from his presence with the Wand of Victory. On the back of the Son of Heaven's letter he scribbled a curt refusal.

But Gordon was thawing towards Li, who paid the E.V.A. quite generously for the capture of Soochow. Moreover the men were restive, and Gordon had to dismiss sixteen officers. As he informed Bruce, 'The rabble called the Quinsan force is a dangerous body – I do not apprehend that the rebellion will last six months longer if I take the field. It may well be six years if I leave.' Sir Robert Hart, head of the Imperial Customs, urged him to stay on, adding significantly, '*Think well before you take another step, but that step determined, stick to it for your own sake.*' Bruce also gave sound advice: 'Do nothing under pressure of excitement, and above all avoid publishing in the newspapers accounts of your difficulties with the Chinese authorities.'[5]

With the loss of Soochow, the Taipings were based on Nanking in the north and Hangchow in the south, 150 miles apart. The obvious strategy was to break through in the centre, across the Tai-ho lake, especially as the rebels had disarmed the *Firefly* to use her guns on land. In bitter weather and snowstorms Gordon's flotilla crossed the lake and sailed past scenes of appalling devastation – children with their throats cut; a woman with her hands tied behind her back, her breasts cut off and her belly ripped open; starving peasants reduced to eating grass and even corpses.

There is a feeling of anti-climax about these operations. Gordon and the E.V.A. were stale. Soochow was to have been their great victory, but it had turned sour. Now they went at their work without zest, wanting only to get it over. Gordon was worn out by the jealousies and squabbles of the 'quarrelsome devils who officer this force'.[6] After some rather muddled fighting, during which he was slightly wounded, they arrived before the city of Hangchow.

This was to be the E.V.A.'s last battle. The great Taiping rebellion was near its end. But the Futai's forces had made little headway against the garrison of tough old rebels from Canton. Li wished the credit to go to his own men, so for the grand assault on 11 May the E.V.A. was relegated to a support role. At first light all the siege-guns opened a tremendous bombardment. At 1 p.m. they stopped, and when the dust cleared, two good breaches could be seen. Both Imperialist columns reached the crest, one was driven back and as it recoiled the 1st Battalion, led by Gordon himself, swept forward in the last charge of the Ever Victorious Army. Up they scrambled, panting and stumbling over the stones and rubble. As Gordon reached the crest he saw, only 150 yards away, the gaping muzzle of the *Firefly*'s 32-pounder, double-loaded with grape, pointing straight at him. It never fired; the powder was damp; and he led his men over the crest and into the town.

One more task remained: the E.V.A. must be disbanded before it set up on its own account. So while Li Hung Chang went on to administer the *coup de grâce* in Nanking, Gordon took the E.V.A. back to Quinsan. By the end of May they had had their last parade, their last grumble, and returned to the water-front of Shanghai and the villages of Kiangsu. Their commanding officer's final verdict was, 'A more turbulent set of men than formed the officers have not often been collected together, or a more dangerous lot if they had been headed by one of their own style.'[7]

Li, not without prompting, recommended him for the greatest honours, and Prince Kung responded. 'We command that Gordon be rewarded with a yellow riding jacket to be worn on his person, and a peacock's feather to be carried in his cap; and that there be bestowed on him four suits of the uniform proper to his rank of *titu* . . . Respect this.' The rank of *titu* was the highest in the Chinese Army, the Yellow Jacket was granted only to fifty mandarins in the whole empire. There were also two specially engraved gold medals, banners, silk robes and hats galore.

There was a special ceremony for his investiture, described by an E.V.A. officer:

All the Chinese officials wore their gorgeous robes and banners and flags of all hues were flying. For some two or three hours Gordon did nothing but put on one suit of clothes, take them off and put on another. The donning of the Yellow Jacket with all its paraphernalia was the climax of this interesting scene. More guns fired, cracker fizzed and burst, gongs were clashed, and huge brass horns brayed ... All the time that this investiture was going on Gordon's face bore a sort of half-amused, half-satirical smile, still he entered into the whole affair with interest, asked about the various garments, and made comical allusions to his appearance in them.

Hart wrote, 'Don't, like a good fellow, reject these things, which you said you would like to have.' Gordon had no intention of rejecting them for he was not as indifferent to honours as was often made out. Years later he admitted, 'It was very much against the grain that the Chinese gave me the Yellow Jacket, but I said, "Give me the Yellow Jacket or nothing." '[8] From Her Majesty's Government he received a brevet-lieutenant colonelcy and the Companionship of the Bath, raising him to the same rank as Foreign Office clerks, the compiler of *Burke's Peerage* and other eminent persons.

His final thoughts on Li Hung Chang and the Imperialists were more objective than they had been at Soochow:

The Chinese are a wonderful people; they seem so apathetic about any changes that I am much afraid of them. The only man I have seen worth anything is the Futai of Kiangsu, Li ... That the execution of the Wangs at Soochow was a breach of faith, there is no doubt; but there are many reasons to exculpate the Futai of his action, which was not at all a bad act in the eyes of the Chinese ... It is a very contested point whether we ought to have interfered in suppressing the rebellion or not; I am, however, perfectly satisfied that it was the proper and humane course to pursue.

On 19 June 1864 Nanking fell at last, after the Heavenly King's suicide and Chung Wang's capture. Gordon was much relieved. 'As long as it held out, my late officers held themselves ready to join the rebels if there was a chance of success; now they will disperse over the globe.' The great Taiping rebellion was over.

With attention focused on Gordon's bravery, piety and eccentricities, his virtuosity as a commander had not been so noticed. He was a master of the 'indirect approach', using the armed steamers and gun-boats which had hitherto been quite unfamiliar to him. He never fell into the fallacy of believing that wars can be won bloodlessly, without fighting battles, simply by manoeuvre. To him, the object of his encircling and outflanking moves was to place him in the best position for a battle. He was always careful of the lives of his men. He mastered the combination of fire and movement. To make what he did of the E.V.A., he must have been a brilliant trainer of troops and military administrator. He was a master of psychological warfare. What other commander has so filled his army with ex-enemies, put them into battle within a few days of their capture and never been let down by them? Gordon has sometimes been written off as a mere leader of irregulars. This is a false judgement. The Ever Victorious Army was not an irregular force, but an imitation, a grotesque travesty, perhaps, of what would now be termed an Infantry Brigade Group with a powerful artillery component, bombardment vessels and transport-boats. Perhaps the greatest proof of Gordon's military genius is not his leadership of so many forlorn hopes and his development of tactics perfectly suited to the situation, but the use he made of such unpromising material.

The fighting over, he completed his survey of the Shanghai area. Then, in November 1864, it was time to go.

He warned his mother not to advertise his home-coming, 'for it would be a signal for the disbanded to come to Southampton, and although the waits at Christmas are bad, these others are worse'; 'they are not gentlemen, and will be up to all sorts of tricks.'[9] Gordon's retreat was meticulously planned. A bowler hat and a reach-me-down suit were purchased for the homeward voyage. Lest their newness draw attention to the conquering hero, the hat was well 'concertinaed', the new suit tied in a bundle and dropped overboard into the muddy Soochow creek. Without a word of farewell, he slipped away from the Mess dinner-table and aboard his launch, where he locked himself in his cabin. But he was not allowed to sneak off like a thief in the night. Chinese troops lined the river with banners, lanterns and blazing torches, rockets and shells were fired, thousands of crackers let off, horns and gongs brayed and clashed to honour 'the Great General Ko', as his launch, decorated with all the Ever Victorious Army's battle colours, sped down the river to the waiting liner.

6

THE GRAVESEND COLONEL

Gordon arrived home in January 1865, to find that he was a celebrity. The press had taken up 'Chinese Gordon' and to the public he was one of Britain's heroes. He went straight to his family, now living in Southampton. Evading those who would lionize him, he escaped social engagements in Southampton by travelling up to London and in London by travelling down to Southampton. He did not enjoy his leave. After seven months he applied to go back to duty.

It is strange that from the age of thirty-one, when he gave up command of the Ever Victorious Army, to his death nearly twenty-one years later he was never entrusted by the War Office with the command of troops on active service. During those years British soldiers fought in New Zealand, Canada, Abyssinia, West Africa, Egypt, South Africa, Burma, Afghanistan and the Indian frontier, but they fought without this brilliant soldier. Gordon's military genius cannot alone account for this, for several able soldiers were positively singled out for command. There was some prejudice in British military circles against officers who had won what were thought to be easy laurels by leading orientals against orientals – but Roberts, Kitchener and many others overcame it. There was also some prejudice against officers in scientific corps where promotion was not by purchase – but Roberts was a gunner, Kitchener a sapper, and purchase was abolished in 1871. Gordon was not personally unpopular: on the contrary, all the evidence is that his brother officers liked him. Perhaps the press had something to do with it, for dislike of the press was almost universal in British military circles.

When Gordon applied, fifteen months before the expiry of his leave, to return to duty, all he was offered was command of the Royal Engineers at Gravesend, where he had to supervise the construction of forts guarding the Thames estuary. He was under no illusions as to the utility of these works, which would hardly have stopped Van Tromp.

He found it profoundly depressing; and his spirits were further lowered by the death of his father. 'I used to walk out to the Chalk, and go into the churchyard and think about my father, and kick the stones about, and walk back again.' His father's death – and, one may think, ample leisure – stimulated his dormant interest in religion, which was to become ever more engrossing, and not (as before) to lapse in the excitement of war. It was from this year that, in retrospect, he dated his conversion. Before this he 'had a belief that Jesus was the son of God, and used to have feelings of deep depression' – not, one must add, apparent to his friends – 'on account of my faults.' Now this belief was strengthened: 'I knew Jesus was my Saviour.' In the aftermath of his father's death, 'God made me count the cost and conclude that His service should *be all*, and that if *everything* was given up He would abundantly repay me in this world . . . He gave me first to see that the fruits of the spirit could be only had by abiding in Christ or being joined to Him, but how joined was still a mystery.'[1]

But what, in Gravesend, was God's service to which *everything* should be given up? He saw it as the relief of the sick, the suffering, the poor; and particularly of poor boys.

It was not in his nature to dabble. Once he had set his hand to it, the days were all too short. He got up early, plunged into a cold bath, said his prayers and read a passage from the scriptures. Nothing irritated him more than being interrupted in his devotions. He hurried through a meagre breakfast and dealt with his correspondence, never letting paperwork accumulate: 'Do it and get it off your mind.' Then he set off to visit the works under construction. He acquired a four-oared gig, the fastest pulled boat on the river. 'A little faster, boys, a little faster!' he would urge his crew as they laboured on a four-mile pull against the tide. Arriving at the works, he would bound up the glacis and hurry round followed by the massive works contractor, two or three foremen comfortable in bulk and some subalterns. He invariably addressed his first remarks to the rearguard. If any work was proceeding at less than top speed, it would be, 'Another five minutes gone and this not yet done, my men! We shall never have them again!' On duty he was always the Colonel Commandant, permitting no liberties. Back then for luncheon, usually eaten at his desk from a half-open drawer which he shut if anyone came in.

Sometimes he had some mapping to do; generally, however, the afternoon was for the dirty little boys of Gravesend, for teaching in the Ragged School, and for visits to an increasing number of poor people, sick people, lonely people and tiresome people whom he befriended.

His closest friends were a quiet, pious couple named Freese, of independent means, living with their children at Milton-next-Gravesend. He used to drop in on them almost every evening 'for talks of intensest interest, varied by laughter and jokes for he had a great deal of humour'. They introduced him to many of the deserving and not-so-deserving poor.

They were not uncritical friends, and Mrs Freese had no hesitation in speaking up on the not infrequent occasions when she deemed him to be holding forth on subjects about which he knew nothing. One of these was music. She well knew that the limit of his appreciation was a lively hymn-tune.

His official residence was the Fort House, a family mansion surrounded by a big, rambling garden with ancient cannon on the ramparts, beehives on the lawn, ships swinging to the tide below, which was used as a sort of public park for almost anyone who asked for the key. 'The human face divine,' he told Mrs Freese, 'is to me much more interesting than any amount of flowers.' He could be very tiresome.

His well-stocked kitchen garden was divided into allotments for his protégés. He gave the fruit to the Workhouse Infirmary. This was little sacrifice for he was indifferent to what he ate: his only indulgence was smoking which he could not give up. Mrs Freese once found him sitting down to a meal consisting of a pot of tea and a stale loaf. 'How very uninviting that looks,' she remarked. His reply was to cram the loaf into the slop-basin and pour tea over it: 'In half an hour it will not in the least matter what I have eaten.' However, when he had guests he ordered a proper dinner and sent a despairing appeal to Freese for some drinkable wine.

It was some time before the Freeses identified him with that hero of the popular press, 'Chinese Gordon'. Then a chance remark caused her to ask, 'Were you ever in China? Did you see anything of the Taiping rebellion?' 'I should think I did,' he replied. 'Why, it was I who put an end to it.' Eventually they dragged the truth out of him.

The highest priority was given to his work with boys, 'scuttlers' or 'kings' as he called them. There were many in the cottages and slum alleys of Gravesend and on the Thames fishing-boats and barges. He ran a free school at Fort House where he taught every evening the 'three r's', varying the routine with cricket in the summer, draughts and chess in winter and with a cheerful hymn shouted at the top of their voices. Finally he would send each scuttler off with a good hunk of bread and cheese inside him.

When they were filthy, they were washed by the Colonel Commandant himself, in the horse-trough. Compulsory ablutions would be followed by a heart-to-heart talk. Planting a newly-cleansed king in front of a mirror, Gordon asked, 'You see a new boy, don't you? Well, just as you are new outside, so I want you to be new inside.' This was not resented: presents of shrimps were brought by the fisher-lads, and in place of more basic graffiti there was chalked on the fence opposite Fort House, 'God bless the Kernel'. To the Sunday School he preached, not very well, and to the 'Ragged School' he gave talks on current affairs and presented the dragon-flags captured in China.

But the most rewarding work he did for his scuttlers – apart from bringing them to the knowledge of God – was to find them jobs in the Army, in barges and warehouses, and at sea. Where necessary he paid their apprentice fees and fitted them out, buying clothes and boots wholesale. He kept a big map of the world, on which pins marked the voyages of Jack, Willie and Harry. Alex, 'a sweet child', jumped his ship in a Spanish port to get involved in a civil war. Gordon thoroughly approved.

The old Adam had not died in Chinese Gordon. When Napier's expeditionary force set off for Abyssinia without him, he suffered agonies of disappointment and frustration. He shut himself up for the whole day and 'went through something'. It required all his resolution to write, 'It is more important (though we may stumble at it) to speak to the scuttlers than to take Magdala.' It was particularly galling to be on the shelf when the army was so badly trained in minor tactics and commanded by generals more ignorant than any subaltern. He pointed out these defects to General Erskine, commanding the Thames defences. 'I made a big map of his district which I placed in his office, and I thought at least that he would study it . . . I told Erskine I would (were I he) take a pack-saddle horse and ride over every bit of my district.' But the General was unreceptive to good advice: 'If you were to ask him how he would get to one of his forts, he could not tell you.'

There was something almost frenzied in his untiring industry. Work, he insisted, was the best cure for 'the doles', and for a fashionable lady's *ennui* he prescribed a good, long day's washing. 'There is nothing like employment for peace and rest . . . hence the poor are so much more cheerful than people in our class of life who have everything.' Yet he had no antipathy towards the well-to-do. 'Christ never took the part of the poor against the rich individually.' Nor did Gordon ever allow the poor to take 'liberties'.

He was a constant visitor to the Workhouse Infirmary with a 'bit of baccy' for the old men, a 'screw of tea' for the old women, a chat and a few verses of scripture. One old woman he found apparently on her death-bed. He lighted her fire, prepared some gruel, fed her with his own hand, found her a nurse, rousted out a doctor – and she lived for many years. He observed, 'You may give away hundreds of pounds and scarcely get any gratitude, but do anyone the least spiritual good and you bind him to you forever.' Generous of money, he was prodigal of time and trouble.

But sometimes his penetration was at fault and those sparkling, lively eyes, just as they were unable to distinguish red from green, failed to see through a plausible rascal. He made a good story of a family he had been helping for a long time with fifteen shillings a week, and frequent visits to hear their tales of woe. One day he made an unexpected call and found them tucking into shrimps and hot cakes. He broke the silence by saying he thought they might at least invite him to the feast he had provided. He never spoke to them again.

An addiction to the bottle was a failing he could not unreservedly condemn, writing tolerantly of one of his old men, 'Less and more steadiness is what he wants.' He had a soft spot for 'the Old Bird', a quite useless jobbing gardener, always on the look-out for a worm and by no means averse to feathering his nest, who spent most afternoons dozing in the conservatory at Fort House.

Towards hypocrisy he was less tolerant. One evening at the Freeses there arrived the agent of a religious society, a compulsive complainer. Gordon, putting his head in his hands, and his elbows on the table, waited patiently till the wearisome stream of words should end. When the man had left, Freese said, 'What do you think of him?' Gordon's reply was a gesture used by Li Hung Chang meaning 'Cut off his head.' Soon afterwards the person decamped with the society's funds.

He had a horror of a death-chamber: 'When a poor partridge or hare is wounded, it gets away from its comrades and dies quietly, and that is what I want to do when the time comes.' Nevertheless he was in constant demand at the bedsides of the dying:

There is a very beautiful young girl dying tonight, in a few short hours she will glide into a bright, balmy land, and see such sights as would pass our understanding . . . She left at ten minutes to 12, very happy and beautifully. 'What are those harps playing for?' she said just before her departure.

> Tune, tune your harps,
> Ye saints in glory.

All is well.

There was Mr Carter, a crotchety old gentleman paralysed for years and by no means disposed to bear his affliction in a spirit of Christian resignation. Gordon hated his perpetual grumbling, but gave him a daily newspaper, a weekly stipend, and a curious frame of gauze-netting, the purpose of which at first escaped the Carter household's comprehension. It was to keep the flies off his head while he was reading.

A sadder case was the widow of an E.V.A. officer to whom Gordon paid so many visits of consolation that she mistook sympathy for a warmer sentiment, and boldly asked his intentions. On such occasions it is well not to hesitate or refine. He said he had none.

Socially he was a dead loss because any fixed engagement bored him. Friendship could only be on his terms: his dedication to those who needed his help made him rude towards those who wanted merely his company. Refusing a dinner invitation, he wrote:

I have much secular work to do during the day and it is as much as I can do to visit the very few people I do go to in the evening. I know you and Mr Freese have every human and many spiritual comforts beyond those of many of our rank of life and therefore though it may be more pleasant there is not any call for me to leave other important work to spend the immortal hours in desultory converse ... I do not see that there is any profit in social meetings for me.[2]

Whether or not Gordon was a saint, surely Mrs Freese was, to put up with this. Apparently the friendship of this extraordinary man, even on his terms, was worth the price.

Official dinner parties, which he could not refuse, were the bane of his life. So were uninvited guests, especially one whom he nicknamed *Auto da fé*, probably Major General Sir William Gordon, no relation but a fellow sapper and friend from Crimean days, suffering from melancholia, who relied on Charley to cheer him up. '*Auto da fé* arrived suddenly ... and is going to stay.' Three weeks later, 'Peace reigns here. *Auto da fé*!!! (hurrah!) will leave (hurrah!) on Monday (hurrah!) though I have asked him to stay.'

Later he visited Sir William in Scotland, and tried to walk him out of 'the doles' by long winter trudges through the dripping woodlands. 'I believe there are many Kings (red-haired) about, but I cannot get at them with facility, as I do not like vexing my old friend who dislikes tracts very much.'

It was not in Gordon's nature to take his religion pre-digested from anyone: he had to work it out for himself, mainly from intensive, detailed study of the Bible. It was a gradual process, most marked during periods of physical inactivity. The result was a highly individual belief. In practice he was perfectly ecumenical, worshipping at Anglican and Congregationalist churches in Gravesend, in a Greek Orthodox church in Jerusalem, a Coptic church in Khartoum. 'Do not forget me in your prayers,' he begged a Catholic bishop, 'Catholic and Protestant are but soldiers in different regiments in Christ's army.'

His constant theme was the need for more Bible-study:

> How little is read of the Bible, compared with man's words. Take a sermon, which lasts from twenty minutes to an hour; as a rule a single verse or two is taken, and the preacher's opinion on that text occupies the time. If people paid more attention to the Scriptures themselves, and less to commentaries on the Scriptures, there would be fewer religious differences: 'Ye do err, not knowing the Scriptures.'

It was while studying the Bible as he dressed for dinner that his attention was caught by 1 John iv, 15, 'Whosoever confesseth that Jesus is the Son of God, God dwelleth in him and he in God.' Suddenly it flashed upon him, as a blinding revelation, that he had discovered a jewel of priceless value. The more he thought about it, the more significant it seemed. It was God's in-dwelling in man that distinguished Christianity from other religions, not bad in themselves but lacking this truth. Gordon felt it with the utmost intensity: it gave him confidence and comfort in all circumstances; it armoured him equally against praise and derision; it made him respect the dirtiest little scuttler, the most drunken old reprobate – so long as they confessed that Jesus was the Son of God – as a temple in which God dwelt.

It seemed a simple truth to be shared with all who were prepared to listen. 'Do you believe in Jesus?' he would ask complete strangers, even Father Wyatt, the Catholic priest. 'Yes,' was the usual reply. 'Then do you know that God lives in you?' Again there would be a slightly embarrassed 'Yes'. He would then talk of the comfort of having God for a friend: 'Talk to your Father often, and tell Him your wants and He will help you.'

He believed in predestination, while insisting that one should use every effort and talent to bring about what one believed to be right. This stimulated his exertions, but freed him from anxiety over the results. 'I believe that not a worm is picked up by a bird without the direct intervention of God, yet I believe entirely in man's free will; but I cannot and do not pretend to reconcile the two.' He read the newspapers 'to see what God is doing and what are His designs'. Providence could have it both ways. If things went well, it was through the merciful dispensation of Providence; if badly, Providence was being inscrutable. In either case it was sure, in the long run, to be all for the best, and in that thought he could always find comfort and reassurance.

He believed that everyone had two natures, the fleshly and the spiritual. The mix varies, some being more fleshly and given to carnal pleasures others more spiritual and seeking heavenly things. Though man's two natures are joined together on earth, there is in everyone a conflict between them which must end in the triumph of the spiritual when the fleshly is destroyed by death. The spiritual in *everyone* was destined for salvation, the fleshly for damnation. 'We are all lepers' – but all would be saved. Why, he asked, were so many good Christians so morose? It was because they were tied to a corpse, their body. 'Why drag this corpse about . . . It is heavy and troublesome. Why not quicken it?'

It followed that death was devoutly to be wished. To Mrs Freese it seemed morbid for a young, healthy man, with no troubles but the frustration of not going to war, to long for death; but to Gordon it was perfectly logical, since only in death could the hateful, fleshly nature be overcome by the spiritual. Yet deliberately to hasten one's death was very wrong, for God had work for us to do. 'No blame is ever given to sons who look forward to the holidays . . . if they ran away and went home, it would be another thing.'

Nevertheless, he gave the impression of a singularly happy man. Even when the Colonel came hurrying into the office in the morning clapping his elbows to his sides and exclaiming, 'Oh, that I had wings like a dove, then I would flee away and be at rest' – even in such eccentricities, nobody thought of him as morose. Indeed he himself, in what was neither the first nor the last of his self-contradictions, wrote, 'I do not think there is so happy a being as I am.'

Holding these views so strongly, he must not – he could not keep them to himself. At first he dreaded accosting complete strangers with the most personal questions. 'There were boys running about worth millions and I could not have the courage to speak to them.' But when he did have the courage, it was richly rewarded. 'Great blessings in Perry Street. Got three rough lads into a room and found they were *kings*! . . . A country lad of Our Lord's, a Hebrew 14 years old, has fallen to me, and I hope to get him a job in the Survey.'

He churned out tracts, printing them at his own expense. Hurrying through the streets, he would press them on passers-by. His subalterns used to watch through a telescope, not without mirth, their Colonel's erratic cross-country progress as he left one tract beside a footpath, stuck another on a wall, darted across a field to hand a third to a scuttler scaring crows. He even scattered them like confetti from the train. But although religion filled so much of his thought, in ordinary conversation he kept off religious topics except with those he was 'sure of'.

On Easter Sunday, 1871, Gordon accepted without marked enthusiasm an offer of the post of British commissioner on the international commission set up after the Crimean War to regulate navigation in the lower reaches of the Danube. There was a farewell to his mother whom he found rather trying with her constant demands on him and her incessant sermons 'on the text I DO NOT LIKE'. The Freeses saw him off. He told Mrs Freese how thankful he was not to be married, the pain of parting from a wife would be too great. Somewhat later he wrote, 'Wives! Wives! What a trial you are to your husbands! Married men have more or less a cowed look. However, it is good discipline, and no doubt wives save men a deal of petty annoyances.'[3] But emphatically marriage was not for him.

On 1 October he took over at Galatz and on the 31st invited Freese to come out as his secretary, 'where you would not have much to do . . . You could bring out a Gravesend laddie with you – little Webster or any other tractable person. You would find everything *comme il faut* – a harmonium, and horses to ride as much as you like, regular quiet hours . . . I think Willie Webster too small – take Bill Palmer, of Chalk; he has been a gentleman's groom.'

What fun it would be, almost like Gravesend with Freese and one of the dear laddies! But Freese could not manage it, so Gordon had to face without congenial companionship his dead-end job and colleagues who gave little thought to eternal things.

He kept up an eager correspondence with Gravesend friends, begging for news of the scuttlers. 'Dear little Arthur, I wish I could see the little wretch . . . but I fear he would fight the Russian Arthurs who are just like him. If his mother would take 15 [shillings], I would buy him.'

Gordon's attitude to marriage and young women, his dedication to boys and the rather maudlin references to them in his correspondence, prompt the question which no honest biographer can ignore.

Nowadays an unmarried man who devotes much of his time to boys is widely assumed to be homosexual. It is an occupational hazard of schoolmasters, choirmasters and scoutmasters. In Gordon's time this was not so. Army officers were not expected to marry young: many schoolmasters never married at all – but no one suspected the numerous bachelor officers and schoolmasters in Kipling's world of being 'queer': it was accepted that a man could do without sex, or amuse himself discreetly with ladies whose profession it was. Nevertheless there seem to have been whispers, even in his own day, that Gordon's devotion to boys exceeded the philanthropical. It was surely to these that his friend, Reginald Brett (later Lord Esher), referred: 'Many lies were told about him, even his moral character was not spared.'[4] Sudanese intellectuals make this assumption, linking him with Romolo Gessi, who seems, however, to have been eminently heterosexual.[5] I have been unable to discover whether these have any source contemporary with Gordon, or are a by-product of anti-colonialism and the modern interest in these matters: certainly there was no public scandal, as one would expect if a man with many enemies had practised sodomy in countries where spies and pederasts abounded.

It is possible that Gordon's nature was homo- rather than hetero-sexual: who can know this about a man who never mentioned the subject and died more than a century ago? That he was ever a practising sodomite is, however, extremely improbable. The modern view of homosexuality as no more morally reprehensible than left-handedness is not one which he would have entertained: he would have been appalled by 'the sin of Sodom and Gomorrah', and had he ever succumbed to this temptation, would have been tortured by a guilt of which there is no sign in his voluminous correspondence.

This view seems to be supported by a remarkable statement which he made at the age of fifty to his friend, the Reverend R. H. Barnes: 'I wished I was a eunuch at 14.'[6]

His letter was written from Haifa, and is probably connected with a passage in his next letter[7] to Barnes, written seventeen days later. Referring to a place where by a projected canal the waters of the Jordan would flow into the Mediterranean, he wrote, 'I call it Perets Uzzah.' *Peretz* is a Hebrew word, the primary meaning of which is a breach or breakthrough, e.g. of water. But it also has a secondary meaning of an outbreak of some outrageous behaviour or an event of unusual harshness. In this sense it is applied in Samuel ii, 6, to the place where the Lord struck dead Uzzah who presumed *to lay his hand on the Ark of the Covenant.*[8] Gordon must have known this, and by a train of thought which is difficult to follow but which was surely on his mind, he wrote later in this letter of his schooldays: 'I remember a deep bitterness then, never can forget it though I was only 10 or 12 years. Humanly speaking it changed my life, it was a Perets I feel sure and was good. I never had a sorrow like it in all my life, therefore I love children so very much, to know they can rest their souls when a Perets happens.' There must have been some connection in his mind between the three 'peretses', and probably some connection between his deep bitterness and sorrow before puberty and his wish at puberty that he were a eunuch. Without any proof, one can deduce that he was the object of some sexual approach or contact by an older person, male or female, and that his reaction was a 'perets' so shocking and powerful as to cure him for the rest of his life of any tendency to carnality. It was therefore 'good' for him. Loving children, he liked to think that if a 'perets' happened to them, it would have the same effect.

'My dear Benjamin,' he wrote to an eighteen-year-old protégé, 'I hear from Mr Lilley you are at Lee Station . . . I dare say that some day you will see me pass your station, perhaps in July, I often speak to a Friend about you, and I dare say you hear Him speak in a quiet loving way to you . . . Talk to that Friend in any difficulty, and He will help you better than anyone else in this world could. Believe me, yours truly, C. G. Gordon.'

It is hardly the sort of letter a homosexual would write to his 'friend', and Gordon prayed for all of his laddies, keeping a long list of them and others. 'Do you know,' he wrote to Mrs Freese, 'my experience is that if you pray for anyone, that person is sure to like you, let him be ever so much against you at the beginning . . . It is even in a worldly way a good investment.'

The commission resembled a combination of the Thames Conservancy and the Elder Brethren of Trinity House, but was less useful than either. He knew he was shelved, despite his promotion in 1872 to regimental major and full colonel in the Army. His letters[9] hardly mention his work, though they are long and detailed.

It is no joke walking over cracking ice with a view of fish swimming beneath you. The great sobs the ice gives, and the wild wail of the wolves makes it cheerful work . . . In driving over the ice the horses will get along without breaking the ice, but the carriage goes through and so you dash along, the horses on the ice and the wheels of the carriage on the bottom. If the horses stop they go in, and then it is a fix.

Galatz was a large, straggling town with mud ankle-deep in the streets, the population cosmopolitan, 'and numbering many Jews who are an evil-looking lot and are much disliked. If you saw the Jews you would certainly wonder that they should have been and are now the chosen people of God, and that our Saviour was one of their nation. They are the leeches of the country.' He seems to have had a prejudice against Jews, evinced, for instance, in his spelling the Conservative statesman's name as 'D'Israeli'.

'Tell Stannard,' he wrote, 'to thank God he was born an Englishman.' This member of the Gordon clan never thought of himself as a Scot or referred to 'Britain' or 'British': it was always 'England' and 'English'.

Early in 1872 his brother Frederick died, leaving a widow and six young children. (Henry and Enderby had even larger families: Gordon was irritated by their 'rabbit-like producing powers'). 'Which would you rather have?' he asked Mrs Freese, '£100,000 in the bank, or the Friend of the Widow? We must say the latter.' Nevertheless he took out an insurance policy for £2,000 on his life for his sister-in-law's benefit.

In the summer of 1872 he revisited the Crimea and on his return through Constantinople happened to meet, at dinner at the British Embassy, Nubar Pasha, the Prime Minister of Egypt. They talked for an hour,[10] and later the Prussian Chargé d'Affaires asked Nubar, 'Do you know whom you were talking with for so long?'

'No.'

'That was Chinese Gordon.'

This meant nothing to Nubar, but he replied wisely, 'Ah!' and hastened to brief himself from a book on modern China. He was looking for a replacement for Sir Samuel Baker, the not altogether satisfactory Governor of the Equatorial Province of the Sudan. Gordon, he decided, was the man; and when they next met, Nubar asked him to recommend someone to establish order and suppress the slave-trade over 200,000 square miles of thorn-scrub and swamp. Gordon recommended himself. But there could be no unseemly haste in Cairo, or for that matter in Whitehall, so he returned home for two months' leave.

This had to be spent mainly in Southampton, for his mother was ailing and demanding. 'I am A.D.C. in close attendance,' he reported to Mrs Freese, 'no chance of getting away for a month.' This was not quite true, for his mother barely recognized him and was as pleased to see the doctor. He escaped to manoeuvres on Salisbury Plain, and found that minor tactics were simply appalling and the two armies behaved like dogs running after one another's tails. 'We haven't any system of modern drill for the men, and it will be some time before the officers, especially the seniors, get out of their level parade-ground movements.'[11]

In February 1873 it was back to Galatz, made more dreary still by news of the deaths of his mother and of various scuttlers drowned at sea, fallen from the mast-head, and died of fever. 'The idleness one has to live in here is insupportable . . . There is a disease called the Doles which is very fatal to the people out here . . . everyone likes to have it and are slightly angry with those who have not got it . . . I have a patient very ill of it at my house and he is not agreeable.'

People at Galatz were more grasping than ever, spotting with practised eyes a soft touch. 'You cannot tell, my dear Augusta, how I am wounded by swordfish in the shape of people wanting money; it is really quite a trial (sent I believe) for me, and I am such a donkey . . . However, the Lord will provide. The only advantages in marriage is, it would prevent these true extravagances.' But perhaps it would promote other extravagances: 'Want of money is a great sore, and yet, to have enough it only requires that we lower our flag a little. Does a new carpet really make you a lot happier?'

That summer an expedition was being prepared against the King of Ashantee. The commander was Sir Garnet Wolseley. The *Daily News*, in criticizing the list of officers appointed to the expedition, denounced the 'systematic neglect of the transcendant claims of "Chinese Gordon" . . . the best leader of irregulars that the world contains'.

Gordon's attitude to the press was equivocal. He was not above resorting to a press campaign, and even 'leaking' information to further some cause he had at heart: Bruce had warned him against this in China, and in later years he was to do it again and again. But this article vexed him, and he denied any resentment at being neglected. The *Daily News*, however, had a point. Wolseley was one of Gordon's friends, prayed for every day. Gordon, he wrote, 'was one of the very few I ever had who came up to my estimate of Christian hero'. He acknowledged that if he had been in Gordon's place in China, he would have made himself emperor. Ten years after the hero's death Wolseley admitted, 'I was never worthy to pipe-clay his belt for him.' Wolseley was notorious for favouritism towards his 'circle'. Perhaps he felt that perfection in a subordinate might be rather trying, and that Gordon might be particularly difficult for a friend to command. For whatever reason, in choosing his team for Ashantee, Wolseley left this paragon kicking his heels in Galatz.

7

⏷ THE NEW BROOM

⏷ Sir Richard Burton, the famous traveller, wrote of Gordon's
'controul'. He should have written 'controuls', for there were two
forever at war within him. One was withdrawing him towards official
obscurity, religious contemplation and unobtrusive good works; the
other, thrusting him on towards excitement, danger, physical exertion
and, above all, power: in a mood of self-examination he listed among his
more conspicuous vices *libido dominandi*, the lust for rule.[1] Perhaps,
though this he would never have admitted, he craved fame, especially
that fame which rewards the victorious commander and which in his
case would be measured not by titles and decorations, but by laudatory
paragraphs in the newspapers and the high opinion of his fellow-country-
men. So now, after lying fallow for eight years, he longed for the excitement and challenge of the Sudan. But he stoically prepared himself for
another disappointment, and 'would not think it unkind of God if He
prevents it, for He must know best'.

His predecessor, Sir Samuel Baker, had been heavy-handed, raiding
villages for cattle and grain if the natives would not supply them, resorting
to Snider rifles rather than tact and persuasion, thus aggravating his
own difficulties. Gordon determined to advance with prudent deliberation, after thorough preparation and fact-gathering. God had allowed
slavery for so many years that a few more months could not matter.
'Born in the people, it needs more than an expedition to eradicate it.
Open the country, and it will fall of itself . . .'; 'My ideas are to open it
by getting steamers onto the lakes, by which time I should know the
perpetrators of the slave-trade and could ask the Khedive to seize them.'
It was to prove more difficult.

Baker, milking the Khedive for huge sums, had set an unfortunate
precedent. 'Your brother,' Gordon told Augusta, 'has been more or less
acted on by sharks, who want to go with me for money. I have told them
that . . . they must belong to the A class – i.e. those who come for the
occupation and interest it may give them and who are content if they are

fairly reimbursed their expenses; not the B class, who go for the salary and only want to make a good thing of it   Pillage the Egyptians is still the cry.' He foresaw trouble from pressure-groups at home – Baker, the Prince of Wales, the Geographical and Anti-Slavery Societies – who expected him to charge bald-headed at the slave-trade instead of adopting the indirect approach.

In December 1873 the job was his, and he returned to England for a round of farewell visits to relatives and friends, including a Miss Dykes, 'the nicest girl I ever knew, but do not be alarmed; the dead marry not.' With much experience of steamers, he saw these as the key to the Nile and the lakes, and consulted Alfred Yarrow, the shipbuilder, on the most suitable model, transportable by land, capable of being hauled up cataracts and of forcing its way through thick tropical weeds. The weeds, Mr Yarrow advised, precluded screw-propulsion; the rocks, steamers with paddle-wheels on each side. He recommended a single paddle-wheel astern, and in due course Gordon remembered and profited by his advice.

A minor Foreign Office functionary saw him off, causing him to leave hat-box and despatch-case on the platform. To the Freeses he sent a farewell postcard with a sketch of himself setting forth from an oasis towards distant hills: '28.1.74. Isaiah 35. Good-bye again.'

Gordon at the age of forty-one, although still incredibly active, was described as 'thick-set'. His temper was shorter than it had been. His extraordinary power to command obedience from his subordinates and secure compliance with his wishes by others was, if anything, increased. Arthur Stannard, a civilian employed with the Royal Engineers at Gravesend, wrote, 'From the unfailing and willing obedience with which his orders were carried out, I fancy that to some extent he unconsciously mesmerized nine out of ten to do his will . . . Had he told me to stand on my head or to perform some impossible feat, I should certainly have tried my utmost to accomplish it without giving a moment for reflection as to whether the order was reasonable or not.'[2] Gordon's judgement being weaker than his determination, sometimes the orders were not reasonable, or were countermanded with the same force with which they had been issued: but they were promptly obeyed. He did not combat opposing counsels, but simply ignored them. When his mind was made up, it did not occur to him that there was any more to be said on the matter – until he changed his mind.

The Cairo at which he arrived on 6 February 1874 was in process of being transformed into the Paris of the Levant. Military bands played airs from *Aida* in the new public gardens, the streets were lit by gas; French-style houses and blocks of apartments, with iron balconies and narrow passages smelling of urine, were springing up all over the place. There were theatres, cafés, hotels, house-boats on the Nile.

The presiding genius was the Khedive Ismail, a bulky, ginger-whiskered Albanian buttoned tightly into a Stamboulieh frock-coat, his *tarbush* rakishly askew. He had a remarkable gift of persuasion, due in part to his invariably conveying the impression that anyone he met was the one person he wished to see: men who went to see him bursting with exasperation would emerge purring with contentment and not realize for several hours that they had been bamboozled. He was adept at reading the character of those with whom he had to deal; to one he would offer money, to another flattery, to a third, a frank man-to-man confidence.[3]

Among his many estimable qualities there was no trace of financial prudence. He spent and borrowed with no thought for the morrow, and as little for the rate of interest (up to 36 per cent for such a risky investment) or his subjects' taxable capacity. Between 1863 and 1877, the public debt rose from £4 million to £87 million, to service which a doubling of the taxes screwed out of the unhappy *fellahin* was totally inadequate. Much of this had been spent on projects with a long-term potential; but vast sums of money had gone on palaces and gardens, opera-houses and theatres, while the pay of army officers and civil servants was months – years – in arrears; and the *fellahin* were taxed to support the Khedive's princely hospitality to kings, opera stars, statesmen and plausible adventurers.[4]

He was himself a slave-owner on a gigantic scale, as were most of his relatives, friends and ministers of state. But this was bad for his image in Europe, and it was on European bondholders that he relied for his funds. According to Nubar Pasha, while instructing Gordon to stop the slave-trade, he counted on this proving impossible, so he himself would continue to enjoy the services of innumerable slaves at the same time as the reputation for an enlightened abhorrence of slavery.[5]

The Khedive and Gordon got on surprisingly well. Ismail thought – or said he thought – that Gordon was his ideal. Gordon was always likely to be taken in by someone with the gift of the gab. 'The Khedive is an honest fellow and I like him very much, but I will not give in to the others.' The others! What a gang of scoundrels! Cairo was a hotbed of intrigue and corruption, and Nubar Pasha, to whom he referred as 'Ha! Ha! Nubar', he could not stand. This capable Armenian Christian was incisive and business-like in his methods, wasting neither time nor undue sympathy. He was wonderfully quick at grasping the essentials of a problem, and had an unrivalled knowledge of Egyptian personalities, politics, law, land-tenure and economics, despite an indolence which evaded embroilment in detail. He served Egypt well, though perhaps the form of government he would have preferred for her would have been a British Protectorate run by a competent Armenian Resident.

'I think,' wrote Gordon to Augusta, 'I can now see the true motive of the expedition, and believe it to be a sham. Nubar thought he had a rash fellow to deal with who could be persuaded to cut a dash etc. etc. and found he had one of the Gordon race. The latter thought it the thing real and found it a sham, and felt like a Gordon who has been humbugged'; 'The Khedive likes me, but no one else does; and I do not like them – I mean the swells whose corns I tread on.' Happily Providence had arranged that the British Consul was a Royal Engineer, Colonel Stanton; but when he warned Gordon not to make an enemy of Nubar, even he was snubbed. Stanton, however, knew his man, and they remained friends.

'I am like Moses who despised the riches of Egypt': Gordon refused the £10,000 a year which had kept Baker beyond the reach of want. In order to set a good example, he asked for only £2,000, thus contributing to a growing belief in well-informed circles that Chinese Gordon was not quite sane.

His most important task in Cairo was to recruit his staff. He regarded his mission not as a British or Egyptian imperial venture, but as an international crusade. His staff must therefore be international.

One had already been chosen, Romolo Gessi. This tough, compact, heavily bearded Italian, born in Constantinople, had served with the Sardinian army in the Crimea, where Gordon had first met him. After more fighting with Garibaldi's Alpini he had run a sawmill on the Danube where they had again met. Gordon wrote of him, 'Cool, most determined man. Born genius for practical ingenuity in mechanics. Ought to have been born in 1560 not 1832. Same disposition as Francis Drake.' Cheerful and gregarious but with a flaming temper, compulsively brave and self-reliant, he was to be Gordon's most useful officer. So Gordon sent for him and Gessi, abandoning with alacrity his wife and family, hastened to the call.

Since Gordon knew no Arabic, he chose as his secretary a Frenchman born in Cairo, Auguste Linant de Bellefonds. A German naturalist, de Witt, asked to accompany the expedition with an assistant, Friedrich Bohndorff. Gordon agreed provided they paid their own way. A third German named Menges came as the Governor-General's servant.

From the staff of an American Military Mission, on the Khedive's pay-roll, Gordon selected Major William Campbell and a young lieutenant colonel, Chaillé-Long, of whom he had heard good reports as a 'sharp fellow'. The latter was a small, slight Marylander, with pop-eyes and a swashbuckling moustache. He was a man of courage and perseverance,

Arabic-speaking and competent at practical things. His weakness was an inordinate vanity which always made him exaggerate his own feats and disparage the work of others.

Gordon's nephew, Willie Anson, threw up a job in the Post Office to go exploring. A marine engineer, Kemp, was engaged to look after the steamers. Frederick Russell, son of the celebrated *Times* war correspondent, came as the expedition's press correspondent.

Gordon turned to the Royal Engineers for the last two European members of his staff. To Lieutenant Charles Watson he wrote, 'There is a Lieutenant R. E. Chippendall* at Glasgow. I want to know what both you and he want per ann. to go up country with me (remembering I engage to no fixed terms of service). I find you subsistence, I find you passage out, I find you arms etc. and you have only to find your clothes.' Watson jumped at the opportunity – but Gordon pushed off into the blue having done nothing more about it. Stanton tied up the loose ends – a somewhat frequent duty of Gordon's friends and colleagues – and the two new recruits eventually received formal offers of appointment in July. 'Curious ways of doing business,' commented young Mr Watson.

Of the Egyptians, Gordon chose one himself, and his two aides-de-camp were wished upon him. Gordon's own choice was Abou Saoud, a former slave-trader and deputy of Baker, imprisoned for treachery to him. Gordon, remembering no doubt his success with Taiping ex-rebels, had him released from jail and saw him in the role of poacher-turned-gamekeeper, or the sinner who repenteth. There were not lacking local experts to warn him that Abou Saoud, despite his distinguished manner and grave deportment, was a scoundrel; but Gordon felt for him an instinctive trust and sympathy. He believed, moreover, that the presence of an ex-slaver in his entourage would make a favourable impression on those whom Baker had antagonized.

The A.D.C.s were sallow, limp young men appalled by the prospect of exchanging the cafés of Cairo for the equatorial wilderness. He met them in Nubar's office, where they resignedly questioned the Minister on the length of their exile, until Nubar lost his temper and chased them out. 'As they don't want to go,' said Gordon, 'never mind.' But Nubar insisted that they go.

After painful visits to the dentist and Gessi's wife ('not over-content'), he was ready to set off, unimpeded by his heavy baggage which his staff could bring up: 'As I am the chief, I do not see why I should not enjoy the advantages of being so.' He had intended to save the Khedive £400 by travelling to Suakim by ordinary passenger-steamer, but Nubar insisted that 'His Excellency General Colonel Gordon, Governor-General

---

* R.E. stands, of course, for Royal Engineers. Chippendall's initials were H.W.

of the Equator', wearing his Royal Engineer undress uniform surmounted by a red *tarbush* ('the effect is very fine'), should travel in state by special steamer. So at midnight on 21 February he boarded a special train accompanied by Long, a German servant threatened with death if he called Gordon 'Your Excellency', and the miserable Lieutenant Hassan Wassif.

After two hours' run across the desert the engine became derailed. 'We were shunted into a common train with a great many people – begun in glory and ended in shame!' The common train was held up by Count Ferdinand de Lesseps, of Suez Canal fame, who wanted a lift. 'Seventy years of age, his wife was confined a few months ago. He is a nice, bright strong old man.' On board the special steamer they found 220 Egyptian soldiers being shipped to the Sudan as a punishment. Dragged from their Delta villages, conscripted into a detestable service, ill-fed, ill-clothed, unpaid, never allowed leave lest they desert, with no hope of discharge short of death or loss of limb, these were the sort of troops with which Gordon would have to suppress the slave-trade, explore the Great Lakes and govern Equatoria. Two of their officers had been degraded for theft.

They disembarked at Suakim and set off across the desert to Berber, on the Nile. The distance is 250 miles, normally covered in twelve to fourteen days by slow camel or eight days by trotting camel.[6] They did it in nine days, hard going for those riding camels for the first time. According to Long, the Governor-General very sensibly rode a good pony 'and thus, comparatively at his ease, tested our endurance in camel-riding . . . When we arrived at Berber we were all extenuated with fatigue.'

From Berber, where the Governor was 'dead against Abou Saoud', they set off on a steamer for Khartoum, a journey of four days expedited by His Excellency's trouserless exertions as he helped the crew shove and haul the boat through crocodile-infested rapids.

At Khartoum a battalion of infantry presented arms, artillery salutes crashed and boomed, the populace ullulated shrilly in welcome and the local Governor-General, Ismail Pasha Ayoub, an agreeable Kurd, fluent in French and Italian and an accomplished chamber musician, entertained his new colleague to a banquet followed by a display of nubile black dancing-girls clad only in bangles and a leather strip round the loins. To the beat of a tomtom and a curious clucking of the lips, they gyrated in slow measure, keeping time with remarkable movements of the hips and torso. The host and his other guests, enchanted with their performance, were about to join the ladies when it was noticed that the principal guest had departed.[7]

The problem of returning Ismail Ayoub's hospitality could not long be shelved. But Gordon had travelled light, bringing no dinner service but only a few tin plates and cups. Long borrowed from Ismail Ayoub a Constantinople cook, and from the government stores damask table-cloths, Sèvres plates, Bohemian wine glasses and ample supplies of burgundy, claret and champagne, all left by Baker. A hundred soldiers, supervised by Lieutenant Hassan and Ismail Ayoub himself, prepared the festive table. Gordon meanwhile had not been idle. He had purchased forty pudding-bowls, and Long found him, coat off and sleeves rolled up, filling these with tapioca pudding. 'What do you think of those?' he pointed, not without pride, at his achievement. Long begged him to rest upon his laurels and entrust all arrangements to his Chief-of-Staff, which he did. The banquet was a great success.

Gordon's first impressions were favourable. Ismail Ayoub, he decided, was 'a first rate man, his troops in first class order, the hospital ditto and also this school'. As for the slave-trade, 'as far as I have seen it is down to a minimum and I have witnessed no signs of it at present.'

This view of the slave-trade was erroneous. The city of Khartoum, with its mixed Levantine population of 30,000 dwelling in close-packed, flat-roofed houses, was a highly prosperous place. Among its gardens of date, lemon and orange trees were schools and hospitals; it was linked by telegraph to the outer world; its Greek-owned shops were stocked with European luxuries – Bass's pale ale, French wines, tinned food, soaps and perfumes, arms and jewellery; every caravan between Egypt and Central Africa must pass through Khartoum. This thriving, stinking, fly-swarming city prospered mainly on the associated trades in slaves and ivory.

Slavery is condemned no more in the Koran than in the Bible. The Prophet commended as a virtuous act the individual freeing of slaves, and set an example, but never condemned the institution. By a strict interpretation of the Koran, slavery should be confined to non-Moslem war captives who refuse Islam and cannot ransom themselves; but these refinements were beyond the man in the *souk*. All the tasks done in middle-class English homes by cooks, parlourmaids, housemaids, footmen, gardeners, grooms were done in Khartoum by slaves. Indeed it would be hard to find any householder so poor as not to own at least one slave. The most pious and humane Moslems were unable to see why Christians made such a fuss about it. When had Jesus (on whom be peace!) ever said a word against it? It might be wrong to enslave Moslems; but the economics of the country required a constant flow of fresh slaves, and the vast majority of these were pagan blacks. Could any reasonable man deny that the life of a Negro – fed, clothed, kindly treated, lightly worked and converted to the Faith – as a slave in Egypt, the Sudan, Turkey or Syria was infinitely preferable to his life in Equatoria or the Congo, poor, nasty, brutish and short?

The possession of slaves was perfectly legal: Gordon's officials and soldiers all owned slaves. It was the traffic in slaves which he had to suppress. It was easy money. Any adventurer could come to Khartoum, borrow money at eighty per cent and equip two or three hundred Dongolawi toughs for an expedition up the Nile. In partnership with some co-operative black chief, the slaver would raid a few villages at dawn; a volley was fired into the huts and as the inhabitants bolted like rabbits a few would be shot and speared, the remainder grabbed. The elders were tortured to make them reveal their hidden ivory. Adults were then secured two-and-two by the *sheyba*, a heavy forked pole resting on the shoulders, the head secured by a cross-bar, hands tied to the pole. Of those who reached civilization, females were allocated to concubinage or domestic service. Most of the males became servants or agricultural labourers; the lucky ones became *bazingers*, slave-soldiers, to carry out raids in their turn; the unlucky ones were castrated for harem service, an operation performed in insanitary conditions, without anaesthetics, which was generally fatal. By-products of the trade were cattle captured and bartered with other tribes for ivory which was carried by able-bodied captives to *nagars* on the Nile, in which the slaves also were crammed like herrings in casks for shipment to Khartoum. In a good season a slaver could reckon on obtaining 20,000 lbs. of ivory worth £4,000 in Khartoum, plus 400 or 500 slaves worth £5 or £6 each. The only concession to the Khedive's law was that slaves were not sold openly within the city. There was hardly an official in the Sudan who was not in it up to the neck.

The leading slave- and ivory-trading company in Khartoum was the Rataz Agat, of which Abou Saoud had been a director. 'About the slavery question,' Gordon wrote, 'I shall have no trouble at all.'[8]

When it was heard that Abou Saoud was on his way, 'Everyone's jaw dropped . . . They said everything they could to dissuade me and the Governor tried several times to get me to give him up . . . Now I am so glad I stuck to him, for I feel sure he will be a very great help.' For Gordon in his character assessment needed advice from no man, least of all from Baker, who gave it at some length. 'All the people are dead against Abou Saoud, but I am faithful to him, and trust to a higher power to bring me through . . . Either there is a God or there is none. That is the whole question!' Abou Saoud was 'built and made to govern . . . the most useful man I have got'.

The most famous slaver of all was a Sudanese named Zebeyr Rahama who with his slave-army ruled a slave-empire, nominally acknowledging the Khedive's suzerainty, in the south-western province of Bahr-el-Ghazal. From thirty *zaribas** his ferociously efficient *bazingers* raided far into black Africa.

Meanwhile, awaiting impatiently the preparations for his onward journey, Gordon killed time in Khartoum. There were flocks of storks assembled for their migration to the Danube, 'I dare say I have seen some of them before, and here they are walking about among the crocodiles 2,000 miles away.' Other manifestations of nature were less agreeable. 'The rats are dreadful at night, circusing about everywhere, and I fear the older ones eat the younger members of their families, for there are great outcries at night, with lamentations and woe, and I found part of a young rat eaten by an older one, and the remnant left for my benefit – a delicate attention!'

The northern boundary of his province of Equatoria was formed by the rivers Sobat and Bahr-el-Ghazal, 600 miles south of Khartoum: its southern boundary was thought to be in the region of the Great Lakes; its eastern and western boundaries, as far as he could push them towards the Indian Ocean and the Atlantic. Effectively, however, his satrapy was some 600 miles long, its width half a day's march on either side of the Nile. At Khartoum he took his first action as governor-general, issuing a decree nationalizing the ivory-trade without which the slave-trade would lose much of its profit. Rataz Agat and other companies were given three months to hand in their ivory. In despair they appealed to Long, who thought it harsh, for the ivory-trade was perfectly legal; but Gordon was adamant: 'Recall the ivory monopoly? Never!'

He proceeded upriver in the *Bordein*, a twin-paddle-boat some 150 ft long with a shallow draft and a 60 h.p. engine burning wood, to cut and collect which required frequent halts. Her maximum speed was only 4 knots, against a current in March of about 2 knots. (None of his steamers was of the type Yarrow had recommended.)

It was dull with nothing to do. It never occurred to Gordon to take Arabic lessons, but the extraordinary variety of wild life along the banks was a diversion. There were the Danube storks in their thousands, and hideous, naked-goitred, big-billed Marabou storks; there were egrets and pelicans; hippopotami bellowing and fighting all night; troops of comical monkeys with tails stuck up like swords at the 'carry'; and crocodiles by the hundred, lying interlaced on the baking rocks, their fanged jaws wide open, birds picking the insects and tasty tit-bits from their gums. He saw buffaloes, 'black as coals'; herds of elephants with

---

* A *zariba* is an enclosure of cut thorn bushes to keep slaves, cattle and camels in, lions and robbers out. It came to mean any defended camp, fort, administrative centre or trading post.

slowly-flapping ears; giraffes nibbling the small green leaves in the flat tops of the acacia trees.

The natives generally fled at their approach; but a bold Dinka chief was induced to come aboard. 'He was in full dress – a necklace . . . He came up to me, took up each hand, and gave a good soft lick to the back of them; then he held my face and made the motion of spitting in it.'

Gordon at first thought well of Long, 'a nice modest fellow, and I am glad I have him with me.' But in less than a month he found Long 'utterly useless. He does not even know the pay or rations of a soldier.' Long was 'always going to do something or other but never does it'; 'I have such a limp personnel up here, all flourish and no result. I have to look after the food myself or we should starve.' Long was to prove brave, tough and self-reliant. But he and Gordon were incompatible – Gordon the perfectionist, the nagger, never able to delegate responsibility; Long with a panache bordering on braggadocio, a tendency to exaggeration which sometimes strayed over the edge of mendacity, and perhaps a certain carelessness about detail.

Gordon's relations with the skipper of the ship and with his A.D.C. were even less happy, and they complained to Long that he had slapped one's face and called the other a baboon, a booby and a baby. Gordon had a flaming temper, which inactivity and boredom aggravated; nothing enraged him so much as indolence and procrastination. After outbursts of temper, his ill-humour passed and characteristically he confessed to Long, 'I have been very low, old fellow, don't be hard on me. This is a terrible country.'

It is a theme on which Long loved to dwell. Gordon, he wrote, could never get on with anyone whom he could not kick, and Gessi, Gordon's 'valet', submitted to being kicked whenever his master was in a bad humour. Gessi, a proud and hot-tempered man, was not Gordon's valet and would never have submitted to such treatment. But Long, when he related these stories, had been mortified by passages in Gordon's published letters to Augusta in which his name was left blank but his identity was obvious. 'The —* is a regular failure . . . There is a set of officers I hate, viz, Captains I-told-him-to-do-it, I-am-going-to-do-it, I-thought-you-were-going-to-do-it.' Two days later 'Feebleness' was too lazy to come on deck.[9]

It took them twenty-six days to reach Gondokoro, Gordon's administrative centre, and it might have taken as many weeks had not Ismail Ayoub recently performed the notable feat of breaking through the '*sud*'. Gordon's description of this strange phenomenon is as good as more scientific studies:

* In the original version of the letter, 'The American'.

A curious little cabbage-like aquatic plant comes floating down, having a little root ready to attach itself to anything; he meets a friend and they go together, and soon join roots and so on. When they get to a lake the current is less strong, and so, no longer constrained to move on, they go off to the sides; others do the same, idle and loitering, like everything up here. After a time winds drive a whole fleet of them against the narrow outlet of the lake and stop it up. Then no more passenger plants can pass through the outlet, while plenty come in at the upper end of the lake.

The result was a solid raft of matted vegetation, blocking the river for several miles above the Bahr-el-Ghazal junction. When Ismail Ayoub with two steamers and three companies of troops had cut a way through, hippopotami were carried down, screaming and snorting; crocodiles were whirled round and round and the river was covered with dead and dying animals and fish which had been crushed.

Gondokoro was a metropolis with 300 soldiers, their women and children, three or four slaves each and miscellaneous followers. Most of the buildings were grass huts with conical roofs, laid out in rows on a bluff on the right bank of the river. The brick church, built by missionaries who had given up the unequal struggle and departed, had disintegrated; but the missionaries had left as their legacy some lemon trees. There was a magazine, built of heavy tins, to hold ammunition and trade stores. The soldiers, their pay four years in arrears, kept up their ration supply by stealing cattle, and as a result could not safely venture half a mile into the park-like country. At the time of Gordon's arrival the grey plain and the flat-topped acacia trees were flushed with new grass and leaves brought out by the early rains. The Governor-General's administration was confined to this and two smaller posts, Fatiko and Foweira, 200 miles to the south: outside these there was no government.

Gordon soon found his predecessor, Raouf Bey, not up to the job, and told him so. A few weeks later, when Raouf departed on leave, Gordon wrote him a glowing confidential report, recommended him for promotion to pasha and for the governor-generalship of Equatoria when his own tour was over. That was typical of Gordon – slate a man to his face, praise him behind his back.[10]

There was a ceremonial visit by the local chief, a magnificent six-footer, stark-naked, carrying a small ebony stool on which he squatted, his genitals dangling almost to the ground. Then Gordon had to hurry back to Khartoum. The reason usually given for this is his discovery that his troops were paid not in hard cash, but in consignments of gin and slave-girls sent up by Ismail Pasha Ayoub. But the source of this story is the Austrian Consul, Martin Hansal, not conspicuously reliable; it is nowhere mentioned in Gordon's voluminous correspondence; and Georges Douin, who examined all the Cairo archives, dismissed it as bazaar gossip. Gordon's own account, that he had to return to chase up his stores and get cash for the soldiers' pay, seems more likely.[11]

He had bones to pick with Ismail Ayoub, and their mutual recriminations deluged the office of Khairi Pasha, the Khedive's Chancellor. Gordon demanded that his province be enlarged, and when Ismail demurred, threatened his superior officer with dismissal. He demanded Remington rifles which had been allocated elsewhere, and was compelled (he complained) to 'bribe the magazine-guards because I could not trust the word of the Governor-General'. He demanded twenty-eight copy-clerks, 'although', wrote Ismail,

we have too few in Khartoum and there are more than enough in Gondokoro. He demanded six field guns although there are eight at Gondokoro and at Khartoum we have no more than a battery. He demanded doctors and pharmacists although he has his proper establishment of each. He demanded 3,400 *ardebs* of corn although the entire stock at Khartoum does not exceed 1,000 *ardebs*. He demanded 15 donkeys, 100 mules, 80 horses, 50,000 dollars. Finally he demanded from me, the Governor-General, that his orders be obeyed within eighteen days.

When Ismail Ayoub tried to pay him an official visit of reconciliation, Gordon went off shooting, writing him next day to say that as Ismail had told him so many lies, he preferred that they meet only on ceremonial arrivals and departures. To Khairi he complained of Ismail's tyranny and mendacity. Ismail in turn complained of 'the intrigues of this colonel, which touch my honour ... If he treats me like this, how will he treat those under his orders?'[12]

Gordon was unreasonable, offensive and domineering, treating Ismail as an erring office-boy; Ismail reacted with obstruction and evasion. The trouble between them was partly due to a faulty arrangement made by the Khedive in February, under which Equatoria would be politically independent of the Sudan, but logistically dependent, indenting for all its supplies on Khartoum and remitting thither its ivory and other exports to help meet the cost. It was not an arrangement conducive to good co-operation, for Ismail Ayoub had no departmental inducement to help Gordon out of his difficulties, and Gordon none to moderate his logistic demands. In the end Gordon had to be content with some Remingtons, 50,000 Maria Theresa dollars* and Khairi Pasha's promise to make him financially independent of Khartoum. He also obtained

* These coins, in common circulation between the Nile and the Indian Ocean, were minted in Addis Ababa with the image and superscription of an Austrian Empress 100 years in her grave.

the services of Ibrahim Fauzi, an officer-cadet of whom he had formed a high opinion. This Egyptian, rapidly promoted to colonel, became one of Gordon's favourites.

Ismail Pasha Ayoub was a good governor who introduced many useful administrative reforms in the teeth of Cairo's obsessive over-centralization. In the end Gordon came to recognize his quality, describing him as 'a great scamp, but the best administrator the Sudan ever had'.[13]

Meanwhile his rear-party with the stores had reached Berber. Here they seemed to be bogged down in total inactivity, taking four days – *four days!* – to transfer the stores to barges. Gordon swept down on them like an avenging angel, and twenty-four hours of his presence sufficed to get them in motion again: 'The utter helplessness of my staff is lamentable. I have driven them like a herd before me.' Only in Linant and Kemp could he detect the rudiments of efficiency: 'You might as well have two ladies as Anson and Russell.' By the end of May he was back in Khartoum complete with staff and baggage. To Stanton he sent an S.O.S. call for Watson and Chippendall, R.E., and set off on 6 June for Gondokoro.

He still took a sanguine view of his prospects. 'I shall not have any difficulty with slavers or the natives. The climate certainly makes one depressed, if one is in the habit of being so, which I am not . . . There is a large amount of passive resistance made, but if you are firm, they give in. I think after a year the Province will pay its way, but when the Baker debt will be paid off, I do not know'; 'I apprehend not the least difficulty in the work; the greatest will be to gain the people's confidence again. They have been hardly treated.' It was extraordinary the hatred they had for Baker.

Nevertheless it was already apparent to him that the problem was more complicated than the Anti-Slavery Society realized. By nagging the Khedive into closing the Nile route to slavers, they had increased ten-fold the sufferings of the slaves who were now marched across the pitiless desert. 'Up to the present,' he informed the Secretary of the Society, 'the slave is worse off through your efforts . . . I am sure a poor child walking across the burning plains would say, "Oh, I do wish those gentlemen had left us alone to come down by boat!" '[14]

8

FRUSTRATION

Gordon now turned to the tasks of administering his province, suppressing the slave-trade and exploring the lakes, according to the detailed instructions given him by the Khedive.[1] Baker had treated it as a military operation, concentrating his force. But this was really a civil operation carried out by soldiers, and the essence of civil administration in a lawless country is to disperse force so that law and order are distributed as widely as possible. The three garrisons were doing nothing but maintain themselves at the natives' expense; they would be far more useful split up between a number of small posts, close enough for mutual support, and on the river so that they could be provisioned, reinforced and supervised by steamer.

The first would be at Sobat, on the junction with the Nile of the river of that name. It was a village of the Shillook tribe, in country of thornscrub and high elephant-grass infested with warthog, lion and buffalo. A post here would block two of the slavers' river-routes. Gordon made it the headquarters of one of the three mudirehs* into which he divided his province, the others being Gondokoro to the south and Rohl to the west. On 19 June 1874 he established it himself, staying there to encourage the soldiers who feared the pestilential climate.

Long was on his way to the court of King Mtesa of Uganda taking with him, at Mtesa's request, one man learned in the religion of Islam, another skilled at performing circumcisions, a third able to blow the trumpet. Gessi and Anson were sent to establish a post at Rabat Shambé, the first firm ground above the *sud*. Campbell and Linant went on up to Gondokoro with five steamers, leaving Gordon one.

All his staff having departed on their several duties, there was nothing much for the Governor-General to do but wait for the slavers to sail down the Sobat or Nile into his hands.

There were three slavers' *zaribas* up the Bahr-el-Ziraf, a loop of the Nile passing through the *sud* south-west of Sobat. To these he sent

* A *mudir*'s district. A *mudir* was the equivalent of a district commissioner.

notice to quit. They did not comply with his wishes, but he intercepted a letter from them promising the *Mudir* of Fashoda a consignment of slaves. It was for these he was waiting, confident that by land or water they must pass close to his camp.

On 20 July Abou Saoud arrived, 'the only man who has a kick in him'. Gordon appointed him deputy governor and sent him up with the last steamer to Gondokoro.

The weary wait continued. With no steamers, Gordon could not move. 'August 6. Still here! What my other steamers are about I cannot tell. They have been away five weeks . . . August 8. No steamers yet . . . August 10. Still no steamers.' On that day came the news that Gessi was very ill and Willie Anson had died of malaria. His nephew's death greatly saddened Gordon, who does not seem to have been consoled by the reflection that the deceased had gone to a far better place.

Gordon busied himself with gaining the confidence of the natives so that one did not have to move through the province as though it were enemy territory. He gave some Shillook a little maize to plant instead of the familiar *dhoora*.* Gradually about sixty families, too poor to have enough cattle to support them, moved in under protection of the post and began to till the land. For four pounds of *dhoora* he bought two Shillook boys, aged nine and twelve, as servants for himself and Bohndorff. It was, perhaps, an equivocal transaction, but if he had not bought them, their father would have sold them to someone else. As it was, their father did not even take leave of them; and on his visits to the *zariba* never noticed or spoke to them. Later Gordon embarked on the task, basic if Africans were ever to be raised above subsistence level, of introducing them to money. He realized that this work was all on a very small scale in relation to the immensity of Central Africa, but reflected that he might do more good by concentrating his effort, 'like a squirt'. It produced results: soon he could go out shooting alone.

He felt for the blacks a deep compassion, writing to Mrs Freese:

I took a poor old bag of bones into my camp a month ago, and have been feeding her up, but yesterday she was quietly taken off, and now knows all things. She had her tobacco up to the last, and died quite quietly. What a change from her misery! I suppose she filled her place in life as well as Queen Elizabeth.

A wretched sister of yours is struggling up the road, but she is such a wisp of bones that the wind threatens to overthrow her . . . I told my man to see her into one of the huts, and thought he had done so. The night was stormy and rainy. When I had got up I went out and peeping through the gateway I

* A cereal native to Central Africa, more resistant than maize to drought, but less nourishing and less prolific.

saw your and my sister lying dead in a pool of mud. Her black brothers had been passing and re-passing and had taken no notice of her, so I sent and ordered her to be buried. She was not more than sixteen years old. I dare say you will see – in fact I feel sure you will see – your black sister some day, and she will tell you all about it, and how Infinite Wisdom directed the whole affair. I know this is a tough morsel to believe, but it is true ... She was deeply lamented by me; not so by her black brothers, who thought her a nuisance.

But although he pitied his black brethren, it was his duty to do so, he could not like them as he had liked the natives of China, Armenia and Gravesend. They were, he thought, utterly callous with no trace of affection for their children. One of his Shillook 'colonists' had two children. He got into trouble, stealing a cow. A few days later Gordon, passing his hut, noticed only one child, and asked what had become of the other.

'Oh,' said the mother with a cheerful smile, 'it has been given to the man from whom the cow was stolen.'

'Are you sorry?'

'Oh no, we would much rather have the cow.' His experiments in cultivation were conducted in a spirit of clinical inquiry, 'to solve the question whether the Negro will work sufficiently to keep himself, if he has security of life and property'.

He was beginning even to have doubts about his mission:

You will perhaps think that the [released] slaves will be very glad; some may be, but I expect the greater number will be sorry. In spite of what Livingstone says, I do not myself find that any affection exists between the parents and children; there is a mutual pleasure in parting with one another. I think the slavers' wars – made for the purpose of taking slaves – detestable, but if a father or mother of their own free will, and with the will of the child, sells that child, I do not see the objection to it.

In a letter to Khairi Pasha dated 11 August 1874, he made the remarkable suggestion that the slave-trade, which he had been sent to abolish, be instead nationalized as a government monopoly under a European director, who would ensure that it be purged of its grosser cruelties. This was not one of his more ephemeral inspirations: five years later he reverted to it, though admitting that it would shock a good many people. It shocked even the Khedive Ismail, who 'repudiated it with indignation'. Fortunately the Anti-Slavery Society never got wind of it.[2]

The Shillook were themselves multiple slave-owners. As they cultivated only a little *dhoora* and their basic food was curdled milk mixed with blood, they had a pretty easy life. The women never had to exert themselves with household work, and the men's only gainful occupations were hunting and fishing. Most of the day they lay stretched on lion skins while slaves massaged them with fat. It was not a life-style of which Gordon could approve. He felt exasperated and baffled at being confronted by a wall of ignorance, incompetence, indolence and apathy. If the blacks were wretched caricatures of humanity, the Arabs (as he invariably called the Egyptian *fellahin* soldiers) were far worse. 'I do not think I ever saw such a tumbledown lot. The slightest pain or ache, and down they are in *articulo mortis*. A man with a headache cannot lift his hand to have his pulse felt. How they were ever a great people I cannot conceive.' One and all they hated Central Africa, to which they had been sent as a punishment. Gordon regarded them as far inferior to the Chinese. The depths of military infamy were plumbed by a captain who sold into slavery six of his own soldiers. The fact that they would far rather be slaves in Cairo than soldiers in Equatoria and had begged to be sold, was beside the point; this sort of thing was not done in the Royal Engineers.

It was the rainy season, and day after day it poured, flooding the flat plain, dripping through the roofs of the straw huts. Clothes in the Central African rains are always clammy for it is impossible to dry them; boots are mildewy; guns and cameras get rusted up in a night. The river bank, heightened by flood-borne vegetation, was actually higher than the inland plain so there was no run-off for the rain which stood in stagnant malarial swamps. The only refuge from mosquitos was in bed, under a net. 'Fancy going to bed at 6.30 p.m. . . . The mosquitos drive you wild if you stay up.' There were white ants, destruction in a night to clothes, books, leather; there were 'safari' ants, crossing the damp ground in shiny black ribbons, millions and millions of them, endowed with a common malign purpose and with pincers to grip fiercely at leg, thigh, or private parts. The rats ran over the mosquito-nets, screamed and fought all night, ate shaving-brush, soap, books and the tops of boots. There were deadly cobras and puff-adders, scorpions with agonizing stings. Lesser pests of the rainy season were eye-flies, which if squashed on the face set up a painful blister; stink-flies, smelling like a corpse; beetles and sausage-flies, buzzing round and flopping into the lamp; myriads of flying ants attracted to any light, losing their wings and falling into one's hair, one's drink, down the back of one's shirt. House-flies, swarming on hands and face, on food, and even on a cup of tea as it was lifted to the mouth, were an intolerable affliction. 'Why should even the alighting of a fly, *his footprints* cause such an irritation to the skin? Why should these countries be so full of annoyances to man? It must be for some good object eventually to be made known to us.' At night one was kept awake hour after hour by the thud-thud of drums, the maddening repetitive chant of Shillook dancers. The food was of the coarsest nature, *dhoora* bread baked hard (because it was then less likely to upset one's stomach), dry biscuits, a few bits of tough meat, and macaroni.

Menges could not stand it and departed. He had been a good servant, 'but the best servant I ever had is myself: he always does what I like.' The interpreter, proved to be in league with the slavers, was sent down-river in disgrace.

Gordon kept fit: he had to. He was careful always to sleep under a mosquito-net, 'more valuable than a revolver'. He boiled his water and prudently mixed it with a little brandy. It was essential to take quinine when tired. He became a fanatical propagandist for Warburg's mixture, a sovereign remedy for almost every tropical illness: 'It throws you into such a fearful perspiration that you think you will flow away altogether.' Since he took proper precautions against the climate, 'the only effect I have noticed is a great shortness of temper, which distresses me and much more those around me.' Sobat was so boring that he decided to go up to Gondokoro, slaves or no slaves, as soon as the steamers arrived. For the remedy for ill-health and 'the doles' was *activity*.

He recorded scraps of information about the blacks: 'Some Shillook gentlemen have a queer way of matting their hair; they plait it in a sort of felt which sticks out quite stiff and is thought very fine. It protects the nape of the neck from rain, and is half an inch thick.' But his interests were not anthropological.

Much more interesting to him were the animals. There were herds of giraffes, splendid when they stood still, but when they lolloped off, pitching and rolling like heavily-laden ships; vultures after a rainstorm 'with their wings outstretched to dry like old coats'; great, fat hippos, gleaming in the moonlight, grunting and blowing all night. He noted the nests of weaver-birds, hanging down from the branches of thorn-trees so that no rain can enter them. Although without relevant scientific training, Gordon could have made a good field naturalist. He was interested in anything unusual in wild life, observing it closely and describing it with meticulous accuracy:

It is curious to watch the ant-lions. They are small insects with a flexible leg. They make a crater and rest in the apex of it, throwing up, now and then, with a flexible leg, a shower of sand. Ants walk on the edge and slip down. As they are getting up the slippery bank, the flexible leg throws up a shower of sand, and then another and another; till at last, as if in the cinders of Vesuvius, the ant gets smothered and falls to the bottom, where a pair of nippers takes him to an inner chamber, and dinner is ready.

Indeed, he had a many-sided nature – now Bayard, now Don Quixote; a touch of St Paul, a touch of John the Baptist; at one moment a Boy Scout – then, suddenly, an amateur Darwin, though he would hardly have approved of some of Mr Darwin's wilder theories.

He read a good deal: the Bible, Greek and Latin classics in translation, books of African travel, Dryden, Trollope, Newman's *Dream of Gerontius* are mentioned in his letters. He surveyed the country. He shot for sport and for the pot: a single hippo would produce a mountain of meat for the soldiers and the Shillook, a duck or a goose a welcome change for himself. Crocodiles, hateful creatures, he 'never spared'. Elephant-shooting he found to be poor sport, 'snipe-shooting much preferable'. He took up photography again, processing, it seems, his own plates.

He wrote to Khairi Pasha nearly 100 letters a year, many of great length and accompanied by maps, all in French which added to the labour. He wrote at great length to Stanton, Mrs Freese, Henry, various Royal Engineers, the Anti-Slavery Society and the Reverend Horace Waller, a Northamptonshire rector who had worked briefly with Livingstone and had a concern for missions, slaves and Africa in general. His real confidante was Augusta to whom he wrote hundreds of long journal-letters. This forbidding spinster was not in the least interested in Africa,[3] but was prepared to correspond endlessly about his religious theories. Her great value to him was that she was never bored by 'eternal things', and never sufficiently interested to gossip about anything else; so he could write safely to her about every subject under the sun. Many of his letters were illustrated with pen-and-ink sketches, rather cleverly done. When he was not letter-writing or working, he mended clocks and musical boxes, and even made a pair of trousers for one of the blacks.

A letter to a Royal Engineer friend perfectly illustrates his boredom and immersion in petty, but necessary, detail:

A is poor and begs to have his tax diminished. B comes up by order of the Government and for some wonderful reason the Governor has refused to pay his expenses. C is the widow of a soldier killed, has nothing to eat, asks to be sent to her home. D's father was a soldier killed and he asks for his father's property. E is a soldier who has not been paid for two or three years. F is an old worn-out creature, a soldier, and asks for his discharge. G wants to be made a sergeant. H wants to be divorced. I is owed something by some other . . . You have nothing but these sorts of things day after day, and all have to be decided in a commonsense way.

His letter was interrupted by a woman who came screeching to him 'and poured out her griefs. Her husband has the amiable wish to strangle her.' No wonder he was 'sorely tempted by cognac and laudanum, but dare not think of it, for my liver rules and will not stand it'.[4]

Though he had time on his hands, he made no effort to learn Arabic or any native language. He had to speak in French to his A.D.C., who would put his words into Arabic, which was then translated into Shillook by one of the soldiers. He cannot have had much idea of what the soldiers, let alone the Shillook, said and thought.

On 16 August the steamer *Khedive* arrived, but a paddle had been damaged by a hippo so it had to be sent on down to Khartoum for repairs. However, next day there arrived from Gondokoro the *Tell Hewein*, so Gordon could move at last. But no – he could not: there was still a few days' delay for cutting fuel. Then, just as they were about to leave this pestilential spot, two boats came downstream and Bohndorff, acting on a tip-off, shifted the firewood on deck and saw under it some woolly heads. There were 96 slaves crammed in below deck, and £2,000 worth of ivory. The same day 25 more freed slaves arrived in a steamer from Gondokoro. It seemed a very satisfactory coup, but Gordon had been hoodwinked: as soon as he had departed upstream, congratulating himself on recovering 121 slaves, 1,600 were passed through Sobat, the *Mudir* having been bribed to look in the other direction.

At Rabat Shambé, Gordon found Gessi, setting up the second new government station. Gessi had malaria, so Gordon took him on to Gondokoro. It seemed as though his staff had no object but to plague him! De Witt, for instance, died on 6 September; and 'there was a glorious tamarisk tree, a regular landmark in this sea of marsh. It was cut down by Kemp, though it took two days to fell and was of no use to burn! How often had its sight gladdened the eyes of those who toiled up and down this stagnant ditch. I can assure you that most of my troubles have come from my Europeans.'

At Gondokoro he plunged into a sea of trouble. He had determined that any of his staff who were discontented must go. He found them not so much discontented as at death's door, though Linant was well enough to intrigue against him.

My place is a complete hospital . . .
Your brother, well but a shadow.
Kemp, engineer, well.
Gessi well; has had a severe fever.
His Greek (servant), ill, more or less. Result, no work.
Berndorf* German, who came up on his own acct and now is my servant, ill; covered with boils.
Menges, German servant, sent back ill.
Russell ill, cannot be moved; invalided.
Anson died.
De Witt dead. Amateur like Berndorf.
Campbell, imposter, but certainly ill. Invalided.
Linant, traitor; very ill, cannot be moved; invalided.
Long with King Mtesa. Have not heard of him for six months . . . Linant and Campbell in huts attended by one of the best doctors (me) that I know.

---

* Bohndorff. Gordon always misspelt his name.

Russell is in my tent, and has constant attacks of sickness ... My temper is very, very short, and it is a bad time for those who come across me the wrong way. Also I have letters to Khedive, money letters of Province, accts of officers going away, arrangements for their going down, watchfulness that they take as little plunder as possible (*no end* of trouble about this). Linant and Campbell well enough to be perfect brigands. Things are in a dreadful muddle, but all is coming right and I do not feel it a bit; on the contrary it rather amuses me.

Campbell is not half as bad as he makes out; if you put *your* finger down *your* throat *you* will be sick.

(Nevertheless he recommended Campbell for promotion.) However the weather was better, and he had a very good bodyguard, Baker's Forty Thieves.[5]

At Gondokoro the river was too shallow for laden steamers to come alongside, supplies of firewood were too distant, and after the rains the water collected in stagnant lagoons ideal for the breeding of the most voracious mosquitoes: 'Trousers, shirt or coat are to them no obstacle. They like a cane-bottomed chair best for you to sit on.' So on 16 September he set off upstream to look for a better site. Before leaving he sent Russell and Campbell down to Khartoum, where Campbell soon died. Gessi stayed at Gondokoro to look after Linant, who died next day. So within six months of their leaving Cairo, four of the ten Europeans were dead and two were far too ill to work. But he was better off without them, and delighted to be no longer paddling about a swamped tent, attending to a sick man at night, with more than a chance of the tent coming down. But why did his staff all fall sick and die? It was a question on which he brooded. 'Have I worked them too much? For as for hardships they really have none to speak of ... To my mind I never work them at all. Perhaps that is the reason.'

For a new station Gordon selected Rejaf, sixteen miles upstream, drier, cooler, with grass and trees on ground rising sharply from the river to a sugarloaf hill behind. It was healthier than Gondokoro, so he moved his invalids there.

Abou Saoud, also ill, now let him down. He misappropriated £6,000 worth of ivory, bullied a *mudir*, intrigued with the soldiers (old Negro-hunters of his), stirred up trouble among the natives, barged in and out of Gordon's cabin without knocking, was bumptious and mendacious. So the erstwhile paragon, unfairly maligned, became a 'despicable creature' and was packed off to Gondokoro in disgrace. He was given another chance, told more lies, and was finally sent back to Cairo. To Stanton Gordon claimed that he had seen through Abou Saoud all the time and was giving him rope to hang himself; but Gordon's earlier letters show clearly that this was not so. As for the *mudir* whom Abou

Saoud had bullied, he was exalted: 'I have given my poor crushed *Mudir* my grand tent and a carpet and made him put up a huge flag, He sits on the throne a perfect king.'

At Rejaf the local tribe was the Niam Niam, occasional cannibals. 'The ladies wear a bunch of leaves as full dress; they are not a bit interested in me or I in them, or, indeed, in the blacks at all. Some wear one scrap, some another. Some pierce their upper lip, and put in a piece of glass; some pierce their ears all round, and put in bits of wood; but they are all black and uncouth creatures, they do not like anything but themselves.' They drummed all night, and could thus communicate over long distances. One of their chiefs turned truculent, surrounding Gordon's tent with 100 armed men and advancing on him with a large knobkerry. Gordon cocked his two guns and laid them on the table. 'Now go,' he said; and the chief, understanding the tone if not the words, went.

Bohndorff, recovered somewhat from his boils, turned out to be a born idiot, quite useless at helping tend the sick. 'It all comes on me, mixing effervescing drinks, medicines etc. . . . It is always my tent, my bed, my etc. etc., that are given up . . . The odd thing of this illness is the sulkiness of the patient. He will scarcely answer you. Will you take some rum water; no answer. Will you take your medicine; no answer.' But Bohndorff did far worse. Borrowing without permission Gordon's elephant-rifle to shoot a hippo, he was knocked over by the recoil and dropped the precious rifle in the water. 'It did not kick if held properly, but Berndorf is a cow.'

It was not Gordon's day. Fuming with rage, he went off to try the mountain howitzer on which the defence of the post largely depended. 'The artillery man, like all that regiment of all nations' was very proud of his weapon until it failed to go off, the Quarter Master at Gondokoro having issued damp priming-tubes to get rid of them. On better days Gordon put on a magic-lantern show for the delighted soldiers; he gave an impressive display of magic by allowing a Niam Niam chief to fire off the gun electrically from 150 yards away.

He was glad when Bohndorff left Rejaf for the delights of Gondokoro. He had no interpreter and no proper cook, only a black who did his best in the kitchen and the two little mosquito-like scraps of Shillook boys whom he had bought in Sobat. They hated one another, being intensely jealous. He could communicate with no one: 'They come, and instinct tells me what they want, and then they go. It is much shorter, and saves a mint of trouble.' He tried to introduce the Niam Niam to the nineteenth century by paying for their ivory in money instead of in beads, and then selling them beads and cattle-bells for their money. Pained to discover how lax his soldiers had been in the observance of their religion, he made Friday a holiday, found them an *alim**, insisted on them keeping the Ramadhan fast and building a mosque. Gordon's attitude to Islam is very remarkable in the context of 1874. Most of his English contemporaries regarded Moslems as idolators, but Gordon had no doubt that Moslems worshipped – albeit with some errors and misconceptions – the God whom he served. The soldiers must have been very puzzled. To them, Christians were unbelievers who never prayed. But here was one who not merely prayed at length and with fervour, but required them to do so.

Gordon used to ask the soldiers' children if they knew God lived in them, and

they understood me. I used to lead up to it by asking them where they would go when they died; they would point to the earth. Then I would ask them if Allah did not care a bit for them, and they would nod acquiescence. Then I would ask them if He would let them lie in the earth, they would shake their heads; then, whether Allah would take them to himself, and often with their eyes moist they would say, Yes. Then I would tell them to thank Him for any good thing they had, to ask Him to help them when they got into trouble, etc. I feel convinced that by leading them up to God thus, it would not have been difficult to let them understand the Redeemer.

For them to understand even Gordon was miraculous, for communication would have to be filtered through amateur interpreters; and with most African tribes nodding and shaking the head do not have the meaning they have for Europeans. However Gordon felt 'sure that the Holy Ghost is in their little black bodies, ready to open their understanding and make clear everything. The natural condition of *all* is blindness . . . The key of the mystery is the fact of God's *actually living in you*. What you need and the black needs is not much explanation but *eyes to see*, but the Holy Ghost is in both of you, to show the truth.'[6]

The primitive nature of the province is illustrated by its monthly expenditure:

Soldiers' pay	£2,397
Engineers' pay	400
Trade goods	200
Administration at Khartoum	150
Cost of steamers and boats	220
Repairs to steamers and boats	120
Miscellaneous	120
	£3,607

* Religious teacher, theologian and prayer-leader. More familiar to Europeans in the plural form, *ulema*.

That was all: nothing on the administration of justice, prisons, revenue collection, education, roads, posts and telegraphs, medical and sanitary services. As for revenue estimates, Gordon could produce none: 'It depends on the natives and on officers' diligence.' Lacking the barest essentials of administration, Equatoria could hardly without absurdity be termed a province. With none of his staff on their feet, and for much of the time no interpreter, there was little he could do to provide the framework of government. So he operated more as a junior district officer than as governor-general.[7]

Baker had left at Gondokoro a small steamer, the *Nyanza*, in sections so that it could be portaged over the cataracts at Dufilé, 134 miles up-stream, and eventually used for exploring the lakes. Kemp, the engineer, had been sent up with 2,000 porters and 200 soldiers to assemble it above the rapids. On 15 October Kemp returned, ill, 'took possession of me as servant and of my things as his; lost his own bed, took mine'. Furthermore he was an ill-bred fellow, who took impertinent liberties with Gordon's private stores. There was an explosion of rage when he borrowed a packet of candles. His resignation was accepted with alacrity – but the storm blew over and he stayed on. Nine days later Gordon found him 'not over-bad' though inclined to pilfer tit-bits.

Gordon now issued positive orders that any illness was to take place away from him, and his staff were not to come near him except on duty. Long elaborates on his 'singular habit of retiring to his hut for days at a time, engaged in the perusal of his Bible and prayer-book'. If for 'days at a time' one reads 'hours at a time', the story is credible; for to officers who came running to him for orders in any difficulty he had at times to be unapproachable, or be driven mad.

However, matters improved with the return of Long who had made fruitful contact with King Mtesa of Uganda; discovered a lake, Kioga, between Lakes Victoria and Albert; and ascertained that the upper waters of the Nile, above Foweira, were navigable. As Foweira could be reached in fourteen days from Gondokoro, Long's journey had been thoroughly worth while. Gordon conceded that he had improved, sent him down to Khartoum on six weeks' leave and recommended him for promotion.

So on the whole things were jogging along fairly well, 'but with much rating and scolding . . . I have given up soft words, if ever I used them, and they get such *digs*!'

9

THE NILE

On 14 November 1874 there arrived at Gondokoro Watson, Chippendall and Ernest Linant de Bellefonds, who had come up as a volunteer to replace his brother. Gordon was overjoyed at this reinforcement: the Frenchman proved to be a great asset; Watson and Chippendall were trained surveyors, 'capital, well-instructed young officers' of the Royal Engineers. 'I cannot,' Gordon wrote to Stanton, 'ever express to you how much I feel indebted to you for them . . . I have been a good deal worn and I fear my temper is *very, very bad.*' Watson and Chippendall, he decided, would in due course take Baker's steamer from Dufilé and survey Lake Albert; meanwhile they were set to work surveying locally. Linant would make a follow-up visit to King Mtesa and try to negotiate a commercial treaty.

Freed from the drudgery of surveying, Gordon could concentrate on administration. But he was again suffering from doubts about his mission. 'The Khedive writes to me quite harshly to stop this slave-trade, and you see his *Mudirs* help it on . . . The real culprits are his local authorities and the Khartoum merchants who are entirely in his power . . . I feel sometimes that, through my influence with the blacks, I am seducing them into a position where they will be a prey to my Arab successor.' He begged Stanton to find out if the Khedive really wanted him to stay on: 'I never put a value on myself, but I can say I am worth more than to perish up here with such a set of incompetent apathetic brutes.'

Gordon's task was made more difficult by events far to the west. The formidable Zebeyr, still nominally the Khedive's Governor, invaded the territory of the Sultan Ibrahim of Darfur and killed him in battle. Thereafter slaves from the Bahr-el-Ghazal could be driven across the desert to Darfur and thence to Khartoum.

However there was nothing Gordon could do about that, so he busied himself with finding a better headquarters site than Gondokoro. He chose Lado, twelve miles down the river. Gessi arrived there and set to work with his usual energy. When some natives appeared the morning after his arrival they were astounded to find the garrison of fifty soldiers safely established inside a high thorn hedge. The only thing this would not keep out was an elephant, which rushed to and fro among the tents uttering panic-stricken screams. The whole country around was full of game, and at night the camp resounded with the deep coughing roars of lions.

Watson and Chippendall continued with their surveying. Both had fallen under Gordon's spell, but were not blinded by it. 'He is very fond of discussions,' wrote Watson. 'He is certainly not a man who runs in an ordinary groove . . . Though professing not to care for geographical discoveries, he does all the time, and I would back him to do work in that line against any man I have ever met.' But Gordon found that they too had the shortcomings which seemed to be inseparable from service on his staff. 'The moment they get a headache they get an abject fear that makes them worse . . . The fact is that they talk, talk and talk, and get all sorts of ideas into their heads, and then bother me with them . . . It is, I suppose, the climate, and having nothing to do in the evenings.' Moreover, 'Watson is a magpie, and an Irishman . . . He will be a fearful bore as he gets older.' Linant found Gordon difficult. Gordon was polite, erudite, far-seeing, the best of men: 'I esteem him, I like him, but I could not live with him, because he is always bothering about my well-being, which annoys him and makes my presence a burden to him.'[1]

In December Watson and 'Chipp' were off with 1,000 porters to establish a base above the rapids at Dufilé; then to push on to Lake Albert. They were provided with detailed written orders. 'The negro is treacherous by nature to some degree and has been badly treated for many years and *ought* to be vengeful even if they are not. Therefore avoid rash adventures, producing no glory but great inconvenience to me. Avoid landing in narrow places among reeds where the natives can jump on boats; and though peaceably received, be ready for war at any time.' Kemp was put under Watson's orders, to get Baker's iron steamer working. All were to study the medical book with the greatest care – much more so than astronomical observations.

Gordon himself, experimenting to find a cure for painful diarrhoea, had discovered that $\frac{1}{2}$ gr. of ginger, $\frac{1}{2}$ gr. of ipecacuanha, and 3 grs. of rhubarb made a splendid daily pill, which kept him in perfect health. Warburg's medicine was most efficacious, 'there is nothing like it, only *you must follow* the directions explicitly.'

Land transport was his great problem; he was trying to get up donkeys, horses and camels, and was manufacturing 200 wheelbarrows. As for his helpless, hopeless staff, they came and went 'like a dissolving view', arriving with almost every boat, departing, shaking with fever or in the throes of dysentery, a few weeks later. Gordon's command of Arabic had not improved, but at least he had mastered a simple formula for the dismissal of the incompetent: '*Imshi Khartoum!*' – 'Go to Khartoum!' – and they went.

On the last day of 1874 there arrived Martin Hansal, Austrian Consul in Khartoum, and a countryman of his, Ernst Marno, with some experience of African travel, who had been sent out by the Austrian Geographical Society. Marno might be an asset; Hansal, a former missionary to Gondokoro, was not. Gordon went to call on him at three in the afternoon, not perhaps the best time. 'He was on his bed, quite incomprehensible either in French or German; discovered at last it was cognac, quite blurred with it; capital man for the Albert Nyanza, would find 60 or 100 lakes for me.' Next day, smiling most benignly, he was '*not very well*, effects telling on him. I never touch any liquor, it is poison to me.'

Actually he did touch liquor, and here a lengthy digression is necessary.

Long returned early in January. He related, or invented, the following incident at Lado:

> The camp was attacked in force one night. Gordon was in his hut and gave no sign of coming out. It was during one of the oft-recurring periods when he shut himself up and placed a hatchet and a flag at the door as a sign that he was not to be disturbed ... I entered abruptly, and found him seated very calmly at a table, on which were an open Bible and a bottle of cognac and sherry. I told him of the situation, to which he made abrupt answer: 'You are commander of the camp.' Whereupon I hastily turned and left him. The savages were finally driven away by a vigorous sortie. The next day Gordon entered my hut in the full-dress uniform of the Royal Engineers and cleanly shaven. He came forward with a quick, tripping step ... and said: 'Old fellow, now don't be angry with me. I was very low last night. Come and dine with me. We will have a glorious dinner.'[2]

The story has been demolished by Bernard Allen in his *Gordon and the Sudan*. Briefly, it may be disbelieved because:

(a) Neither Gordon, nor Marno who was present and kept a very full diary, mentions any attack.

(b) The story is not included in Long's book *Central Africa*, published in 1876, although several pages are devoted to his sojourn in Lado. It first appears in his book *My Life in Four Continents*, published in 1912. By that time Long had been mortified by Gordon's comments on his feebleness, procrastination and inefficiency, published in *Letters of General C. G. Gordon to his Sister* (1888). These did not give his name, but the identity of the officer whom Gordon so mauled is obvious.*

* See p. 77.

Long's books might well have passed almost unnoticed had not Lytton Strachey sieved through them for prosecution evidence. He makes a small but significant amendment to Long's story: instead of inviting the American to 'a glorious dinner', Gordon invites him to 'a good breakfast – a little b-and-s'. There is no authority for this: it is the product of Lytton Strachey's desire to disparage eminent Victorians by irony and innuendo. On another occasion Gordon is described by Long as suggesting brandy-and-soda for breakfast, but not on this occasion.[3]

Bernard Allen goes to great pains to prove that Gordon was never immoderate in his consumption of alcohol; he calls several witnesses to this effect. Nevertheless he does not have the last word on this delicate matter. It is notoriously difficult to prove a negative; and there were the rumours, heard by Wilfred Scawen Blunt long before Long's allegations and Strachey's feline essay. Gordon himself saw in drink a weakness in his defences against the world, the flesh and the devil: 'I am always open to attack on that flank.' He admitted that brandy made him talk too much. On one of his many resignations, he wrote to his brother, Henry: 'Nubar, Rivers Wilson & Co. will say, "it is on account of his LIVER! SMOKING! COGNAC!" I wish I had some now, I never take it with me.'* There are, moreover, witnesses unknown to Bernard Allen. One is Miss Sauer, a very old lady still living in Cape Town, whose father knew Gordon well. 'Gordon,' she says, 'seemed to drink excessively, but had an extraordinary ability to hold his liquor.' Twenty-seven years after Gordon's death Lord Cromer, who as Sir Evelyn Baring had known and disliked Gordon, wrote in a private letter, 'There is not in reality the least doubt that he drank deeply.' The wording suggests that Cromer was writing from common report rather than from personal knowledge, just as Miss Sauer was merely repeating what her father had told her. But there was an eye-witness, very favourably disposed to Gordon. Joseph Reinach, Gambetta's private secretary, made friends with him in 1880, and describes him in a bad mood as sitting alone with a Bible and a half-empty bottle of whisky, and also as a prodigious consumer of cognac.† [4]

The picture comes into focus. Apart from Marno's silence about the 'attack' on the camp, it is inconceivable that Gordon, drunk or sober, remained skulking in his tent while a fight was going on fifty yards away. It is extremely improbable that he was a habitual soaker; neither his health, his work nor his reputation in the Sudan could have stood it. Sometimes, on leave or when his work would not suffer, he drank heavily, but because he could hold it, no one ever saw him the worse for liquor. Burton, though they met only once, probably got it about right: 'For

* i.e., by implication, he never took it on safari.
† See p. 161.

months he would drink nothing but water; and then prefer, very decidedly, water mixed with whisky.'[5]

Although Long was much improved, he and Gordon were incompatible. Moreover he had committed the grave error of providing the province with the wrong kind of reinforcements. 'Oh, my dear Augusta, for two days I dared not ask Long (who had told me he had applied for 400 soldiers) whether these were Arabs or black troops. At last I asked. They were Arabs! Now, out of 250 Arabs I brought here, I should say half were dead and 100 were invalided, so you can imagine my horror.' Within three weeks, 270 out of the 400 were sick.

So Long was again in disrepute, having tumbled back into procrastination and forgetfulness. Gordon took the opportunity, when they were in good tempers, to point out that they would never get on together: 'He neglects everything, and, I may say, it is the hunting season, with me for hunter and with nearly everyone else for the hunted.'

But how could Long be eased off? He was, after all, a colonel, highly praised in Gordon's official reports, recently promoted by the Khedive. He could not be disposed of by a curt '*Imshi Khartoum*'.

Gordon had an inspiration. For a long time he had worried about his unsatisfactory line of communication, 3,080 miles up the Nile with its *sud* and its rapids and its ever-diminishing supplies of firewood for the steamers. From the Great Lakes to the East African coast would be far less, especially if (as he erroneously believed) Lake Baringo was an arm of Lake Victoria. He consulted Burton. Where was the northern frontier of Zanzibar? Had the natives fire-arms? Was the Tana river navigable between Mount Kenya and the sea, and hence by international law open to shipping of all countries, including Egypt? Burton, Long and Augusta were enjoined to secrecy, for it appeared that Britain might not want Egypt debouching onto the sea. Although Gordon claimed to have been assured that Britain had no interests in this area, one is left with the impression that, out of loyalty to the Khedive, he was less than frank with Her Majesty's Government. Indeed he later admitted this.

So the project was put to the Khedive; and Long, recommended for command of the exploratory expedition, was sent down to Cairo with presents for His Highness – a daughter of Mtesa, a monkey, a tame buffalo, and a female pigmy of Tiki-Tiki.

In the event the plan fell through, for the British Government had ideas on East Africa incompatible with its annexation by the Khedive. They treated His Highness, wrote Gordon in disgust, like a Hindu rajah. But the East African project brought Gordon into correspondence with Sir William Mackinnon, a Scottish shipowner with interests in East Africa who was also an agent for the King of the Belgians' Congo

Company. He became a useful and generous friend, positively pressing on Gordon loans and cheap passages which were not refused.

Gordon's main object in the early part of 1875 was to improve communications by establishing along the Nile a chain of posts not more than a day's journey apart; for 'now we do not hear from a station for six months, and then 100 men must go.' For this he needed competent, fit officers, and where was he to find them? Gessi was in Khartoum, Linant on his way to Mtesa's, Chippendall somewhere between Dufilé and Lake Albert, Kemp invalided off to Cairo, Watson had returned from Dufilé with 'his clothes hanging on him like a pole', so rotten with malaria that Gordon feared he would never reach Cairo alive. 'Poor Watson, he feels so much going back.' But Watson, according to Long, stopped in Khartoum to draw £2,000 for his few weeks' work, 'paid with many grimaces and contemptuous criticisms'. Gordon was more tolerant of his Royal Engineers who were 'a hard bargain for the Khedive', but 'I did not make the contract, so they have pretty pickings.'[6]

He had himself to sort out trouble at Sobat, where he found Captain Frederick Burnaby, who gave *The Times* a vivid picture of Gordon at work:

Nearer and nearer came the steamer ... The one bugler nearly burst his lungs in ringing out the clear strain of a General's salute, the black captain lowered his sword, and the seventeen men comprising the garrison brought their arms to the 'Present' as a short, thick-set man, who appeared to be in the picture of health and was attired in the undress uniform of a Colonel of Engineers, hastened down the ship's side and ... rapidly inspected the men and their accoutrements. The number of things he had to settle would have been enough to turn the head of any ordinary mortal, but the Colonel went steadily ahead, giving out one order after another, administering justice to the natives, censuring or praising the officials, ordering punishment here and reward there, all this through an Egyptian interpreter who gravely rendered every word of Gordon's French into Arabic.[7]

It was a *personal* administration, a personal justice, based on no court procedure, no code but common sense, in which Gordon was himself judge, jury, counsel for the prosecution and for the defence. It was quick: the delinquents were forthwith flogged. It worked: it was popular with the natives. But it worked only because of Gordon's personality. With someone less fair and conscientious, it might have led to monstrous injustice.

Gordon returned to Rejaf where the chief, Bedden, had been troublesome. Gordon had made polite overtures and been told that his next messenger would be killed. Bedden had sent his fighting men against a friendly chief. Recalcitrant pastoral tribes are not easy to deal with:

they are more mobile than troops, and when the arm of government stretches out to grab them – they are not there. Burning down their villages does them no harm, for their huts are temporary affairs of sticks, mud and mats which can be rebuilt in a day. Their Achilles' heel is their cattle which in the dry season can always be found within ten miles of permanent water to which they must go at least every other day. If these are seized, the toughest tribe must come to terms – paying the fine, handing over the murderer, returning the stolen beasts.

In this case some cattle *zaribas* were on islands, others along the banks. Gordon planned as carefully as in China, sending 60 men up the east bank, 100 up the west bank, while he with an officer and ten men would land on the islands. They set off at ten o'clock so as to come upon the miscreants' *zaribas* at dawn before the cattle had been let out to graze. With a bright moon Gordon's own approach was not a difficult operation, but it was too difficult for these troops. The officer and eight men lost themselves, and two hours before dawn Gordon found himself with only two soldiers and his interpreter. It was a situation such as governors-general seldom encounter; his party could easily be overwhelmed by a rush of spearmen, and were too few to drive away the cattle while the owners were doing all they could to obstruct. Gordon's *razzia* had all the makings of a fiasco, even of a disaster.

However, he managed to find his stragglers and, imperturbable when action was imminent, went to sleep. Just as the sky was beginning to redden three rifle-shots rang out, and a drum beat an alarm. As it grew light Gordon saw that what he had been told were the huts of a *zariba* were nothing but rocks. Eventually, with the help of some warriors from another tribe, they collected about 600 cattle, some of which were later proved not to belong to Bedden's people at all. The eastern party had done better, rounding up about 2,000 head. The western party had lost their way. It was a typical little operation, in which nothing went according to plan, but which was in the end more or less successful. 'I do most cordially hate this work; but what are you to do? You must protect your own people and also the friendly sheikhs; and you cannot make them give in, except by the capture of their cattle.'

Seventeen days later Gordon happened to meet Bedden sitting under a tree, and was pained to find that he was almost blind. 'Poor old man! . . . I tried to be civil to him and said if the tribe behaved well nothing would be taken from them.' Bedden made submission, and received back some of the cattle, a coil of copper wire and a pair of scissors.

Gordon planned to establish four posts between Rejaf and Dufilé. These would be at Bedden*, Kerri, Moogie and Laboré, respectively

* African places are often named after a local chief, and changed when he dies.

15, 45, 57 and 72 miles above Rejaf. At Kerri he experienced yet another of those frustrations inseparable from tropical Africa, and so damaging to his temper. His camp was apart from the native huts, which he had forbidden his soldiers to enter. In the course of a thunderstorm several shots were fired, his soldiers cried out that they were under attack and in retaliation pillaged the huts. 'I saw no enemy . . . It was all a ruse . . . Cowardly, lying, effeminate brutes, these Arabs and Sudanese! I wish they had one neck and someone would squeeze it! I keep as far as I can from them, out of earshot of their voices . . . Oh! I am sick of these people. It is they, and not the blacks, who need civilization. There is little difference between white and black men, I feel more and more assured.'

It was not exactly the opinion on Negroes that he had been expressing eight months earlier, but Gordon never set a high value on consistency. He was suffering from disillusion: 'I do not care if there is one lake or a million lakes, and I do not care if the Nile has a source or not. Some philanthropic people write to me about "noble work, poor blacks", etc. I have, I think, stopped them writing by acknowledging ourselves to be a pillaging horde of brigands and propose to them to leave their comfortable homes and come out to their favourite poor blacks.' Not even missionaries earned his approval:

One wrote me word, 'that fine fellow Young goes out to Lake Nyasa with a fine set of young fellows, and the first *dhow* with slaves he meets, he will run her down with his steam-launch.' How like Mr Young's proceedings were to the Apostles' ditto! Mr Young goes out as a missionary with no earthly weapons, only a lot of Sniders! Old Livingstone wanted chains for his porters! . . . Be a geographical explorer or not – be a brigand or not – but sail under true colours. 'We do not want your beads, we do not want your cloths' of the Moogies rings in my ears. 'We want you to go away.'

Whatever the trials of Equatoria, he was at least spared those of England. 'Fancy having to go to a Horticultural Show or to the Crystal Palace! . . . No hard labour is equal to that sort of society. Fancy a picnic! What more utterly melancholy than a *fête champêtre* or a masked costume ball!'

At least he was denting the slave-trade. Writing on 9 March 1875 to the Secretary of the Anti-Slavery Society, he could report that the price of slaves at Khartoum was falling owing to slaves taking every advantage of the law to claim their freedom, as they could legally do if they had been taken from their homes by slave-hunters: 'People will not buy with the chance of a total loss in a few weeks.' But Gordon was too sanguine: the very captains of his steamers were carrying slaves to Khartoum. Nevertheless the whole question of slavery was not nearly so cut and dried as the gentlemen in England believed. He proceeded to enlighten the Anti-Slavery Society about some of the facts of life in Equatoria. 'I have never witnessed the harrowing scenes related by other travellers. The slaves I have come across never will return to their tribes. I can only account for this by the consideration that they have found it much more amusing to be in civilized parts than where life is monotonous and food is scarce.[8]

There was no reluctance on the part of the blacks to leave their distant homes: the hordes of women and children who infested his military posts were the greatest curse, causing endless trouble, for no black woman would remain faithful to the same man for more than a few months; but nothing would induce them to return home. Most blacks would 'give their all to be enslaved in a good Cairo house'. Slave-*raiding* was cruel and evil, but the way to stop it was not by churning out pamphlets in London and badgering him to hang all slavers, but by some of the wealthy members of Society making sacrifices – of their wine, for a start – in order to finance more consulates, which would advertise widely the slave's right to be set free whenever he wished. Warming to his work, he recommended that a party of English clergy be sent out to advise him *on the spot*. Their expenses might be met by his home-based critics, and he himself would gladly contribute £100. His desire for clerical counsel was not to be gratified, but he enjoyed teasing the Reverend Horace Waller who through Livingstone and the slave-trade had worked himself into a good living from a poor one.[9]

On 16 April Chippendall rejoined him at Kerri, having been prevented by a smallpox epidemic from reconnoitring the river as far as Lake Albert. Gordon believed, from instinct and hearsay, that when the Nile rose in April, he would be able to get boats up to the Fola Falls: but beyond that? All depended on Baker's levels, most of which Chippendall had checked. But Chippendall had been inexcusably careless, arriving from Dufilé with no maps, no pedometer, no chronometer, no instruments nor nautical almanac. 'I do not think he has the least idea where he has been, though when pressed by your brother he used to say this or that.' So Chipp was harried, chased, nagged, subjected to interminable cross-examination about the inland route, the mountain and those all-important levels. Soon his hero-worship was diluted by a liberal dash of exasperation, and he unburdened himself to Watson:

Oh! How he bores me night after night about the levels and the distances! I should not mind if he would have one good night of it and settle it; but every night to discuss whether Baker's levels are right; whether the distance is this or that, what you think; then, if you give an opinion, to be nailed until out of sheer fag you agree to any proposition he likes to put forward ... Gordon treats one so much as an equal, and then one has to be careful not to forget he is one's superior officer, that really I often feel quite mad. He ought to keep one more at arm's length, because one is nearly certain some day or other to treat him as an equal, and then there will be a row.

During May Gordon was to-ing and fro-ing between Kerri and Lado, bringing up boats, garrisons and stores through gorges and rapids of great difficulty and danger. Hippos were troublesome: 'We were afraid every minute of being swamped by them. Sometimes they are very fierce and bite the boats in two.'

Chippendall, meanwhile, was constructing a station at Kerri. First, there was a rectangular thorn *zariba*, high, wide and dense; some thorns were like miniature stilettos, two inches or more long, others were wicked, hooked 'wait-a-bit' thorns. The bushes were cut and laid with their stumps on the inward side, so that they could not be pulled out by a native creeping up in the dark. Outside the *zariba* was dug a deep ditch, and at the corners were emplacements for the 6-pounders. Inside were the straw huts for the soldiers and officers, an office and a guard-room. The store and magazine was a more solid structure of mud and wattle. There was a wooden quay for steamers; and a flag-pole, on which the Khedive's flag was raised at dawn, lowered at sunset, while the Quarter Guard presented arms and a bugler sounded Reveillé and Retreat. No *zariba* could keep out elephants: three broke into Lado and spent the night devastating the vegetable garden.

Gordon complained that there was not a single branch of the administration that he had not to attend to personally. Chippendall took a somewhat different view of the Governor-General's attention to detail. 'He seems always to think that nobody but his blessed self can even screw a box-lid on . . . But he is devilish kind to one, and really I fear he will almost spoil me for future service.' But Chippendall developed a huge growth on his neck, and by the end of July was on his way down to Cairo. 'I cannot tell you my sorrow at leaving Gordon, for with all his faults one can't help but love him.'

So Gordon was left with no company but Arabs and blacks with whom he could not communicate, no reliable subordinates but the indestructible Gessi, now in Khartoum organizing the punctual despatch of stores, and Ernest Linant, somewhere between Kerri and Mtesa's. Gordon was incapable of relaxing. 'Inaction to me is terrible. I really do not know what on earth to do from morn to night.' So, when he was not feverishly busy, he complained of having nothing to do, made work for himself, made himself a perfect nuisance to everyone else. He killed time by constructing a rocket-launcher. It was apparently the governor-general's duty to order crate after crate of trade-goods – coloured umbrellas and blankets, hatchets and hoes, knives and scissors, fish-hooks and lines, needles and thread; and, of course, endless quantities of beads, opal, blue, coral, chalk, ruby, amber, turquoise, striped gold-and-silver. If he had left it to his quartermaster, the fool would have ordered beads with gold mounting, quite useless, 'for your black brethren are greasy and grease is deadly on Birmingham gilt'.[10]

The stores at Lado kept him busy for days. Watson would

rejoice to hear that chaos ceases to exist in the magazines. Now each tar-tin, soap-tin, oil-tin is with its brothers, and you no longer find a bullet-mould with a mass of beads, screwdrivers, magnets, needles and thread; tents have their poles and mallets; things are in a certain order. I had, of course, to do it myself ... How wretchedly ignorant we are in practical things. What is the advantage of material soft soap over hard soap? What is the advantage of using linseed oil in paint? And how (oh dear! this is bad!) do you make paint?

So he slaved away in the steamy heat, sweat pouring off him as he created order from chaos, brought the stores ledgers up-to-date, oiled and greased everything which was rusty or mildewy or cracking in the heat. It was not, perhaps, how the governor-general should occupy himself, but if the quartermaster was incapable, what else could one do? 'Altogether there is a universal wish for the steamers to come to be rid of me ... Bear in mind the great maxims, "Never do to-day what you can put off till to-morrow", "Never let your duty interfere with your pleasure." What is a drier in paint? Turps is, I think. How are screws designated in trade? When does a nail become a spike?' It was lamentable how little of practical use even Woolwich cadets were taught. He had to repair his own boots and a nice mess he made of it. If he had sons, he would certainly teach them boot-making, tailoring, carpentering, black- and tin-smithing – all of which seemed to be essential qualifications for the Governor-General of Equatoria.

Clients came to him to redress the smallest wrong.

I must say your black sisters stick up for their rights – slaves or no slaves. It frequently happens that one of them comes and stands before me. I know what is meant. I make the sign that someone has beaten them, and they assent; they are then sent to my filthy kitchen for the night and given refuge. Then they disappear, having found another husband. When they repeat this very often I am obliged to remonstrate with them for their inconstancy ... You might as well marry a cock to his hens as one of them. The semi-civilized black woman is a true horror ... One of them was nearly caught by the hostile natives the other day, she squawked loud enough.

However he could detect some results for his eighteen months' hard labour. When he first arrived, thanks to Baker's depredations and the rapacity of the soldiery, one could not move without an escort of sixty soldiers, and even then the blacks would conceal themselves in the grass and stick a spear into the hindermost. Now two men could move safely, with no fear of every clump of high grass. The blacks were even beginning dimly to comprehend that there was a rule of law, and that they could obtain justice even against the Governor-General's own servants.

Week after week Gordon waited for his steamers to come up from Khartoum. 'It is a country of delays . . . The rudder is always out of repair; when you get in a boat the rowel-pins are never fastened in properly.' He fretted endlessly. For the river was higher than in living memory, and with sufficient muscle-power he hoped to be able to haul even the steamer *Khedive* up to Makade. 'Oh the worries I have had! Sentries asleep and taking off even their clothes, wretched creatures of officers not fit for buglers' . . . but the greatest worry of all was the failure of the steamers to arrive. And when they did arrive, could he haul them up the rapids without good ropes? But one must never forget that there was a Higher Purpose, as yet unfathomed and unfathomable, even in the most infuriating delay. 'There is some deep and wonderful design in all these trying obstacles.'

At last the steamers arrived, on 20 July, and he set off with 100 soldiers, 80 porters to haul each boat, and at least 120 soldiers' 'wives' and children. There followed three weeks of prodigious labour. 'In one place the current came down from both sides of a mass of rocks, besides which the channel curved and the force was terrific . . . A small boat broke loose and it was nearly four miles down the stream before it was secured . . . It is the violent eddies which are so terrible . . . Often and often the ropes break and it all has to be done over again.' After the worst of the rapids had been passed – at Bedden, with the aid of a helpful witch-doctor striking the water to make it give passage – he thought that all would be plain sailing to Laboré. But a mile above Moogie a *nagar* broke loose and grounded on some rocks in midstream. Two more boats were sent to rescue the first; one capsized, the other grounded, and aboard the former was all the spare tow-rope. He could move no further until he obtained more rope; and meanwhile, to protect the boats, must camp on the spot.

A further complication was trouble from the natives, here of the truculent Bari tribe, who began stalking the camp with hostile intent. A few long-range shots made them think differently, and next day their chiefs came in to apologize. But an ominous sign was the disappearance of their women. Witch-doctors seemed to be performing some cursing ceremony, which Gordon terminated by a shot into the ground beside them. At night arrows were shot into his camp (making the women 'squawk') from a nearby patch of *dhoora*, which he blasted with his duck-gun. 'People laugh at bows and arrows, but at night they are very disagreeable.' When Linant arrived with his soldiers, he really would have to 'tax' the Bari by taking some of their cattle.

On 22 August Linant arrived, with hair-raising accounts of conditions at the court of Mtesa. This moved Gordon to some general reflections on imperialism. 'The chiefs have a right to resist, and our right is only our might . . . Australia was a fair colony, Canada and America ditto – but not New Zealand or India which were already peopled sufficiently for the land.'

With Linant there came a really good officer from Fatiko, Nuehr Agha. 'Now for the taxing!'

The Bari again surrounded Gordon and his escort, who had to drive them back with volleys. They proved extraordinarily difficult to hit, running forward while the soldiers were loading, falling flat as soon as the soldiers took aim. Gordon tried a few shots himself: 'I shoot fairly, but three times missed.'[11] Double-barrelled guns with slugs were better than rifles against them.

On the 25th Linant volunteered to cross the river and burn the huts of the hostile natives. Gordon sent with him forty-three men of his own bodyguard, and off he went, gay and gallant in a red shirt Gordon had lent him. There was intermittent firing, but through his telescope Gordon could see them apparently in control of the situation. In the evening a man wearing clothes came to the far bank and a boat was sent to bring him across. He said he was the sole survivor: the others had all been slaughtered.

With only thirty demoralized soldiers and a mob of women and children, Gordon, as night fell, was in a position of the utmost danger. He decided to withdraw to Moogie, no easy operation in the circumstances, but accomplished without firing a shot – except one fired accidentally which nearly blew off his head, 'for which I gave him a box on the ear which he has not forgotten'. The Bari let them go, only one mocking them in the early morning: 'I made him see that the top of a rock 500 yards distant was not a healthy place to stand on.'

Next day he crossed the river to search for survivors. Five crept out of the bush, and Linant's tattered corpse was found, with gaping spear-wounds in back and neck. It would never have happened with proper troops, and Gordon objected most strongly to conducting operations with a mob of untrained, undisciplined soldiers cluttered up with their women and children. 'We derided the poor blacks who fought for their independence, and now God gave them victory.' But he could not leave them, truculent and unrepentant, on his line of communication. So to 'tax' the offending Bari he recruited auxiliaries from the fierce Niam Niam, but the tax-hunting *razzia* was not a great success. In dense bamboo jungle intersected by narrow paths known only to the Bari, the bag amounted to no more than 200 cattle and 1,500 sheep.

Gordon protested often his abhorrence of war; he truly sympathized with the tribes resisting his aggression. But it is clear from the zest and detail with which he described these skirmishes and cattle-raids that he enjoyed every minute of them. Nor did he eschew the tactics of 'divide and rule'. When the natives attacked him, he refrained from punishing those near the river, in whose territory he needed to cut firewood for the steamers, but burned the villages of those further away, which led to much recrimination between them.

In the pocket of Linant's blood-stained shirt had been found a letter from Stanley to the *Daily Telegraph* recommending the despatch of missionaries to Mtesa's. As that monarch was in the habit of supervising every day the execution of several of his subjects chosen at random, it was clear that his court was a fertile and virgin field for missionary endeavour. Stanley's letter resulted in the establishment of the first station of the Church Missionary Society in Uganda.

While these operations were in progress the officer in charge of Kerri had let the men get drunk and then admitted hundreds of armed warriors inside the *zariba*: nothing but the fortuitous arrival of a steamer prevented a disaster. 'I quite despair with those brutes . . . *the very worst* troops, unworthy of the name of soldiers, I ever saw. I shall certainly strain the Military Law to have this officer shot.' (In the event he fined the officer three months' pay and reduced him to the ranks.)

At last, on 15 September, new ropes and some big blocks and tackle arrived. He was in a position to press on up to the lakes with steamers and all. But should he? What right had he 'to place a despicable unworthy race in authority? The Arabs are an effete race and the Sudanese fit only to be slaves. Think, my dear Stanton, why should I stay? "We want to be left alone" rings in my ears.' Once he had placed his chain of stations and put steamers above the Fola Falls, could he not leave? He had no wish to explore the lakes: some geographical society could send someone up. 'Yours sincerely, C. G. Gordon, tired out with wear and tear and finding fault with those poor devils who I suppose do their best.'

So he asked Khairi Pasha to arrange for his relief in eleven months' time. The only way, he advised, to run the country was by a cadre of Sudanese officers, caught young enough to be taught reading and writing, the elements of administration, agriculture and commerce.[12]

Next day they failed to haul the steamer off the rocks, the strap of the block breaking at a critical moment owing no doubt to the expertise of a hostile witch-doctor on the opposite bank. (The *Mudir* wanted to open up with artillery on him. 'I never saw such people!') However, eventually they succeeded, and the appalling labour of hauling the *nagars* and steamer up the cataracts began again.

With ropes leading to each bank the boats had to be hauled not merely upstream, but from side to side to avoid rocks and take advantage of slack water. This required exact timing and co-ordination between the two hauling teams, one slacking off as the other pulled; and for muscle-power he must rely on scores of local warriors who an hour before had never even seen a boat bigger than a dug-out canoe. Every order – even an order to deal with a sudden crisis – had to be given in French and passed on by interpreters ignorant of nautical terms, through Arabic to the local dialect; 'before it is in Arabic the mischief is done.' The soldiers moved as though they were at a funeral, and if the eye of authority was not on them, would go off and hide in the grass; they would lackadaisically stand watching others hauling on a rope till their eyes started from their heads – but never think of helping. 'Oh dear! what a people to slave for! They never have a knife, nor a hammer, nor a bit of yarn, nor anything of the sort . . .' And all in savage heat: 'Pour the Nile down your throat and it does not appease your thirst. The immense amount of perspiration exhausts the body.'

A newly-posted Arab lieutenant reported for duty, a pitiable sight. He was muffled up like his veiled wife, weeping and begging to be sent back. When Gordon raised a *courbach*,* he flopped on the ground and kissed the interpreter's feet. 'These officers have committed some crime in Cairo and are sent here for punishment.' Again and again Gordon raged against 'those wretched little mushrooms' of Egyptian officers, '. . . *I hate them*, a two-penny half-penny nature!' In comprehensive condemnation he found them to be idle, selfish, deceitful, cowardly and cruel. 'As for the blacks, it is a farce to call them Mussulmen, their women and their stomachs are their gods . . . They are a hopeless, hopeless, hopeless lot indeed.'[13]

If he really so despised Egyptians, Arabs and Sudanese, he could hardly have got the best out of them. But one must always take Gordon's private letters with a pinch of salt, for they were the safety-valve for his temper. The measure of his exasperation was that he could now think better of his predecessor. 'I now see that Baker had very much to contend with, and I quite whitewash him of any failure. For with ten times his power and means, I have had a sickener.' Indeed he even apologized to Baker, 'I call your attention to the fact that I have been swayed by a desire to disparage your efforts.' This was the start of a long correspondence which was to continue until his death, with Baker acting almost as his unofficial adviser on Sudanese affairs.[14]

* Hippo- or rhino-hide whip.

Gordon was suffering from a severe attack of 'the doles', and was even 'dolishly inclined' to run away. However there was, thank heaven, Nuehr Agha from Fatiko, who would be judged a good officer anywhere. Moreover a friendly chief invited Gordon to his territory and promised to supply meat and *dhoora* at a fair price. So the new station of Laboré was established.

10
⌘ THE GREAT LAKES

Merely to push on to the lakes would present little difficulty. But Gordon was determined not to be absorbed in 'all this geographical business'. For the time being, however, there was little else for him to do. His chain of government stations along the Nile prevented slavers from using that route except with the connivance of his colleagues at Fashoda and Khartoum, and the desert-routes from Bahr-el-Ghazal to Darfur and Khartoum were far outside his province.

In a rare mood of self-congratulation he reflected on his success. The natives could see that the government was there to stay: they could not, at least in the dry season, evade it by moving away from the river, because neighbouring tribes would not let them have grass or water. The river was proved now to be navigable as far as Laboré by small boats all the year round, and by steamers in the rains. With posts so close to one another, patrols and officers on tour could be assured of food without pillaging the natives. With the exception of the Bari, the river tribes had been brought to a state of reasonable grace; he had even established some resemblance to law and order along the river.

Yet again and again he was tormented by doubts. What benefit could possibly accrue from these conquerors? The only difference between them and the natives was that one spoke a bastard sort of Arabic, wore clothes and had a gun. In Equatoria the dividing line between right and wrong was painfully obscure:

Here is a stretch of conscience. When we got up here the natives who were friendly would not sell us *dhoora*. What was there to be done? I must feed the men. There was a rather hostile, not very hostile, sheikh near us, and so I sent and took the *dhoora* from him. This is harmful work to me, but what can I do? ... All these questions are difficult ones of right and wrong ... What right has a man of one nation in another nation's territory? What right has he to subdue that nation?

It was a dilemma from which there was no escape. A few weeks later he was forced by the sheer necessity of feeding his men to take 140 head of cattle from a tribe which was 'certainly *semi*-hostile, but it is no excuse'.

However he was, for good or ill, still in the Khedive's service; so to the task of getting steamers onto Lake Albert he directed his formidable energy and ingenuity, taking advantage of the second rains which were due to start in October.

He could not do it alone, and Nuehr Agha did not pretend to expertise on river navigation. The man he needed was Gessi, not only experienced, but a man of his own age; and Gordon had already noticed that only middle-aged men could stand the climate, the exasperation and the monotony. Gessi was summoned in October. Meanwhile Gordon, having sent for his horses, rode up to Dufilé, and then made his way down the river to examine the cataract at Fola. 'It is ALL OVER!... it was appalling to look at, far less to think of getting anything up or down except in splinters. Above it the water was smooth, and 80 to 150 yards wide; and here it was suddenly contracted to two passages of 15 and 20 yards wide. It boiled down, twisting into all sorts of eddies . . . for two miles.' It was hopeless to think of taking a big steamer up the lake: nothing could go which could not be carried past these falls. Gessi would have to rely on Baker's little steamer, still waiting to be assembled at Dufilé, and on two iron life-boats rusting in sections at Gondokoro.

Dufilé was a place of silence and solitude, like the end of the world. Gordon had no interpreter, for the doctor, a delicate, fragile creature, who had been acting in that role, had died in Laboré. 'Poor little doctor! He was so looking forward to ending this work.' No longer did Gordon see death as a happy release: such thoughts were for Gravesend: death in Equatoria, breathing all the time over one's shoulder, accompanied by the awful sweating and chills of malaria or the gut-agonies of dysentery, had a less agreeable image.

He was in constant expectation of an urgent message that some garrison's food was finished. 'You never get any warning. When all is finished, then you hear.' He got instead a report from Lado that the natives meditated an attack. As there were eighty soldiers there, four or five 'hare-brained officers' and a strong stockade, he merely recommended keeping the sentries awake. He had given up all hope of improving these useless soldiers: 'The only way they should be governed is by the whip.'[1]

It was great country for elephants . . . 'What a number of poor beasts have died for this ivory!' He himself had sworn off elephant-shooting, but shooting for the pot was another matter. 'You can scarcely conceive the desire one has for a change of food and how glad one is for anything to shoot.' When the snipe came in he had excellent sport. He could find no work that needed doing but the triangulation of a fifty-mile sea of high grass.

On 20 November 1875 there arrived a packet of letters, including one from the Khedive containing nothing but pettifogging complaints. In a fury he dashed off three telegrams of resignation. Fortunately they were not despatched, for next morning he opened another letter from His Highness containing nothing but warm thanks and praise. So he set off downstream to meet Gessi.

What a relief! In Gessi, bearded and sunburnt, no callow youth but a stern, seasoned soldier and pioneer, expecting and exacting prompt obedience – or, at least, obedience as prompt as possible in Africa – Gordon at last had 'a smart fellow, better than many a R.E.', who did not need to be herded to his work and supervised every minute of the day. Within ten days they had divided the iron-boats and stores at Gondokoro into 1,000 porter-loads and set off on their march, the heavier pieces being dragged along on carts, Gessi riding up and down on his tough little Abyssinian pony. At Moogie they stopped a few days to teach the Bari a lesson. 'Sons of dogs!' the warriors shouted across the river. 'Come over here, and we will sit under trees and send our children to destroy you.' So they went over and took 1,500 cattle, after which the Bari were more polite. On 29 December Gordon watched the single file of Gessi's porters winding up the hill past Fola.

There was a glamour attached to the Great Lakes and the sources of the Nile. For decades they had attracted the most famous explorers. To discover whether the Nile actually passed through Lake Albert was to geographers a matter of great importance, and to put a Khedival steamer on the lake had a high political priority. Gordon had every excuse for grabbing at this glittering prize of exploration. Indeed this had been practically ordered by the Khedive. Furthermore the mapping of unknown country had always been his great interest, and no one was better qualified to survey the lakes. But he had not the slightest intention of doing so. He rationalized his refusal by explaining that to be boxed up for a fantasy in a fifty-foot steamer beside a hot boiler would kill him. His real reason was a distaste for 'the inordinate praise given to an explorer'; he did not wish to be classed with mountebanks like Livingstone and Stanley. So, leaving Gessi and a rather efficient Syrian engineer named Ibrahim to assemble the boats and steamer, he set off on foot to inspect the long-neglected posts at Fatiko and Foweira.

Gordon was not very fit for a foot-safari, and made heavy weather of it. He took a jaundiced view of this wilderness of thorn-scrub, high elephant-grass and red laterite soil. Elephants had uprooted the trees and laid them across his path, which was pitted with their gigantic footprints, made during the rains when the ground was soft, a foot deep, now baked hard as brick and hell to walk over. Although dog-tired every evening, he seldom had a good night's sleep, and was glad of any excuse to take a little laudanum. At last his constitution was beginning to falter: 'Out of sorts again with bleeding at the nose; nearly suffocated last night with blood. Poor sheath! It is much worn.'

He sent Nuehr Agha 200 miles on to establish stations at Urondogani (Murchison's Falls) and Kossitza (Ripon Falls). The latter was near Mtesa's country, and that potentate had to be handled with caution because, having recently announced his conversion to Christianity, he was the favourite of the mission societies. Meanwhile he established another new post on the Nile 143 miles above Lake Albert. This too was a politically sensitive area, being on the eastern boundary of Unyoro, realm of the unpredictable Kabarega, who had forced Baker to beat an inglorious retreat, losing twenty of his men, his scarlet and silver-laced deputy county lieutenant's uniform (which Gordon later ransomed for £30) and his musical-box (which Kabarega later sent to Gordon for repair).

Gordon was beginning to dwell on the pleasures of home leave next winter, oysters, lying abed in the mornings, travelling first-class in the train, and (D.V.) resting a while. 'But,' he begged Waller, 'let me ask you to leave me alone. I want quiet when at home. I do not want to go and stay or dine out *anywhere*, and I do not want to see any of the men who worry about Africa.'[2]

But that was still many months ahead: here, right beside him, was the problem of Kabarega, who was reported to have decamped from Masindi, taking with him his ancient, magic ceremonial stool, symbol of royalty. So Gordon sent an Arab officer to establish a post at Masindi, and another to Magungo, near the north-eastern end of Lake Albert. Then he returned to Dufilé to see how Gessi and Ibrahim had done with the boats.

They had done very well, one life-boat was complete, another nearly so, and the steamer well on. This was a minor miracle, seeing that for years they had been lying at Gondokoro and Dufilé, exposed to rust and to the attentions of pilferers who required copper-piping for bracelets, nuts for knobkerries, iron rods to beat into spears.

On 7 March 1876 Gessi set off with the two life-boats, three dozen Dongolawi rowers, two dozen soldiers and stores for Magungo. He was accompanied by Carlo Piaggia, a free-lance traveller of good repute, who had arrived a few days earlier. The steamer would soon follow. Gordon walked at a leisurely pace down to Kerri, mapping the Nile as he went.

It was almost a holiday. His health improved and he positively enjoyed himself. Now that the most difficult part of his work was nearly accomplished, he could look back on it with modest pride. Baker had placed troops in Gondokoro, Fatiko and Foweira, 'all more or less in misery and years behind in their pay . . . These were the province of which I was to be Governor-General. It was a farce!' Now law and order prevailed along the river. His map was almost complete. Slavers had ceased from troubling his riverine tribes. With home-leave approaching, he was building castles in the air about a blissful time to be spent searching well the scriptures and studying the mysteries in some quiet place. Elated at the prospect of getting back to England alive, he pointed out to the Insurance Office their folly in refusing to insure his life two years ago and invited them to do so now.

He could even take a more kindly view of Arabs and Egyptians. They were indolent because everything they produced was taken from them in taxes, afraid of responsibility because they were punished so severely if things went wrong, deceitful because honesty had been bred out of them.

On 29 April Gessi made a triumphant return. He had explored Lake Albert and survived a prodigious storm which nothing but his life-boats could have weathered. 'NUNC DIMITTIS,' Gordon exulted to Mrs Freese. 'The Lake is surveyed and it is over.' More specifically it had been proved that the Nile ran through the lake's north-east corner. Moreover, by strict international law, he noted with satisfaction, the lakes would be the Khedive's, as he had hoisted his flag first on them. One might argue that on these grounds they belonged to Mtesa and Kabarega, but Gordon was not in Mtesa's or Kabarega's service.

It was very wrong, however, to give any of the credit to himself: 'I am the chisel that cuts the wood, the Carpenter directs it.' So he 'resigned the government of the province to the Friend . . . He will use me so long as he pleases.' In a mood of introspection he examined one of his principal shortcomings. 'Some of my letters are written by one nature, others by another nature'; 'Talk of two natures in one, I have a hundred, and they none think alike, and will all rule'; 'I never know my own mind for two days consecutively. "You ought to know your own mind" is to me as if you said "You ought to have red hair". I wish I was more decided . . . and I envy Gessi, who knows his mind.' Most people in positions of responsibility, if some new plan or policy occurs to them, reflect on it before putting it forward as a considered recommendation. That was not Gordon's way. Increasingly, as soon as he had a new idea, he must commit it to paper in private letters, official memoranda or long encyphered telegrams. Officials in Cairo or London, assuming that he had thought the matter out, were then puzzled or exasperated by his recommending the exact opposite a week later. He realized he was often inconsistent, but would not change his ways. 'How odd it is that we judge one another as if each one of us was consistent. "Why, yesterday you said so-and-so, and now you say the reverse." It is quite possible for a person to have been sincere in his expression in both cases at the time he expressed himself.' Quite possible, but inconvenient for those who must assess and perhaps act on his suggestions. 'My letters and my journal are impressions of the moment. I cannot be bound by them.' How, then, could others be bound by them? 'Do not put any confidence in what I say or do.' The confusion so produced contributed not a little to his final tragedy.[3]

In May there arrived a German–Jewish doctor named Schnitzer who had worked for years in Turkey, turned Mussulman and now pretended that he was a Turk and that his name was Emin Effendi. ('He thinks I do not know, but, my dear Augusta, I am a Gordon, and very little passes that I do not know.') Gessi thought him unequalled in hypocrisy, meanness and deceit; but Gordon discerned the quality of this queer, cringing fellow and in this case Gordon's judgement was not at fault, for Emin was to make his mark on Africa. For the moment, however, he was to be the provincial medical officer, and it was a great relief to have one.[4]

Gordon's heaviest cross at this time was laid on him by Stanton who sent up, with letters of introduction from exalted persons, a young Englishman, Louis Lucas, with useful social connections, but no experience, no manners, no tact and a violent temper. He fell ill from smoking all day and taking no exercise. In Khartoum he had distinguished himself by shooting an Italian's dog, flying the Union Jack over his house despite the Governor-General's order to remove it, enticing away a Maltese lady's servant, and drawing his revolver on a camel-driver whose beasts could go no further without water. Gordon's letters resound with denunciations of this wealthy oaf. 'Who are the fathers and grandfathers of Lucas? He is not a gentleman, I feel sure, of more than one generation . . . He appears to me to be a sort of man whom cab-drivers will always be in altercation with, for 6d.' Unfortunately, Lucas greatly admired him, so Gordon could not shake off the incubus, but had to take him when he went south to settle the problem of Kabarega.[5]

Gessi returned to Khartoum, and Gordon went all the way back to Lake Albert, checking and revising his map. He had great difficulty in finding the Nile's exit from the lake, which was blocked with papyrus, a horrid end of the world place, swamps and gloomy silence, inhabited only by a herd of elephants who were 'chucking the grass into their mouths, with their trunks'. Baker's map, to his surprise, proved '*wonderfully correct'*. Lucas, after striking a sergeant and receiving one of the Colonel's crushing reprimands, became so subdued that Gordon was quite anxious for his health. 'My dear Stanton, why did you give him such a good letter of introduction? He is such a snob.' But poor Lucas went quite mad and had to be sent back, stark naked, for he tore his clothes in shreds and at times was most violent. He soon died.[6]

On 1 August there came dramatic news from Nuehr Agha who had been sent south in January to establish two new posts. Mtesa, hoping to use the Khedive's troops for his own purpose, had suggested that instead they be placed at his capital. Nuehr Agha had used his own initiative and done just as Mtesa asked. Gordon, rather surprisingly, approved. He had not intended to deprive Mtesa of his independence, but since that monarch had voluntarily given it up, so be it. With 160 of Gordon's least bad soldiers, commanded by an efficient officer, at his capital Mtesa would be virtually annexed to the Khedive's empire; and the rich ivory trade of Uganda, hitherto directed towards Zanzibar, would henceforth flow down the Nile. 'So far it is very well for the Egyptian Government... and quite unsought by me.'

His previous denunciations of Egyptian imperialism all forgotten, Gordon decided to see the situation for himself. It was one of his hardest safaris. From the steamer nothing could be seen but waving papyrus grass, thick jungle and shoals of crocodiles. To map the river's course he had to walk through a jumble of steep hills and ravines running across his path. The lower slopes were of clay, very slippery in the pouring rain. Sometimes wild vines and convolvulus bound them hand and foot. He was utterly prostrated with a deadly cold and stomach-cramp.

At Foweira Nuehr Agha reported the latest development, which caused Gordon to have second thoughts on the prudence of his enterprise. Mtesa had immobilized the soldiers by making difficulties in the supply of porters and food. 'Mtesa has annexed my soldiers, he has not been annexed himself.' There was the additional embarrassment that Mtesa had done this under cover of the Union Jack supplied by Stanley. 'This is a nice mess we are in,' Gordon told Stanton, 'do not say much about this.' To Khairi Pasha he made the astonishing suggestion that Ismail Ayoub be sent up to sort out the mess: 'I shall not be angry.' Meanwhile he must extricate the troops. So he sent Nuehr Agha with 90 more men to withdraw the 160.[7]

In this withdrawal he wondered if he was really motivated by his passionate longing to be out of the Sudan? He could (D.V.) be home on 5 February. 'My present idea is to lie in bed till eleven every day. I want OYSTERS, they are good for the brain, with brown bread and lots of them, not a dozen but four dozen.' And no dinner parties. He sent for his fur coat to be despatched to Cairo, where he would arrive in mid-winter. By a natural transition of thought his mind turned to Heaven. 'The future world has been somehow painted to our mind as a place of continuous praise; and, though we may not say it, yet one cannot help feeling that, if thus, it would prove monotonous. It cannot be thus. It must be a life of activity, for happiness is dependent on activity.'

Nuehr Agha extricated his troops safely, leaving Uganda for a few years to itself. Gordon determined to march overland to Niamyongo and return by boat, surveying Lake Kioga.

The march was unpleasant and dangerous, through elephant-grass and thick forest, stagnant marshes and mosquitoes in myriads. This was hostile territory, Kabarega's kingdom. Gordon felt thoroughly uncomfortable moving in single file through country so perfect for an ambush, much more dangerous than regular war. The blacks could throw their spears accurately up to fifty yards, he had no confidence in his troops and was carrying no gun since both hands were occupied in fending off tsetse flies and mosquitoes. Once there was a volley of shots twenty yards behind him: one soldier had been speared and Gordon's butter-tin broken. It was with considerable relief that they reached an open site suitable for their camp.

Now for Kabarega, reported to be a fugitive in the bush. So Gordon set off first to Masindi, on a visit of inspection. When, however, he was within a few miles of it, he was appalled to learn that the officer he had sent to occupy the place had never been near it. Although reporting that he was there, he had stopped two days' march away. Gordon was in a position of some danger, in thick bush well known to the enemy, with only 100 very scared soldiers, including boys of sixteen. All around them they could hear Kabarega's warriors drumming and blowing horns: they expected for every moment of two days to be attacked. Gordon was furious with the officer who had let him down; 'however, after a fearful row, as mercy had been showed me, I did the same.'

Leaving Kabarega to be '*razzia*'ed' by his officers, on 28 September he turned his face towards Southampton. Five days later he received from the Khedive the Order of Medjidieh, First Class, as his award for occupying Mtesa's capital. 'This is dreadful, for it was obtained under false pretences.' It was a supreme irony that the man who scorned orders and decorations and disproved of annexations, should be decorated for annexing Uganda when all he had done was to withdraw from it.

At Khartoum there was the first taste of home, English sparrows in the dusty streets. Gessi was there too, and they seem to have had a row when Gordon was tactless enough to say, 'What a pity you are not an Englishman!' However they travelled on to Cairo amicably together, and

Gordon warmly recommended Gessi to Burton, then Consul in Trieste.[8]

Gordon arranged for a competent American, Colonel Prout, to look after Equatoria in his absence, but had not decided whether to come back:

> Comfort of Body – a very strong gentleman – says, 'You are well; go home; go home; and be quiet, and risk no more.' Mr Reason says, 'What is the use of opening more country to such a Government? There is more now under their power than they will ever manage. Retire now, and avoid trouble.' But Mr Something (I do not know what) says, 'Shut your eyes to what may happen in the future; leave that to God, and do what you think will open the country thoroughly to both Lakes. Do this, not for H.H. or for his Government, but do it blindly and in faith.'

But on his way he heard of the treatment meted out to Ismail Pasha Sadyk, Finance Minister, who had just passed down the Nile on his way to exile. The Khedive had, in the most friendly manner, inspected a steamer with him, taken him down to a cabin, said, '*Restez ici*' and gone ashore – leaving him locked in a cabin with the windows nailed up for his long, sad journey into exile. 'What an affair . . . I have (D.V.) made up my mind to serve H.H. no longer.'

On 3 December he 'went in to H.H. with an angry face and heart, determined not to go back'. But Ismail, sitting as usual with his own face in shadow and his interlocutor's in full light, turned on all the formidable charm – praise, thanks for great work, deep interest and appreciation. 'Well, the end of my interview with H.H. was that I agreed to go back, so much for making up my mind.' Like many others who had been subjected to the full treatment, Gordon a few hours later felt that he had been conned. He tried casting responsibility for a decision not on a Friend but on the Foreign Office, suggesting that they recall him; but the officials would not play, so that was that.

Gordon had been nearly three years in Equatoria, the hardest three years of his life. The province when he had taken it over was effectively about 600 miles of the Nile. The rest was unexplored jungle, swamp and thorn-scrub, supporting an unknown number of savages. Its only exports were a small quantity of ivory and a large number of slaves. All Baker had done was to map part of the river and dump in three posts 300 miles apart about 600 miserable, unpaid convict-soldiers engaged solely in living at the expense of the natives. There was not even the most basic administration and the soldiers could not move half a mile from their posts except in large armed gangs. Slavers operated without let or hindrance, from merchant princes dealing in human beings by the thousand to small traders picking up job-lots of half-a-dozen in a country where a healthy young female could be bought from her parents for a packet of needles.

Gordon's most important work was to increase Baker's three stations to sixteen. Except where the Nile passed through the *sud* and the papyrus swamps south of Dufilé, these stations were one or two days' journey apart. The object of this was not so much mutual support as to enable military patrols and officials to carry with them all the food they needed for a journey, so that they did not need to pillage the natives *en route*. As a result it had become fairly safe to move from one station to another in parties of three or four. The natives were beginning to graze their cattle in the open, within sight of the river.

He had made a thorough survey and a map of the river, on a scale of half-inch to the mile, from Sobat to within sixty miles of Lake Victoria. In his task of suppressing the slave-trade Gordon had been less successful. Indeed all he had really achieved was to divert it from the Nile to the desert routes, to the doubtful benefit of the victims. He thought he had succeeded in making the province pay its way: with the increased export of ivory, due to improved security and the government monopoly, it should no longer be a burden on the Khedive's rickety finances.

It does not seem much for three years' work. There are glaring *lacunae*, whole areas of administration untouched. His writ, for instance, operated only along the river: a few miles from it, the natives hardly knew that the Khedive's government existed. This was because he had not solved the problem of overland transport. Before the development of veterinary vaccines, tsetse fly and African horse-sickness closed much of Equatoria to horses and camels; mules were scarce, donkeys carry very little. There were no roads for wagons. The Khedive had promised six trained elephants, but Gordon was sceptical of their value, and was proved right. The fifty camels he imported were a modest success, but too few to solve his problem. The best overland transport was by porter, but the natives felt no inclination to exert themselves in the Khedive's service. So, just as later colonial officials have sometimes been road-bound, Gordon was distinctly river-bound.

He made no attempt to tax the natives, except by an occasional *razzia* on their cattle which was collective punishment rather than revenue-raising. He introduced not even the simplest code of law and legal procedure, except for trying his own soldiers by court-martial. Nor did he show any interest in the province's economic potential. Emin, as governor three years later, busied himself with the possibility of developing a hides and skins industry with local tanning media; he experimented in cultivating wheat, rice, sugar, tobacco, cotton, rubber and coffee; he tried distilling, and the manufacture of vegetable oils.[9] But Gordon cared for none of these things. Of course Emin did not have to get steamers up to the lakes and establish new stations. To criticize Gordon for not doing more is rather like denouncing Columbus for not going on to discover Australia. But the contrast between what he did and what Emin tried to do does indicate in Gordon a lack of interest in economic affairs.

It is also a just criticism of Gordon that he made no effort to get closer to his soldiers or to the natives. 'I cannot govern,' he admitted, 'without knowing the language ... I am quite like a blind man, I grope my way by instinct.' This being so, he should have learned it, as countless other officers have done in less than three years, rather than rely on amateur interpreters and on English and French, spoken louder and louder, with vigorous gestures and miming. If he had been able to communicate with them, he might have found that not all Egyptians and Sudanese were useless.

His performance must be judged in the light of his resources. His officers and troops were largely such as would be sent to a punishment station. His mudirs were corrupt and involved in the slave-trade. Of Europeans, only Ernest Linant, Long and Gessi stood the climate: Linant was killed, Long was away most of the time, and Gessi was essentially a field officer. So Gordon had no staff. 'I surely should be supplied with an intendant to look after the supplies of the troops, etc., I have none, and have to do it myself. Surely I ought to have a man to look after the discipline of the troops, etc., I have none; all falls on me.' Yet this was partly his own fault, for he would not delegate, and though complaining constantly of his Arab officers, he told Stanton, after all the Europeans had died or been invalided out, that he would have no foreigners but Gessi.

The wonder is not that Gordon achieved so little, but that with so little he achieved so much. Perhaps his biggest achievement was to instil into the tribes the first dim realization that the conquerors from the north could perhaps do something to improve their lot. He set an example of alien rule, not over-sensitive, not particularly sympathetic to human dignity, but incorruptible, conscientious and even-handed. With such exiguous forces he could never have imposed even a modest degree of tranquillity without a large measure of consent. Fifteen years after his death his countrymen, with many times his resources, returned and did his work all over again, and much more as well. A half-century later nowhere in all Africa was the departure of the colonial power regretted more deeply than in Gordon's Equatoria.

His personal finances had prospered modestly. 'You know how penniless I am always, well, in 2½ years I have made:

$£$

	£
Clear gain	3,000
Paid the Linants £980	1,080
and Marno 100	
Pitched away	920
	5,000 $= 2\frac{1}{2}$ years' pay.'

This enabled him to capitalize the annuity he paid to his brother's widow, and to let Augusta have £500 to buy a small house. As for the £920 pitched away, 'I have been,' he confessed, 'as usual an ass . . . and have been careless in my private accounts . . . Someone has got it, and that person or persons was destined to get it. It was but lent to me, and He who lent it has given it to someone else and not told me.'

In the twentieth century it was considered that officers serving in the Sudan required three months' home leave every year. Gordon, with no modern medicine, no refrigerator, no regular mails and no social life had three years on end without a day's leave. Although he was very tough, and dosed himself regularly with quinine and Warburg's medicine, this had taken a toll of his health. He had frequent diarrhoea, his liver troubled him and in the retreat from Masindi he complained for the first time of a sharp pain in the heart which was to recur whenever he drove himself too hard. He himself thought he had aged in those three years, and his hair had turned grey: Linant had remarked, on his return from a nine months' absence, that his chief had aged ten years. But he must have made a quick recovery – or perhaps there was a touch of hypochondria in his complex character; Edwin de Leon, an American who met Gordon in Cairo late in 1876, thought that for a middle-aged man just returned from a land where 'pestilence walketh in the noon-day', he looked remarkably youthful and fit, 'as though he had just come from promenading on the shady side of Pall Mall'. De Leon also remarked that, normally sparing of speech, absentminded in common intercourse and with a shy, reserved manner, 'when interested or excited, or in the vein with congenial companions, he can talk fast and fluently, and with great felicity of expression . . . He seems to be swept away by the rushing flood of feelings and thoughts long pent up in his own breast . . . He is a man terribly in earnest.'[10]

With his impulsive garrulity on matters which interested him, Gordon in Equatoria must have found the loneliness more trying and more damaging than the climate. He was always conscious of the presence of a Friend, but his was not the temperament of a hermit; he was a man who needed and appreciated human companionship. This, no doubt, was at the bottom of Chippendall's complaints that 'Gordon ought to keep one more at arm's length' and 'I am too young to be a companion to Gordon.' He pined for the companionship of men with his own background, but Watson and Chippendall were years younger, and with him only for a few weeks. Gordon liked Americans, but he and Long were incompatible. Gessi and Gordon were more of an age, they had known one another for a long time, but they were together for only three short periods in three years. The other foreign officers Gordon hardly saw except when they were desperately ill. As for the Arabs, Sudanese and Nilotic tribesmen, he was capable only of the most basic communication with them. So for the greater part of those three years he had no meeting of minds with another human being.

This for him was a new experience. In the past he had been able to discuss his plans with others and 'do his thinking aloud'. In Equatoria his communication with others was on paper, so he fell into the habit of doing his thinking on paper, giving an impression of vaccillation of which there is not a hint in his earlier career. Moreover it was a singularity of his nature that he was unable to see more than one side of a question at a time, but this he saw with clarity and expounded with vigour. Later he would examine the same question from another point of view, and argue with equal force in the opposite sense. This puzzled those with whom he dealt, who charged him with irrationality.

He was inclined to be too immersed in detail. This became very marked in Equatoria. It was really none of the governor-general's business to be personally checking the quartermaster's stores or taking part in a *razzia*. He was bad at delegating authority – or perhaps one should say reluctant to delegate authority except to Gessi.

Gordon's life in Equatoria was an alternation of enforced idleness and hard labour, of mental stagnation and extreme exasperation, in one of the worst climates in the world, with a temperature of up to 120° F. in the shade, enervating humidity and an extraordinary variety of insect pests. In these conditions his temper, always quick, became 'very, very bad'. His rages were terrifying – and very effective in rousing his torpid subordinates into unaccustomed activity. As he was quick to wound, even to cuff and kick, so he was quick to apologize. However furious he might be with his Arab officers, when he cooled down he reflected that God, for his inscrutable purpose, had made them cowardly, indolent, corrupt and mendacious, and one should no more blame them for these defects than one blames a cow for being a cow.

It was exasperation with his officers, with Africans, with prickly heat, diarrhoea, boredom and the vigorous insect life of the Nile, which filled his private letters with querulous complaint. But letters were his safety-valve; there is nothing in the evidence of Long, Watson, Chippendall,

Gessi and others to suggest that he was eternally complaining; to them he appeared a lively, cheerful, friendly person, though at times very trying. Raouf Bey, by no means one of his favourites, found him thoughtful and polite, too trustful perhaps for the rough circumstances of Equatoria.[11]

It is in his relations with his officers, white, black and brown, that he showed up at his worst. He was a tiresome perfectionist. Whenever things went wrong, his first thought was to find someone to blame. Even his family were not exempt: he could interrupt a diatribe against Arabs, blacks and the Sudan in general by informing Augusta, 'It is the fault of those who persuaded me to come (viz. Rose's, Henry's and yours).'[12] His officers had their shortcomings, but it was he who had selected most of them, and in some cases against the unanimous advice of people who knew them and knew the Sudan. He prided himself on his acumen in judging character, but again and again he was taken in by some rogue, trusted him and was then furious at being let down.

No doubt he believed that one Englishman was worth five foreigners, but never that one white was worth five blacks. It was inefficiency, mendacity, indolence and indecision that he hated, whether in whites, browns or blacks. Indeed he complained far more of his white than of his black officers. On a later occasion, when a European asked a Sudanese officer to pass him a mug of water, Gordon called him sharply to order: 'Are you not aware that Yusuf Pasha, in spite of his black face, is very much your senior in rank?'

His bark was worse than his bite. His reprimand was terrifying – eyes flashing, voice shaking with rage, hand barely restrained, or not restrained, from violence. But although in letters he boasted of being a tyrant and promised to inflict the most draconic punishments, hanging and shooting, when he had simmered down the culprits were let off lightly. Similarly he cursed his officers for malingering – but when he found that Campbell and Linant were really dying, Russell, Watson and Chippendall desperately ill, he gave them the most devoted nursing. Officers whom he had abused in private letters, and sometimes to their faces, were given glowing confidential reports.

There is something about Gordon which eludes us: despite his occasional priggishness, his bad temper, his fussiness over trifles, his incessant nagging, he never lost his power to compel love as well as fear, exasperation and obedience: those bright blue eyes in the sunburnt face could 'charm the birds out of a tree'.

11

⌂ THE GOVERNOR-GENERAL ON A CAMEL

⌂ Characteristically, the first thing Gordon did, on arrival in England on Christmas Eve 1876, was to visit the sister of poor Lucas, who had married a Jew and adopted the Hebrew faith. He 'spoke to her of Jesus and she seemed not to feel it . . . and asked her if she knew God dwelt in her, and she said Yes.' He visited the Freeses, and kept the boys agog by his vivid description of an elephant kneeling on a man, breaking every bone in his body, and then picking up the body with its trunk and throwing it over his head as a dog throws a rat. Otherwise he presumably spent his time between London and Southampton, lying in bed in the mornings and eating oysters. But soon these sybaritic delights began to pall, and he was racked by indecision about his future. Should he return to Egypt or not?

On his way home he had contacted Nubar Pasha, repeating again and again, '*comme un enfant qui se butte à son idee*', that nothing would induce him to go back, since the Khedive had conned him. 'Then don't go,' advised Nubar. But how, Gordon asked, could he abandon 'his' poor blacks? 'Then go,' advised Nubar. The Secretary for War said he was in honour bound to resign, the Duke of Cambridge that he was in honour bound not to. To H. C. Vivian, Stanton's successor in Cairo, he communicated his irrevocable decision to quit. But Ismail knew his man: 'I refuse to believe,' he telegraphed, 'that when Gordon has once given his word as a gentleman, anything will ever induce him to go back on it.' Gordon decided to leave the decision to a Friend: 'After preparation, tossed.' The coin fell head-up, showing that God wished him to leave the Sudan; but Waller then shoved his oar in, assuring him that 'everyone' in the Anti-Slavery Society thought that as an honourable man he could no longer remain in the Khedive's service. That settled the matter: he booked a passage to Port Said for 31 January 1877, after less than six weeks in England.[1]

Before departure he had just the sort of evening he enjoyed, a quiet dinner at the Club with Watson and his friend of Crimea days, Colonel Gerald Graham, v.c., also a Royal Engineer. They persuaded Gordon, who needed little persuasion, that as the slave-routes were now across the desert from Bahr-el-Ghazal to Darfur, he could do nothing to stop the trade by returning to Equatoria: if he remained in the Khedive's service, it must be as Governor-General of the whole Sudan, with his headquarters in Khartoum.

In Cairo he was immediately invited by His Highness to dinner. 'I pleaded fatigue . . . If I go to dinner H. H. will only humbug me into some admission or promise.' However, after some preliminary negotiations, he went to the Khedive, who could no more resist Gordon's charm than Gordon could resist his. 'He looked at me reproachfully, and my conscience smote me . . . Then I began, and told him all; and then he gave me the Sudan.'

He resumed his practice of recording his work in immensely long, journal letters addressed to Augusta, but having a wider circulation, since they were sent to her after being read by Sherif Pasha, the Minister responsible for the Sudan; and by her to Henry and Lord Salisbury, the Minister for Foreign Affairs. Gordon could perhaps in this way express himself more pungently than in official correspondence, though even in the most formal despatch he was seldom inhibited.[2]

Gordon's Sudan was 1,640 miles long and averaged about 660 miles wide: there was in addition a detached province of Harar on the Gulf of Aden. The first task laid upon him was to settle disputes between Egypt and Abyssinia, which was in a state of confusion and misrule under a military usurper.

The main obstacle to harmony was a border baron named Walad al Michael. With a large private army and hereditary fiefs in both countries, he was advantageously placed to play off the Khedive Ismail and Johannes, King of Kings, against one another, and his latest outrage had been to plunder an Abyssinian district and slay its governor. Since the miscreant was nominally an Egyptian subject, Johannes would not be reconciled with the Khedive until he had been handed over for blinding and castration; but Walad al Michael, with 3,000 warriors and 700 Remingtons, was too hot for the Khedive to handle. In addition to this quarrel, Johannes claimed the port of Massawa and the district of Bogos which Egypt had grabbed some years earlier. Since his master was basically in the wrong, Gordon was negotiating from weakness, his only assets being the recently conferred rank of Egyptian marshal and a gorgeous gold-braided uniform.

On camel-back he rode from Massawa through the mountains to Keren, exasperated by the pomp of his exalted office, ten men to help him dismount, circles of sentries (all asleep) round the tree under which his camp-bed and table were set at night. At Keren he met Walad al Michael. The only thing to do with this mean-faced scoundrel was to buy him off, so Gordon confirmed him in the governorship of his Egyptian fief so long as he behaved himself. Gordon formed the worst possible opinion of Abyssinians, 'a furtive, polecat race'. Everyone was a soldier or a brigand, terms which were synonymous. Walad al Michael's Nestorian chaplain maintained that Jesus was killed by accident; 'he did not seem to know that He died for the world.' Meanwhile King Johannes was drawn away by trouble elsewhere: so was Gordon, who must turn his mind to more important matters.

The most important thing was to *see* the whole Sudan – or, perhaps more important, to be seen by it. This would necessitate 5,000 miles of camel-riding, from Keren through white limestone hills to Kassala, and then across the desert to Khartoum. Darfur was in a state of rebellion, so there he must ride next; first across the scorching sands of Kordofan, then through the wooded uplands of the Jebel Marra to his western boundary, 750 miles from Khartoum. To his northern boundary he must go, 500 miles away; north-east across desert and stony steppes to Suakim; perhaps back to the steamy heat of the Great Lakes; and finally to his detached province of Harar.

Much nonsense has been written about Gordon's camel journeys; averaging $32\frac{1}{2}$ miles a day, they were hard rides, but there was nothing prodigious about them. Distance and speed depend (when one has become tolerably competent) on the terrain and the type of camel. Across the mountains from Massawa to Kasala a camel could only walk, but over the desert, on gravel or hard sand, much better speeds are possible. The ordinary caravan uses baggage camels, which move at not more than 3 miles an hour for not more than six hours a day as they must have time to browse. But Gordon used thoroughbred racing camels, capable of long journeys at an average of 7 miles an hour. Moreover they were grain-fed, so did not need hours a day to browse; and he owned five, so they were not overworked. In such conditions the French-officered *Meharistes* in the Sahara averaged 40 miles a day; and Wilfrid Thesiger as a district commissioner in Western Sudan did rides of 115 miles in twenty-four hours and 450 miles in nine days on a single camel. So Gordon's performances were creditable for a middle-aged man who had never ridden a camel, but not prodigious. The feats of endurance were by his escort and servants, pounding along in his wake on inferior beasts.

A camel's walk is uncomfortable to the rider as he lurches backwards and forwards. Gordon wore a sash wound tightly round his waist, another below his arm-pits, as supports. But the trot of a well-bred camel is a joy to the rider, so smooth that he can read as he rides along. Thus Gordon's letters, written when he was a beginner and travelling through country too stony for a camel to trot, complain of the intolerable jolting 'shaking one's organs out of place'; and of the camel as a cross-grained, ill-natured beast hating mankind and always miserable. But a month later, in the good going of the desert near Khartoum, he found the camel a wonderful creature, and so comfortable with its silent, cushion-like tread. Later still, trotting across the Kordofan desert, 'I have a splendid camel – none like it; it flies along and quite astonishes the Arabs.'

He stopped briefly at Kasala to be entertained by a military band playing martial airs (generous *backsheesh*) and to review a troop of horse all wearing mail and helmets of the Crusader pattern, and carrying long, straight, cross-hilted swords. Then on to Khartoum, his mind churning with the problem of the slave-trade.

Once he had believed he could easily stop it. Now he knew better. Trotting across the desert hour after hour, in the cool mornings, the evenings, and under the brilliant night-sky, he came to the conclusion that the best tactic was again the indirect approach. Nothing could stop the trade so long as there was an insatiable demand for slaves in Egypt: end this demand, and the trade would wither away. But there were moral and political difficulties. Had not slave-owners their rights? The owner-ship of slaves was permitted by the law of their land and the religion of their fore-fathers. So long as slaves were humanely treated, as was generally the case, slave-owners regarded their case as morally unassail-able. In 1833 the British conscience, motive force of the anti-slavery movement, had provided £20 million of taxpayers' money to compensate West Indian slave-owners, and still hundreds were ruined by emanci-pation; but no one proposed compensating Egyptian slave-owners. 'Consider the effect of harsh measures among an essentially Mussulman population carried out brusquely by a Nazarene – measures which touch the pocket of everyone. Who that had not the Almighty with him would dare do that? I will do it.' But trust in God did not preclude making use of all the craft and common sense God had given him; compensation being ruled out, the demand for slaves must be reduced gradually, giving slave-owners time to adjust themselves to the new order. So he advised:

1. The law by which runaway slaves were returned to their masters, which in recent years had been in abeyance, should now be enforced.

2. But only for slaves who had been legally registered.

3. The registration of slaves should cease on 1 January 1878; after which, although the ownership of registered slaves would continue to be legal for a number of years, no new slaves could be acquired.

His advice was not taken.

At the beginning of May he rode into Khartoum and found himself living in a riverside palace with all 130 windows smashed and all the divans cut to pieces by Ismail Pasha Ayoub's sister ('What a cat!') in her rage at his supercession. He was driven almost out of his mind by hordes of servants who did nothing but stand staring at him; even a eunuch 'though why, with no harem, I am obliged to keep this individual, I do not know'. Worst of all were the interminable interviews with notables who came just to exchange stilted civilities. By oriental custom it is for the host to terminate a visit: for a guest to go before 'the permission' is the height of ill-breeding. Eventually he developed a technique of saying briskly, in English, 'Now, old bird, it's time for you to go.' This was what they had been waiting for; though they may not have understood the words, the meaning was obvious; so, as relieved as he was, they went. Gordon considered that his first duty, however boring, was to be freely accessible to petitioners. He put outside his gate a box for written petitions. But being accessible was not as easy as one might think. He soon found that his clerks and servants received a tip from anyone admitted to his presence. So valuable was this perquisite that bribes up to £600 were paid to his head clerk by aspirants to places in the palace of which the salary was no more than £20 a month.

He announced plans for Nile water to be pumped into the town, a great boon as many houses were a long way inland; he abolished the bastinado, flogging with the *courbach* on the soles of the feet; and he announced simply at his investiture, 'With the help of God I will hold the balance level.' He believed the people rejoiced at his presence.

It is necessary here to qualify Gordon's judgements. The bastinado, cruel by the standards of Gravesend in 1877, was probably a milder punishment than the flogging administered to British sailors and soldiers a generation earlier. As for popularity, any ruler of any oriental or African people will be told how much better liked he is than his predecessor.

With an eye to public relations he restored Abou Saoud to the Khedive's pay-roll; and on several learned *ulema* he conferred robes of honour and privileges removed from them by his predecessor. With the Christian missions his relations were less happy: he was obliged to complain to the Pope about the 'arrogance of the Catholic Mission in giving asylum to runaway slaves'.[3]

After only three weeks in Khartoum Gordon set out for Kordofan and Darfur. The journey gives an opportunity to examine factually the legendary speed of Gordon's camel-travel. El Obeid, capital of Kordofan, was 180 miles, twelve caravan marches (by walking camel) or five post marches (by trotting camel) across a fairly flat, hard, sandy desert, ideal 'going' for camels. Gordon did it in six days.[4]

The inhabitants of the western desert were nomadic Arab tribes whom

Gordon called Bedouin. More properly most of them were known as Baggara, a term used for nomads who lived mainly on the milk and meat of their cattle. The Baggara owned large numbers of horses, cattle and slaves: the latter grew a little *dhoora* in the oases, but their masters considered that a gentleman's only occupations were cattle-herding, hunting, robbery, slave-raiding and war. There were also the Fors, semi-negroid agriculturalists in the oases.

After Zebeyr, greatest of slavers, had condescended to acknowledge the Khedive's sovereignty without actually obeying the Khedive's orders, Ismail made him a pasha, and invited him to Cairo. Once there, Zebeyr had been prevented from returning. He was not under house-arrest, and certainly not a prisoner; indeed in the Russo-Turkish War 1877 he commanded the Egyptian contingent with the Turkish army; but he could not return to his slave-empire, and his twenty-year-old son, Suleiman, governed in his place.

In the winter of 1876–7 Haroun al Rashid, nephew of the Sultan of Darfur whom Zebeyr had slain, rebelled against the rapacious Bashi-Bazouks – irregular cavalry employed in aid of the civil power – and tax-collectors whose favourite instrument of fiscal assessment was the *courbach*. He hemmed in at El Fasher, Dara and Kolkol 16,000 Egyptian soldiers under Hassan Pasha; and in Bahr-el-Ghazal young Suleiman, with his father's formidable slave-army, showed every sign of joining the rebellion. An Egyptian force at Foggia, on the eastern frontier of Darfur, had made no move to intervene. It was to stimulate their efforts that Gordon set off from Khartoum on 19 May.

On 7 June, accompanied only by his guide and one orderly, one and a half hours ahead of his escort, he came within sight of Foggia. The garrison were busy with their usual occupations – the sentries dozing or down at the well drinking; the *Mudir* resting from his exertions; arms piled. Before they could identify the distant riders and fall in a Guard of Honour, the Governor-General, in his gold-braided marshal's uniform, came flying down upon them. 'I could not help it . . . The Gordons and the camels are the same race – let them take an idea into their heads and nothing will take it out.'

On the 15th he heard that El Fasher had been relieved. This was welcome news as with his 'rag-bag and bob-tail' force of 2,700 Egyptian soldiers, Bashi-Bazouks and 'loyal' tribesmen he had no wish to get involved against Baggara rebels who could field 6,000 horsemen. The revolt was all the fault of the Bashi-Bazouks, 'scum of Cairo and Stamboul'; he was confident, however, that God would enable him to make friends with the tribes. 'The danger to me, if He does this, is that I may be puffed up.'

He moved on to Toashia, to evacuate it and concentrate his force along the road between Foggia and El Fasher. On the way they passed some huge hollow fig-trees, which should contain as much as a ton of water, cool and fresh. The amiable Bashi-Bazouks, to save themselves the trouble of climbing to the top and drawing water properly, used to shoot at the trunk, drink what they wanted as it spurted through the hole and let the rest drain away.

At Toashia he found the garrison demoralized, a mere set of brigands. (They had been three years without pay.) He therefore sent them back to El Obeid to be disbanded, and moved on to Dara, whence the enemy had withdrawn. Here too he took the garrison by surprise, swooping down on them out of the desert. He discovered that the mosque had been requisitioned for use as a powder-magazine. Iniquitous! Like Christ cleansing the temple, Gordon cleansed the mosque, endowed a *muezzin*, and restored it for worship. 'They blessed me and cursed Zebeyr Pasha who took the mosque from them.'

He had a respect for Islam. 'Now this strong feeling and attachment of Mussulmans to their religion, is it to be understood as uncontrolled by God? Does He still *wink* at it?* You know Mohamad claimed only a divine mission: he did not claim divinity. He does not deny that our Saviour had a divine mission, but he denies His divinity'; 'I find the Mussulman quite as good a Christian as any Christian . . . He is not ashamed of his God; his life is a fairly pure one; certainly he gives himself a good margin in the wife-line, but at any rate he never poaches on others.'

His ideas of an after-life were changing. 'This life is only one of a series of lives which our incarnated part has lived. I have little doubt of our having pre-existed; and that also in the time of our pre-existence we were actively employed. So, therefore, I believe in our active employment in a future life, and like the thought.' This applied to every human soul, good and bad: there was no question of eternal bliss for the one and damnation for the other: each would continue its existence in some other incarnation, 'actively employed' (for any other state would indeed be Hell) and moving gradually towards perfection.

The doctrine of the transmigration of souls owes much to Plato and Pythagoras and is akin to Buddhism and Hinduism; but it is incompatible with the Christian doctrine of the resurrection of the body, which implies that life after death is wholly the gift of God, whereas Gordon and Plato and the Buddhist sages believed that it was due to the inherently immortal nature of man's soul, good or bad. Well might Augusta reproach him for heresy, but without causing him a moment's concern.

He stayed three weeks in Dara, contemplating a sea of trouble. The

* A reference to Acts xvii, 30: 'And the times of this ignorance, God winked at.'

closer he came to Zebeyr's slave-empire, the capital of which was Shaka, 100 miles to the south, the more visionary seemed the expectation in England that he would promptly abolish the slave-trade. 'Imagine to yourself,' he invited Waller, 'immense arid countries inhabited by huge Bedouin tribes and bordered on the south by negro tribes . . . [These Bedouin] have from the beginning preyed on the negro tribes, who in their turn have preyed on their neighbours, and so on, to the Cape of Good Hope.' The Baggara raided the Bahr-el-Ghazal for blacks whom they sold to middlemen, not locals but men from the Dongola-Berber area, known generally as 'Jalaba'*, itinerant retailers on quite a small scale, taking their wares to market in Lower Egypt. Gordon believed, erroneously, that large caravans of slaves, linked by the *sheyba* and herded along by whips, had been stopped. But how could anyone stop the petty slavers? 'I am quite nonplussed what to do.'

As for the possession of slaves, putting an end to it was far easier said than done. There were several categories of slaves. First, there were thousands owned by the Baggara. If they were Fors, negroid agriculturists but nevertheless Mussulman, he could legally order their release, for the enslavement of Moslems is forbidden in the Koran, and they could return to their homes not far away. But if they were heathen when captured, they could be freed legally only if compensation were paid to their owners, and there was no money for compensation. To free them without payment would start a serious revolt.

Next were slaves intercepted in transit, many of them (sold by their parents) 'poor little wretches only stomachs and heads with antennae for heads and arms'. These could legally be freed because the trade was illegal; but what would happen to them? What would they do? Who would feed them? How could they return to their homes hundreds of miles away? If he let them loose they would be picked up in every direction, for an escaped slave was the property of the finder. If he forbad the merchants to operate, they would smuggle their slaves through by unfrequented desert tracks and half would die of hunger and thirst. 'Shall I be cowardly and do this for fear of what ill-informed Europe will say? No, I will legitimize their transport, and let them say what they will.'

Finally there were Zebeyr's *bazinger* soldiers, 5,000 of them, ferociously efficient slave-hunters and themselves slaves to a man, including their officers. They formed the best army in the Sudan, far too formidable to be disarmed by the wretched troops at his disposal; and if he told them, 'You are free' they would laugh in his face.

In his own caravan he had no doubt that there were a hundred slaves. 'I ask one man who those seven women are. He says, "My wives". How

* Gordon called them 'gallabats'.

can I disprove it? Can I risk the imputation of taking away one of his wives? Besides, what could I do with the black slut? Another says, "These three boys are my sons." How am I to disprove it? Am I to go into the question of whether he did beget them or not?' He wished he had with him some of the Anti-Slavery Society who thought he had only to say the word and slavery would cease.[5]

He decided that the slave-hunters and the slave-caravans would be suppressed, but small-scale slaving by the Jalaba must be tolerated. To draw Suleiman Zebeyr's teeth he would buy the best of the *bazingers* for his own army and use them against the big slavers. 'I want you to understand this, for I doubt not people will write and say – 1. Colonel Gordon buys slaves for the Government. 2. Colonel Gordon lets the Jalaba take slaves. To No. 1. I say, "True, for I need the purchased slaves to put down the slave-dealers." To No. 2. "True, for I dare not stop it for fear of adding to my enemies before I have broken the slave-dealers at Shaka. I should be mad if I did." '

In August 1877, the Anglo-Egyptian Slave Convention was signed. It did not much help, for Gordon's difficulties lay in the practical enforcement of the law. Moreover there were differences between the Convention and the Khedive's decree supposedly promulgating it. The Convention said that 'any person engaged in traffic of slaves shall be considered guilty of stealing with murder', the punishment for which was death. But the decree permitted the sale of slaves from family to family for seven years in Egypt and twelve years in the Sudan, a qualification which would enable any astute slaver to escape conviction. The possession of slaves would be illegal after twelve years, but 'it makes one wink to think how on earth the slaves of all these Bedouin tribes are to be freed. When the trees obey me, then will the tribes liberate their slaves. The only thing the Government can do is to prevent them getting new ones.'

There were other problems besides slavery – famine, for example. In Darfur and Kordofan the months of regular rain are June, July and August, but this year the rains had been poor, and three years of anarchy, with no great hopes of reaping what one had sown, had caused a great shortage of *dhoora*. 'The stench of the putrifying dead (men and animals) is terrible.' The water-holes were thirty and forty miles apart. 'What very little sin was the murmuring of the Israelites for water. What was it to them that they had seen wonders? When their little ones were thirsty, that would not make them less thirsty. And yet how hardly the pulpits judge them.' He felt at times like Moses, surrounded by those importunate Israelites. 'Imagine the weariness of Moses for forty years in Mount Sinai – a man accustomed to a court life. He must have suffered a good deal.'

It was more healthy than Equatoria, hot by day, but with a dry heat and cold, bracing nights. But there was the usual plague of petty irritations, such as the man who dropped Gordon's Express rifle, broke the stock and said not a word about it until Gordon called for his rifle to shoot an antelope. It would have been awkward if he had called for the rifle to beat off an attack. There were forty donkeys with the caravan. 'When I heard one bray, I knew all the rest would bray, and so it went on last night . . . It generally took five minutes for the whole to perform.'

But all would come right in the end: and if he were killed, that would be by God's will because his work was finished upon this earth. 'I own nothing and am nothing, I am a pauper and seem to have ceased to exist. A sack of rice jolting along on a camel would do as much as *I think* I do.' So the desert, the long, lonely camel-rides, worked upon him as they had worked on so many others – Moses, John the Baptist, the Prophet Mohamad and a certain Mohamad Ahmed who was fasting and contemplating 'eternal things' in a lonely cave south of Khartoum. The desert strengthened the strains of asceticism and mysticism already strong within him; and of fatalism, for what desert-dweller can be anything but a fatalist when his life depends on the next shower of rain or on finding a single small water-hole in 10,000 square miles of desolation? He noted that no one in the Sudan ever made any statement of intent, or of the future, without adding '*Inshallah*' (God willing). He had exactly the same habit, but spelt it 'D.V.' 'I own nothing and am nothing': Mohamad Ahmed, soon to proclaim himself as the Mahdi, the Expected One, could hardly have put it better.

There was a complicated situation with Haroun in open rebellion in northern Darfur, Suleiman Zebeyr to the south loudly protesting his loyalty, offering to suppress Haroun (i.e. plunder his territory) but on the point of rebellion himself; and various southern tribes, sympathizing with Haroun, refugees from Suleiman, flocking to Dara for food Gordon could not provide. ('They are like a white elephant as a present.') He longed for a reliable governor of Darfur, and asked Burton to take it on; but the explorer refused, 'I could not serve under you nor you under me.'

The nearest threat was from the fierce Leopard tribe, moving against Toashia, whom Gordon decided to discipline himself. Fortunately he had with him more than the Egyptian regulars and Bashi-Bazouks who, for all their prancing and sword-waving, were a set of arrant cowards. Some friendly Baggara horse came too, and it was well they did, for none of the others would fight. When 700 rebels demonstrated against a *zariba* held by 3,500 troops, so bad was the soldiers' musketry that not a single enemy was killed. 'The way the artillery handled their guns and rocket tubes made one creep. Fancy, the enemy came within ten yards of the stockade and I think got off scot free.'

The Leopards were subdued by occupying all their wells, so that they had to submit, coming over the desert one by one, like flies on a wall, for water. The soldiers captured hidden stores of *dhoora* by probing the ground for covered-in pits and by putting captives to 'the question', which he could not prevent.

There was a murder in the camp, a slave of one of the soldiers shooting an Arab. Gordon settled the case characteristically. Cocking his rifle and pointing it at the 'poor, black, ivory-toothed murderer', he asked the elders of the dead man's tribe, 'Shall I shoot him now, and leave him a stinking carcase? Or will you take him and make him work for the family he has bereaved?' They chose the latter.

El Fasher was more or less hemmed in by Haroun's men, so Gordon took 150 men to relieve it. Three days march away, under the lethargic Hassan Pasha Helmi, were 1,500 soldiers, who had done absolutely nothing for eight weeks. 'I hate (there is no other word for it) these Arabs;* and I like the blacks, patient, enduring and friendly, as much as the Arab is cowardly, cruel and effeminate. All the misery is due to these Arab and Circassian Pashas and authorities. I would not stay a day here for these wretched creatures, but I would give my life for these poor blacks.'

He must do something about Suleiman, whose 5,000 slave-soldiers were far more dangerous than a mere tribal revolt. At the end of August, while he was engaged with the Leopards and Darfur rebels, Suleiman moved in silent menace to a camp near Dara. Gordon was determined to have him court-martialled and shot.

So to Dara Gordon went, meeting on the way a lieutenant-colonel who was allowing his Bashi-Bazouks to rob right and left, stealing a boy or a girl with as little compunction as a fowl. He had furthermore lost thirty-one confidential despatches to the Khedive. 'Poor wretch! He cried to my clerk.' Having ridden eighty-five miles in a day and a half, about seven miles from Dara Gordon 'got into a swarm of flies and they annoyed me and my camel so much that I jolted along as fast as we could . . . I came upon my people like a thunderbolt. My poor escort! Where was it? Imagine to yourself a single, dirty, red-faced man on a camel, ornamented with flies, arriving in the divan all of a sudden. The people were paralysed.' Gordon had little vanity, except on his judgement of character (which was deplorable) and his camel-riding. 'I gain a great deal of prestige by these unheard-of marches.' He enjoyed the drama of swooping alone on the lethargic garrison of a remote desert outpost, leaning forward in the

* By implication and context he meant Egyptians, not the Baggara whom he admired.

high saddle, legs pressing the camel's shoulders. His well-known statue shows him in uniform on his camel, but he generally wore plain white trousers and shirt, sleeves rolled up, and a hat or *tarbush*; often he carried an umbrella. On rare ceremonial occasions he was very grand, donning his gold-encrusted marshal's uniform and white kid gloves in the sweltering heat.

He slept well, though stiff and tired. In the morning he put on uniform, mounted his horse and with an escort of Bashi-Bazouks rode out to the camp of the other robbers. He was taking his life in his hands, but showed no apprehension. His Bashi-Bazouks would certainly bolt at the first sign of trouble: Suleiman had 300 slave-soldiers, 'smart, dapper-looking fellows like antelopes; fierce, unsparing, the terror of Central Africa, having a prestige far beyond that of Government troops'. But the Governor-General, glittering with gold lace, showed no sign of having come on any errand but to admonish a youthful, erring subordinate.

Suleiman Zebeyr was 'a little chap, wearing a blue velvet riding coat' and an air in which cockiness, impertinence and apprehension were mingled. He arrived at the divan armed to the teeth, a grave breach of manners. 'He has no sense of propriety – lolls about, yawns, fondles his naked feet, and speaks as if he were a street boy.' This unlicked cub with the terror of his father's name had kept his tough free-booters in a state of abject submission. Gordon treated him as a spoilt child in need of a good shaking.

In 'choice Arabic', the wide gaps in his vocabulary filled in by pantomimic gestures, the Governor-General berated the chiefs for their evil intentions. They listened in silence, went off to consider what he had said, and submitted. Zebeyr's son was heartbroken because his chiefs would not fight. 'Poor little chap! . . . Brought up in the midst of the most obsequious people and slaves, accustomed to do just what he liked, to think nothing of killing people, or of their misery, and now to be nothing! "And David said, 'Deal gently, for my sake, with the young man.' " I will try to do so if I can.'

The reason why Gordon had to address the divan himself in his kitchen-Arabic was that his 'first class secretary' and interpreter had been detected taking £3,000 in bribes – 'a man whom I trusted. I declare I am sick at heart.' The culprit was sent under arrest to Khartoum for trial. Nothing much happened to him.

Without ever making an issue of it, Gordon simply assumed that Zebeyr's son and all the slave-soldiers were under his command. Suleiman, having recovered his cockiness, asked for a Robe of Honour and a governorship. He received a dusty answer: 'The little chap is very irate with me.' Gordon asked one of the chiefs if he did not think a good flogging would do the cub good, with which he agreed. 'Ruffians as they are, I rather like having a chat with them.' He paid an informal visit to his new soldiers, some scowled, some smiled. One commanded 400 *élite* troops, and Zebeyr's son told Gordon to his face, 'He belongs to my house.'

Willingly would Gordon have given £500 to have had the Anti-Slavery Society in Dara: 'A bad fort, a cowed garrison, and not one who did not tremble; – a strong, determined set of men accustomed to war, good shots, with two field-pieces.' Addressing his stay-at-home critics, he wrote, 'Now understand me. If it suits me I will buy slaves [for my army]. I will let captured slaves go down to Egypt, and I will do what I like and what God in His mercy may direct me to do about domestic slaves; but I will break the neck of the slave-*raids**, even if it cost me my life.'

He rode the 100 miles to Shaka. 'You are my father,' said Suleiman, looking daggers at him. 'Will you stay at my house?' Gordon accepted the invitation. He rather liked the young ruffian, who had lived all his few years a life of brigandage. This did not, however, mean that the cub would be made Governor of Bahr-el-Ghazal: on that Gordon was adamant, despite the offer of a wedge of gold and the privilege of having his feet embraced by the applicant for office. Instead he made Suleiman second-in-command to Idris Abtar, one of Zebeyr's principal officers, a veteran slaver but ostensibly reformed. The cub took it badly, sulking on the verandah to excite pity. They parted on better terms after Gordon had presented him with a gun.

So ended one of the most dangerous periods in Gordon's life. He had suppressed an incipient revolt, cut Zebeyr's son down to size, outfaced the robber chieftains of Bahr-el-Ghazal, disbanded half the slave-army and taken the rest into his service – all without firing a shot, with nothing but bluff, self-confidence and his overwhelming personality. The experience convinced him that there were no limits to what he could achieve by audacity and trust in God.

Leaving Haroun to Hassan Pasha Helmi, he rode back to El Obeid. One night a big black woman crept into his tent. She could not bear the tribesman who owned her, and fancied someone else. Gordon gave her thirty dollars to purchase her freedom, and she went to her new man. 'She was a huge woman, and had a nice black face.' As before, there were hordes of women and children, reputedly the families of his soldiers, attached to his entourage. 'I strongly suspect that I am conveying a caravan of slaves . . . When you have got the ink which has soaked into blotting paper out of it, then slavery will cease in these lands.' He encountered two slave-caravans, but all he could do was to order the

* Author's italics.

removal of the *sheybas* and allow them to proceed to Lower Egypt in charge of their owners who, 'looking on them as valuable cows, will look after them'. He could not 'free' the slaves, who would either starve or be re-enslaved the instant his back was turned. 'No person under fifteen years is safe in Darfur or Kordofan.' Nor, it seems, were variants such as an albino Negress. 'I shall give her to the convent at Obeid. I know of a male albino negro in Darfur. I shall try to marry the two. I shall make the convent people report on the result, whether it is white or black.'

He was inclined to think it would be best to leave the Baggara alone, subject to payment of £1,000 a year tribute-money. This would save the cost of a garrison, and there would be no Bashi-Bazouks provoking rebellion. He would discourage slave-trading by allowing the Baggara to capture slave-caravans passing through their country. But would it be better for the slaves to be kept by the Baggara? Would they not be happier with more civilized owners in Egypt? Would it be right to set one class of subjects against another? There was no easy answer to these questions.

On 15 October, after an absence of nearly five months, he was back in Khartoum to deal with a mountain of official correspondence. He was salaamed on arrival by the six elephants which the Khedive had sent up for work in Equatoria, which proved quite useless.

Gordon hated living in Khartoum. A Report on the Sudan compiled in 1883 says practically nothing of his governor-generalship except, 'He spent most of his time travelling'.[6] The implication is that he did not spend enough time governing. The situation in Equatoria had required a robust man of character relying on common sense. But the Sudan proper had enjoyed – or at least experienced – a regular administration for half a century: there was an established governmental machine run by *mudirs* with all their junior officers, clerks, cashiers and tax-collectors; there were civil and criminal courts of first instance and of appeal dispensing justice according to the Turkish Law Code; there was a fiscal system with methodical assessments: there were roads, a postal service, a public health department. Under the Director of Telegraphs, Carl Christian Giegler, a German whom Gordon held in high esteem, the major administrative centres were being linked by telegraph lines. The economy was quite advanced, with an annual yield of 12,000 tons of cotton and as much gum; there was a flourishing export and import trade, and the railway from Cairo had almost reached the northern border. Perhaps none of this worked very well, but it was Gordon's job to see that it worked better, and he had been given the job, at the age of forty-five, with no relevant experience. No wonder he felt oppressed by the complex problems of finance, revenue, economic development and litigation which he could not now ignore. In Dufilé and Darfur he had been in his element, but in Khartoum he was out of his depth, and he knew it ('All seems at 6's and 7's . . . I am enveloped in trouble like a web').

He hated the shoddy pomp and ceremony, the dusty palace with its long colonnades and verandahs, its punkahs flapping the stale air; he detested the paper work, and the interminable petitions which he could not understand. 'Your brother is much feared and I think respected, but not overmuch liked . . . "NEVER!" is the answer to many requests, shouted in a loud voice, and followed by "Do you understand?" and "Have you finished?" Then they begin again, and when they own to having finished, I give them the same answer.' The more ceremonious citizens, when dragged to a chair by *cavasses* (footmen) and forced to sit down in the Presence, were sometimes so upset that they forgot what they had to say. His disrespect for ceremony and red-tape extended even to the Law. He summarily hanged a notorious murderer, and the city was quieter for it.

After only eight days in Khartoum, he set off on his second tour, to Berber, Dongola and the north. The unusually low level of the Nile had caused a food-shortage, and every plucky young Dongolawi had gone south to seek his fortune in the slave-trade. Those that remained ran alongside the boat shouting their lamentations. There were no funds for famine relief. He could reply only that he too was miserable.

He was recalled from this depressing experience by more trouble in Abyssinia – Walad al Michael and King Johannes, as usual. He could not escape the fact that Johannes, unpleasant though he might be, was basically in the right, since he only wanted to recover the territory which Egypt had grabbed.

Gordon had to tackle the unprepossessing Walad al Michael in his mountain stronghold. Was he honoured guest or prisoner in this flea-ridden little hut inside a ten-foot fence? However, God pulled him through, after he had increased his host's allowance by £1,000 a month. 'How I hate these Abyssinians! My Bedouin Arabs of Darfur are fine, handsome fellows and quite gentlemen. They do not loll about, or spit about, or smell like these.'

He returned via Massawa, visiting a Swedish Mission which served, so far as he could see, no useful purpose. The encounter with these good people impelled him to tell Augusta some home truths about missionaries, including 'the idol, Livingstone', whom he did not hold in high esteem:

The Roman Catholics in China were certainly far more self-sacrificing than the Protestants . . . Why does the Romish Church thrive with so many errors? It is because of these godly men in her who lead Christ's life. For devotion, for self-denial, the Roman Catholic Church is in advance of present-day

Protestantism ... A man must give up everything, understand *everything*, *everything* to do anything for Christ here. No half or three quarter measures will do ... I cannot help thinking ... that God has not yet decided to open these countries to know His Son. I do not think the time has come for the gathering in of the heathen. The first thing which has to be done is to open communication with their countries. Next, to let the natives mix with more civilized races, so as to acquire their language, their own native tongue being so poor as to contain not more than 300 words. [How did *he* know?] It is remarkable that, as a rule, the Apostles went to more or less civilized countries which, though pagan, had some germ of the old truth in their religions. I look upon the negro races as I would look on children of three or four years of age, incapable of understanding these truths until more matured in knowledge.

Yet they were nice, quiet people, in many ways an example to Europeans.

On his return from Abyssinia Gordon was summoned to Cairo to sort out the Khedive's chaotic finances. It was a singularly inappropriate choice, for Gordon's imprudence in his own finances was hardly less than His Highness's, though not on so majestic a scale. This he realized. However, to Cairo he went, encountering on the way the palatial houseboat of the Earl and Countess of Aberdeen, on their honeymoon. They invited him to dinner, and no sooner had he stepped aboard than they asked him for a tow down to Cairo, for the Countess, 'a great fat girl', had seen enough of the Nile. 'I expected that,' he replied, and she had the grace to blush. After that, he did not count on an invitation to Aberdeen Castle for the grouse-shooting.

Gordon viewed with dismay the prospect of a long stay in Cairo. *Dinner parties!* But he had hardly arrived at the station, on 7 March 1878, when he was whisked off, dirty and covered with dust, to dine with H.H. at the palace (where Madame de Lesseps was scarcely more clothed than the black ladies he had photographed) and then to another palace where he had to stay, pining for his camel. So far as it is possible to live like a hermit in a palace, Gordon did so: 'Everyone laughs at me, and I do not care.'

Two years earlier the full horror of the Khedive's financial position had burst – if not upon him – upon those who had lent him nearly £81 million, much of it at an interest which reflected their scepticism at his ability and willingness to repay. Most of these bond-holders being European, four Commissioners of Debt – British, French, Austrian and Italian – had been appointed to ensure that they got their pound of flesh. In November 1876, these multitudinous debts had been funded, and two Controllers General, an Englishman to supervise the Khedive's receipts and a Frenchman to supervise his expenditure, had been appointed to secure the repayment of interest on the loan at six per cent, plus one per cent for a Sinking Fund to reduce the principal. This would swallow up five-sixths of Egypt's tax-revenue.

War and bad harvests reduced the tax yield despite the most rigorous application of the *courbach*, and there was nothing for the salaries of civil servants and army officers.

The Khedive Ismail, having evaded the duns for so many years, at last seemed cornered by the insistence of the Controllers General on his setting up a Commission of Inquiry charged with the examination of the whole Augean stable of Egyptian finance. The Commission would include the Controllers and the four Debt Commissioners; but the Khedive insisted on appointing the president, and had been awaiting, with all the anxiety of a besieged commander watching the slow approach of a relief force, the arrival of his faithful servant, Gordon Pasha. He offered the post after dinner the first evening and Gordon rashly accepted, provided the Debt Commissioners were not members of his commission as he felt they could not be impartial in their deliberations.

It was unfortunate, indeed pregnant with future disaster, that the British Debt Commissioner was Captain Evelyn Baring, then at the outset of a career which was to make him, as Lord Cromer, Britain's most eminent proconsul. Baring, a member of the banking family, was what would nowadays be stigmatized as an 'Establishment figure'; and Gordon was instinctively anti-Establishment. Baring had been a regular soldier, but in the wrong corps, for Gordon had a prejudice against gunners. In an ante-chamber of his palace, he met Captain Baring, and took an instant dislike to him. 'Now Baring is in the Royal Artillery, while I am Royal Engineers. Baring was in the nursery while I was in the Crimea. He has a pretentious grand patronizing way about him . . . When oil mixes with water, we will mix together.' Nor could he approve of the Khedive's financial agents with whom he was supposed to work in close accord: one had a name like an Italian opera singer's, and the other parted his hair down the middle.

Gordon had no knowledge of the money market, no particular desire to keep the bond-holders beyond reach of want. It did not escape his notice that European officials drew punctually their own 'enormous salaries',* and he thought that at least as high a priority should be given to the payment of Egyptians' salaries, which were two years in arrears, forcing officials into corruption, peculation and slave-trading. Baring, whose job was to look after the interest of the bond-holders, held that people who lend money to a government are entitled to their interest before any other of the government's commitments are met.

Gordon conferred with de Lesseps and agreed to recommend that

* In this he was unjust at least to Baring, whose salary was months in arrears.

payment of the current year's interest be suspended to release some money for government salaries; and that thereafter interest be reduced to three per cent. Only then could the Commission proceed to a thorough examination of the country's finances. It was a fair proposal, and close to the conclusion which Baring was eventually to reach. But as Vivian, whom he remembered as 'a pretty, black-eyed boy at the R.M.A.', pointed out, Gordon was positively 'red republican' in his opinions, and a financial ignoramus, so it was hardly necessary to take his recommendation seriously. The consuls, the Debt Commissioners, the Controllers General, the foreign residents in Cairo united in denouncing it. The Khedive, under overwhelming pressure, gave way.

Gordon 'left Cairo with no honours, by the ordinary train, paying my passage. The sun, which rose in such splendour, set in the deepest obscurity.' The whole episode cost him £800, which he could not claim as there was no money in the kitty. His principal contribution to Egypt's financial stability had been to cut his own salary from £6,000 to £3,000 a year – a quarter of what he had originally been offered. This he did in protest against the exorbitant emoluments of 'a detestable little tyrant' sent out from England to report on the slave-trade. His glimpse of financial imperialism confirmed his dislike of the 'D'Israeli' ministry. He would be glad to see the Liberals come in, especially if Gladstone did not come in with them.

12

⚑ THE GOVERNOR-GENERAL IN KHARTOUM

⚑ Gordon's next tour was to Harar, where he found installed his
Gondokoro acquaintance, Raouf Pasha, 'a great tyrant who
strangled the Emir of Harar'.* The turbulent Somali tribes were ardent
slave-traders. He intercepted and confiscated £2,000 worth of coffee
which Raouf Pasha was sending to Aden on his private account, meaning
to buy there general merchandise which he could then sell to his own
soldiers at exorbitant prices.

At the gate of Harar he found the palpitating carcase of two cows, their
throats ritually cut in honour of his arrival, and at the entrance to the
divan a third sobbing her life out, blood pumping over the threshold.
Two weeks in the province of Harar were enough, so back he went to
Khartoum, removing *en route* Raouf Pasha, three generals of division, one
general of brigade and four lieutenant-colonels. But it was really no use
removing them if the Khedive would never dismiss them: most of them
appeared at receptions in the Abdan Palace within a few weeks of being
sent down from the Sudan in disgrace. Gordon prided himself on his
ruthlessness with incompetent officials. Many were indeed lethargic and
corrupt; but, because of his anti-Egyptian prejudices, they were too often
replaced by Sudanese ignorant of the first principles of civil administration and by Europeans who were nothing but adventurers. These up-
heavals and sudden improvisations in the machinery of government may
well have been more damaging than a modicum of corruption and
indolence.

Gordon did not like Harar, and was pleased to be relieved of it in
December 1878.

There were in colonial days two types of officials, the district officers
and the secretariat officers. Gordon – except for his ignorance of the
language – was an archetypal district officer. His idea of administration

* Gordon was quoting a rumour which the Khedive believed to be untrue.

was riding round the country and dealing with problems on the spot, dispensing justice under a tree, making instant decisions and issuing verbal orders at divans attended by scores of tribal notables. This is well suited to a people whose social and political organization is tribal; but it is the job of the district officer or *mudir*, not the governor-general: if the latter immerses himself in local problems, broader issues tend to be neglected. Baring was eminently a secretariat officer, remote from the heat and burden of the day, dealing with ministers and heads of department rather than chiefs and village elders, taking a broad view of problems but knowing little of what actually went on in the *fellahins'* fields and the grazing grounds of the Bedouin – and not caring much either, provided that the year's estimate of tax was collected, canal and road-building proceeded according to schedule and the statistics of violent crime showed a satisfactory annual decline.

For the next nine months Gordon had to be a secretariat officer, wrestling with problems which were wholly unfamiliar in an atmosphere wholly uncongenial to him. Moreover he had not the facilities enjoyed by governors in more advanced countries – chief clerks and cashiers, financial and legal experts who knew far more than he of their expertises. Whenever Gordon asked for advice, he was met by a sickly smile and 'You know best'. The trouble was that he did not.

From June 1878 to March 1879, with only one short break, he remained in Khartoum, under-exercised and over-irritated, chained to the palace by the manifold responsibilities of the governor-general. 'Since the lonely camel rides are at an end, I have no nice thoughts.' He had directly under him eleven *mudirs*, of whom four (at Berber, Massawa, Suakim and Kassala) could be instructed and admonished daily by the telegraph. But the others he really could not supervise as he would wish, so he refrained from interfering unless they were outrageous in their conduct. Or so he said. What he could supervise were the local barracks, hospitals and prisons, the state of which gave him a good idea of the efficiency of local officials. The prisons he found to be dens of injustice, with prisoners in many cases shut up for years pending trial. He found time to look into every case. The courts were unsatisfactory, largely because the presidents were quite untrained; the members were unpaid local notables and therefore corrupt, biased, and irregular in attendance; and witnesses were reluctant to come forward except when paid to give false testimony. He therefore found it necessary to interfere a good deal in the muddy course of Egyptian justice, as when he had a man hanged for castrating a slave.

He was up by seven, and in the comparative cool of the morning inspected some government installation. He saw his chief clerk, ran through twenty or thirty telegrams and issued orders for the day. Then breakfast. From ten until one o'clock he sat under the swinging punkah, while sweat trickled down his face and soaked the paper under his hand, listening to petitions, going through his official mail, reading judgements, drafting memoranda, totting up long columns of accounts. He chain-smoked fat cigarettes, rolled by a *cavasse* standing behind his chair with one ready to slip between his fingers when he silently held up a hand for it. After luncheon, 'nothing much till four, when more telegrams'. In the evening he might go for a walk or ride. He dined at six and went to bed early. His temper became very short; a clerk who arrived late would be greeted with a swinging box on the ear, a *cavasse* who inadvertently burnt a bag of official papers felt the weight of His Excellency's whip. The monotony was deadly.

In 1877 expenditure had exceeded revenue by £92,000. The public debt was £327,000, nearly sixty per cent of the annual revenue. This was serious, for the Khedive had no use for the Sudan unless it was self-supporting. Besides, a massive deficit reflects on a governor: either he has been over-optimistic in his estimates, or he has been incompetent in his collection.

A peasant was supposed to pay in tax about one-tenth of the value of his annual produce. This was collected not as a simple tithe, but in a multitude of different taxes on his house, his livestock, his water-wheel or bucket-irrigation, his date-palms and his irrigated land. Bedouin paid only on their livestock. In addition there were taxes on professions, legal stamps, tobacco, boats, market dues and much else. It was a complicated system for a rather moderate revenue staff. The assessment was on the village or nomad clan, and it was up to the sheikhs to divide the total between individuals. 'We never get in so much as five-sixths of our revenue: the collectors say to the heads of communities, "Pay me four-sixths of the sum due, and give as *backsheesh* to me one-sixth; then I will certify that you cannot pay the remaining sixth".'

Gordon did remedy abuses such as collecting taxes on young date-palms before they could bear, on land which had been swallowed up by sand-drifts or washed away by the river. But he could not collect taxes save by methods which he deplored. 'The people unless they are physically coerced by the whip will not pay their taxes . . . By putting them in prison you would need a huge prison for defaulters . . . so they must be beaten into it.'[1] He made major economies such as withdrawing from all the Equatorial posts south of Dufilé; but could not stop innumerable leaks in the system. In his efforts to close the gap between revenue and expenditure he was singularly unsuccessful. For the five central, more-or-less settled provinces of the Sudan the annual deficit (in round figures and making an adjustment for a change in the financial year) was:[2]

1874/5	£49,000
1875/6	£96,000
1877	£92,000
1878	£109,000
1879	£115,000

Finance was not his *forte*. But all who have wrestled with similar problems will share his pleasure in proving that, so far from the Sudan owing Cairo £30,000 as the Cairene financial experts maintained, the boot was on the other foot to the tune of £9,000.

To C. Rivers Wilson, a civil servant on loan to the Khedive as finance minister, his attitude was anything but friendly. When the Finance Minister incautiously addressed to Gordon Pasha a query about military finances, the Pasha replied, 'I beg you, *Monsieur le Ministre de Finances*, to inform me, since when has His Highness the Khedive of Egypt entrusted to you the administration of his army?' Later, however, when they met, Gordon characteristically apologized for his rudeness.

On the question of the Sudan Railway he could speak with more authority, as a colonel of the Royal Engineers. This was the brain-child of the Khedive, fathered on him by various European contractors such as Messrs Appleby to whom His Highness (through failure to read the small print of the contract) found he owed £540,000 for £150,000 worth of material delivered at railhead. Gordon condemned the whole project as a complete waste of money. He insisted that an efficient steamer-service was the answer to the Sudan's transport problem. When Colonel Prout was invalided home from Equatoria, Gordon commissioned him to order five steamers of the type Mr Yarrow had specially recommended for the Nile – stern-wheelers, capable of being taken to pieces for portage overland. They did not arrive during this governor-generalship, but were to play their part later.

In Khartoum Gordon was more single-minded about the slave-trade than he had been in Darfur. By the end of July he had captured twelve caravans in two months. One of these was found to be escorted by Suleiman's *bazingers*, now in government service; by the time it was intercepted, after crossing 500 miles of desert, only 90 out of 400 slaves survived. Few were over sixteen, some of the girls had babies, and there were many small children. 'It is much for me to do to keep myself from cruel illegal acts towards the slave-dealers; yet I think I must not forget that God suffers it, and that one must keep to the law. I have done the best I can, and He is Governor General.' But the greatest slaver of all he would allow to return.[3] Gordon could never quite conquer his admiration for Zebeyr's ruthless ability.

In his belief that he was on top of the slave-trade he was grievously mistaken. The very *mudirs* he had appointed were in it up to the neck, using government troops to facilitate their operations. A particularly scandalous case was that of Ibrahim Fauzi, whom he had promoted to succeed Prout in Equatoria. To decide his fate Gordon, 'after asking God to settle it', tossed a coin. It fell with the Sultan's fatal cypher uppermost, 'so unless He intervenes, Fauzi will be shot'. Actually it was Giegler who intervened: 'But for Giegler, I should have shot Fauzi today . . . But he has been sent to Sobat in chains and perhaps he will die.' Ibrahim Fauzi still, however, had a part to play.[4]

Gordon was 'striking deadly blows at the slave-trade', when suddenly, in July 1878, Suleiman Zebeyr attacked the garrison of Dem Idris,* killed Idris Abtar of whom he was bitterly jealous, seized the garrison's rifles and cannon and declared his independence. Gordon decided to blockade him into submission, and fortunately there was in Khartoum the very man he needed, Gessi.

The Italian's relations with Gordon had not been easy since they parted in January 1877. Gordon had formed the opinion that Gessi was 'utterly devoid of principle', besides being 'very much too grand, giving himself airs and forgetting his place'. Europe and the pleasures of family life had soon palled, so Gessi had asked Gordon to take him on again. Gordon had refused, and Gessi in a rage had threatened to publish Gordon's letters, which 'only shows the vindictive state of the Italian whom I kept from starvation'. Gessi, however, on a private venture, arrived at Khartoum shortly before news of Suleiman's revolt. Despite his shortcomings, he was a fine swashbuckling soldier, so Gordon invited him to resume his Egyptian commission and 'smash the Cub'. Gessi could not refuse and (borrowing Gordon's elephant-rifle) set off upriver to collect some 2,800 men from the garrisons for his campaign. They were not the most promising material, since many were martyrs to syphilis and 'the itch' and none had been paid for two years. Moreover Gordon could not but regret that they invariably cut their prisoners' throats, and many were addicted to cannibalism. He promised Gessi £1,000 if he caught Suleiman: 'I hope he will hang him.'[5]

A. B. Wylde, former British Consul in Jeddah, visited the Sudan in 1878 to report on the slave-traffic. Gordon disliked him ('inclined to imbibe'). He believed that Wylde's statistics of the traffic across the Red Sea were swollen by the iniquitous practice of giving the Royal Navy £1 a head prize money for every slave they 'rescued', which caused them to classify every Negro as a slave. While Gordon was harassing the traffic to

---

* Dem Idris is 'the fortified town' of Idris: Suleiman's headquarters were known as 'Dem Suleiman'.

Lower Egypt, Wylde found that slave-caravans moved freely from the Nile to the Red Sea coast, and thence across to Jeddah. There was no difficulty in buying slaves in the Sudan. Slaves were more profitable than general merchandise because they walked, while gum, cotton, coffee, ivory, etc. had to be carried on camel-back and were often damaged by rain. A good slave made a 1,000 per cent profit. He found the slaves generally quite content, not ill-used, and by no means pining for their own countries.

One characteristic example of Gordoniana is recorded by Wylde. Gordon had ordered that the governor of any district through which a captured slave-train was proved to have passed should forfeit a quarter's pay. But he was hoist with his own petard, for while he himself was at Massawa, a Royal Navy vessel captured a large slave-ship just off-shore; so he solemnly handed over three months' of his own salary. It was the sort of gesture which built up the legend.

He continued his correspondence with the Anti-Slavery Society, whose pomposity, unction and pretensions to omniscience he found insufferable. It was infuriating to be congratulated on 'realizing an "*imperium in imperio*",' as independent of the Khedive as the Khedive was of the Sultan of Turkey, when he was scrupulous in his loyalty to Ismail. 'We submit,' pontificated Mr Aaron Buzacott, Secretary of the Society, 'that within the limits of your jurisdiction you might establish the fact that no title of slaves would be hereafter recognized.' How could he establish such a fact when the law said that slavery was legal until 1889? . . . 'As was recently done on the Gold Coast with the happiest effects.' What had the Gold Coast to do with it? That was a British colony, the Sudan was a Province of Egypt . . . 'The faculties afforded by the absolute despotism which you wield and represent . . .' But he was not the despot; that was the Khedive, whose law permitted slavery. Did these fools mean he should break the law he was employed to enforce? 'To restore a slave [to slavery] entails complicity with slave holding.' And what if hundreds of slaves were 'freed' in a waterless desert? Would not that entail complicity with their death by hunger and thirst? It seemed that the Society assumed a sort of general interference-licence in Africa: 'Will you tell Mr Sturge* that he is silly to write those things, S,I,L,L,Y, *silly*.'[6]

The unfortunate Waller was unmercifully harried.

Excuse my remarking on your regiment, but you must be congratulated on the loss incurred by the enemy when your missionaries were attacked the other day and of whom, the papers say, one of your officers killed twelve before he fell. It quite recalls one to the apostolic times and will no doubt

* Honorary Secretary, later Chairman of the Society.

do much to civilize the natives. I think I shall claim the title of Reverend, for I declare I am only a shade more energetic and zealous . . . 'Take care of that box of Bibles, but for goodness sake do not let that box of powder get wet.'

Of the C.M.S. mission on its way to Mtesa's he formed a more favourable opinion. They had been apprehensive of their reception at Khartoum. 'Please understand,' he had written acidly, 'that I am equally and even more anxious for the welfare of mankind as you are.' His telegrams which they had received at Alexandria had not been models of clarity. But at Khartoum all doubts were set at rest. A little man they took to be a butler was showing two *cavasses* how to lay a table. On their arrival he came running up. 'How d'ye do? So glad to see you! Excuse shirt-sleeves. So hot! Awful long voyage. I'll make a row about it. Are you very angry with me?' He put them up, showed them his bedroom (furnished only with a chair and a camp-bed) and his 'Prayer Book', a thick notebook filled with the names of those for whom he regularly prayed. After they had sufficiently rested he sent them on their way with much practical advice, plenty of cash and two large bags of macaroni. It was a typical, unobtrusive kindness to pay their entrance fees to the Royal Geographical Society.[7]

For light relief he had a baby elephant and four little hippopotami, 'like huge pigs, plump and soft and cool-skinned. The little elephant smelled them, but did not like them at all. The hippopotamuses would have been friendly with the elephant, but after a few overtures on their part he butted at them, and flicked water at them with his trunk . . . The hippopotamuses do not smell a bit, and are lovable animals.' He also kept in his palace grounds two tame ostriches which were far from lovable. They attacked a slave, striking him with their toes, tearing off his nose and almost killing him. 'The culprits I have ordered to be sold into slavery and annually plucked. The proceeds of the sale is to be devoted to purchasing the freedom of the wounded slave and to giving him a good *backsheesh*.'

He had not enough to do. He spent ten days on the congenial task of making a big map of the Sudan: 'Now it is finished I am again utterly at a loss how to employ my time. You see, one lacks books.' He repaired clocks, pulling them to pieces and putting them together again, but a cuckoo–clock defeated him. It was a sickly season: more than half the Arab officials were ill, or said they were, as were his entire domestic staff, with malaria, diarrhoea, boils or prickly heat.

The companionship of the Friend was his unfailing solace, but this Friend was not the God of the Victorian pulpit:

What pleasure would it be to Him to burn us or torture us? . . . Would it show His power? Why, He is omnipotent. Would it show His justice? He is righteous . . . We credit God with attributes which are utterly hateful to the meanest of men . . . Is not the preaching of every place of worship you have ever entered, this? 'If you do well, you will be saved; if you do ill, you will be damned.' Where is the Gospel or Good News in this? . . . The Good News is, 'Whatever you do, God, for His Son's sake, pardons you.'

I will tell you a story of 1,848 years ago. There was a workman of Bethlehem who did not agree with the great teachers of an old religion, who answered them roughly and who did not conform to their view or pay them the attention to which they were accustomed. He was always in the slums with very dubious characters . . . He did not look upon them as pariahs. He did not think it beneath him to call on worse than 'Divorced' . . . His strong rebukes were against the white-robed, clean, respectable people . . . Well, you know the story. The *good people* could not bear the home-thrusts they received, and so they murdered him.

Gordon's Friend is perhaps more recognizable to us than to his contemporaries – this working-class Saviour, 'the carpenter, the bastard son of Yusuf', murdered by the Establishment for his radical views and dubious associations.

Gordon did not share the prevailing English self-satisfaction. 'I declare the products of Great Britain have terribly fallen off. You can never get a good thing nowadays . . . My dear Augusta, I feel sure it is nearly over with us. I hope it may come after our day, but I think we are on the decline . . . You must see it yourself in the things you buy . . . Now falsehood in trade shows want of morality in the nation, and when morality – i.e. honesty – is lacking, the end is not far off.'

He must attend again to the 'cub', Suleiman, who was believed to be egged on by his father, now residing in Cairo. Some months earlier, before the rebellion erupted, Zebeyr had consigned to his son forty richly ornamented saddles and magnificent sabres. It was surmised, since owing to tsetse fly and horse-sickness there were no horses in Bahr-el-Ghazal, that they were intended to subvert the chiefs of the Baggara. The saddles and sabres had been intercepted in Khartoum, but the Darfur tribes under Haroun and some of the Baggara under a former officer of Zebeyr's named Shabahi had rebelled. So in March 1879 Gordon set off for the west to support Gessi and prevent the three rebellions linking up. Before departure he gave up smoking – not for the first or last time.

He moved by easy marches through great heat and a desiccated country. He had another 'first class secretary', Barzati Bey, who really was a success. He was a cadet of an aristocratic Khartoum family, about twenty-nine years of age, a man of courage, of erudition and an encyclopaedic knowledge of the Sudan: he could 'write in several cyphers without looking at the keys'. Gordon set much store by his advice; particularly as 'he had the invaluable quality of telling me when he disagreed with me.' His black eyes used to 'twinkle with delight' when the Governor-General was in full oratorical flow on his favourite subject, Arab shortcomings. Scoffers might call him 'the black imp', but he was Gordon's closest friend and best adviser.

They had the usual encounters. 'I smell slaves,' said Gordon one day to Barzati Bey. 'Look under those trees.' The bag was fourteen slaves being taken to market by three Bashi-Bazouks whom Gordon had summarily flogged and dismissed. Another party of twenty-three slaves had struggled across the burning desert from Shaka and were in a pitiable state. How could he dispose of them? They could not make their way back to Bahr-el-Ghazal. So he enlisted the men and boys in his army, told off the women as 'wives' of his soldiers, and arranged for the children to be escorted in the rains to El Obeid. The slavers were jailed; he could not follow the advice of a clergyman in England to 'stretch the law a bit' and shoot them.

The law was not helpful to a man whose enemies in Cairo were eagerly awaiting a chance to trip him up. Gordon listed its more conspicuous imperfections:

1. I have an order signed by the Khedive to put to death all slave-dealers or persons taking slaves.
2. I have the Convention which calls slave-taking 'robbery with murder'.
3. I have the Khedive's decree, which came out with the Convention, that this crime is to be punished with five months to five years prison.
4. I have a telegram from Nubar Pasha, saying that 'the sale and purchase of slaves in Egypt is legal'.

Armed with such instructions, the man on the spot could hardly do right. None of the wise men in Cairo seemed to have given thought to what would happen when, in 1889 under the Convention, slavery suddenly ceased. Seven-eighths of the population of the Sudan were slaves; the country's revenue would fall by two-thirds.

On 7 April he arrived at Shaka, that 'den of iniquity', whence he expelled 100 slave-dealers despite their lamentations. A few days later there came Suleiman's chief secretary and three of his clerks, sent to explain that he had never wavered in his allegiance. However, Suleiman had 'tried this trick too often'. The unlucky four (were they not envoys?) Gordon had court-martialled and shot, because they had massacred the defenders of Dem Idris.

Gessi was doing splendidly against the Cub, and Gordon provided him with compromising letters in Arabic to be dropped near Suleiman's camp to cause dissension among his chiefs. He also gave Gessi a number of signed pardons, with names left blank: 'Let me know what promises you have made to your prisoners when you send them to me so that I may not cause you to break your word.' To tighten the blockade of Bahr-el-Ghazal, Gordon reversed his previous policy of tolerating the Jalaba petty slavers and, instead, authorized the Baggara to arrest them. This was effective against Suleiman, cutting off his supplies of arms, ammunition and consumer-goods which they brought him to barter for slaves; but it had wider effects which Gordon did not appreciate. The Jalaba were not mere individuals; they were the commercial agents of powerful tribes. In 'making friends' with the Baggara, who naturally took his instructions as a licence to plunder, he antagonized all the Jalaba families and business associates. He prided himself on being crafty, but in buying the friendship of the fickle Baggara by making enemies of the agriculturists of the Nile valley he was making a bad long-term bargain. Meanwhile the Baggara were obeying his instructions with zest and the desert was full of liberated slaves wandering about without food and water until re-enslaved by their liberators. They had no other hope of survival.

'What a terrible time these poor, patient slaves have had for the last three days – harried on all sides and forced first one day's march in one direction, and then back again, and then off again in another. It appears that the slaves were not divided but were scrambled for. It is a horrid idea, for of course families get separated; but I cannot help it, and the slaves seem to be perfectly indifferent to anything whatsoever.' Where the demand was slack he had to allocate 'freed' slaves to the Baggara. A little wretch named Capsune gave useful information about the slavers. After being 'freed' he was re-sold, not against his wish, in El Obeid, and after several changes of ownership passed into the hands of the missionary, Felkin, who took him to England. There Gordon was to meet him again.

Gordon has been denounced by post-colonial historians for acting, in respect to the slave-trade, like a bull in a china shop. This is unfair: he acted with circumspection. But licensing the Baggara to harry the Jalaba – intended not so much to suppress the slave-trade as to tighten the blockade on Suleiman – was hasty and ill-judged; and, it seems, did little to help the unfortunate slaves.

On 25 June Gessi reported in person, delighted with his gratuity of £2,000 and with being made a pasha. His campaign, after prodigious exertions and much fighting, had been successful, and Suleiman was now a fugitive. Since Haroun and Shabahi were small fry, Gordon left them to Gessi, and returned to Khartoum.

There was a sequel, which was to have a bearing on Gordon's life and death. On 15 July Gessi caught up with Suleiman who surrendered; but during the night (according to Gessi) he planned to escape with eleven of his brigand-chiefs, and had a dozen horses bridled and saddled for a getaway. So Gessi with or without good reason, and certainly without a trial, had them shot. Gordon had no compunction about the death of this young ruffian and, though far away at the time, accepted full responsibility: 'Gessi only obeyed my orders.'[8]

What he wanted was proof that Zebeyr had instigated his son's rebellion. This (he was told, he could not himself read it) was found among papers captured by Gessi, a letter from Zebeyr to Suleiman. As the Khedive would not send Zebeyr to Khartoum, he was court-martialled *in absentia*, found guilty and condemned to death; 'but I expect they will do nothing to him.' Actually Gordon himself asked the Khedive to pardon Zebeyr, about whom his feelings were always ambivalent.[9]

While Gordon had been harrying the slavers in the desert, the Khedive Ismail had been harried with equal pertinacity by his creditors in Cairo. To obtain from Messrs Rothschild a further £8½ millions to meet government salaries, he had been obliged to hand over to the State his personal landed property and accept Rivers Wilson as his minister of finance. It was discovered that much of the land had already been assigned to earlier creditors. There was thus a delay while the priorities were investigated by the International Courts.

Meanwhile 2,500 military officers were put on half-pay. This provoked an officers' mutiny, which was bought off from a special advance on the Rothschild loan, and next day Nubar Pasha resigned. Mutiny had succeeded, and the young officers had tasted power. On 7 April the Khedive made a bid for nationalist support by dismissing Rivers Wilson and appointing a purely Egyptian cabinet. Gordon approved. 'I admire the Khedive exceedingly. He is the perfect type of his people, a splendid leopard! Look at the numberless cages out of which he has broken his way, when it seemed quite impossible for him to do so.' But the leopard was at the end of his tether. Under pressure from France and Britain, the Sultan of Turkey deposed him, and his son, Tewfik, reigned in his stead.

Gordon heard the news at Foggia on 1 July and was saddened by the thought of the sufferings of 'my poor Khedive Ismail'. He had already, in March, given notice of his intention to resign. After five and a half years in the Sudan his health was failing. His heart was giving him from time to time sudden agonizing stabs of pain; he had a horror of food, and no wish for anything but sleep. A newly arrived officer, a Viennese named Rudolf Slatin, met him on his way to Khartoum, exhausted after his long ride and suffering from sores on his legs. He had finished with the Sudan, and went to Cairo to tell them so. As for Egypt, he 'rather laughed in his sleeve' at the mess the English and French had got into by meddling: they had eaten the sweet things, and must now eat the bitter.

He regarded himself as friendless in Cairo; he refused a special train ('they would have charged me for it') and when offered palatial accommodation, was inclined to insist on putting up instead at Shepheards. However, Barzati Bey dissuaded him from snubbing the new Khedive, whom he went to see the next day. Tewfik accepted his resignation with equanimity, but Gordon found this clumsy, solid Turk better disposed than he had expected. Tewfik did not believe in the rumours, industriously fabricated by Gordon's enemies, that he plotted to set up an independent state of the Sudan with himself as sultan.

Tewfik begged Gordon to undertake one last mission – to King Johannes, who had assumed a belligerent posture. Gordon was charged with patching up a peace without compromising any Egyptian interest or giving up an inch of the province of Bogos. He pointed out to the Commissioners of Debts that, in the bond-holders' interests, their governments should dissuade Johannes from starting a war which would cost Egypt a mint of money. As a precaution against kidnapping by the King of Kings, he arranged for the 'black imp' to be provided with a French passport. Then he embarked for Massawa. There he discovered that the Abyssinians were already in possession of Bogos, and from Tewfik he received orders to avoid a war but cede nothing. It was not a promising basis for negotiations.

He left Massawa on 13 September. Riding – or, more often, leading – his mule up and down steep mountain tracks, he found the road terrible, his temper diabolical; with palpitation of the heart, prickly heat and boils, he was 'a perfect Job'. On the 16th, wearing marshal's uniform, he dragged his mule past the Guard of Honour (who remained squatting on their heels) into the Abyssinian headquarters. Their General was so muffled up, face and all, that Gordon wondered if he should feel his pulse. He motioned Gordon to a low stool and Barzati Bey (looking daggers) had to squat on the ground. After a long, objectionable silence, he asked why Gordon had come. Gordon (sending away the black imp who by then was in such a temper as to be a diplomatic disaster) explained his mission. They had no fruitful dialogue, either socially or diplomatically, so after four days of premeditated slights and frustrations, Gordon rode slowly on 'over the world's crust', thirty-nine days' march to the King's presence at Debra Tabor.

The Lion of Judah never smiled nor looked one in the face, but 'when you look away he glares at you like a tiger'. Those who displeased him by smoking or taking snuff were punished by having their noses cut off: more serious offenders had their feet or hands amputated, hot tallow poured into their ears. But much bad temper may be excused a man who has to be dosed every ten days for tapeworms picked up in eating raw meat. Gordon felt quite kindly disposed towards Lord Napier and his expedition. Dispraise of Abyssinia could go no further.

'What have you come for?' asked Johannes.

'Have you not read His Highness's letters?'

'No.' After a great search the letters were found and the Chief Clerk received forty strokes for not producing them before. The letters were read to him by Johannes's Italian interpreter, 'a great scamp'.

'You want peace,' said the King of Kings. He then proceeded to make preposterous territorial and financial claims, far exceeding Bogos. 'And you must send me an *abouna*.'*

Gordon asked to be given these demands in writing, and six months for the Khedive's reply, which was agreed.

The Lion of Judah's next demand was that Gordon should go to the bath with him. This was a hot spring, bubbling up through a bamboo stem in the floor of a hut two days' journey away: 'His object was to drag me in triumph through the country.' Gordon said he could not spare the time. He then asked what Johannes would do if the Khedive did not make these territorial cessions.

'I shall then know my enemies and fight you. Come to the bath with me.'

The dialogue proceeded on these unpromising lines for some time, with the King every now and then reproaching Gordon, a Christian, for wishing to spill Christian blood.

'Come to the bath, friendship business, perhaps I will change my demands.'

Gordon was playing a weak hand with considerable skill. The real danger to Egypt was not the barbaric empire of Abyssinia, but Britain and France, with their stranglehold on Egypt's finances. If Egypt were to be involved in a frontier war, it was vital to have their diplomatic support; they must be convinced that it was in the bond-holders' interests that Egypt should not be defeated and humiliated. They would certainly not support Egypt's claim to Bogos, but they could hardly countenance the more outrageous demands of the King of Kings, especially that for a port on the Red Sea. Gordon's orders were to cede nothing, but he did hint at concessions. He required in turn that Johannes put his preposterous demands, not in a verbal altercation which could afterwards be denied, but in a formal letter to the Khedive. Johannes saw the snare set for him, and was not going to be hustled into writing that letter.

* A bishop of the Coptic Church. Johannes, fearful of spiritual back-sliding in Abyssinia, wanted an *abouna* from Egypt.

Half an hour after their conversation, His Majesty went off to the baths and stayed there for nine days.

At their second interview, thirteen days later, Johannes asked, 'Have you anything more to say?'

'I only want that letter.'

'I will write a letter about this. Go to your master.'

Gordon saluted his 'dear Christian friend and bolted with precipitancy. Having my baggage packed, I struck tents. Down comes interpreter with a letter and sack of 1,000 dollars.

' "How are you? How are you? His Majesty says, and sends a thousand dollars." '

Gordon refused the money but, once clear of Debra Tabor, opened the letter to the Khedive, as was his duty, to see what it really contained. In it was written: 'Johannes the God-given King to Mohamad Tewfik. I have received your letter by that man. You have robbed me and struck me. Eight Kings knew not of it. You now want peace like a robber. If you want peace eight Kings must have cognizance of it.' The 'eight kings' were the governments of Britain, France, Germany, Austria–Hungary, Russia, Italy, Greece and Turkey. Johannes knew what he was up to, and the need for international support. His letter was offensive in wording, style and innuendo: it addressed the Khedive merely as 'Mohamad Tewfik', without titles; it *tutoyéd* him as an inferior; and it referred insultingly to his envoy as 'that man'. So Gordon wrote a protest, and received a reply that His Majesty had done as he thought fit.

As there was nothing more Gordon could do but fill the uncomfortable role of murdered envoy, he set out on a ghastly return journey to Massawa. With only six Sudanese soldiers and 'escorted' by a mob of Abyssinian soldier-brigands who did not conceal their hatred of a foreigner, he was in such peril that he burned all his secret papers. To lighten his baggage he discarded his tents, and found that his road passed through snow and ice. He was arrested, released, re-arrested, insulted, bullied and plundered. It was not pleasant sleeping between two of these brigands with a third at his feet. He had to spend £1,450 on 'purchasing every yard of the road'.

On 8 December he arrived at Massawa where, to his great relief, he found H.M.S. *Seagull*. He also found a telegram from the Council of Ministers calling upon him to explain why his tax-collection had fallen short of estimates. These wretched pen-pushers in Cairo! What did they know of conditions in the Sudan? Did they not realize that in the past year he had spent less than three months in Khartoum? What was more important, collecting their trumpery taxes, or suppressing rebellion and the slave-trade? Was it by his choice that the Khedive had set him off on a fool's errand to Abyssinia? Ignoring these maggots, he suggested to the Khedive that Italian support be obtained against Johannes by territorial concessions. To his fury garbled versions of both this top-secret proposal, and of the reprimand administered to him over tax-arrears, appeared in the Cairo press. This seemed to him the last straw, confirming his resolve to resign.

Moreover he had serious doubts about whether it was right for foreigners to serve a country such as Egypt. Mendacity, lethargy, peculation and corruption were endemic from top to bottom, and not really much resented. They might perhaps be eradicated by annexing the state and ruling it *in toto*, but not by a few individuals. Any people must resent the occupation of high places by strangers, however good or honest. When once the slave-trade had been suppressed, he had no hesitation in saying that an Arab governor suited the people better and was more agreeable to them than a European. (It was not quite what he had previously written about Arab governors.) So long as the voice of the Egyptian people was smothered, so long must Egypt be the basest of kingdoms. The rights of bond-holders? Nonsense! 'If people go on what is evidently rotten ice, it is their own fault if they fall through.' Holding these views he could not remain in the Khedive's service.

In Cairo he met Vivian's successor, a diplomat named Edward Malet, who found that 'his thoughts and ways seemed always to be at war with received usages and conventionalities. Even the ordinary questions of life appeared to assume a different aspect to him from that which they present to other people.' Malet invited him to dinner next day, but Gordon refused. 'Dinner parties are not in my line.' Nevertheless, just as the guests were going in, His Excellency Gordon Pasha was announced, explaining airily that he had changed his mind and not in the least put out by the fact that a place had specially to be laid for him, making thirteen at the table.

A few days later he took Malet's breath away by announcing that he proposed to call out Nubar Pasha for making disparaging remarks about Vivian. Nubar's observations could hardly have been more injurious than those Gordon had made on more than one occasion, but 'Vivian is a C.B. and I am a C.B. too. I will not permit anyone to speak in such a way of a man who belongs to the same Order of Knighthood as I do. Nubar Pasha must apologize or fight.' Confronted by a paladin who insisted on applying to the nineteenth century the code of the Chevalier Bayard – indeed of Don Quixote – the astonished Nubar showed a marked disinclination to do either, but was eventually persuaded that the former was the lesser evil, so Gordon was appeased.

After being very rude to the Khedive – whose Minister-in-Waiting bolted from the room as soon as Nemesis entered – and giving Baring a piece of his mind, he left Egypt, in December 1879, never, he hoped, to return.

Gordon wrote, 'I never was, am not, never shall be and never want to be a great man.' He summed up his work in the Sudan with disarming and perhaps misleading modesty, 'I am neither a Napoleon nor a Colbert; I do not profess to have been either a great ruler or a great financier; but I can say this – I have cut off the slave-dealers in their strongholds and I made all my people love me.'[10]

He might have proved a great captain, but the War Office never gave him the opportunity. He was not a great ruler: he had immense energy, a dynamic personality, a spirit of dedication; but besides being ignorant of the language he lacked the experience of administration and of governing a Moslem people which were essential for the governor-general; he had never served a relevant apprenticeship as district officer or under-secretary. Others have been pitchforked untrained into colonial governorships and have acquitted themselves well. But they were advised by professionals; Gordon was not, and if he had been, he would have ignored them. 'There was never a greater mistake than in thinking that I ask other people's advice . . . though it may suit me to let people think they guide me. I paddle my own canoe.'[11] Such sturdy independence, which he liked to think characteristic of 'the Gordon tribe', would have been the more admirable had he known the Sudan and understood civil administration.

In his dismissals and appointments he was too capricious, inclined to be swayed by instant hunches which were later found to be erroneous. Virtually the only experienced officials in the Sudan were Egyptians and Circassians. They had their shortcomings, but their wholesale replacement by Sudanese, many of whom took with alacrity to slave-trading and corruption, and by *condottieri* like Gessi, was not necessarily conducive to efficiency. Nevertheless the charge that he filled the Administration with Europeans can be pressed too far. Of fourteen *mudirs* when he left, only four were European, and one of these, Emin, was a Moslem. He preferred native *mudirs*, at least for provinces where the slave-trade was not a major problem: Europeans were far too expensive, and thought they conferred a favour by coming.

'I think,' he wrote in May 1879, 'that the slave-trade is definitely over. I shot nine of the runaway chiefs when I was in Shaka.'[12] It was not over, but his campaign against it had caused far more economic confusion and distress than perhaps he realized, though he was more perceptive than his home-based critics. The Jalaba were the commercial agents of powerful tribes; when they were suppressed, ruin and resentment spread up and down the Nile. The whole economic infrastructure of the Sudan was shaken loose by his vigorous interference.

His claim to have 'made all my people love me' is obscured by rival ideologies. The circumstances of Gordon's death and the surge of late Victorian imperialism ensured that to most of his British contemporaries and early biographers it was unthinkable that he should not have been beloved by all 'loyal' natives. He had given up his life for them, had he not? He had abolished the *courbach*, stamped on corruption, freed those who had been unjustly imprisoned and liberated the poor slaves. They *must* have loved him: it was part of the mystique of Empire that they should have done so. But now the received wisdom is that a colonial governor, however high-minded and just, is worse for a country than an indigenous president, however despotic and self-seeking. A modern Sudanese historian describes Gordon as a complete failure because he was unable to get the best out of his subordinates.[13] Somewhere between the two extremes lies the truth, and it is difficult to discover because nearly all the direct evidence is from Europeans who, although often exasperated, were impressed by his extraordinary personality. But did Arabs and Sudanese come under the wand of the magician? On that we have only hearsay evidence from the long years of Anglo-Egyptian rule during which the Gordon legend was lovingly cultivated.

Moreover Gordon's own thoughts on the subject were conflicting. In one mood he claimed to have been loved, in another 'I cannot think that any people like being governed by aliens in race or religion. They prefer their own bad native government to a stiff, civilized government, in spite of the increased worldly prosperity the latter may give.' Of over-emphasis by 'Rivers Wilson & Co.' on efficiency he wrote, 'I only hope that in a future world we English may not be judged after this hard, cruel rule.'[14] What cause had the Sudanese people to love him?

We can dismiss at once his campaign against the slave-trade: this was almost universally resented. 'Certainly,' wrote Gessi from the Bahr-el-Ghazal in May 1880, 'your dismissal causes pleasure here, for everyone thinks . . . he will be able to resume his past habits of slave-trading and brigandage.'[15] His attack on corruption won him few friends, for Arabs and Africans have learned over the centuries to live with official corruption, which oils the wheels of government and is to them less objectionable than incomprehension. Any improvement he made in the administrative machine would have been a grievance rather than an object of gratitude, for it would be reflected most conspicuously in more efficient tax-collection. However, his gaol deliveries and the abolition of the bastinado must have pleased circles far wider than the criminal classes; for the most respectable citizen might, if he fell foul of authority, be flung into gaol for months without trial; or for the most trivial offences – delaying payment of tax until after the harvest, arguing about his assessment, refusing a tax-collector the customary *backsheesh* – be up-ended and bastinadoed till the soles of his feet were raw pulp.

No doubt Gordon's remission of taxes and the provision of piped Nile water for Khartoum were greatly appreciated, as was his harrying of 'Turkish' *mudirs* and their replacement by Sudanese officers, no less venal but at least not foreign. It was probably of acts such as these that the Mahdi was thinking when he praised Gordon.*

Tribalism and, in the case of Moslems, religion, dictate African loyalties, and there is little doubt that the Sudanese view of Gordon was formed largely by tribal and religious factors. He was probably popular among the natives of Equatoria who saw him as the man who had, at least temporarily, freed them from the Moslems of the north. But in Khartoum his ignorance of Arabic must have set up a barrier between him and 'his' people, making it impossible for him to gain friends through an interest in local culture, sports, or normal social usages. No doubt the Baggara were appreciative of his licence to plunder the Jalaba, but the governor who hopes to draw consistent support from his ephemeral popularity with such as they is doomed to disappointment. It is likely that many Sudanese with whom he was in regular contact were devoted to him; Barzati Bey certainly was, and some of his officers, in the desperate days of 1884, were to fight like tigers against their own kith and kin in a cause which they must have known was lost. But it is doubtful if his charisma operated on those who rarely or never saw him. His occasional acts of quixotic and eccentric generosity, related and exaggerated by the story-tellers, probably gave him the semi-popularity accorded to a 'character'. He hit the nail on the head when he wrote, 'This sort of thing, *tours de force*, though expensive, give me great influence with the people; and the only regret is that I am a Christian. Yet they would be the first to despise me if I recanted and became a Mussulman.' But no Christian could be generally 'loved' by the Moslem Sudanese, least of all one who was unable to communicate with them.

Yet despite this failure in communication, he was more sympathetic even to Egyptian Arabs than were many of his countrymen. 'If the Arabs *could* like an European,' he wrote, 'they would like me, for I am never hard on them.' Yet he could on occasion be utterly ruthless, writing to Gessi, 'I quite approve the execution of the greater criminals, for prisoners are always a great trouble . . . I shoot and do not hang, it is shorter work.'[16] Gordon himself was perhaps close to the truth when he wrote,

* See p. 286.

'Your brother is much feared, and I think respected, but not overmuch liked.' His prestige was higher than his popularity.

Clearly this prestige was not the handmaiden of success, for he failed more often than he succeeded. There was something in his character which compelled respect and obedience. A Catholic missionary bishop, when asked the secret of Gordon's prestige, replied, 'His chastity.' It was an unexpected reply, made in the context of a country where the only white women were a handful of nuns, and where Europeans often took slave-girls. There is little evidence that Sudanese disapproved of the custom, though they might resent the influence a mistress might use on behalf of her tribe, family and friends. Male chastity is not venerated by Moslems; the bishop conceded that it was almost incomprehensible to them, but insisted that it seemed to raise Gordon to a position of mystical and almost divine character. While acknowledging a Catholic Missionary Bishop's high authority, one may doubt whether his evidence on the political value of chastity was entirely objective.[17]

A dynamic ruler is generally respected, even though his dynamism be sometimes misdirected. Gordon wrote, 'It is only by hard camel-riding that I hold my position among the people.' There is something in this. Nomads who think nothing of walking forty or riding seventy miles in a day are impressed by a European who can do nearly as well. Besides, it is of the utmost importance that the administrator should meet people in their environment, not his. Arabs and Africans in the tribal stage of cultural development appreciate personal rule; they require that their ruler be always accessible to the petitioner, the tribal dignitary, the oppressed – not sheltering in an office behind clerks and *cavasses* who must be bribed before one can reach the presence. They like their justice to be quick and clean, rather than distorted by lawyers and delayed by legal procedures: and if it is sometimes capricious, with irrational pardons and an occasional stretching of the law to hang a culprit who richly deserves hanging, on the whole they approve. They do not understand the separation of judicial and executive powers, and their ideal judge is also the ruler, dispensing justice, issuing orders, punishing wrongdoers, assessing taxes not in some distant city but in his tent or during his midday halt under a tree. Gordon was always accessible, always quick (though not always prudent) in his decisions. Such personal rule has its drawbacks when seen from above, but its virtues are appreciated from below. Because he was accessible, the Sudanese could forgive his irascibility and incomprehension. A touch of eccentricity is no harm in a ruler, and Gordon was never dull.

It used to be said by the intellectually superior that district officers were overgrown school prefects. In Gordon there was certainly a streak of boyishness. It shows in his attitude to authority: he delighted in setting off squibs under the ponderous backsides of the beaks in Cairo. He took pleasure in craftily confounding his enemies by setting one off against another. He was inclined – his handling of the Jalaba is an example – to be too clever by half, a habit which on several occasions recoiled against him. He chortled at the dismay of isolated garrisons caught with their pants down by his sudden arrival, swooping out of the desert. He boasted naively of his feats in camel-riding. This boyishness need not have detracted from his performance as governor-general, but Baring, Nubar Pasha and Rivers-Wilson found him unpredictable and incomprehensible.

It has been remarked that Arabs govern but do not administer. Like most generalizations, it will not stand too close an examination, but it is relevant in any estimate of Gordon. So long as he merely governed – arbitrarily, often unreasonably but always with an innate decency and sense of justice – he was understood and tolerably successful. In Equatoria, for instance, it was government that was needed: any competent battalion quartermaster could have coped with the administration. But in Khartoum the governor-general had also to administer, in accordance with established rules and precedents, and in this Gordon was less successful.

A reluctant admiration rather than the tepid 'respect' or the fulsome 'love' perhaps describes the Sudanese feeling for Gordon. It was there, without a doubt, showing clearly even in the Mahdi's correspondence with him. Most Sudanese were of warrior race, valuing courage very high among human virtues, and Gordon's courage was unquestioned and unquestioning. Warriors are always susceptible to the elusive, indefinable quality of leadership, which he surely possessed. Most of them were Moslems, with a zeal always on the edge of fanaticism. No doubt they resented having a Christian as their governor-general, but they would prefer a devout Christian, worshipping God with open piety albeit with grievous errors, to one who really had no religion at all. Moreover this Christian, unlike many, did show a proper respect for Islam.

Although they might not themselves always emulate it, they probably appreciated his truthfulness and integrity. Although deploring his irrational attacks on the slave-trade, no doubt they respected his zeal and energy. Compassion is a quality valued in Moslem countries (even though it sometimes seems to have a scarcity-value), especially if it is dramatically displayed, and Gordon's compassion for the poor and the oppressed was obvious to all. So were his sudden bursts of blazing temper: 'In matters like my head camelman giving me a stumbling camel or placing my camel-saddle badly, etc., etc., I use my whip.' One day his servant brought him a bad egg for breakfast. Gordon, in a rage, gave him a jab in the wrist with his fork. A cruel act of arbitrary tyranny? Well, yes, one might call it so. But half a century later the victim, a be-medalled and battle-scarred veteran, used to tell the story, point to the scar and say, '*That* is the wound I am most proud of!'[18]

It is likely that Gordon was admired more for what he was than for what he did, more for minor, humanitarian reforms than for great administrative changes. No one could have done more for the Sudan, in the colonial context, than Kitchener, who was moreover a fluent Arabic speaker and Near East expert. But when, as part of the Independence celebrations in 1953, the statues of Kitchener and Gordon were triumphantly overthrown, the slighting of the former passed without comment, but the injury done to Gordon's memory was widely resented by the older people of Khartoum.[19]

When all is said, the secret of Gordon's prestige among the people at large, as well as the devotion he inspired among his immediate associates, still eludes us. He himself would have said that the power was not his, but God's working through him; and in later years the most common judgement on Gordon by old Sudanese who remembered him was, 'He was a man of God.'

13

♠ THE HERO ON THE SHELF

♠ On board ship Gordon made friends with a French passenger, Joseph Reinach, Gambetta's secretary, and they spent several days together in Naples, visiting the ex-Khedive Ismail and going to the ballet. The show was *Sardanapalus*, not perhaps well chosen for Gordon who was so upset by the half-naked chorus that he stumped out exclaiming angrily, 'and you call that civilization!' At one o'clock in the morning Reinach found him in his room in his dressing-gown, reading the Bible, on the table a half-empty bottle of whisky. Reinach wrote, '*Il buvait terriblement de brandy. Plus tard, à Paris, il venait souvent me voir le matin. Et, au bout de cinque minutes, il demandait du cognac.*' Reinach added some singularly perceptive comments: '*C'était un héros, a très court vue comme beaucoup d'héros, un mystique qui se payait de phrases, et aussi, comment dirai-je? Un peu "un fumiste". Il ne croyait pas tout ce qu'il disait. Dans les lettres de lui que j'ai conservés, il traitait (?) volontiers Dizzie et ses amis de* Mountebanks. *Il était, lui-même,* Mountebank . . . *Il m'a beaucoup interessé, beaucoup amusé.*'*[1]

It was a common reaction among retired pro-consuls to fret about their successors reversing their policies and ruining their achievements. Gordon was succeeded in Khartoum by Raouf Pasha, a more competent civil servant than he would acknowledge but not a strong character. 'Everything I have done in the Sudan is being obliterated,' he wrote. So obsessed was he with his forebodings that in Paris he called on the British Ambassador, Lord Lyons, and said he would ask the French Government to appoint his successor. In view of the Anglo-French rivalry in the Near

---

* Like many heroes he was a hero in the short term, a mystic who liked the sound of his own voice and also, how should I put it? A bit of a humbug. He did not believe all he said. In the letters from him which I have kept, he quite happily treated Dizzie and his friends as mountebanks. He himself was a mountebank. He greatly interested and amused me.

East, it was a staggering suggestion, which shocked Lord Lyons out of his diplomatic urbanity. 'That,' he exclaimed, 'I forbid you to do.' Gordon replied that it was his duty to obey his lordship, but his lordship's duty to forward to the Foreign Office his memorandum incorporating this suggestion and concluding, 'Anyhow it matters little, a few years hence a piece of ground six feet by two will contain all that remains of ambassadors, ministers and your obedient, humble servant, C. G. Gordon.' Lord Salisbury, the Foreign Secretary, summoned Rivers Wilson to ask tactfully if Gordon was all there. Wilson, who must himself have harboured occasional doubts on this very point, replied, 'Well, I should never recommend Your Lordship to send Gordon on a delicate diplomatic mission to Paris, Vienna or Berlin; but if you want some out-of-the-way piece of work to be done in an unknown and barbarous country, Gordon would be your man. If you told him to capture Cetewayo*, for instance, he would get to Africa, mount on a pony with a stick in his hand, and ask the way to Cetewayo's kraal, and when he got there he would sit down and have a talk with him.'[2]

Gordon called on the Foreign Office to press his scheme in person, but without success. 'I have written letters to the F.O. that would raise a corpse; it is no good. I have threatened to go to the French Government about the Sudan; it is no good. In fact I have done for myself with this Government.'

But there was still his reputation as a character to be kept up, and when the Prince of Wales invited him to dinner, what could Gordon do but refuse the invitation? To accept would be a betrayal of his image. An Equerry called to protest. 'But you cannot refuse the Prince.'

'Why not? I refused King Johannes, and he might have cut my head off. I am sure H.R.H. will not do that.'

'Well then,' suggested the Equerry in desperation, 'let me say you are ill.'

'But I am not ill.'

'Give me *some* reason that I can give the Prince.'

'Very well, then,' said Gordon, 'tell him that I always go to bed at half-past nine.'

At a Levée, however, H.R.H., who had a sense of humour, whispered in Gordon's ear, 'Come and see me at lunch-time on Sunday.' This invitation was not refused.

Watson got engaged, which gave Gordon the opportunity of expressing his views on marriage: 'A man's wife is his faithful looking-glass; she will tell him his faults . . . Therefore I say to you "Marry!" Till a man is married he is a selfish fellow, however he may not wish to be so . . . You

---

* Actually Cetewayo, the Zulu king, had just been captured.

Before Sebastopol, Crimea, 1855. Gordon's first duty under fire ...
was to effect a junction by means of rifle-pits between the French
and English sentries who were stationed in advance of the trenches

Gordon leading an attack against the Taiping rebels. 'He conceived it the duty
of a commanding officer not only to direct but personally to lead the critical assaults,
smoking a cigar and carrying only a light cane.'

Captain Gordon, R.E., c. 1860 with an unidentified child

Left: A narrow escape on the Patachiaou Bridge near Soochow. September 1863.
'ne evening Gordon was seated alone on the parapet of the bridge smoking a cigar. when
o shots in succession struck the stone on which he sat.'
ght: The death of Captain Perry at the storming of Leeku. 'A ball struck Perry in
: mouth. He fell screaming into Captain Gordon's arms, and almost immediately expired.'

Gordon in 1863

Gordon in his Chinese General's uniform

A Dervish preaching the Holy War to Arab chiefs

Major J. D. Hamill-Stewart

Sir Evelyn Baring

Towing an armed steamer over a cataract

Zebeyr

The Mahdi

The slave market. Khartoum, before Gordon's time

say, "Why do you not follow your own advice?" I reply, "Because I know myself sufficiently to know I could make no woman happy." '

He was no admirer of the English public school ('That wretched Wellington College! The Baylys would have done much better at Southampton Grammar school'); at the end of February 1880 he went abroad to arrange for the education of Enderby's son. In Brussels the King of the Belgians wished to view this elusive celebrity and perhaps enlist him for the service of his private company formed for the exploitation of the Congo. The idea rather appealed to Gordon. His experience in Equatoria and the Sudan had convinced him that the slave-trade could not be stopped by setting up a block between the Congo, where most of the slaves were captured, and Egypt, where most of them were sold. Effective action could only be taken in the Congo and in Egypt. So he had a talk with King Leopold who 'was very civil . . . He is quite at sea with his expeditions [Congo] and I have to try and get him out of it.'

Leopold was certainly not at sea, though possibly Gordon was in dealing with that very crafty character. Writing to Mackinnon, he explained that the King wished only to help a wretched people, suppress slavery and promote Christianity – all under an international flag. But it would be difficult to get the flag generally accepted. Besides, Gordon could never work with Stanley whom he did not admire. Imagination boggles at the thought of Gordon in the black heart of Leopold's Congo, where every kind of atrocity was perpetrated to extract more profit for the royal entrepreneur. But for the time being Gordon would not enter the Congo service.

At Lausanne there was another visitor, the Reverend R. H. Barnes. One day Barnes, entering Gordon's room, found him perusing some Arabic documents.

'They are death warrants,' said Gordon.

'Death warrants! Why, who are you?'

'Don't you know me? I have been Governor-General of the Sudan and still nominally retain the position; but nothing now remains for me but to sign these papers – that will be the end of it.'

Back in London he made friends with Florence Nightingale. Among the few men who had earned her respect was Lord Ripon who, after the victory of the Liberals in the General Election of April 1880, was appointed Viceroy of India. It was possibly through Miss Nightingale that Gordon was offered the post of the Viceroy's private secretary.

Apart from generally liberal views, Gordon had nothing to qualify him for the appointment. He was strongly prejudiced against both Indians and Britons who served in India. For Indian sepoys he had an ill-informed contempt. 'I hate these snake-like creatures.' Anglo-Indian officials he despised as over-paid and under-worked. India was 'the centre of all petty intrigues, while if our energy were directed elsewhere it would produce tenfold. India sways all policy to our detriment.' Moreover he conspicuously lacked the local expertise, the tact, the social and political contacts, the *savoir faire*, the self-effacement, the deference always to his master's wishes, which are essential qualities in a viceroy's private secretary. 'I am too truculent,' he boasted.

However, his judgement perhaps warped by joy at the glorious over-throw of Disraeli's 'proud military-feeling ministry', Gordon accepted the offer early in May, and promptly regretted doing so. To Waller he wrote, 'The post is very unlikely to suit me, or me it,' and to a sapper friend, 'Transition from a comet to a satellite is not over pleasurable to yours sincerely.' At a farewell banquet for Ripon he insisted in eating all courses from the same dish. To agitated protests he replied, 'We shall have to rough it out in India, you know, so we may as well start now.' Did he really visualize Viceregal Lodge as an Asiatic Gondokoro, or was this the schoolboy letting off a stink-bomb on Speech Day, the mountebank acting – grossly over-acting – the part of the cynic? The latter, one suspects.

Lord Ripon was kindness itself. With his Jesuit chaplain Gordon became very friendly, though calling him always 'Mr Kerr'. But by the time the ship reached Aden Gordon was determined to break away. As an ironic protest against the pomp of viceroyalty, he wore a formal black frock-coat through the heat of the Red Sea. But this sartorial splendour did not survive his arrival in Bombay, for when bidden to a gala dinner the Viceroy's Private Secretary had no dress clothes. A hasty whip round produced a bizarre mixture of civilian and military evening garb. After dinner, when he was required to support His Excellency through an evening's conversation, the Private Secretary was nowhere to be found. He was eventually tracked to his room where he was peacefully smoking, his legs on the table, his borrowed plumes strewn over the floor.[3]

Next day he resigned, on the characteristic grounds that he was expected to say, on receiving an Address, that His Excellency had read it with interest and would give his opinion in writing. 'You know perfectly well that Lord Ripon has never read it, and will never write, and I can't say that sort of thing.' There was more to it than that. In September 1879, the mutinous Afghan army had massacred the staff of the British Legation. In retribution, Lord Roberts had occupied Kabul; the Amir, Yakub Khan, assumed to have been at the bottom of the trouble, had been deported; and the soldiers were engaged in the perennial debate on whether the Afghans were more of a nuisance inside or outside the empire. Gordon held that as there was no proof against Yakub Khan, he should be reinstated. 'Take him back yourself, my lord,' he urged Ripon. 'You can easily do it with 3,000 cavalry. If you succeed, you will be looked upon as the greatest Governor-General India ever had, and if you are killed you will have a splendid marble monument.' But Ripon 'did not seem to see the monument'. He would neither ride to Kabul himself nor allow his Private Secretary to do so, and Gordon resigned. They parted the best of friends. Indeed after his resignation Gordon continued to advise Ripon, recommending him to engage Baring, with a K.C.B. and £10,000 a year, as his financial secretary: 'He would be an immense help.'[4] Gordon was delighted to be rid of the most wretched of countries where 'the way Europeans live is absurd in its luxury . . . I declare I think we are not far off losing it, and the sooner the better. It is only the upper ten thousand of England who benefit by it.'

His resignation was accepted on 3 June 1880. That night he received a telegram inviting him to go to China, the scene of his greatest triumphs, to which he often looked back with nostalgic longing.

The Celestial Empire was on the point of going to war with Russia, and needed its Field Marshal. The title, salary and duties of his appointment were all left for him to decide. He replied, 'Will leave for Shanghai first opportunity; as for conditions Gordon indifferent.' To the Deputy Adjutant-General he wired, 'Obtain me leave until end of year; never mind pay; am invited to China; will not involve Government.' To this the D.A.G., not unreasonably, replied, 'Must state more specifically purpose and position for and in which you go to China.' This was easily answered: 'Am ignorant; will write from China before the expiration of my leave.' On 11 June authority replied, 'Reasons insufficient; your going to China is not approved,' and on the 12th Gordon wired, 'Arrange retirement, commutation or resignation of service. My counsel, if asked, would be for peace, not war.' Then, without waiting for a reply, he took passage. He was granted leave on condition that he undertook no military service in China. To this he agreed, adding virtuously, 'I would never embarrass the British Government,' an undertaking which must have raised bureaucratic eyebrows.

At Shanghai many old comrades, now 'moon-faced veterans', were awaiting him. Lar Wang's son was a bulky red-button mandarin; and Quincey, the urchin he had rescued from the battlefield, 'a first rate young fellow'. But the situation was complicated: the hawks were in power in Pekin; his old friend Li Hung Chang headed the doves. The European ministers, in unusual accord, wished to preserve peace by promoting a coup by Li; and the German Minister made the startling suggestion that Gordon march on Pekin, depose the Son of Heaven and install Li on the throne. Gordon replied that he was equal to a good deal of filibustering, but that this was beyond him. However, he felt an obligation to remain in China to protect Li from his fiends, and again resigned his commission. 'Li Hung Chang is a noble fellow and worth giving one's life for; but he must not rebel and lose his good name.' Gordon went on to Pekin to dissuade the Grand Council from a suicidal war. Prudently evading the British Minister, he harangued the resentful mandarins on their military incompetence. At one point the interpreter refused to translate the impious expressions. Gordon thereupon seized a dictionary and pointed out the Chinese word for 'idiocy'. His arguments were so unanswerable that the peace party prevailed and Li Hung Chang, who had been in some danger of decapitation, rose to power.

By the end of October, his resignation having been refused, he was once more installed at Augusta's house in Southampton, where he was permitted to smoke only in the kitchen. He was bothered at this time by Dr Birkbeck Hill, who wished to edit his letters from the Sudan. Gordon had consented on condition that the book contained no praise of himself and no ill-natured remarks about anyone likely to read it, especially Watson, Chippendall and Russell. Barzati Bey must receive a special eulogy. Hill need have no hesitation in setting out his religious views, which 'were and are a great-coat to me'. Hill had to edit the letters without ever meeting or corresponding with the man who wrote them. But the book, though names are left blank, frank opinions omitted and the text bowdlerized for evangelical consumption, remains an important quarry for Gordoniana.

Gordon achieved the accolade of an 'Ape' cartoon in *Vanity Fair*. The artist found that he was 'all eyes', and was privileged to hear an exposition of 'the great truths'. The cartoon does not suggest the hero or, indeed, the soldier of any kind. There is a stoop, an untidy moustache, a simple, snub-nosed face with a smile of singular diffidence and charm, but also of mischief. A word-portrait accompanied the cartoon of

the grandest Englishman now alive ... Colonel Gordon is the most conscientious, simple-minded and honest of men. He has a complete contempt for money, and after having again and again rejected opportunities of becoming rich beyond the dreams of avarice, he remains a poor man with nothing in the world but his sword and his honour. The official mind regards it as a sign of madness . . . He is set down by officials as being 'cracky' and unsafe to employ ... He is very modest and very gentle, yet full of enthusiasm for what he holds to be right. This enthusiasm often leads him to interfere in matters which he does not understand, and to make in haste statements he has to correct at leisure. But he is a fine, noble, knightly gentleman, such as is found but once in many generations.

So what was the knight-errant to attempt next? Where could he find wrongs to right, abuses to remedy? He did not have to look far. In November he packed his bags and gun (but forgot his game-licence) and set off for West Cork for some rough shooting and to 'study the question'.

It certainly required, if it did not repay, study. During the late 1870s a fall in world crop prices and a series of bad harvests had brought the familiar tragic pattern of semi-starvation, eviction, rural unrest and assassination.

Six years ago, angry with Watson, Gordon had written, 'I do not like the Irish, never did, and do not believe in their being such good soldiers.' Now his opinion had changed. From Eccle's Hotel in Glengarrif he toured the poverty-stricken countryside, peered into smoky cabins, inspected National Schools compared to which those in Khartoum were like palaces. He was appalled. 'Poor wretches of Irish! I think they are more to be pitied than co-erced. They live in the West and South-West in a more pitiable condition than any people of Turkey, China or Africa, and the landlords have no sympathy for them.'

He set out his views in a memorandum of which he left one copy at Number Ten for Gladstone, sent one to Lord Northbrook at the Admiralty, and a third to his Royal Engineer friend, Colonel Donnelly, who forwarded it to *The Times*.

Gordon proposed that the Government purchase the rights of the landlords over the greater part of the south, west and midlands. The lands would be Crown lands, administered by a Land Commission and leased to working farmers. For the rest of Ireland he advocated free sale of leases, fair rents, and a government valuation.

I believe that these people are patient beyond belief, loyal, but at the same time broken-spirited and desperate, living on the verge of starvation in places in which we would not keep our cattle. The Bulgarians, Anatolians, Chinese and Indians are better off than many of them are. The priests alone have any sympathy with their sufferings, and naturally alone have a hold over them . . . In common justice, if we endow a Protestant University, why should we not endow a Catholic University in a Catholic country? . . . I am not well off, but I would offer Lord Lansdowne or his agent £1,000 if either of them would live for a week in one of these poor devil's places, and feed as these people do.

Such a letter from a national hero provoked an uproar of partizanship, ranging from the Dublin *Freeman's Journal* which noted that one of the most remarkable men of the time had reached the same conclusions as the Land League, to the *Standard* which deprecated this 'superficial glance at the disquieted island'. It was his foray into the Irish problem which convinced the Establishment that Gordon 'did not seem to be clothed in the rightest of minds'.

It was not only on Ireland that he favoured Her Majesty's Government with his unsolicited advice: his views on subjects as diverse as harbour lights, Constantinople and the Red Sea reached ministerial in-trays – where, it seems, they rested. The satisfaction of seeing his views headlined in the press was a pleasure he sought time and again. 'How dreadfully one is continually cropping up in *The Times*,' he lamented, with, however, an undertone of satisfaction; later he wrote more frankly, 'Newspapers feed a passion I have for giving my opinion.'[5]

So he gave it on Afghanistan, advising that the Afghans be left alone to perform the task for which nature and Providence had designed them, of acting as a buffer between Russia and India. He wrote with authority on colonial warfare. The enemy, he pointed out, is tougher, more mobile and knows the country better than the British soldier, whose only advantage is discipline and the consequent ability to fight a long war. Regular forces should therefore be in no hurry for time is on their side. They should operate only near secure bases, while irregular corps did most of the fighting 'untrammelled by regulations'. Untrammelled, too, by artillery. There are few soldiers so flexible in mind as to be able to unlearn the lessons of the glorious campaigns of their youth. In China the enemy had to be turned out of fortified places by heavy artillery; in the bush, artillery, he thought, was more trouble than it was worth.

Wilfrid Scawen Blunt, friendly but perceptive critic, remarked that 'Gordon's only failing – for that of drink with which he has been charged was not a serious one – was a certain tendency to court publicity.'[6] Gordon linked this with worldly ambition, personified by a wily imaginary tempter named 'Agag' who sorely tried him during these months of idleness. It was Watson, years younger and junior in rank, who took him to task about his press-addiction: 'Agag *smothered*. I promised Watson not to write to the papers about *anything*.'[7] But Agag, 'a clever, shrewd fellow' was to crop up again in Gordon's career. Nor had the papers finished with him.

Staying with the Wallers he was persuaded to take Holy Communion, which he had not done for many years. That one should do so, he explained to Mrs Freese, was 'the last wish of our dying Saviour . . . The Lord's Supper in His Levée.' He found in it an intense spiritual joy, an assurance, a refreshment: 'It ought to be taken very often'; he rejoiced in the novel experience, taking it as a pleasure of which he could never be sated. 'I have had many Comns and have a good many in prospect up to Easter Monday.' Two days later he was 'revelling in Comns'. Moreover the 'Comn is a deadly weapon against envy, malice and all uncharitableness,' and it really did seem to calm his temper and soften the asperities of his judgement. He was not disposed to keep this exciting discovery to himself, but wrote a pamphlet, *Take, eat*, which Mrs Freese criticized as being a defence of the Roman doctrine of transubstantiation.

Colonel Donnelly urged him to stand for Parliament. It is hard to see what Party could have accommodated his views. In colonial and Irish affairs he was closer to Gladstone than to 'the mountebank d'Israeli'. But Gladstone would hardly have approved his plea for compulsory, universal military training, to meet the naval and military threat from Germany which, years before anyone else, he foresaw. Nor could Gordon have stomached the element of social levelling which was beginning to permeate the Liberal Party. For though he felt a compassion for the poor, his sympathy was *de haut en bas*; he was always the Colonel, permitting no liberties. His real objection to Kemp was that the fellow was no gentleman. Khartoum Europeans, being of 'the working class stamp', were dull company. Even Rivers Wilson and the great Sir Evelyn Baring were 'a mushroom lot, and would not have to go back to any remote period to find that their family mansions were probably near the Tower, or Minories, and that the head of the family knew the value of partly worn apparel.'[8] He lamented that 'our class of life are going down a little, and the class below us are rising up.' Lucas was 'not a gentleman of more than one generation, if so much': indeed Lucas was 'a snob', a term which in those days meant a self-made man, and the use of which indicates that there was in Gordon a streak of snobbery in the modern sense. He disapproved of competitive examinations for the public service, and of reforms in the Army designed to open a way, however narrow, for classes which had hitherto found it almost impossible to achieve officer-status: 'I wonder at anyone going into the army now, it seems as if all the foundations were shaken.'[9] In hundreds of letters I have found only three references to the Queen, two of which were faintly disparaging; perhaps he was one of those Victorians who did not like Queen Victoria. The Whiggery of Charles Fox, the aristocratic republicanism of Dilke, might have suited him better than contemporary Liberalism, but he could hardly have approved of Fox's and Dilke's moral laxity. So perhaps it was as well that he decided Parliament for him was 'not for the present'.

He spent much time visiting his friends, but not, strangely enough, the Freeses whom he never saw after February 1880. There is a hint of coolness: Gordon was disillusioned with a bossy lady whose name Augusta carefully deleted; he was vexed by Mrs Freese's criticism of *Take, eat*; and on departing from England in January 1884 he noted, 'Allen and Waller were at the station Freese *not*.'

He did not totally shun Society, only 'refusing when it is possible, and when I go, getting humiliated or being foolish . . . I dwell more or less under the shadow of the Almighty, when I go out of that refuge I get often wounded by shafts of ridicule . . . One's inclination is, having a quiverful of the sharpest arrows, to shoot back . . . I know I am feared because of this, but it is not fear one would wish to meet, but love.'[10] The letter gives a strange picture of Gordon – prickly, sensitive to slights, yet needing affection. He was not, however, above occasional tittle-tattle, remarking after a social call, 'Mrs Vivian had a packet of charcoal biscuits. That means more children.'

He was saddened by news of Gessi's death as a result of appalling privations when his steamer was stuck without food for ninety-nine days in the *sud*. 'Gessi! Gessi! How I warned him to leave with me! When at Toashia I said to him, "Whether you like it or not, and whether I like it or not, your life is bound up with mine!" '

With Gessi's death Dr Hill had more than ever to be circumspect in relating his exploits, for these seem to have been amatory no less than military. 'Italians are a queer lot, and he might have a deal of trouble with Gessi's widow . . . Better let Burton do it, if he likes.'

On 21 March 1881 the Scroll began again to unroll. He met a friend, Colonel Sir Howard Elphinstone, lamenting that he had been posted to command the Royal Engineers in Mauritius, a backwater so stagnant that officers resigned their commission rather than go there. Gordon offered to go instead.

He left England early in May. The voyage gave him ample time for self-examination. 'Go not to the Table for salvation or in fear. I go because the antidote to the poison in my flesh is there.' The flesh was represented by his liking for cigarettes and spirits. So 'I have today smitten that immense serpent . . . and for six months no spirits at all and only 15 cigarettes a day. Terrible work with that snake. However, there is the pledge for six months.'[11]

The ship's slow passage through the Suez Canal moved him to reflections in conflict with the imperial strategy of his day. Malta, the Canal, the whole Mediterranean were, he argued, useless to Britain, since the Canal could easily be blocked by the sinking of a single ship, and the Mediterranean was a saucer dominated by the powerful nations along its rim. The only safe route to India and the Far East was by the Cape, to secure which coaling stations and naval bases should be established in the Indian Ocean, especially in Diego Garcia. Gordon was a 'blue water' strategist, and had the habit of being right in the long run.

After many a Communion, he could report to Augusta that he had kept intact his pledge to give up spirits. But it had been a grim struggle, for 'I am always open to attack on that flank . . . So today I have given it up altogether and mean D.V. to take no wine at all. Next Sunday is another Comn, and if God wills I hope to offer up another victim, but I am not sure what. It will be with respect to smoking.' Actually the next sacrifice, a very great one, was the English newspapers, for 'as long as we prefer the paper of today to the Bible, things are wrong with us, yet I greet the paper with greater joy than my Bible.' With the newspapers he hoped would go his passion for politics.[12]

The social life of Mauritius was hateful with its garden parties, archery parties, lawn-tennis parties and dinner parties. Militarily it was a dead-end. The whole concept of dumping 400 men in the middle of the Indian Ocean to defend Mauritius, the Seychelles and Chagos Islands was ludicrous; it was a job for the Navy. But the 400 men were commanded by a seventy-year-old veteran retained, apparently, for the sole purpose of depriving him of command-pay. Chinese Gordon's more humble task, as officer commanding a detachment of Royal Engineers, was the maintenance and repair of barracks, drains, ablutions and latrines. 'My dear Elphin,' he wrote to the man whose place he had so quixotically taken, 'it is only fair to let you know what you have escaped. They say that H.R.H. in one of his furies with someone said to the Adjutant General, "Send him to hell." The A.G. said, "We have no station there, Your Royal Highness." At which H.R.H. replied, "Then send him to Mauritius." ' They could not even manage, in this military backwater, a simple ceremonial parade: the General appeared wearing his cocked hat back-to-front. 'I thought the R.E. were the only people who did these things.'[13]

Nevertheless even here he could find things to interest him, and was soon absorbed in botanical and biblical research. These led him to report with modest satisfaction to Waller, 'You will be interested to hear that I can show that the District and Garden of Eden are near Seychelles.' (Five years earlier he had placed them in the vicinity of Lake Albert; and one suspects that, had he been posted to Ceylon, Malta or New Zealand, there too he would have located the Garden.) More specifically, the site of Man's Creation and Fall was Praslin, a volcanic island in the Seychelles group.

Gordon's theory,[14] which has failed to gain general scientific acceptance, was based on the remarkable similarity between the ripe fruit of the Coco de Mer, a gigantic palm-tree, and Eve's *pudenda*. This, then, was the Tree of Knowledge of Good and Evil. The Breadfruit, with its equally striking resemblance to Adam's organ, was clearly the Tree of Life. And both are native to Praslin Island. To clinch the case, he found on Praslin a small serpent.

It was all worked out in talks and correspondence with W. Scott, Superintendent of the Royal Botanical Gardens at Pamplemousses, clarified by maps, sectional diagrams, anatomical sketches of Eve's reproductive system executed with rather less precision, and enlarged photographs of the plants. Mysteriously sandwiched between the Jordan valley and the female ovary, tubes, uterus and womb is a description of the development, month by month, of the human foetus: undoubtedly this paper is pregnant with the Great Truths, but without a personal explanation, its significance eludes us.

All these had to be studied prayerfully in the light of Holy Writ. We know, from Genesis iii, 24, that Cherubim with flaming swords were posted at the gate of the Garden to keep the way of the Tree of Life; and there was a close connection (1 Kings vi, 24, 32, 35, and Ezekiel xlv, 18, 19, 23, 25) between Cherubim and palm-trees. The identification of the Breadfruit tree, which is root-propagated, with the Tree of Life was confirmed by Isaiah xi, 1, 'And there shall come forth a rod out of the stem of Jesse, and a branch shall grow out of his roots.' Moreover the Breadfruit was made up of many flowers or fruits, and yet was one, as in 1 Corinthians x, 17, 'For we being many are one bread and one body.' But was the flower of the Breadfruit male, female or hermaphrodite? Scott must look into this. Scott too must put him in touch with the Liverpool doctor who had examined a pregnant man.

Gordon's discoveries made 'a long story', with little bits of evidence fitted into one another and cemented by faith into an edifice of revealed truth. But eventually he had 'pretty well settled the site of Eden of the Garden and the Trees of Knowledge and Life'. Moreover, to cap it all, 'Milton wonderfully works it to my idea.'

> And all amid them stood the Tree of Life
> High eminent, blooming ambrosial fruits
> Of vegetable gold.

One may, perhaps, surmise a connection between these researches and Gordon's demi-official recommendation that the Seychelles, an up-and-coming colony, be separate from the Mauritius, 'played-out and over-officialed'. But before he could pursue further this hare, he was promoted to major-general, on 24 March 1882. Mauritius was a colonel's command, so General Gordon had to go.

At this juncture the Government of the Cape invited him to take up an unspecified post at an unspecified salary and settle the Basuto question. So, without quibbling, to the Cape he went as Commandant-General of the Colonial Forces. Having failed in his attempt to secure a cheap passage in a British India steamship (he was always asking Mackinnon for reduced passages), he travelled on a 300-ton sailing ship, a nightmare voyage through monsoon storms, with sea-water in the drinking tank and the bilge stinking of decayed sugar. 'I am not generally sick at sea, but I was literally dead.'

14

♠ THE BASUTO PROBLEM

♠ Gordon arrived at Cape Town on 3 May 1882 and was immediately bidden to dinner by the Governor, Sir Hercules Robinson. It was a bad start, made worse by his treading on his hostess's train and inadvertently calling her Lady Baker, 'a person she hates'.

Already he had formed strong opinions on South Africa. The Boers, who had recently thrashed a British army at Majuba, were men after his own heart, pious, frugal and brave: he regretted having signed an Address of the Anti-Slavery Society exposing their shortcomings. He admired the colonists too. As for the natives, they had been badly treated and promises made to them had been broken.

In exile at Cape Town was Cetewayo, the Zulu King. A call on him was practically obligatory for English visitors. Like many others, this visitor was captivated by Cetewayo's jovial charm: 'When I told Cetewayo . . . that he must have hope, with a deep "Ah!" he pointed upwards. He is a fine savage.'

So were the Basutos,* that was half the trouble. They had adopted with some success the horses, rifles and tactics of the Boers, with whom they had for thirty years been at intermittent war, losing their lowlands but holding their mountain fastnesses. In 1869, at the request of the great Basuto King Mosheshwe, the British Imperial Government (which he regarded as the lesser evil) had annexed Basutoland lest it be absorbed by the Orange Free State; but in 1871, for administrative convenience, had handed it over to Cape Colony. The Basutos learned the use of the plough, worked in the diamond fields and prospered, spending much of their wealth on the purchase of rifles. But with Mosheshwe's death, tribal discipline disintegrated. This alarmed the Cape Government, which in 1879 imposed on the Basutos direct rule by magistrates and tried to disarm them. The disarming failed: the Basutos kept their rifles. Thereafter it was government policy to reduce them by exploiting the jealousies of the sons of Mosheshwe. The most formidable, Masupha,

* Or, more accurately, the Sotho.

remained truculent and suspicious, in possession of Mosheshwe's old stronghold on the flat-topped mountain known as Thaba Bosiu.

What exactly Gordon was to do about the Basutos was not quite clear. Had he been summoned to suppress a smouldering rebellion, or in the more congenial role of peacemaker? He assumed the latter, and at Communion 'asked Christ that He should take the post of Commandant-General, and that I should be passive in the matter'.

Passivity, however, was not his most conspicuous quality. Twenty-three days after arriving at Cape Town, and without setting foot in Basutoland, he sent the Colonial Government a *resumé* of his views. The general sense of these was that the Imperial Government had twice taken the Basutos under its protection but had handed them over, without consultation, first to the Boers, then to the Cape Government. This should now be remedied by calling a national *pitso* (assembly) to air the tribe's grievances and hear how they wished to be governed.

To Thomas Scanlen, the Premier of the Colony, it must have seemed that St George, invited to slay the dragon, was instead lecturing the Princess on the error of her ways. It was one of those occasions when Gordon failed to see the trees for the wood. The trouble with the Basutos was not whether they should be ruled by one set of white men rather than another, but dislike of being ruled and taxed by any white magistrates, aggravated by the dynastic quarrel between the Paramount Chief, Letsie, and his younger brother, Masupha.

While the Cape Government was digesting his memorandum, Gordon turned to his duties as commandant-general of the Colony's forces. It was his foible at that time seldom to wear uniform, and he astonished the Cape Mounted Rifles by reviewing them dressed in a shabby frock-coat and top-hat. His informality was embarrassing to his Military Secretary, Colonel Ffolliott, whom Gordon not merely convinced of the indwelling of God, but even, by fining him one shilling for each offence, broke of the habit of repeatedly addressing his chief as 'Sir'. After running up a fine of fifteen shillings, 'Ffolliott lost all respect for me, and I can never get a "Sir" out of him.'

He deplored the formation of the Cape Infantry Regiment, and deprecated as costly and useless the Cape Field Artillery. The only effective local force was the Cape Mounted Rifles (though in 'a semi-insubordinate state, officers and men'). A Frontier Police Force should be formed, partly officered by natives – a startling suggestion, on which he later had second thoughts.

He was asked to investigate and report on the activities in Transkei of the trek-Boers who had no business to be there. He took the opportunity to recommend a wholesale reconstruction of the Native Administration, and to embody in his reports some scathing criticism of native policy, without consulting Mr Sauer, the Secretary for Native Affairs. 'Much in these memorandums,' he confessed to the Colonial Secretary, 'is out of my sphere as Commandant-General; but perhaps you will excuse this.' The Colonial Secretary may have excused it, but it is doubtful if Mr Sauer did. Nor did Gordon neglect the spiritual welfare of the Boers. Years ago, in Gravesend, he had had one of his tracts translated into Dutch. He had copies sent out by Augusta and scattered them round the countryside for the God-fearing burghers to peruse.

In July he sent the Prime Minister (again by-passing Sauer) fresh proposals on Basutoland. These, too, were rejected, but it was agreed that Gordon and Sauer should together visit Basutoland and examine the situation. They arrived in early September, in the depths of winter, with snow on the heights. Gordon distributed to the shivering Basutos blankets purloined from government stores, and airily brushed aside the protests of Arthur Garcia, the Paymaster-General, who had to account for them: 'Don't be angry, my dear fellow, I gave them to these poor natives who had so little clothing.' Garcia was not angry, and remained Gordon's firm friend.

Gordon produced yet another memorandum, recommending that the head of the magisterial administration be sacked; that Paramount Chief Letsie should not be pressed, as was present government policy, into action against his younger brother, Masupha; that the Cape Mounted Rifles be withdrawn and replaced by Basuto police; and that Basuto 'loyals', who had supported the Government in the recent rebellion, be compensated for their losses and resettled elsewhere.

The last proposal was uncontroversial, and a commission was formed to assess compensation. One member of the commission was a brash thirty-year-old businessman named Cecil Rhodes. The man of God and the man of mammon got on well, especially when Rhodes agreed that the Basutos had a perfect right to buy rifles with the money they had earned in the diamond diggings. When the commission's work was completed, Gordon suggested that they remain and work in Basutoland together, but it was too small a field for Rhodes' ambition. 'There are very few men,' said Gordon, 'to whom I would have made such an offer, but of course you will have your way. I never knew a man so strong for your opinion; you think your views are always right.' Rhodes, in turn, thought that Gordon was 'a ready listener, but self-willed to a degree . . . Extraordinary man – and yet so practical.' He could not understand anyone being indifferent to money. Gordon had once refused a roomful of Chinese gold; Rhodes would have taken it, 'and as many roomfuls as they offered me. It's no use having big ideas if you haven't the cash to carry them out.'

When Rhodes heard of Gordon's death he repeated again and again, 'I am sorry I was not with him, I am sorry I was not with him.' Yet there was no money to be made in Khartoum.

To tackle the central problem of Masupha, Gordon offered to go to Thaba Bosiu and have a straight talk with him. To this Sauer agreed on condition – specifically confirmed by Gordon in writing – that he went in a private capacity with no power to make promises: he was simply to discover whether Masupha would now accept government authority, personified by a magistrate, collect and pay his clan's hut-tax and generally behave himself.[1] Gordon arrived at Masupha's stronghold on 25 September, accompanied by Garcia and by a missionary named Keck, acting as interpreter.

Gordon's first move, clearly in his *official* capacity, was to state unequivocally that he would never fight the Basutos; nor would the Paramount Chief, Letsie, be 'set against' Masupha. 'So now, after this, my written promise, you may trust me that I will not break my word.' But the Government must remain in Basutoland to protect it against Boer encroachments, and the Basutos must pay for this protection. 'I think Government wants you to take a magistrate, and to order your people to pay a hut-tax.' Switching now to his private capacity he added:

Now this which I now write is from myself and not from Government. (a) I think you can ask the Government to give you the magistrate you like. (b) I think you can ask the Government to order this magistrate to consult with you on all large matters . . . (c) I think you can ask the Government to let you and the magistrate agree how to spend the hut-tax money . . . (d) I think you can ask the Government to let you arrange about the Police on the Free State frontier, with the magistrate.

These observations were submitted to Masupha in writing on 25 September and verbally on the 25th, translated by Keck. It is clear that Gordon was in breach of his agreement with Sauer: he was, for at least part of the time, speaking in his official capacity; he did make specific promises; he was in fact negotiating with Masupha, which he was not authorized to do. As Keck had no English, Garcia no French, and neither he nor Gordon a word of Basuto, it is possible that there was some failure in communication. It is unlikely that Masupha appreciated the distinction between General Gordon speaking in an official capacity, and the same person speaking as a private individual. In any case, assured that no action would be taken to coerce him, Masupha was prepared to spin out negotiations indefinitely, and returned no answer.

Sauer had for some time, most recently on 16 September in Gordon's presence, been upbraiding Letsie for his flabbiness towards Masupha and urging him to exert his authority. Gordon did not approve of this pressure on Letsie, and did not believe that Letsie would come up to scratch. But he knew of it: in an undated note he wrote, 'I knew Sauer was going to try the useless expedient of an expedition against Masupha.'² It was therefore, to say the least, imprudent to promise Masupha that Letsie should not be 'set against' him. On 26 September Sauer heard that Letsie was now sending an armed force under his son, Lerothodi, to bring Masupha to heel. Sauer did not believe that Gordon would succeed in talking Masupha into obedience: if Gordon failed, coercion would be necessary and the Paramount Chief must be supported. He could not hold Lerothodi's commando for more than a day, as he could not feed them: if they dispersed, it would be difficult to assemble them again. So he wrote at once, warning Gordon of what was happening, and specifically asking him to be out of Thaba Bosiu *by the following morning, the 27th*, so that he would be clear before Lerothodi arrived. To Garcia he wrote, 'Don't let Masupha prolong negotiations and so destroy the chance of getting Letsie to act. Impress this upon the General. If Masupha refuses to meet the General, you should leave. If he agrees to a meeting, he must do so at once.'

Gordon replied, through Garcia, that he would wait for an answer from Masupha until 9 a.m. on the 27th, and if none was received, he would then leave. He informed Masupha of this intention. During the night of the 26–7th Masupha heard of the approach of Lerothodi, and wrote to Gordon expressing astonishment as he had, he asserted, decided to agree to the Government's terms. But it was too late: Gordon replied that he would leave at 9 a.m. and at 9 a.m. he left.

Gordon was furious at what he saw as Sauer's bad faith, and slammed in his resignation. When he saw Sauer at the railway station, he said very loudly, 'I am not going into the same carriage as that fellow'; at the East London hotel, he refused to sleep under the same roof. His biographers have all more or less accepted his version of the incident, and some suggest that Sauer plotted to have him murdered by Masupha. But the Cape Government records show that Gordon's account is by no means accurate, and there were faults on both sides. Sauer was a decent, mediocre Cape Liberal opposed to whittling away native rights, whose main fault was indecision. He did not deceive Gordon, or arrange that Gordon deceive Masupha; for their meeting took place on condition that Gordon make no promise; and when Gordon set off for Thaba Basiu, Sauer had no idea that Lerothodi's commando had been mobilized. It can be argued that he should have delayed Lerothodi for more than one day, but that was the worst with which he can be charged. Gordon undertook in writing not to make any promises, and to speak only in his private capacity; and under both heads he breached the agreement in letter and in spirit. He did not heed Sauer's warning to be clear by the morning of 27 September. If he was in danger, he was to blame for it; but Sauer categorically denied in the Cape Parliament that Gordon was in danger; and Garcia, Gordon's fervent admirer, in several letters written during and after the mission to Masupha, does not suggest that he apprehended any peril.

It was certainly not the first, and arguably not the last occasion on which Gordon turned a blind eye to instructions of which he disapproved. Of course he did so from the best motives. He believed that his way of dealing with Masupha was better than Sauer's. He was sure he had done his best for the Colony.

To his letter of resignation Scanlen replied, 'After the intimation that you would not fight the Basuto, and considering the tenor of your communications to Masupha, I regret to record my conviction that your continuance in the position you occupy would not be conducive to the public interest.' After justifying his actions in a telegram of some 800 words, Gordon departed in a huff because it was 'not possible to do anything with such a weak, vacillating Government'. The Cape ministers, he told Augusta, were 'conies' (his favourite pejorative term). 'We are a pig-headed race, we Gordons . . . What a queer life mine has been, with these fearful rows continually occurring.'[3]

15

REFLECTIONS IN PALESTINE

On leaving the Cape in October 1882, Gordon reverted to his idea of service under the King of the Belgians. In July Mackinnon had sent a glowing account of the Congo – based on a talk with King Leopold – as throbbing with purposeful development, a-glow with good intentions; and 'His Majesty is more impressed than ever that you alone of all the men he knows anything of can control and work out the great problem of African civilization towards which his aims and efforts have been directed.' Why King Leopold sought Gordon as governor-general is a mystery: perhaps he wanted a respectable cover for the infamous deeds of his company's servants, or perhaps he wanted to stop the export of slaves whom he needed to collect rubber. Gordon seems to have come round to the idea that an international flag was practicable. He agreed to enter the Congo service when the question of a flag was in a fair way to settlement, and there the matter rested.

In London he breakfasted with the Blunts, fellow eccentrics on whom he made a very good impression. To Lady Ann he seemed 'in perfect possession of perfect commonsense. So much has been said to imply his being "touched" in the head that I put this down as being a very distinct impression.' She added, however, 'He does not, I think, quite know the state of feeling in the Mohamadan world.'[1]

Gordon could now fulfil a cherished ambition, to spend a year in research in the Holy Land. Travelling on a reduced fare by courtesy of Mackinnon, on 16 January 1883 he landed at Jaffa and pushed straight on up to Jerusalem. He rented a house at Ain Karin, a village among rocky hills some three miles west of the city, and settled into what was perhaps the happiest year of his life. He was his own master, with no helpless subordinates; he acquired two good horses; there were no dinner parties, fêtes, receptions or other manifestations of the world. He followed an equable routine of prayer and Bible-reading, purposeful walks and rides round Jerusalem and its environs, designing the Nablus Mission house, and discussions on great matters with a few kindred souls.

He was not the only eccentric in Jerusalem. There was an American commune of what would now be called hippies, addicted to spirit-writing, anointing one another with oil, and feeding the poor on such a scale that they ran into financial difficulties. There was a retired sea-captain, claiming to be Christ risen from the dead, who spent his time carrying a nine-foot cross round the Holy City, and preaching when the spirit moved him. There was a seventy-year-old American who was convinced that he was immortal. Miss Poole, 'the Prophetess', went in for astrology and painting 'most extraordinary' pictures. Among their idiosyncrasies, Gordon's passed almost unnoticed.

To the French Consul his activities were incomprehensible, except as cover to the most nefarious francophobic machinations. He had to shake off the Consul's spy by walking rapidly down to Haifa where he dropped in on Laurence Oliphant, an old acquaintance, and in a single evening argued with equal conviction, and equally convincingly, that China would never find salvation until every foreigner had been expelled, and that the only hope for China was a foreign occupation, the first task of which would be to hang every mandarin in his own courtyard, beginning with 'that scoundrel' Li Hung Chang.[2]

In July he moved down to Jaffa, renting a house near Simon the Tanner's. He rode out to the site of Coeur de Lion's victory at Arsouf – capital cavalry country; visited the place where Peter had had the vision of clean and unclean beasts; identified the exact spot where Elijah had slain the prophets of Baal. There was at Jaffa a clergyman of the Church Missionary Society, a Jewish convert named Schapiro, whom Gordon at first found a splendid man, quite after his own heart. But, alas, by November Schapiro was 'not a worthy man; how very easily I am deceived, for all my experience!' Another burden at Jaffa was his correspondence with an ardent admirer, Mrs Surtees Allnatt, who bombarded him with letters though he besought Augusta's help in choking her off. Finally she sent him a splendid dressing case, worth £8 or £10 – 'I am greatly distressed by it.'

Every now and then he gave up all hindrances to a spiritual life: 'Smoking knocked off, never D.V. to be resumed.' Like many a sportsman in middle age, he felt a sudden aversion to killing birds. 'My servant brings up a hen-partridge, alive . . . Its wings were tied, it had been captured on its nest, such beautiful bright eyes and red bill, such a beauty. I took it to cut the string, and whilst doing so, I felt it struggle, then flutter, and it was dead. I felt it very much, and do still, though I am accustomed to death and think it no loss; however, that day the gun was doomed.'

He investigated the possibilities of a canal from the Mediterranean to the Jordan, replacing the politically sensitive Suez Canal. 'If the Palestine Canal is completed, we shall abandon Egypt, which will then get self-government, and will succeed under God's blessing for it.' For a paltry £10½ millions Britain would be rid of an intractable problem. He found authoritative backing for his ideas in Zachariah xiv, 8: 'And it shall be in that day that living waters shall go out from Jerusalem; half of them towards the former sea and half of them towards the hinder sea.'

He spent hours every day on his correspondence – writing to some of topography, to others of theology, and not forgetting Capsune, the boy he had rescued from the slavers, now established in England with Miss Felkin, sister of a Uganda missionary:

You are one of Jesus's lambs, and He lives in your little body. Take care of it. Ever since you met me, every day I prayed for you . . . every day I have remembered the little chap who stood under the trees and told me of the slavers . . . My dear little fellow, pray for me and you will give me more than all the millions of the earth . . . I see your little brothers often in their black satin coats, some of them come from Darfur and . . . they make me think of you. I am glad to hear of your canary and hope it will get tame. I am also glad you get on with your lessons.

But Gordon could never be happy unless he was busy, and what made him happy in Palestine was his absorption in several important problems:

1. The place of the Crucifixion.
2. The place of the Holy Sepulchre.
3. The boundary between the tribes of Benjamin and Judah.
4. The relation between the various Gibeons of the Bible.

The Crucifixion, he decided, had taken place outside the north wall on a hill shaped like a skull, to which he referred as 'skull hill' or 'the Rock'. (Golgotha, he discovered, meant 'the place of the skull'.) 'I think that the Cross stood on the top of the skull hill' whence 'the whole city would be embraced by those outstretched arms. "All day long have I stretched forth my hands onto a wicked and gain-saying people." (Romans x, 21 and Isaiah lxv, 2) . . . *There* Jesus suffered without the gate.' To Oliphant and later to the King of the Belgians he expounded this theory with the aid of a plaster model.

Furthermore (it was wonderful how all the secondary evidence dove-tailed in so neatly if viewed with the eye of faith and a detailed knowledge of the Bible),

the little hill on the side is just the place where the woman would look on afar off, ready to run away by the road if molested . . . Evidently Peter had been hanging about the place of Crucifixion and burial the whole day of the Resurrection, and then took off to Emmaus as an out-of-the-way place. He would not like to go to Bethany where he was so well known to be connected with Jesus. All seems so natural that seeing it is a real pleasure . . . Put yourself in the actors' skins and you will feel as Peter and the others did, and know their motives. The situation at Emmaus quite suits the sort of place a timid man would go to for hiding – a wild, stony country with caverns all about.

The Holy Sepulchre was not, as was generally believed, 200 yards east of the Rock, but a similar tomb in what had become the Russian Garden.

Gordon was not the first to place Calvary on the Rock, and a respectable body of expert opinion supports this view. Less support is given to his identification of the Tomb, though people who have visited it testify to a strong feeling that this is a holy place. Nevertheless 'Gordon's Calvary' and 'Gordon's Tomb' became the subjects of serious controversy among savants.

'The ravines round Jerusalem,' he reflected, 'are full of the dust of men, for over a million bodies must have been slain there. What a terrific sight the Resurrection there will be!'

The maps produced by the Palestine Exploration Society placed Jerusalem entirely within the boundaries of the tribe of Benjamin. 'All Bible maps are wrong!' The experts might divide Jerusalem as they liked, 'but it is not Scripture that the Temple, which was the type of Our Lord's body, should be in Benjamin, for He was of the tribe of Judah . . . It is wrong doctrine.' With support from 2 Kings xiv, 13 and 2 Chron. xxv, 23, Gordon divided the Holy City along the line of the brook Gihon, allocating the eastern, and holiest half, to Judah, the western half to Benjamin. 'I think this settles the boundaries; but it took a lot of study, and was at first seen only spiritually.' In other words, he intuitively decided that Jerusalem *must* be so divided, and then sought evidence to justify his conclusion, a process of rationalization to which he was addicted.

As for the numerous Gibeons, they presented no problem to a Royal Engineer. The most cursory study of the books of Joshua, Judges, Chronicles, Samuel, Isaiah and Kings, read with the Septuagint and Josephus, proved that the Palestine Exploration Society had got it all wrong, scattering Gibeons all over the map. Gordon perceived that there was but one Gibeon, and that, naturally enough, was near Jerusalem.

It was extraordinary what deep truths one could unearth about Jerusalem. There was, for instance, the vexed question of the Ark. It was constructed, according to Moslem tradition, at Ain Judeh, twenty miles from Jerusalem. How could it possibly have drifted thence to Ararat? Genesis xi, 2 implies that on disembarking from the Ark, the passengers journeyed eastwards into Mesopotamia, but Mesopotamia lies south of Ararat: it is, however, east of Jerusalem. Shem, alias Melchizedek, was not likely to have moved far from where the Ark rested, and he met Abraham at Shanek, near Jerusalem. Ham named his son Canaan. 'My idea,' explained Gordon, 'is that the Dead Sea was originally a bed of rock-salt and gypsum, and that when the Flood came, the extra weight broke through the crust, and the superfluous waters made their way into the bowels of the earth.' (According to the Koran, Noah prayed, 'Oh Earth, swallow up thy waters!') So with water escaping as though through the plug-hole of a bath, all floating objects would be drawn towards it, 'and one notable floating object was the Ark'. Clearly, then, Noah's dove picked up a twig from the now exposed Mount of Olives, and the Ark drifted from Ain Judah eastward until it grounded on Mount Zion. Moreover the Koran records the tradition that Adam's body was carried in the Ark; so it was highly probable that the Father of Mankind was buried on the Rock, at the precise spot where the Cross was to stand, and that the sacred blood soaked through the soil onto his skull, as in the original rendering of Ephesians v, 14, 'Awake, thou Adam, and the Messiah will touch thee.'

From these comparatively well-trodden fields of research, Gordon launched happily forth into the wildest seas of speculation. Before the Creation, the Earth, a hollow ball filled with fire, was encased in a cocoon of water which was Satan's particular domain. The Creation was God's invasion of Satan's kingdom, 'the calling up of a dead world out of the grave of the waters'. The first dry land to emerge from the waters was the Rock. God's voice was first heard on the Rock, and at that the Devil beat a precipitate retreat to the point furthest from the Holy Place, viz latitude 31°47'S., longitude 44°45'W., close to Pitcairn Island, where, significantly enough, the *Bounty* mutineers were to settle. Adam was created out of clay from the Potter's Field, adjacent to the Rock, and migrated to the Garden of Eden on Praslin Island. But there Satan shrewdly counter-attacked by persuading Eve to eat of the Forbidden Fruit. After the Fall, Adam and his erring wife returned to till the earth out of which he was taken, bearing within them the taint of evil. But in the last days the Devil and all his seas will be sucked down, through the Dead Sea, into the centre of the earth and there perpetually imprisoned; and the New Jerusalem, constructed by celestial hands, will be established around the Rock.

If Satan's base was in the deep waters, where, exactly, did God reside? In every man, to be sure, but where, so to speak, was his H.Q.? This question Gordon answered in a long letter to Scott. The ground-plan of the Temple of Solomon was in the shape of a shadow cast by the Cross. It was, indeed, the shadow of the True Cross vertical and invisible to our eyes.

Now here is an interesting point. Our Lord is a man, as a Man He must be in some definite place. Where is He? He rose and ascended from Mt Olives. He descends (Zach. xiv) on Mt Olives. Where is He now? He is in the *true* Temple above the Altar, just over Jerusalem. You are at Port Louis, I am here, A is at Cape of Good Hope, B is in America. All prayer must pass by and through Him. He is above Jerusalem where Stephen last saw Him, all our prayers ascend by and through Jerusalem as per sketch.

The sketch showed the Temple as a sort of celestial telephone-exchange, with one line going up to heaven, others radiating out to Mauritius, the Cape and the United States.

It is impossible in one book to do full justice to his discoveries or to give more than a summary of his more remarkable conclusions. His investigations were not confined to history and topography. Those more narrowly theological were set out in his own slim volume, *Reflections in Palestine*, published during the following year while the world waited with bated breath for news from Khartoum. In this little book he took far more pride than in all the big books describing his exploits in far-flung lands.

Eve's taking of the Forbidden Fruit he saw as a sort of diabolic Eucharist, an evil mirror-image of the Communion. It was

a fellowship with Satan . . . communion with him . . . There was a real, spiritual entry of Satan into her body by the fact of her eating. Place before a child 999 lozenges and prohibit the eating of one, and the child will yearn after that one. And so with Eve . . . She trusted in herself, distrusted God, and so communed with Satan . . . and acquired his *attributes of evil*, viz she was poisoned by evil introduced into her actual body . . . the fruit was the vehicle of the virus of evil.

(Almost as an afterthought he adds, 'In speaking of Eve so often, I mean Adam as well.') Moreover, since one human body is as like another as one Enfield rifle is to another, the virus of evil was inherited from Eve by *all* her descendants. To Eve's poison the antidote is the Bread and Wine of the Communion. These Gordon believed to be literally the Body and Blood of Christ, not by transubstantiation but descending in minute particles from Heaven. To the obvious quantitative argument he had a ready retort: the blood of an average man contained 3,840,000,000,000 corpuscles and one corpuscle was sufficient to establish a communion of blood and body.

If his religious opinions were held with the utmost earnestness, his expression of them could be flippant. Slapping a friend on the back, he would ask, 'Well, how is the Tabby?' – the Tabernacle of the body in which God dwelt.

Agag, however, would not be denied, and was dragging him back onto the 'tram of the world'. Besides, on half-pay he was finding his long holiday expensive, and had to borrow £250 from Mackinnon. Among all Gordon's inconsistencies, few are stranger and less in character than his exploitation of this obliging shipping magnate. In October Mackinnon reminded him of his half-promise to King Leopold, and although the question of an international flag was unresolved, he applied to the War Office for permission to enter the Congo service. This was refused. A certain confusion was caused by the Turkish telegraphist's error in writing 'decides to sangdon' instead of 'declines to sanction'; but when this was corrected, Gordon determined none the less to ask King Leopold to guarantee his pension should he defy the War Office and resign his commission.

With this intent he left Palestine for Brussels on 18 December 1883. When Oliphant asked if he would be staying at the royal palace in Brussels, 'Certainly not,' replied the Mountebank playing the Cynic for all it was worth. 'I shall stay at a hotel, I don't want the King's servants to see my old comb.'

16

THE EXPECTED MAHDI

During Gordon's four-year absence there had been great changes in Egypt and the Sudan. In September 1881, Arabi Pasha, a colonel of *fellahin* stock and nationalist convictions, had by a military coup compelled the Khedive Tewfik to install a government of the Army's choice. Nine months later, following a massacre of Christians in Alexandria and obvious preparations to bottle up the British and French warships which were in the harbour, the British Admiral bombarded the town. At this show of strength the Khedive dismissed Arabi Pasha and Gladstone reluctantly authorized a British expedition under Wolseley to protect the Khedive against his army and foreigners against the mob. On 13 September 1882, Wolseley routed Arabi Pasha's spectacularly incompetent army at Tel-el-Kebir, and Britain began an occupation of Egypt which, intended originally to be very brief, was to last for seventy years. With the French withdrawing and the Sultan declining to intervene, the British Government found itself saddled with a responsibility for propping up the Khedive which it did not want but could not discard.

This came at an inopportune time, for there was trouble in the Sudan. It originated from a man of whom Gordon had probably never heard, Mohamad Ahmed ibn Abdullah, son of a Dongolawi Sharif* boat-builder, who was living as a hermit on the island of Aba, 200 miles up the White Nile from Khartoum. In May 1881, at the age of thirty-eight, after years spent in prayer, fasting, Koranic study and contemplation of the decay of Islam, he had proclaimed himself in a triple role: as the Imam, holding temporal authority over all Moslems; the Successor of the Prophet of God, implying that he had a spiritual authority and a task similar to that of the Prophet in restoring the purity of Islam; and the Mahdi, the Expected One, the eschatological figure whose advent foreshadowed the end of the world in its present state. To all *mudirs* and sheikhs he sent letters (and to the Governor-General a telegram) setting

* The Ashraf (sing. Sharif), descendants of the Prophet, are found in many tribes of Arabia, Sudan and Somalia.

forth his claims and calling for their support because 'whosoever doubts my mission does not believe in God or his prophets, and whosoever is at enmity with me is an unbeliever, and whosoever fights against me will be forsaken and unconsoled in both worlds.'

The messianic belief in a Mahdi is not held by Moslems of the majority Sunni sect which was dominant in Turkey, Egypt and Arabia. But in the Sudan Sufi orders proliferated; their spiritual leaders and teachers known as *fakis*, and their dervish disciples, were numerous and influential, not least because they were exempt from taxation. Among these it was widely believed that in the year 1300 of the Hegira, 1882 of the Christian calendar, the Expected Mahdi would reveal himself. They were therefore predisposed to accept the claim of Mohamad Ahmed, who was himself a member of the Sammani order of Sufis. He came from the west of the Moslem world, not, as had been predicted, from the east; but otherwise he was everything the Mahdi should be – devout, eloquent, virtuous, learned in Islamic lore, descended from the Prophet, of the right age and the right name. He even carried the sign of a mole on the right cheek. There had been other *soi-disant* Mahdis, but none so closely fitting the bill. The Khartoum *ulema* denounced him as an impostor; but the ordinary tribesman was not given to doctrinal hair-splitting, and between the *fakis*, indigenous holy men, and the *ulema*, a Turkish creation (many indeed on the Khedive's pay-roll), there was professional jealousy.

His cause had three main inspirations. By far the strongest was the religious appeal: all who accepted Mohamad Ahmed's claim owed him implicit obedience as Imam, unquestioning belief as Successor to the Prophet; and, of course, their lives, but what were these when the end of the world was nigh and the martyr's reward was eternal bliss? Secondly, there was widespread resentment of the rule of the 'Turks', in which pejorative term were included all non-Sudanese officials. Contemporary Europeans were probably wrong in interpreting this as a reaction against corruption and tyranny: the *fakis*' objection to the *Turkiya* was that it was non-Islamic. True, the Khedive, his ministers and *mudirs* for the most part called themselves Moslems, but the ethos of the *Turkiya* seemed to owe more to European notions than to the *Sheria*, the Moslem Law – witness the European officials in key positions, and the persecution of respectable traders. Thirdly, attacks on the slave-trade had brought economic chaos, bankruptcies and ruin to thousands, and wrecked the way of life of the whole Jalaba community which was particularly numerous among the Mahdi's own tribe, the Dongolawi, and the neighbouring Jaalin.

At the same time the fabric of the state had been first strained by Gordon's tempestuous energy, then weakened by his capricious dismissals of experienced, if corrupt, 'Turks', and their replacement by inexperienced Sudanese and Europeans – the latter totally ignorant of Arabic and the Sudan. The provincial administration, thus weakened in *esprit de corps* and self-confidence, was in no state to face the challenge of the Mahdi; and Gordon's successor, Raouf Pasha, a competent pen-pusher, was afflicted by a nervous paralysis of the will when confronted by a crisis. Finally, the best troops were withdrawn to Egypt by Arabi Pasha, and what was left was an armed rabble.

The Mahdi's support came from three groups: the *fakis* and dervishes who responded to his religious appeal; the riverine tribes whose prosperity had depended largely on the slave-trade; and the Baggara nomads who were basically against any government, which to them meant taxes and the interruption of their agreeable pursuits of raiding and slaving: so when the Mahdi forbade the payment of taxes, the Baggara were unanimously for him. Later, in the eastern Sudan, the nomadic Bija tribes, of which the best known was the Hadendowa, joined him for similar reasons.

Just as Europeans attributed to the Sudanese that abhorrence of the shortcomings of the Khedive's government which they themselves felt, so modern Sudanese nationalists tend to see the *Mahdiya* in terms of modern nationalism, and the Mahdi as the Father of Independence. This is probably an anachronism: it is unlikely that the Mahdi or his followers had any sense of a Sudanese nation. His appeal was both wider – to the whole body of Islam – and narrower – to those tribes and economic groups with special grievances. Driving the Turks from the Sudan was to be merely the first step of a *Jihad* to cleanse Islam of its impurities.

This is reflected in the hierarchy which the Mahdi established and in the battle-order of the Ansar.* Like the Prophet, he appointed four *Khalifs* or Companions to deputize for him. One, the head of the Senussi order, ignored him. The other three were notables of the Baggara, of the Dongolawi, and of those tribes who inhabited the Gezirah plain between the White and Blue Niles. Each was to command a division of the Ansar. The entire Ansar wore as a uniform a patched *jibbah*†, symbol of poverty.

But this was for the future. In May 1881, the newly-proclaimed Mahdi was still on Aba Island, and skippers of government steamers sounded their sirens in salute as they chugged past the abode of sanctity.

In July 1881 the egregious Abou Saoud was sent to Aba Island, with four trusty *ulema*, to point out to the imposter the error of his ways and

---

* The Ansar is the proper term for what Europeans generally called the Dervish army.

† A garment similar to a nightshirt. The patches of black, red, white and yellow symbolized man's four natural colours, of the hair, lips, teeth and nails.

summon him to Khartoum for a wigging. Finding him defiant, they withdrew. Abou Saoud returned in August with 240 soldiers. While these floundered ashore through the mud, they were set on by dervishes armed only with sticks and clubbed to death, save a handful who escaped to the steamer from which Abou Saoud was watching the fray. A minor nuisance had grown into a minor rebellion.

The Mahdi, imitating the Prophet, made his *Hegira* to the Jebel Qadir, a rocky hill in the Nuba mountains of Kordofan, where the Baggara joined him in their thousands. Three punitive expeditions were annihilated, and his rebellion throve on a diet of victory. His forces were strengthened by a contingent of Zebeyr's old *bazingers*, armed with Remingtons, who became the core of the Mahdi's *Jihadiya*, regular black infantry who fought for him as stoutly as they had fought for Zebeyr and the Khedive. In the summer of 1882 the rebels were strong enough to march on El Obeid, administrative centre of Kordofan.

Gordon thoroughly approved of these revolts. He sympathized with Arabi Pasha and denounced the occupation as solely in the bond-holders' interests. He was 'quite comforted about the Sudan. God is working out an intricate scheme . . . but I believe it will be good . . . Wonderful are the works of God in the Sudan. They will get their liberty from the oppressing pashas; He has permitted this revolt, which will end, I believe, in the suppression of the slave-trade . . . I forsaw the Egyptian and Sudan affair and was not listened to.' Not long before he had described Nubar Pasha as a gangster and double-dealer: 'He is my horror.' Now Nubar was 'the only man who can give hope to Egypt and some hope of benefiting the *fellahin*'. The sensible thing was to negotiate with the Mahdi; and, if he proved obdurate, threaten him with a coalition of Sudanese sheikhs.[1]

Before departing to Palestine, Gordon had assured the Foreign Secretary, Lord Granville, that the rebellion was much exaggerated. This was just what Granville wanted to hear, for the Liberal Government were determined not to be involved in an Egyptian responsibility, to be shouldered by the Khedive without help or even advice from Her Majesty's Government.

Gordon's views on the *Mahdiya* were not shared by Sir Charles Wilson, Wolseley's chief intelligence officer, who, to obtain accurate information, sent an officer on a special mission to Khartoum. He was John Donald Hamill-Stewart, an Anglo-Irish major in the 11th Hussars whom Major Herbert Kitchener, R.E. considered 'the finest soldier I ever met'. It is no disparagement of his brother-officers to suggest that Stewart, who had passed first out of Sandhurst, was more intellectually gifted than most. His interests were wider, his experience more varied.

He had made hazardous journeys through Central Asia and Arabia, travelling hard, sleeping on a rug laid on the ground, subsisting on tea, rice, biscuits and the milk and camel-meat of the nomads. Two years as vice-consul in Anatolia had given him a close-up view of Turkish administration. He did not speak much more Arabic than Gordon, but had a knowledge of Turkish. Although he distrusted Gladstone, his politics were distinctly liberal, or at least un-conservative. On the Eastern question he believed that his own job, of propping up and reforming the Turkish empire, was a waste of time. If left to 'stew in their own sauce', the Turks would collapse and 'we should then be at full liberty to give all our sympathy to the rising races.' He was friendly with the anti-imperialist traveller, Wilfrid Scawen Blunt, who stayed with him in Aleppo: as for Lady Ann Blunt, she was 'a clipper, a jolly plucky woman with lots of brain, a good traveller and, withal, exceedingly lady-like . . . I am quite in love with her.'

His report was to cover every aspect of the Sudan administration, civil and military; the slave-trade; the origins and extent of the revolt. He was to draw up a plan for the defence of Egypt proper against a Mahdist invasion. Finally he was to 'examine the possibility of making a strategical frontier by abandoning useless territory' – all this without entering the disturbed districts or taking part in military operations. It was quite a tall order. Stewart, however, was confident that he could carry it out, provided he was not impeded by a useless clutter of officers whose presence would excite in Khartoum 'vain hopes of British military assistance'. His mother was not to be uneasy about him, for 'by the last accounts, the Mahdi's cause is not flourishing'. Actually, it was – largely because the Egyptian troops, with a record of unbroken defeat at his hands, were terrified of his dervish army. Even the officers of the battalion which accompanied Stewart to Khartoum were apprehensive that their powder would turn to water if they fired on those holy men.

Arriving at Khartoum on 16 December 1882, within four days Stewart was recording in his journal his first impressions of the Mahdi's revolt. Like Gordon and most Europeans, he believed that the main cause was misgovernment by Turkish and Egyptian officials: 'Only the worst are sent to the Sudan.' In his belief there was, perhaps, an unconscious element of rationalization, since British intervention in Egypt was justified only by the misdeeds of the pashas. It is by no means certain that the Khedive's Sudan was governed as badly as they believed, or that the Sudanese particularly resented corruption and the liberal use of the *courbach*. The *Turkiya* was odious because it was non-Islamic, and it could not be made acceptable merely by bringing in better officials. Secondly, he attributed the revolt to the partial suppression of the slave-trade, bringing miseries almost as great as those which it set out to cure. The nomads were taxed by collective tribal assessments. It was against all their traditions and instincts to sell cattle and camels to pay taxes, since livestock were the nomad's savings, his earnings and his status symbol. So they raided for slaves among the Negro agriculturalists to the south; merchants paid the tribes' taxes, and then recouped themselves by buying slaves from them and selling these at a handsome profit. But Gordon's activities had upset these arrangements; the *mudirs* had been obliged to collect taxes with the assistance of the infamous Bashi-Bazouks, who applied fiscal pressure by pillage, rape, seizures of cattle, and the *courbach* vigorously applied to the soles of tribal chiefs and elders. Stewart saw that the Mahdi's main military strength lay in the Baggara, and that he was supported by the *fakis* and their dervish followers. But he underestimated the movement's religious inspiration.

He ate his Christmas turkey and plum-pudding at the house of a Greek merchant, sitting beside Abdul Qadir, the Egyptian Governor-General, whom he found to be a very capable man. After dinner they were entertained by the customary display of naked dancing girls: 'The way they waggled their hips was perfectly astounding. Altogether a novel way of spending Xmas.' He had a satisfactory row with Giegler. 'There is nothing like wheeling these gentlemen into line as we say in the army. All or most of these Europeans in the Egyptian service . . . get enormous salaries for which they do absolutely nothing. It is revolting to see these people decorated with orders up to the eyes.'

For the next few weeks Stewart was engaged in his *Report on the Sudan*. Detailed and exhaustive to the last degree, it was an astonishing production for a major of hussars. It concluded with the recommendation that all the provinces south and west of Khartoum should be abandoned: 'I am not altogether sure that it would not in the end be best for all parties if the Mahdi or some other leader were successful, and the Egyptians compelled to restrict their territory to the right bank of the White Nile.'

As for the Khedive's troops, 'I believe an army of old English-women armed with broomsticks would have beaten them . . . You can have no conception of the crass ignorance of the officers, not the faintest idea of drill, manoeuvring or outpost duty. Quite a third of the troops are ignorant of the use of the rifle and would be more formidable if armed with sticks.'

The wisdom of Stewart's advice was emphasized by the fall of El Obeid in January 1883. The black garrison now joined the Mahdi with their Remingtons and modern artillery. But the Egyptian Government, headed by Sherif Pasha, had no intention of giving up the Sudan, which was a source of prestige, if not profit, establishing the Khedive's credentials as an empire-builder. They wished to relieve Abdul Qadir of his military duties by appointing a general to command the troops, with a British chief-of-staff. The most competent Briton in the Egyptian service was Valentine Baker Pasha, Sir Samuel's brother, but as he had been cashiered from the British Army for an alleged indecent assault on a young woman in a railway carriage, it was felt that there might be difficulty in finding British officers on secondment to serve under him. So Sherif Pasha's choice fell on Suleiman Niazi, a miserable old man of seventy-five, to command the troops with instructions to defer always to the mature advice of his Chief-of-Staff, Colonel Hicks, an extinct military volcano retired, none too soon, from the Indian Army. Hicks's leisurely progress brought him early in March 1883 to Khartoum, where he was generally expected (but not by Stewart) to 'wheel the Mahdi into line'. Stewart handed over to him and returned home on leave.

Lord Dufferin, British Ambassador to the Sublime Porte, in Cairo on a watching brief, agreed with Stewart that the south and west of the Sudan be abandoned, but did not press this on Her Majesty's Government. Sherif Pasha did not agree, and urged Hicks to deal with the Mahdi. So on 8 September Hicks, accompanied by 10,000 useless soldiers and an immense quantity of baggage, marched off into Kordofan. On 5 December his rabble was annihilated, he himself being killed with all his officers. In the same week there was a disaster in the eastern Sudan. A retired slave-trader named Osman Digna had declared for the Mahdi and raised in rebellion most of the Hadendowa tribe. These besieged two small forts at Sinkat and Tokar and destroyed an Egyptian force moving out of Suakim to relieve them. This closed the Suakim-Berber route, by which Khartoum could most easily be reinforced.

In September Baring arrived in Cairo as Agent-General and immediately made his weighty presence felt. Still forbidden to advise the Egyptian ministers on the Sudan, he felt no inhibition against warning the British Cabinet that it was impossible to maintain a purely passive attitude and give no advice whatsoever. His opinion was that the Egyptians should 'fall back on any points on the Nile they can hold with confidence'. Granville merely replied that there were no troops available to help the Egyptians who should abandon the Sudan 'within certain limits'. But Baring was still not authorized to press this advice on Sherif Pasha.

To retrieve the situation round Suakim Valentine Baker was sent with 2,500 para-military gendarmerie and 6,000 Sudanese. The latter were to be commanded by Zebeyr, still in Cairo. But to this proposal Gladstone's Cabinet, which had hitherto refused to advise in any way, suddenly objected, out of deference to the anti-slavery lobby. The 6,000 Sudanese, deprived of the only commander in whom they had any confidence, refused to embark for Suakim and had to be rounded up by cavalry and herded aboard like cattle on the way to an abattoir.

British public opinion was confused and divided. In principle, Liberals wanted to get out of Egypt and keep out of the Sudan. They sympathized with the Mahdi as a freedom-fighter. Yet many Liberals, especially those who felt strongly about the slave-trade, doubted whether this policy would really be conducive to the greatest good of the greatest number. Might not some form of British protectorate be best for the natives? With these views many Conservatives agreed, partly from concern for the empire's life-line, partly from a simple wish to paint the map red. But on both sides of the House economy was regarded as a cardinal virtue, and military operations in the Sudan would be expensive. In the Cabinet itself most of these views were held, so its handling of the problem was fumbling and hesitant.

Meanwhile in Khartoum Colonel de Coetlogon, left by Hicks to command the shaky garrison, telegraphed on 26 November 1883 that the town was untenable as there was food for only two months; and Frank Power, a young Dubliner acting as consular agent and *Times* correspondent, wrote of 2,000 soldiers confronted by 300,000 dervishes armed with rifles and artillery. 'It is perfectly useless to hold this place, where the population is a slumbering volcano; the land line of retreat is closed, the river line may be closed tomorrow.'

The prospects for Khartoum were certainly in the long run unhealthy; but it does seem that de Coetlogon and Power over-estimated the immediate danger. There was hardly a dervish nearer than El Obeid, 200 miles away; and Khartoum, with its garrison of 6,000,* had, as Power reported on 19 December and as events were to prove, food for over a year. However the situation was certainly worse than in March when Stewart had recommended a limited withdrawal; so General Sir Frederick Stephenson, commanding the British troops in Egypt, and General Sir Evelyn Wood, Sirdar of the Egyptian Army, recommended a withdrawal to Wadi Halfa and the re-opening of the Suakim-Berber route to facilitate this. On 3 December Baring passed on their views to Granville.

At this point Gordon comes into the picture. He had a large circle of friends, bound to him by correspondence and prayer. They included army officers, evangelical clergymen, African experts, philanthropists and business magnates. Outside these there was a wider circle of admirers, including the Queen and the Duke of Cambridge, who hardly knew him

---

* In early January 1884 three outlying garrisons came in to strengthen the garrison of Khartoum.

but had read of his exploits. This hardly constituted a 'Gordon lobby'; there was no concerted effort to further his interests. But many of his 'fans' had influential connections, and some were compulsive letter-writers to the press. Despite, or because of, his ostentatious avoidance of publicity, Gordon was news. To all his friends and admirers, except perhaps Burton, it was axiomatic that as governor-general he had been a brilliant success; and that because he had abolished the slave-trade (he hadn't) he was universally loved by the Sudanese (he wasn't).

It was therefore not surprising that on 24 November 1883 the Chancellor of the Exchequer, Erskine Childers, should receive letters from two officers of the Royal Engineers: 'There is one man who is competent to deal with the question – Charley Gordon'; and, 'If the Mahdi is a prophet, Gordon in the Sudan is a greater.' The suggestion was passed on to Granville two days before Baring's telegram of 26 November recommending that the Sudan be evacuated. The nation's mood demanded an act of vigour, and the Cabinet's principles were such that action must cost very little and commit H.M.G. to no military adventure. Granville therefore consulted Gladstone. 'Do you see any objection to using Gordon in some way? He has an immense name in Egypt – he is popular at home. He is a strong, but sensible, opponent of slavery. He has a small bee in his bonnet.'[2]

Two ideas are here discernible, which were to govern Cabinet thinking on the Sudan for several weeks: the hope that Gordon's employment would placate public opinion, and the delusion that his name in the Sudan was one to conjure with.

Gladstone being prepared to take a chance on the small bee, Baring was asked on 1 December if Gordon would be 'of any use to you or to the Egyptian Government, and, if so, in what capacity'.

Gordon was the last person Baring wanted at this time, with his unpredictable inspirations, his changes of mind, and his tendency to treat orders as a basis for discussion, to be obeyed if he (and a Friend) happened to approve, otherwise to be evaded or ignored. So he replied that the Egyptian Government thought it unwise to employ a Christian in suppressing a Moslem religious revolt. But he begged Granville to take some positive line with the Egyptian Government: 'At present they are drifting on without any definite or practical plan.'

On 13 December Granville at last authorized Baring to advise a withdrawal to Wadi Halfa, while still refusing any military aid other than keeping open the Red Sea ports. Sherif Pasha, however, refused to take this advice; so on 22 December Baring recommended that Her Majesty's Government insist on the Sudan being abandoned: if Sherif Pasha would not do this, his Ministry must be replaced by one that would. At the same time he made the recommendation, pregnant in misunderstandings and fateful in its consequences, that an 'English officer of high authority' be sent to Khartoum 'with full power to withdraw all the garrisons in the Sudan and make the best arrangements possible for the future government of the country'.[3]

While Baring was awaiting a reply, Power in his consular capacity reported to him that Khartoum might within three days be in rebel hands; and de Coetlogon telegraphed, 'Were we twice as strong we could not hold Khartoum against the country which without a doubt are one and all against us.'

On 4 January 1884, the British Cabinet at last insisted that the Khedive's ministers either carry out the evacuation policy, or forfeit their offices. At this, on the 7th, the Ministry of Sherif Pasha resigned and Nubar Pasha formed a government prepared to evacuate the whole of the Sudan except Suakim.

Gordon had arrived in Brussels on New Year's Day to arrange the terms of his employment in the Congo, including compensation for the loss of his British Army pension. He received there a letter from Sir Samuel Baker, who had written in similar terms to *The Times*, suggesting that he go to Khartoum as British High Commissioner. Perhaps Baker would not have made this approach had he known that Gordon had just written to Felkin's sister, 'I feel for the rebels, and am proud of their prowess, and Our Lord will work good for them out of it.'[4] Citing the warning of 'an inner voice', Gordon refused Baker's suggestion: he was all set to go to the Congo.

Wolseley, the Adjutant-General, was not pleased: 'I hate the idea of your going to the Congo. Our very best man, burying himself among niggers on the Equator. If ever I have the power, the first man I should ask to take employment would be yourself.'[5] (He had the power: he was notorious for packing his staff with his favourites.) He invited Gordon for a talk about the Sudan. *The Times* on 5 January echoed his regrets. But on the 7th Gordon, from Southampton, posted to the War Office his letter of resignation.

On the following day there arrived at Southampton Captain Brocklehurst, one of those on Gordon's prayer-list, who was working at the War Office and was not averse to enlisting press support against what he conceived to be the mistaken policy of Her Majesty's Government. He was accompanied by W. T. Stead, editor of the *Pall Mall Gazette*, whose aim it was to make his paper the voice of God in Britain. Stead persuaded Gordon to give his opinion on the Sudan. Gordon was later to say that he did not then realize that the British Government had decided on evacuation. This seems unlikely, since the *Pall Mall Gazette* on the previous evening, and *The Times* that very morning, had carried the news of Sherif Pasha's resignation and its reason. But he had now formed views on the Mahdi and the Sudan very different from those he had previously expressed; and, not for the first or last time, he intended to use the press to promote these views.

Gordon now declared[6] that the conquest of the Sudan by the Mahdi would inflame the whole Moslem world, and that to concede him this victory was quite unnecessary. The eastern Sudan, between the White Nile and the Red Sea, should and could be held. Nubar should be 'left untrammelled by any stipulation about the evacuation of Khartoum. I imagine he would appoint a Governor-General with full powers and furnish him with £2 million, which would be needed to relieve* the garrisons and quell the revolt.' The sole cause of the rebellion was misgovernment by Egypt: it was entirely wrong to regard the Mahdi as a religious leader . . . he personified popular discontent . . . 'The movement is not really religious but an outbreak of despair . . . The egg of the present rebellion was laid in the three years during which I was allowed to govern the Sudan on other than Turkish principles.'

So far his views were very similar to those expressed by Stewart nine months earlier. But the situation in January 1884, after the destruction of Hicks Pasha's army and the spread of the rebellion to Suakim, was far worse than it had then been.

The real answer to Mahdism, Gordon told Stead, was to quell the revolt and then introduce a new constitution for the Sudan, prohibiting the entry of any Turks or Circassion officials. It ought then to be possible 'to come to terms with the rebels, to grant them an amnesty for the past and security for decent government in the future. If this were done and the government entrusted to a man whose word was truth, all might yet be re-established.'

Evacuation was totally impracticable:

You have 6,000 men in Khartoum. What are you going to do with them? You have garrisons in Darfur, in Bahr-el-Ghazal and Gondokoro.† Are they to be sacrificed? . . . How will you move your 6,000 men from Khartoum – to

---

* Not 'evacuate'.

† The Darfur garrison, under Slatin, had just surrendered, but this was not yet known in Cairo. The Bahr-el-Ghazal garrison had been cut off for several months. The garrison of Equatoria was never seriously threatened. There were also garrisons at Suakim, Sinkat and Tokar on the Red Sea coast, beleaguered by Osman Digna; at Sennaar, 200 miles up the Blue Nile from Khartoum, also besieged; at Qallabat, Gern, Amondib, Senhit, Gedaref and Kassala, along the Abyssinian frontier, of which the two last were besieged; and at Berber, not yet threatened. Their total strength amounted to about 15,000 (without the Khartoum garrison), rather more than half being black, the rest Egyptian.

say nothing of other places – and all the Europeans in that city through the desert to Wadi Halfa? Where are you going to get the camels to take them away? Will the Mahdi supply them? ... You cannot evacuate, because your army cannot be moved. You must either surrender absolutely to the Mahdi, or defend Khartoum at all hazards.

Next day, 9 January, an account of the interview appeared in the *Pall Mall Gazette*, together with a leader headed 'Chinese Gordon for the Sudan': 'We cannot send a regiment to Khartoum, but we can send a man who on more than one occasion has proved himself more valuable in similar circumstances than an entire army. Why not send Chinese Gordon with full powers to Khartoum, to assume absolute control for the territory, to treat with the Mahdi, to relieve the garrisons, and to do what he can to save what can be saved from the wreck in the Sudan?' Most newspapers republished the *Pall Mall Gazette* interview, and *The Times* regretted that Gordon's services had not been secured for the Sudan. The press was in full cry, with one paper after another following Stead's lead.

It has been conjectured that Gordon's friend, Reginald Brett, played a part in these events. As private secretary to the Secretary at War, and with large financial interests in *The Times* and the *Pall Mall Gazette*, he was in a position to act as link between the War Office and the press, but there is no proof that he did so.

It was not the first time that the press had urged the claims of 'the best leader of irregulars the world contains'; but it was the first time those in power paid any attention. The Queen jogged Granville; and Lord Hartington, Secretary for War, suggested to him that as Nubar had replaced Sherif, another approach to Baring might be made. This was done on 10 January, and again Baring, after consulting Nubar, turned Gordon down.

Nubar selected the competent Abdul Qadir to conduct an orderly evacuation. The latter estimated that he would require several thousand camels and seven to twelve months for the job. When he learned of the Government's intention to give advance notice of the operation, he refused to have anything to do with it. Abdul Qadir having declined the poisoned chalice, Baring again, on 16 January, asked for a British officer 'to go to Khartoum with full powers, civil and military, to conduct the retreat'.[7]

Gordon meanwhile had been staying with Barnes near Exeter. He took Communion; startled Bishop Temple by the uncanonical suggestion that Sudanese converts be allowed three wives; and went for a long drive with Barnes and Baker, who again pressed him to go to Khartoum as governor-general if the job were offered him. Never did Agag wrestle so fiercely. Although Gordon made no reply, 'his eyes flashed and an eager expression passed over his face.' Later that evening he said softly to Barnes, 'You saw me today.' 'You mean in the carriage?' 'Yes; you saw *me* that was myself – the self I want to get rid of.'

But to a Royal Engineer friend he wrote, 'The deed was done, on the 7th January, resigning my commission, so I cannot help it. I also promised the King, and I cannot break my word ... As for Tewfik, I could never serve him, so there is an end of that.' In a letter to *The Times* of the 13th he suggested that a force of 4,000 Turkish reservists and 2,000 Indian troops be placed under Valentine Baker to re-open the Suakim-Berber route.

On 15 January, at Wolseley's invitation, he went to the War Office, ostensibly for a talk on his resignation and pension rights. These had been a worry to Granville and Hartington, who felt that if Gordon lost his pension, the Government would appear to be acting meanly, and it would be 'awkward to quarrel with so deservedly popular a man'. On the 14th Granville had written to Gladstone at Harwarden a long and revealing letter:

There is rather a mess about Chinese Gordon. In the autumn Hartington asked for a Foreign Office opinion whether to give him leave to act in the King of the Belgians' African Association. I gave my opinion against an officer on full pay being connected with this nondescript Association. Hartington accordingly telegraphed 'The Secretary of State declines to sanction the appointment.' Gordon came from Syria and agrees with the King. The result is that Gordon loses his rank and pay in the English Army. On the other hand people are clamouring for Gordon to be sent to Egypt. I have twice asked Baring whether Gordon would be of use. He has agreed with Sherif and now with Nubar to answer in the negative. But it is said that there has been an old quarrel between Baring and Gordon. Wolseley is to see Gordon tomorrow and ask him as a friend what are his views. If he says he cannot go to Egypt, or that he cannot go without a considerable force such as he mentions in a rather foolish letter to *The Times* today, we shall be on velvet. If he says he believes he could, by his personal influence, excite the tribes to escort the Khartoum garrison and inhabitants to Suakim, a little pressure on Baring might be advisable.[8]

Granville was under pressure from Hartington, and Hartington from Wolseley, to send out Gordon; to himself, however, as this letter shows, the ideal solution would not be Gordon proceeding to Khartoum and there solving all problems with neither expense to the British taxpayer nor outrage to the Liberal conscience, but Gordon refusing to go for reasons which could be leaked to satisfy public opinion. But if he did go, Granville contemplated his having some authority in dealing with the tribes.

Gladstone, according to G. W. Smalley, his Private Secretary who knew him well, hated Gordon. They had never met, and there was no discernible reason for this strong prejudice, but something about Gordon put the Prime Minister's hackles up.[9] However, he telegraphed his consent to the proposal.

Wolseley, therefore, at their meeting, first told Gordon that the Government had withdrawn its objection to his serving in the Congo, so there was no need to resign his commission. They then started discussing the Sudan. Gordon insisted that the revolt was caused entirely by Egyptian misrule, and certainly in the eastern Sudan it would fizzle out as soon as the tribes were promised that they would be governed by an English officer independent of Cairo. Wolseley asked, 'What would you do?' Gordon promptly replied, 'I would send myself direct to Suakim without going to Cairo.' At this Wolseley asked if he would be willing to 'go to Suakim to enquire into the condition of affairs in the Sudan'. Gordon assented, adding that, without examining the situation on the spot, he could not now say what he would recommend: it might be a complete withdrawal, or it might be his own appointment as governor-general to restore the situation. On Wolseley's suggestion, Gordon drafted some notes on his proposed mission, the salient points of which were:

'1. To proceed to Suakim and report on the military situation of Sudan and return. Under Baring for orders . . .

2. I understand H.M.G. only wish me to report and are in no way bound to me.'[10]

These instructions, drafted by Gordon himself, fell far short of the governor-generalship for which the press was agitating; of Baring's repeated requests for a qualified officer to conduct the retreat and settle the country; and even of the modest executive functions implied by Granville's letter to Gladstone. But neither the officials at the Foreign Office to which Gordon's notes were immediately conveyed, nor Baring to whom a summary was telegraphed that night, nor Granville who forwarded them to the Prime Minister, nor Gladstone himself remarked on these discrepancies. Gladstone merely warned Granville against getting committed to following Gordon's advice: it must be made quite clear that his mission was only advisory.[11]

Baring erroneously assumed that the proposal to send Gordon was in response to his own latest request for an officer with executive powers. On 16 January he wired a cautious acceptance:

General Gordon would be the best man if he will pledge himself to carry out the policy of withdrawal from Sudan as soon as possible, consistently with saving life. He must also fully understand that he must take his instructions from the British Representative* in Egypt and report to him ... I would rather have him than anyone else, provided there is a perfectly clear understanding with him as to what his position is and what line of policy he is to carry out.

In Baring's own account of these events he states that he added, 'Otherwise not. Failing him, consider Stewart. Whoever goes should be distinctly warned that he will undertake a service of great difficulty and danger.' As these words are not included in the copy of the telegram held in the Public Records Office, they presumably formed part of a private communication to Granville. Granville was glad to get Baring's approval of Gordon: 'He may possibly be of great use and the appointment will be popular with many classes in the country.' Neither Granville nor anyone else noticed that, while the Cabinet intended Gordon's mission to be advisory, Baring assumed it would be executive.[12]

On the 16th Gordon went to Brussels to confirm or extricate himself from his engagement to King Leopold. To Lord Northbrook, First Lord of the Admiralty, he wrote a letter remarkable for its misunderstanding of the situation: 'The Mahdi's kingdom will fall to pieces ere long. The man I most fear is Tewfik, he is a little snake, and Nubar must be the ferret to get rid of him or keep him in order. My instinct tells me this.'[13] He was elated by the prospect of returning to the Sudan on a mission which would be the greatest challenge he had ever met. But he must not count his chickens, and from Dover he scribbled a note begging Wolseley, if any hitch occurred, to 'bury the whole matter of yesterday'; he would not have 'the slightest flutter of hurt about it', and 'it was known to no one outside the War Office but himself.' He then disclosed to Augusta that he might go to the Sudan for a couple of months, not as governor-general, but 'only as a military officer to report on affairs'; she must keep it a dead secret. His mind was set at rest by a telegram from Wolseley on the 17th ordering him to return.[14]

He made his excuses to King Leopold who was 'furious' and was in London by six o'clock next morning. In the highest spirits he sent a note asking Henry to pack his uniforms and sword, a Koran and, significantly, a life of Zebeyr. He had two talks with Wolseley before meeting a Cabinet committee at the War Office at 3.30.

In marvelling at the confusion and cross-purposes which attended the despatch of Gordon to Khartoum, we must remember that there was no Cabinet secretary to take minutes of meetings, no secretariat to ensure that decisions were unambiguous and were translated into action. Indeed ministers were not supposed to take notes of Cabinet proceedings lest

* i.e., Baring himself.

secrecy be compromised. It was therefore not uncommon for ministers to have conflicting ideas of what had been decided.

Gladstone and most ministers being out of town, an *ad hoc* Cabinet Committee met consisting of Granville, Hartington, Northbrook and Sir Charles Dilke (President of the Local Government Board). The departmental responsibilities of the last two seem irrelevant, but no others could be rounded up. Moreover they had sat in December on an informal committee held to discuss the Sudan, so were not wholly unfamiliar with the background. Northbrook was a cousin of Baring. All favoured evacuation, though Hartington had some doubts about its practicability.

Gordon wrote, within the next four days, two accounts of the meeting to Barnes and one to Augusta. Since these do not differ in essentials, it is enough to quote only his longer account, written to Barnes on 22 January:

> Wolseley came for me and took me to the Ministers. He went in and talked to the Ministers and came back and said, 'H.M.G. want you to understand that they are determined to evacuate the Sudan, for they will not guarantee future government. Will you go and do it?' I said, 'Yes.' He said, 'Go in.' I went in and saw them. They said, 'Did Wolseley tell you our ideas?' I said, 'Yes, he said you will not guarantee future government of Sudan and you wish me to go and evacuate it.' They said, 'Yes.' and it was over and I left at 8 p.m. for Calais.[15]

His accounts, and later conversations with Graham and others, leave no doubt that Gordon was under the impression that he was to *conduct* the evacuation; though the day before he had told Augusta that he might be going to *report* on the situation; and he had himself, with Wolseley, drafted his own instructions for a *reporting* mission.

It seems, however, that there was some preliminary conversation, which Granville a week later related to Dilke who had arrived late at the meeting. 'It appeared in his conversation with Wolseley on Tuesday . . . that he was as likely to recommend one course as another when on the spot. I told him that we would not send him out to re-open the whole question, and he then declared himself ready to go out merely to help in the evacuation . . . He is not remarkably precise in conversation, though I found him much more so than Wolseley had led me to expect.'[16]

One can only say that if Gordon was not remarkably precise, nor was Granville: to Dilke he wrote of Gordon being sent 'to help in the evacuation'; but he drafted on War Office paper (and therefore, presumably, immediately after the briefing) a telegram for Baring in which it was stated that Gordon was to

proceed to Suakim to report on the military situation in the Sudan and on the measures to be taken for the security of the Egyptian garrisons ... and of the Egyptian population at Khartoum. He will consider the best mode of evacuating the interior of the Sudan and of securing the safety and good administration by the Egyptian Government of the ports on the Red Sea coast. He will pay special attention to what steps should be taken to counteract the possible stimulus to the slave-trade which may be given by the revolution which has taken place. Colonel [sic] Gordon will be under the orders of H.M.'s Minister* at Cairo and will report through him to H.M.'s Government and *perform such other duties as may be entrusted to him by the Egyptian Government through Sir Evelyn Baring.†*

Similar instructions in writing were later handed to Gordon at Port Said; these, however, left it open to him, if he wished, to go via Cairo to Khartoum.[17]

Thus Granville started by describing Gordon's mission as purely a reporting one; but in the last eighteen words opened the door to unlimited possibilities.

Northbrook wrote immediately to Baring:

The upshot of the meeting was that he leaves by tonight's mail for Suakim to report on the best way of withdrawing the garrisons, settling the country, and to perform such other duties as may be entrusted to him by the Khedive's government through you. He will be under you and wishes it. He has no doubt of being able to get on with you. He was very hopeful as to the state of affairs, does not believe in the great power of the Mahdi, does not think that the tribes will go much beyond their own confines and does not see why the garrisons should not get off. He does not seem at all anxious to retain the Sudan and agreed heartily to accept the policy of withdrawal.[18]

Thus Northbrook's account agreed substantially with Granville's, though adding details which make it clear that there was considerable discussion.

Dilke wrote in his confidential diary for 18 January, 'Cabal at the War Office ... Decided to send Colonel [sic] Gordon to Suakim to report on Khartoum.' Elaborating on this some years later he wrote, 'Gordon stated danger at Khartoum exaggerated, that the Englishmen there had too much whisky. He would be able to bring away the garrisons without difficulty. We decided that he should go to Suakim to collect information and report on the situation in the Sudan. This was the sole decision taken, but it was understood that, if he found he could get across, he should go to Berber.'[19]

Although Dilke stated specifically that 'the sole decisions taken' was that Gordon should go to Suakim and report, and made no mention of

* i.e., Baring.
† Author's italics.

him performing other duties entrusted him by the Egyptian Government, yet there are hints in his account that the ministers envisaged more than merely making a report. Why, otherwise, should Gordon go to Berber? Did anyone, when he spoke of being 'able to bring away the garrisons without difficulty', reply, 'But we're not asking you to bring away the garrisons. We're only asking you to report on how they might be brought away'?

Finally there is Hartington's account, important because he undertook to inform the Prime Minister at Hawarden. He simply repeated what Gordon had told Wolseley three days earlier, enclosing the draft notes Gordon had made on that occasion, which implied that it was an advisory, non-executive, reporting mission. To this Gladstone telegraphed his consent – but he consented to Hartington's version of the ministers' decision, which made no mention of conducting the withdrawal, settling the country, or performing other duties entrusted to him by the Egyptian Government through Baring. When, therefore, Gladstone later charged Gordon with going far beyond his brief, his accusation was to some extent based on a false premise.[20]

There was only one point on which the ministers were unanimous and adamant. In Hartington's words, 'He left this country with the most clear and distinct understanding, repeated over and over again by myself, that the mission on which he was going to undertake was only to be undertaken with such resources as he might find on the spot, and that there would be no British expedition for the relief of Khartoum or any other garrison in the Sudan.'[21]

Our knowledge of this briefing leaves many questions unanswered:

1. Why did Gordon, who three days earlier had drafted his own brief for a reporting mission, and one day previously had informed Augusta in similar terms, now assume that he was armed with executive powers? It is possible that he was informed by Wolseley of Baring's request for a qualified officer to conduct the retreat, and assumed that he was that officer. But this is mere conjecture: there is no evidence that Gordon, or even Wolseley, knew of Baring's request.

2. Why did Gordon agree to evacuation which a few days earlier he had denounced as impracticable? Reginald Wingate suggested that he regarded his instructions as an exhortation to do his best, not as a clause in an international treaty to be interpreted by jurists. Quite so. But this does not explain his *agreement* with the policy, which is made quite clear in a letter to Barnes: 'Government are right, if they will not guarantee future government of the Sudan, to evacuate it.'[22]

Blunt deduced a conspiracy between Wolseley and Gordon to send the latter out ostensibly on a reporting mission which would later be changed to one of conquest. Gordon could be deceitful in a good cause, but one cannot quite see him entering into a plot so devious. Of Wolseley one cannot be so confident. He was a born intriguer, and he thought it 'the worst of ignorant, cowardly folly to force Egypt to give up the Eastern Sudan'. In the course of briefing Gordon to go and report on evacuation, he may have hinted at a different outcome.

3. Why did Granville insert into Gordon's instructions words which could, and did, result in a reporting mission becoming an executive one? That it was not a mere mental aberration is proved by his telegram to Baring of the same date, 'Gordon suggests that it be announced in Egypt that he is on his way to Khartoum to arrange for the future settlement of the Sudan.'

4. How was it possible for Gordon, a few hours after a vague verbal briefing, to set out on such an important mission with no written instructions? One can only attribute this to lack of a Cabinet secretary. If before his departure he had been presented with the formal instructions he was eventually to receive at Port Said, many a misunderstanding might have been discussed and eliminated. As it was, from Dover all the way to Cairo, he churned out telegrams, memoranda and draft manifestoes which were perfectly appropriate coming from a governor-general elect, but not from a major-general sent out to report on the military situation.

Childers, among others, wondered who was to be Gordon's master. Gordon himself said to Hartington, 'I shall be under General Stephenson, and if I do anything wrong, he can try me by Court Martial.'[23] But there is no record of his having any communication with Stephenson. The chain of command, vital in any operation, was in hopeless confusion, and in Gordon's case it was particularly desirable that it be absolutely clear. It is possible that behind the scenes there was a departmental dispute about Gordon's role, with Hartington and the War Office wishing him to go out purely as a military officer to advise, through the proper military channels, on the problems of evacuation, while Granville and the Foreign Office wished to give him wider powers while controlling him through Baring.*

Gordon asked for Stewart as his staff-officer, 'for his reports seemed so good'. Stewart, on leave, had been summoned to advise on the military problems of evacuation, which he believed to be possible only if a relief force were sent to Berber or Kassala. He was found at his club and was brought to the War Office to meet Gordon. They took to one another, and each described the other as a first-rate man. Although he had not even his uniform with him, he agreed at once to accompany Gordon, leaving by that night's boat-train.

* See p. 210.

The intervening hours Gordon spent dining with Brocklehurst and visiting his friend, Reginald Brett, walking up and down the nursery with the Brett baby in his arms. Henry found him in the most buoyant mood, all cares cast aside. On being asked why he needed his uniform, he replied, 'I am off to the Sudan.' 'When?' 'Tonight!' Then he took a cab to Charing Cross. Lord Granville bought his ticket, Lord Wolseley carried his bag down the platform, the Duke of Cambridge opened the carriage door for him. He had forgotten his uniform-case, which was brought along just in time by Henry's son, and his money, so Wolseley pressed on him his gold watch and chain and all the cash in his pockets. Then the train pulled out of the dimly-lit station, carrying Gordon and Stewart to their deaths.

17

THE ROAD
TO KHARTOUM

Within hours of Gordon's departure Granville was asking, 'Are you sure we did not commit a gigantic folly?' To us it is apparent that they did. If it were incumbent on Britain to extricate the Egyptian garrisons – the case was arguable – it could be done only by sending a relief force to Berber. If it were decided instead to send a single man to overawe or negotiate with a Messiah whose inspiration was Islamic and xenophobic, then it was foolish to send a Christian European. If a British officer had to be sent to preside over an ignominious scuttle, it was a mistake (as Gladstone afterwards acknowledged) to send a hero of heroes, but mercurial, flighty in his opinions, unpredictable and uncontrollable. The Government's decision is comprehensible only in the light of the Gordon *cultus*. It was almost universally believed – and the nobility of his character silenced dissent – that he was the greatest living expert on the Sudan, whose name was magic there. If he said that Mahdism would soon collapse and that he would have no difficulty in carrying out his mission (whatever that might be), then it could do no harm to send him, and in the context of party politics it could do a lot of good. But in fact Gordon's reputation was exaggerated. Seven years earlier he had made a great impact on the tribes of Equatoria, but these were irrelevant to the present situation. Five years earlier his courage and masterful personality had made a considerable impression among the Baggara, but these to a man had joined the Mahdi. Among the Jalaba slavers between Berber and Dongola – of crucial importance to a withdrawal – his attempts to destroy their way of life were bitterly resented. Only in Khartoum did he have anything like the influence attributed to him, and that after four years must have faded. The Sudan of 1884 was very different from the Sudan he had left in 1879. Gordon was the most dangerous of advisers: the local expert, or supposed expert, whose authority is unquestioned but whose knowledge is a little out of date.

All this was apparent to Baring. He knew Gordon was not the man for the job, largely because the circumstances of his career were such that he had never been subjected to healthy public criticism. He had twice refused the offer of Gordon's services and to the end of his life he bitterly regretted not persisting in his refusal. But having been persuaded, largely by Wood who was himself influenced by Watson, he gave Gordon all possible support, and it was a great reassurance to him that Gordon was accompanied by Stewart, for he had seldom been so impressed by anyone as by this 'cool, sagacious and courageous officer'.

Stewart was the perfect foil to Gordon. His temperament was calm, while Gordon's was hasty, his mind logical and disciplined, while Gordon's was impulsive and erratic. He believed that orders were to be obeyed. He was inclined to cynicism, or at least to realism; and Gordon was far off the mark when he wrote that Stewart 'never thought of danger in perspective; he was not a bit suspicious (while I am made up of it).' His journal and long, shrewd letters are the best source of information on the journey to Khartoum and early weeks of the siege. Singularly enough they made no mention of Gordon's religious views: presumably Gordon thought that Stewart would not be interested in endless discussions on 'great matters'. Stewart was a man of the world: it would never have occurred to him to walk out of a display by naked dancing girls, any more than it would have occurred to Gordon to record in his journal an explicit description of the pre-nuptial customs of certain Sudanese tribes. Encouraged by Gordon to express his own opinion to Baring, Stewart did so fully but without disloyalty to his chief, playing the difficult part of link between two men who had a strong mutual aversion.

Gordon never doubted that, 'if He goes with me, all is well.' Stewart did not have this assurance. Though he wrote to his sister, 'Keep your pecker up, I assure you this job is not nearly so dangerous as it looks', to his solicitor he described it as a very dangerous expedition. As for his General, he was 'an Englishman of the very noblest type . . . a charming chief and companion'. They were often to differ, but only once quarrelled, after which Stewart let himself go in a letter which, at his request, Baring destroyed. Baring had enormous confidence in Stewart's judgement, and it is not too much to say that he accepted Gordon's recommendations only when Stewart supported them.

Harking back to the Sudan he had known five years earlier, Gordon thought first of Zebeyr, evil genius of the south-west who nevertheless had 'some idea of government'. Not without reason, he believed Zebeyr to be his enemy, and untrustworthy: if he had been sent to Suakim, Zebeyr would have managed to be taken prisoner and lead the revolt. Certainly Zebeyr bore him a grudge: up to the eyes in debt, the great slaver blamed Gordon for his misfortunes. But it was entirely wrong to believe that the rebellion was mainly a revolt of the slave traders and that the Mahdi was Zebeyr's creation, 'a mere puppet put forward by Elias, Zebeyr's father-in-law and the largest slave-owner in Obeid'. Acting on this erroneous assumption, Gordon telegraphed Baring asking for Zebeyr to be exiled to Cyprus.

The policy of evacuation, he thought, was the right one: he assured Northbrook that he had no doubt about this, and anticipated no difficulty in carrying it out. A far more difficult problem was that of leaving behind some settled government after the legions had departed – a task which, though not included in his written instructions and barely hinted at in Northbrook's letter to Baring, occupied his mind more than anything. To Baring he wrote that the irrevocable decision to evacuate 'as far as possible involves the avoidance of fighting'. His idea was that the Sudan should be handed back to the petty sultans who had ruled it before the Egyptian conquest; these, in some loose confederation, would be a counterweight to the Mahdi. There would be difficulties in finding hereditary rulers for towns such as Khartoum which were practically the creation of the Egyptians, but they could certainly be found for the tribal areas. Whether they would stand up to the Mahdi was another matter. Nevertheless he did reiterate his belief that evacuation was the only practicable policy: 'H.M.'s Government will now leave them as God has placed them.'

On his way across Europe Gordon drafted four proclamations, which he sent back for Granville to approve and telegraph on to Baring. Two called upon the tribes of eastern Sudan to meet him at Berber to discuss arrangements for facilitating the withdrawal and for the subsequent government of the country. Two announced his appointment as the Khedive's governor-general for the purpose of evacuating the Sudan and returning it to the native rulers. (To Stead Gordon had stressed 'the impolicy of announcing an intention to evacuate'.) These and other draft telegrams surprised the Cabinet, for they implied that Gordon was to be governor-general with executive powers to conduct the retreat. Granville, however, made no protest, having 'not local knowledge sufficient to judge'; he considered that events (and Gordon) had gone beyond recall and authorized Baring to accept Gordon's recommendations. Baring approved of these: 'They quite harmonize with the lines on which we have already been working.'

It seems strange that Gordon should have been instructed by Wolseley, on his own advice, to proceed to Suakim, which besides being 'out on a limb' was loosely invested by Osman Digna. In 1884, however, the Suakim-Berber route was normally the quickest way to Khartoum; and

Gordon, who had pardoned one of their sons under sentence of death, was confident that he could persuade the Hadendowa sheikhs to escort him to Berber. By now he assumed that he would have executive authority and would go to Khartoum. Another question is why he made the astonishing decision to go *direct* to Suakim, instead of breaking his journey at Cairo to consult those whose co-operation was essential. The probable explanation is that he was at variance with the Khedive Tewfik, with Wood and with Baring, so he wished to see as little of them as possible. If Baring wished to talk with him, he could meet the ship at Ismailia.

The possibility of a tug-of-war between the War Office and the Foreign Office is to some extent confirmed by a note of E. W. Hamilton on Wolseley's opinions:

> He believes that the point at which the Government is really open to attack is that, instead of allowing Gordon to go out, as originally intended, to *report* on the state and outlook of things in the Sudan, he was waylaid by Baring at Port Said, brought up to Cairo and despatched to Khartoum as Governor-General, a distinct departure from the terms on which he left England and the consequence [sic] of all subsequent troubles.[1]

Baring wrote promptly to Granville:

> It is absolutely essential that Gordon come to Cairo. He cannot get to Khartoum by any other route, and so marked an act of disrespect to the Khedive would do harm ... Moreover it is useless for him to go until he has fully concerted measures with Nubar Pasha, Wood, myself and others ... I hope you have made clear to him that he is not to carry out the policy set forth in his letter [sic] to the *Pall Mall Gazette*. If not, I anticipate a good deal of trouble.

Two days later Baring added, 'It is well that Gordon should be under my orders, but a man who habitually consults the Prophet Isaiah when he is in a difficulty is not apt to obey the orders of anyone ... He really ought to see the Khedive. His dislike of him is rather silly.'[2]

So when Gordon reached Port Said on 24 January 1884, he was met by Wood, whom he disliked ('wrapped up in the things of this world'), with a civil letter from Baring explaining why he must go via Cairo to Khartoum where he could 'arrange for the withdrawal of the Egyptian garrisons etc. as rapidly as is consistent with (1) the saving of life and so far as is possible, property; (2) the establishment of some rough form of Government which will prevent, so far as is possible, anarchy and confusion arising on the withdrawal of the Egyptian troops.'[3]

This, of course, put Gordon's mission on a very different basis from that envisaged by the Cabinet in London. Watson was at Port Said too, with a personal appeal from Gerald Graham who was in Cairo. 'My dear Charley, do come to Cairo . . . Throw aside all personal feeling, if you have any, and act like yourself with straightforward directness.' So Gordon went to Cairo where he stayed with Wood. His first official act, on 25 January, was to pay his respects to the Khedive and apologize for his former rudeness.

From the palace, he returned to Wood's house where there was an *ad hoc* committee meeting of Baring, Wood, Graham, Nubar and Stewart, to settle the details of the mission. The important decisions were:

(a) that the Government place a credit of £E100,000 at Gordon's disposal;

(b) that the evacuation be gradual;

(c) that two *firmans** be given Gordon: one, for public consumption, appointing him Governor-General of the Sudan; the other, to be kept secret until it could be most advantageously revealed, instructing him to evacuate the Egyptian garrisons and officials, and set up a purely Sudanese administration;

(d) that Gordon have an interview next day with Zebeyr, who was still in Cairo;

(e) that as a counterweight to the Mahdi in the west, some member of the former ruling house of the Fur be provided with £2,000, a gold-laced gala uniform and the biggest decoration that could be found, and sent to Darfur.

Gordon was to go to Khartoum in a double role – as the Khedive's Governor-General and the Queen's High Commissioner. If Her Majesty's Government were surprised by the rapid escalation of a reporting mission, they had only themselves to blame; for Gordon's new responsibilities were certainly 'entrusted to him by the Egyptian Government through Sir Evelyn Baring'.

On the following day, 26 January, Baring collected to meet Gordon a number of officers with experience of the Sudan. Among these was a very tall, very thin Sudanese, aged about fifty-two, dressed in a black frock-coat and *tarbush*, whose face (according to Graham) resembled a death's head tenanted by a demon. He was introduced to Gordon as Zebeyr Pasha. There are several accounts of this momentous meeting, the most circumstantial[4] being by Reginald Wingate, Wood's A.D.C., who was probably the only person present throughout who could speak, read and write Arabic and English:

When Gordon held out his hand to Zebeyr, the latter refused to shake hands. Gordon, furious at this discourtesy, turned angrily on Zebeyr and asked

* Khedive's commissions.

his reasons – Zebeyr, at once replied, 'You signed the death warrant of my son, Suleiman; how can I touch the hand soiled with the blood of my son?'

To this Gordon instantly replied, 'Zebeyr *you* – not I – are responsible for your son's death; you wrote to him from Cairo instigating him to revolt; your letter is attached to the Court Martial proceedings and must be in the Cairo War Office.'

Zebeyr replied, 'This is not the truth – I never wrote to my son as you say – let my letter be produced."

I* was then ordered to go to the War Office, search the records, and bring the Court Martial proceedings. I left the room at once and, after a short search, the Court Martial proceedings were found, they were written entirely in Arabic (Gordon could neither read nor write Arabic).

The documents were carefully examined but no trace of the supposed letter from Zebeyr to Suleiman was discovered, nor was there mention of any such letter – clearly Gordon had been imposed upon and Zebeyr was right.

Meanwhile, pending the result of the search, the meeting in the Agency had been adjourned till the next day.

Baring sent Granville a long description of the meeting, including a furious altercation between Gordon and Zebeyr. Strangely enough he did not include the important point that Zebeyr's letter could not be found. Some weeks later a document in Arabic, purporting to be this letter, reached the Foreign Office via Egmont Hake, Gordon's biographer, and Sir Henry Gordon. It was translated but not, apparently, examined to establish its authenticity. Wingate remained convinced that it was a forgery; Baring was of the opinion that it 'did not confirm Gordon's statement, but did to a certain extent implicate the father as well as the son'.[5]

At this second meeting Gordon was given his formal instructions, drafted by Baring as a result of the previous day's decisions. These dwelt in more detail on the problems of evacuating the garrisons and the 12,000–15,000 civilians – Christians, Egyptian government employees, their wives and children etc. – who would not wish to be left behind when the garrisons departed. 'As regards the most opportune time and the best method for effecting the retreat . . . it is neither necessary nor desirable that you should receive detailed instructions . . . You will bear in mind that the main end to be pursued is the evacuation of the Sudan . . . I also understand that you entirely agree on the desirability of adopting this policy.' At this point in reading out the instructions Baring stopped and asked Gordon if he did in fact agree. Gordon replied 'in the strongest terms' that he did; and at his particular request Baring inserted, after the word 'policy', the words 'and that you think it should on no account be changed'.

* i.e., Wingate.

Baring continued:

'You consider it may take a few months to carry out in safety. You are further of the opinion that the restoration of the country should be made to the different petty Sultans who existed at the time of Mohamad Ali's conquest, and whose families still exist; and that an endeavour should be made to form a confederation of these Sultans. In this view the Egyptian Government entirely concurs. It will of course be fully understood that the Egyptian troops are not to be kept in the Sudan merely with a view to consolidating the power of the new rulers. But ... you ... are ... given full discretionary powers to retain the troops for such reasonable period as you may think necessary in order that the abandonment of the country may be accomplished with the least possible risk to life and property.'[6]

The discussion then turned to Zebeyr, who was summoned. Gordon went up to him, held out his hand and apologized for his accusation. Zebeyr said, 'I feel sure that my enemies imposed upon you, knowing that you could not read Arabic, and had shown you some Arabic paper saying it was a letter from me to my son. I am glad that I am cleared of a disgraceful insinuation. We are now friends again, I give you my hand on it and I am your slave for life and will do anything you wish.' They shook hands, and Gordon then astounded the company by saying, 'I wish Zebeyr to come to the Sudan with me.'[7]

At some point during the past twenty-four hours Gordon had put this proposal to Baring. Zebeyr, he wrote, 'although the greatest slave-hunter who ever existed', was the ablest man in the Sudan and a capital general. 'He has a capacity for government far beyond any man in the Sudan. All the followers of the Mahdi would, I believe, leave the Mahdi on Zebeyr's approach, for the Mahdi's chiefs are ex-chiefs of Zebeyr.' The only way to avoid civil war in the Sudan after the evacuation was to install as ruler Zebeyr who would 'end the Mahdi in a couple of months'. If he were merely to evacuate the Sudan, he needed no Zebeyr; but if he was to leave behind any sort of stability, then 'Zebeyr becomes a *sine qua non*'. He had, he explained, 'a mystic feeling that I could trust him'.

The real point, which he had failed to make, was that this was a religious revolt, and that Zebeyr was a Moslem with the most impeccable credentials, claiming descent through the Abassid Khalifs from the Prophet, of such piety and prestige that he had been asked, some years ago, to declare himself the Mahdi. He was a member of the large and warlike Jaalin tribe, inhabiting the country round Berber; he was respected and greatly feared.

There followed a heated discussion. Watson, now a lieutenant colonel in the Egyptian Army, quoted local opinion in saying that if Gordon and Zebeyr went to Khartoum together, one would not come back. Baring, who had no confidence in decisions based on mystic feelings but had himself been half-inclined to send Zebeyr, mentioned that within twenty-four hours he had received one recommendation from Gordon recommending that Zebeyr be deported to Cyprus, and another that he be sent to govern the Sudan. He thought Gordon needed more time to examine the matter. Eventually Gordon's proposal was put to the vote – a somewhat strange procedure in the circumstances – and narrowly defeated.

Gordon was furious and made plain his displeasure that evening in Wood's house where a large farewell dinner had been arranged for him. He entered the room wearing his ordinary day-clothes – black frock-coat, black gloves, *tarbush*.

'Gordon,' said the Sirdar, 'I told you there was a farewell dinner for you tonight, the guests will be here in a few minutes – you have not much time to get ready.'

'You were one of those who voted against Zebeyr coming with me to the Sudan. I will not attend the farewell dinner and prefer to have a plate of soup in my bedroom.'

With that he walked out.

He was still angry at the railway station later that evening, but somewhat mollified when Baring promised, if Gordon on reaching Khartoum still wanted Zebeyr, to support his request. ('Your nephew,' wrote Gordon to Lord Northbrook a few days later, 'is very kind and is up to his post.') Having shaken hands with Baring, Wood and Watson, and endured the ordeal of Nubar's embrace, he stepped aboard the train. He had exactly a year to live.

Mercifully the high drama of Gordon's departure, with all its potential for tragedy, was lightened by the misfortunes (described by Stewart) of his travelling companion, Abdul Shakur, the newly-appointed Sultan of Darfur. Extra carriages were needed for his twenty-three wailing wives and vast quantities of baggage; at the last moment it was discovered that his gala uniform was missing, and there was a great commotion until it could be found. Next morning at Assiout, where the party transferred to one of Messrs Cook's river-steamers,

the Sultan stepped from his carriage in gorgeous array, in a uniform bedizened with gold lace and with the broad ribbon and plaque of the Medjeduha Osmania slung across his shoulders. With long and rapid steps, followed by a motley crowd of ragged and dirty women and men he passed us on his way to the steamer, occupied every now and then in hitching up his ribbon which would perversely attempt to slide off his shoulder. Arrived at the steamer he and his court took possession of the main deck cabin, but was speedily and ignominiously expelled by Gordon Pasha.

Gordon gave him a good talking-to and warned him to make himself less conspicuous, or he would certainly be murdered on arrival at Darfur, if not before. At this, the Sultan had recourse to the bottle and remained in Assouan. As the representative of the former rulers to whom the Sudan was to be returned, he did not inspire confidence.

After Gordon's departure Baring telegraphed Granville, 'There is no sort of difference between his views and those entertained by Nubar Pasha and myself.' However in a private letter he added a word both of warning and of reassurance:

> Most of what I have to say about Gordon can best be said privately . . . He is certainly half-cracked, but it is impossible not to be charmed by the simplicity and honesty of his character . . . He was most anxious that I should tell you, in his own words, that he had not 'kicked over the traces' . . . I am very glad he has come, for I believe he is the best man to send. My only fear is that he is terribly flighty and changes his opinions very rapidly. I am glad that Stewart, who impressed me very favourably, is going with him, but I don't think Gordon much likes it himself. He said to me, 'They sent him [Stewart] with me to be my wet-nurse'.[8]

The party included Graham and Colonel Ibrahim Fauzi who was in official disfavour having sided with Arabi Pasha. But Gordon was the last to hold that against him, and had specially asked for the services of his former protégé. He loved to chaff Ibrahim in his execrable Arabic – nouns indifferently used in singular and plural forms, and verbs with no regard to person or tense. Ibrahim put up with this good-humouredly and used to call him 'Father'. Nubar Pasha refused to confirm Gordon's impetuous promotion to the rank of general of this officer who had only eleven years' service, with no regimental experience, whose contemporaries were lieutenants and captains and who in that exalted rank would be 'a burden on the War Office budget for the rest of his life'. Ibrahim, however, justified Gordon's trust at Khartoum and, later, as the Mahdi's captive.

Graham did not believe in evacuation, and argued the point with quotations from the *Pall Mall Gazette* interview. Gordon replied that evacuation was the Government's policy, and he could give effect to it with least chance of disaster. He assured Baring that he would 'keep in view that evacuation is the policy of H.M.G.', but it did not interest him nearly as much as setting up a successor government.

At home the press campaign was stoked by Gordon's friends and admirers. *The Times* and the *Pall Mall Gazette* repeated over and over again that Gordon had not gone to the Sudan to preside over a disgraceful retreat. He would proceed to Khartoum, said *The Times* of 20 January, escorted by the Hadendowa, call a conference of chiefs and, in the name of Her Majesty's Government, restore to them their liberty. 'An honest and capable administration at Khartoum would win us the respect of the natives . . . It can hardly be doubted that Gordon would be in favour of this.' The most picturesque proposal, in the *Pall Mall Gazette*, was that Gordon would 'Sarawak the Sudan', setting up there a semi-independent kingdom with himself as sultan. The Cabinet was displeased. 'The papers,' complained Granville, 'seem to think that Gordon is a new discovery of the Government under pressure of the Press.' Dilke wrote to Granville, 'I am alarmed at Gordon's hints to the Press, for I think they must come from him. When I was at the War Office I heard nothing of his going to Khartoum or anywhere but Suakim. But if he goes up towards Khartoum and is carried off and held to ransom, we shall have to send a terrible force after him, even though he should go without instructions.' Granville, however, doubted 'whether we have the right to say he has changed his instructions. It appeared in his conversation at the War Office that he was as likely to recommend one course as another.'[9]

Nor were the ministers reassured when they received Gordon's memoranda written on board ship. One trouble, Hartington observed, was that they could not agree on what they had told him. Gladstone took the point. 'My belief,' he noted,

that Gordon has a perfect freedom of action under our last two telegrams is confirmed by a reference to his own memorandum. The irrevocable decision of which he speaks is not a decision under no conceivable circumstances to employ a soldier in the Sudan, but the decision to evacuate the territory . . . This decision '*as far as possible* involves the avoidance of fighting' . . . I much regret that we had not the expression of General Gordon's views . . . before us yesterday.[10]

It was Stewart's duty to compile the mission's journal and send it in instalments with covering letters to Baring. In this he found unexpected difficulties, notably Gordon's incurable telegraphic diarrhoea. Chugging up the Nile for three days in a small steamer, Gordon had nothing to do but fire at Baring a succession of long telegrams, letters and memoranda, many of them flatly contradicting one another. Long before he had had any chance of examining the situation on the spot, basing his ideas on third-hand reports and intuition, he sent Baring an undated memorandum containing his master-plan. In it he defined the areas of rebellion as Kordofan, where the Mahdi was too strong to be touched; the Gezira, where it was a matter of raiding tribes hemming in the garrison of Sennaar; and the Suakim area, where the revolt of the Hadendowa (he supposed) had no connection with the Mahdi. He proposed to evacuate

Egyptian officials and replace them by Sudanese; relieve Sennaar; send up five steamers to bring down the garrisons of Equatoria and Bahr-el-Ghazal; arrange for the retreat of the Darfur troops ('if they still exist') to Dongola; and organize a movement by friendly tribes to open up the Suakim-Berber route. For the last operation he would require five British officers. A few days later he believed that the only area in danger was Darfur and cancelled the request for British officers, as the Suakim-Berber route would soon be opened by the *Mudir* of Berber.

After by-passing the First Cataract by train, they embarked on another steamer. 'He has now got hold of the idea,' wrote Stewart, 'of getting the King of the Belgians to take over the Equatorial and Bahr-el-Ghazal Provinces.' This inspiration was the fruit of an evening's talk with Graham. 'A capital plan!' Gordon exclaimed at 11 p.m. 'I will write to the King tomorrow.' So he did, fortunately sending a copy of the letter to Baring with a covering note: 'Here is a letter I have written to the King of the Belgians. His Majesty told me he would take the two provinces if I could get them when I was in Brussels. You might mention this to the Foreign Office, and send them a copy of the letter. *It would settle the slave-trade.*' It would also mean that he need not return to Cairo and Europe. The reaction of Her Majesty's Government was wholly unfavourable: the letter, noted Granville, 'contained strange advice', and Gordon was categorically forbidden to go south of Khartoum. He returned again and again to the charge, but Baring and Granville were unmoved by his arguments.

He asked that Suakim and Massawa be placed under his direct control as soon as Hussein Pasha Khalifa, the *Mudir* of Berber, had opened up the Suakim road, which was promised in a few days. ('But,' Stewart warned Baring, 'it remains to be seen how far he will be able to fulfil his promise.') He suggested that extracts from his telegrams and memoranda be published in the Cairo press. ('But, of course,' wrote Stewart, 'you are the best judge.') This sort of thing put Stewart in an awkward position. If he merely forwarded these effusions without comment, either Baring would be strengthened in his conviction that Gordon was cracked; or he might act promptly on some recommendation, and then have it cancelled. So Stewart slipped in a few words of warning:

As you are aware, General Gordon is rather hasty ... As regards the letter to Slatin Bey, please detain it, as it is very likely that ... its purport may be more or less altered. I shall be very glad when we are actually in Khartoum and face-to-face with the situation. Gordon is so full of energy and action that he cannot get along without doing something, and at present he revenges himself for his forced inactivity by writing letters, despatches etc. and sending telegrams.

Gordon was particularly concerned with Slatin and his troops who in December, after a valiant resistance, had surrendered to the Mahdi. Gordon felt a strong obligation to ransom them, and charged Stewart with 'great cold-bloodedness' in arguing that the return of Slatin was all that mattered, since his soldiers, nearly all blacks, would happily merge with the local population or join the Mahdi, as indeed they did. Gordon would not have felt so strongly had he known that Slatin had adopted Islam and was now in the Mahdi's entourage, sometimes as a despised and humiliated slave, sometimes almost as a private secretary. Since there was no other way, Gordon wrote offering the Mahdi £10,000 for them. Another problem was when to disclose the secret *firman* in which the policy of evacuation and handing over to a purely Sudanese government was set out. The intention was thereby to stimulate a native opposition to the Mahdi: but the mere mention of evacuation might make all the fence-sitters vault down on the Mahdi's side. Gordon in the *Pall Mall Gazette* interview had for that very reason condemned it, but was now not so sure. 'It seems to me,' wrote Stewart on 1 February, 'that the most sensible plan is not to publish abroad throughout the Sudan that we mean to leave . . . Whether it will be possible to induce Gordon to remain silent in the matter is however more than doubtful.'

The third problem was to find a Sudanese to stand up to the Mahdi, or perhaps make peace with him. 'Gordon,' wrote Stewart, 'is still hankering after Zebeyr, says he feels a sympathy for him, etc. It is impossible to say that he may not of a sudden request for him to be sent up. Should this be the case, I trust you will not let him leave Cairo unless under very cogent reasons. I am convinced that this would be a most dangerous experiment. It is also quite possible that he might not have the influence attributed to him now that it is said his Bazingers have ceased to exist.' (Most of them had joined the rebels.)

Gordon was encouraged by their reception en route and by over 400 applications for appointments, taking this as evidence that the Government was not regarded as *in extremis*. The slow progress of the steamer gave time for reflection, and he hit belatedly on one truth which corrected his previous misapprehensions: 'The rising is, by all accounts, that of the Sudan people, not of the slave-dealers.'

On 29 January there came aboard a French merchant from Khartoum, who reported panic in the city, hardly lessened by Gordon's telegram from Cairo, 'Do not be panic-stricken. We are men, not women. I am coming.' Two days later they reached Korosko, where they left the steamer for a six-day desert journey to Abu Hamid, by-passing the great loop of the Nile with the Second, Third and Fourth Cataracts. Graham must now return to Cairo:

About eight o'clock Gordon mounted his camel and said good-bye, but I walked beside him, and he shortly got down and walked with me. At last I left him, saying 'good-bye' and 'God bless you.' Then he mounted again, and a handsome young Arab, Ahmed, son of the Sheikh of Berber, rode beside him on a beautiful white camel. At the head of the caravan rode Ahmed's brother, both armed with the great cross-hilted swords, and shields of rhinoceros hide, which Soudan warfare has now made familiar. These swords, together with a couple of very old double-barrelled pistols with flint locks, made up the Arab armament. Gordon carried no arms, but Stewart had a revolver. Before Gordon left he gave me a long, heavy silver-mounted *kourbash* of rhinoceros hide, and told me to say that was a token that the reign of the *kourbash* in the Soudan was over. In exchange he took my white umbrella, having lost his own ... The desert there is covered with a series of volcanic hills ... nothing between the hills but black basins or ravines, dry, dark, and destitute of vegetation. I climbed up the highest of these hills and through a glass watched Gordon and the small caravan as his camels threaded their way along a sandy valley until he turned the dark side of one of the hills and I saw him no more.

The 260-mile desert journey was tough even by Stewart's standards – baking hot by day, freezing at night. They slept on rugs on the hard ground, 'roughing it with a vengeance'. There was no water save in a few brackish wells. Gordon, aged fifty-one, who had not ridden a camel for four years, must have suffered. The worst was over by 7 February, when they reached Abu Hamid; from there to Berber, riding up the right bank of the Nile with here and there some cultivation, they could take it easy.

They were well received by the villagers of Abu Hamid who crowded round to kiss Gordon's hand and hear what he had to say. This pleased them even more than his arrival: taxes halved and arrears remitted; an amnesty for all offences; Sudanese in all high places; government by kindness and justice.

There was no mention of evacuation or the end of Khedival rule. Indeed Gordon, encouraged by his reception among tribes hardly yet affected by Mahdist propaganda, recommended to Baring on 8 February that, as the country was less disturbed than had been reported, and the prestige of the Cairo government so little shaken that Egyptian employees 'would very probably refuse to leave even if they were dismissed and their expenses paid to Cairo', the Khedive's sovereignty over the Sudan should continue, exercised through Sudanese officers. This startling suggestion was in flat contradiction to his instructions, but he urged that the secret *firman* be changed accordingly.[11]

Gordon could not wait until he reached Khartoum before repeating his request for Zebeyr, writing to Baring on the 8th, 'He is the only man who is fit for Governor General of the Sudan if we wish it to be quiet . . . I wish you would see more of this remarkable man . . . I wish Lady Baring would see him.' In a third telegram also dated 8 February he assured Baring that tranquillity would be restored in a month and 'Mohamad Ahmed will no longer claim to be the Mahdi. It was Raouf Pasha who gave him that name.'[12]

He had his programme set out in leaflets distributed along his route. It seemed to make a good impression, though Stewart doubted the people really understood.

Lying under the stars on rugs reeking with camel-sweat, they discussed endlessly the problems before them. Gordon had learned that the Mahdi was the nephew of his best guide in Darfur. Surely he could come to a sensible arrangement with a man who was almost one of the family? He had contemplated going in person to see the Mahdi, prudently omitting to mention the idea to Baring. Baring, hearing of it indirectly, forbad it, as he could not risk Gordon being held prisoner. If Gordon could not go, he must write. Two days before reaching Berber he had a letter written to the Mahdi, wrapped in silk and forwarded to El Obeid together with a scarlet Robe of Honour and a *tarbush*. In this Gordon 'appointed' Mohamad Ahmed Sultan of Kordofan, and intimated that as he, Gordon Pasha, was *Hukumdar** of Khartoum, they were colleagues, and should not quarrel. He enlarged on the sin of Moslem slaying Moslem, and asked the Mahdi to release all his European prisoners, encourage trade with Khartoum and restore the Khartoum-El Obeid telegraph line to facilitate co-operation between them. This communication shows astonishing misconception of the Mahdi: a man who regards himself, and is widely regarded, as having God's commission to reform Islam is hardly likely to be bought off by a Robe of Honour, a *tarbush* (symbol of Egyptian rule), and the empty title, bestowed by a *Nasrani†*, to a province which he has ruled for a year by right of conquest. Hussein Pasha Khalifa, *Mudir* of Berber, assured Gordon that he had done well so to write. On the same day he assured Stewart that the letter was nonsensical.

Before arriving at Berber, Gordon heard that the Khedive had recently appointed a Circassian in place of Hussein Pasha Khalifa. Promptly he cancelled the appointment, and announced that he would do likewise for any other 'Turks'. Stewart cynically commented that handing over the Sudan to the Sudanese would only make a change of oppressors, but in Berber it was certainly popular.

They reached Berber at the head of a chaotic cavalcade – Bedouin cavaliers galloping about to display their horsemanship, men on camels

* Governor-General.
† Christian.

and donkeys and on foot, tomtoms thudding and women ululating in compulsive rhythms, all in dense clouds of dust. There were flags and guards of honour and a formal reception, beginning with the *ulema*, continuing with officers, officials and prominent merchants. Gordon, through an interpreter, made his usual speech, oxen were slaughtered for the soldiers, charity distributed to the poor. At the end of it Stewart broke to Gordon the news, received in a cyphered telegram, that Valentine Baker's force, which might have opened the Suakim-Berber route, had been massacred by a rebel army of less than half its strength. 'The people,' wrote Stewart, 'seem heartily glad to see Gordon. At the same time it is necessary to be on one's guard in judging of popular feeling anywhere, but particularly so in the East where dissimulation is so common. As yet, Baker's defeat is not known here, which is fortunate.'

Stewart added some words which warned Baring that Gordon might have third thoughts about evacuation: 'Gordon is so full of sympathy for these people that he is inclined to use every effort to mitigate the effect of our withdrawal, but I am convinced that no effort of his will prevent the reign of anarchy. Personally, though I regret the unavoidable, still I am persuaded that the evacuation policy is the right one and that it will probably in the end be best for all parties.'

On 12 February, four days after Gordon had written, and eleven days before Baring received, the recommendation that the Khedive's suzerainty over the Sudan continue, Stewart was 'called up at 5 a.m. by General Gordon who, having pondered all night, had come to the decision of opening the Pandora Box and openly proclaiming the divorce of the Sudan from Egypt . . . At 8 a.m. Hussein Pasha and Mohamad Tahir, a Judge of the Civil Court, a man we have every reason to believe is a friend of the Mahdi', were shown the secret *firman*. On the following day a proclamation was made announcing the independence of the *Mudiriyat* from Egypt but its subordination to General Gordon as H.M.G.'s commissioner; and a local council of notables was appointed. So far as Stewart was able to judge, the people appeared to approve.[13]

Amid a torrent of petitions – for jobs, arrears of pay, transfers, promotion, passes to go down to Cairo – which overwhelmed half a dozen clerks, a deputation arrived to ask a vitally important question. With the Sudan's independence from Egypt, would all slaves be freed in 1889 under the Anglo-Egyptian Convention of 1877 ? Gordon naturally replied, 'No', and published a proclamation that 'whoever has slaves shall have full right to their services and full control over them.' This pleased the people more than anything else.[14]

The publication of the secret *firman* also seemed to cause astonishment and delight; but, wrote Stewart, 'we have tried to fathom what those present really thought, and we are told it was a mistake to have shown it.' Gordon argued that it would be a sharp spur to make the people organize their own government; but Stewart thought that the disclosure was premature. It is significant that Hussein Pasha Khalifa and all the Berber notables soon defected to the Mahdi. To Baring Stewart wrote, 'Gordon has taken his leap in the dark and shown his secret *Firman*. How it will act and what will be the result, goodness only knows. At any rate the deed is done, and we must now abide by the result and hope for the best.' On 14 February, six days after recommending that the Khedive's sovereignty over the Sudan continue, Gordon recommended that all communication between Cairo and the Sudan cease in three months' time.

There is little doubt that Gordon's 'leap in the dark' was a mistake. He himself soon realized this and later admitted, 'I showed it not knowing well its contents' – a remarkable confession. On Hussein Pasha Khalifa's advice he published a few days later the open *firman* which merely appointed him governor-general. But the damage was done: the news spread and, predictably, reached the Mahdi who issued a proclamation of his own asking those who were still uncommitted what they hoped to gain by supporting a Pasha who was on his way out. All the consequences flowed from this error which Gordon himself had predicted to Stead. It was probably in an attempt to retrieve his mistake that he hinted to a Berber notable that once the Egyptian yoke had been lifted, the Sudanese, if they feared being sundered from the comity of nations, might apply for British protection.

They were now in the country of the Jalaba slave-traders. It was clear that what really interested them was Gordon's statement that slavery would continue. Undoubtedly, thought Stewart, this would do more than anything to facilitate their task, but he realized that it was bound to cause trouble at home. It did. The anti-slavery lobby was not numerous; but with its humanitarian motivation, its prosperous, upper-middle class composition and its links with the churches and the politicians, it was very influential. No British Government, particularly no Liberal Government, dared offend it. Varying in its view of Gordon between hero-worship and dark suspicion, at the news that he was perpetrating slavery it boiled with righteous indignation. An article in the influential *Fortnightly Review* compared him to a Home Secretary visiting a den of thieves to assure the inmates that the police would in future regard their operations with indifference: of course Gordon – always prepared to 'temporize with injustice' – thereby procured a friendly reception, but 'what is the use of his prestige if he has to do this?' Yet Gordon's announcement was no more than a statement of the obvious: if the Egyptian Government withdrew from the Sudan, of course slavery would continue, for there would be no one there to stop it. Naturally he hoped to make political capital out of 'this proof of my clemency towards you'.

Gordon was now consulted on how to make the best of the situation produced by Valentine Baker's defeat. In response to a telegram from Granville asking whether he should be recalled and whether it would be helpful to send British reinforcements to Suakim, which would cost but a fraction of an inland expedition, he replied in a series of telegrams from Berber:

(a) that his recall would reflect great discredit on the British name;

(b) that nothing should be done at Suakim but invite the local chiefs to Khartoum for a conference;

(c) that rumours of British intervention at Suakim would be more helpful to him than actual intervention;

(d) that a local force be raised;

(e) that the tribes should be promised peace if they accepted unspecified terms 'which I am authorized to offer';

(f) that consideration be given to raising 3,000 Turkish troops in British pay with a view to creating 'unofficially fear of a Turkish invasion';

(g) that no precipitate action be taken which would 'throw well-disposed people into the hands of the enemy'.

Baring, forwarding these 'fairly rational' telegrams, assured Granville, 'I am very favourably impressed by Gordon's messages . . . Please remember that his general ideas are excellent, but that undue importance should not be attached to his words.' Baring recommended accordingly that no British troops be sent to Suakim except for the protection of the town.

This conflicted with advice submitted four days earlier by Wolseley to Hartington, that the whole policy of evacuation be reversed, with everything east of the Nile being ruled by Sudanese officials under British supervision; and that a British force be sent to Suakim to deal with Osman Digna and another to hold Wadi Halfa. This, said Wolseley, 'would so strengthen General Gordon's hands that he would be enabled to carry out whatever policy he deemed advisable'. Otherwise an expedition would sooner or later have to be mounted to relieve Khartoum, 'a very long and tedious operation'. He added the warning that Gordon was inclined to attempt too much with too little.[15]

'*Whatever policy he deemed advisable*'. But had not Gordon already received clear – well, fairly clear – instructions to advise on – or execute – a policy of evacuation? Suspicion of military wire-pulling, never absent from Liberal minds, must indeed have been roused by these words. Meanwhile *The Times* demanded that the rebels be taught a lesson.

Otherwise, after Baker's defeat, 'it would be idle to hold that even Gordon's extraordinary personal influence could produce a pacification of the country and secure the withdrawal of the garrisons.'

Faced with conflicting advice by Gordon, Baring and Wolseley and angry discordant growls from the British Lion, the Cabinet havered, with ministers holding, and indeed expressing, different opinions. They were, as Gladstone informed the Queen, 'only too sensible of their responsibility, which in case of any miscarriage will be pretty promptly visited upon them'. On 12 February the reluctant decision was made to send a British brigade, under Graham, to relieve Tokar and protect the Red Sea ports. The conflict between this patently war-like operation and Gordon's peaceful mission was rationalized by the fiction that the Suakim area was not really part of the Sudan; the real point was that Suakim is on the sea, Khartoum is not. It resulted in more cross-purposes and confusion: Gordon asked for the Bija chiefs to be sent to confer with him at Khartoum, but the Admiral in command at Suakim refused to 'ask them to leave their people' when British troops were about to be sent against them.

Gordon and Stewart were beginning to regret their ignorance of Arabic. 'We have been greatly puzzled by the varying geographical positions of Obeid . . . Sometimes 250 miles to the west of the White Nile, and at other times within a few hours of Khartoum . . . We have at length solved the problem. It would appear that the Obeid near Khartoum is not a town but . . . a very holy sheikh . . . This closes the episode of the wandering city.' But it did not clear the mist of incomprehension in which Gordon moved.

Having appointed an Italian merchant, Giuseppe Cuzzi, as his liaison officer in Berber, and telegraphed to Khartoum sacking the Circassian acting Governor-General, he left Berber on 14 February on the last lap of the journey.

On the 17th they met Hussein Pasha Serri, Gordon's dismissed predecessor, 'the vanguard of the exodus of Pashas, women and children'. When Stewart heard about this person's doings in Khartoum and saw the effect of the bastinado applied to an old man's feet, he asked Baring to 'give that rascal a warm reception in Cairo. He is a cowardly, bribe-taking scoundrel . . . He is also addicted to an eastern vice which shall be nameless.'

18

THE ARRIVAL AT KHARTOUM

Arriving at Khartoum in the morning of 18 February 1884, Gordon was received by a row of officials in gold-laced uniforms and a throng of excited citizens. Whatever his repute elsewhere, his personality and energy had impressed the polyglot population of Khartoum. Most of the merchants dreaded the puritanical Mahdi and the fierce, acquisitive Baggara; and whatever rumours they might have heard from downriver, they expected Gordon to save them from worse than death.

The official party proceeded to the Governor's palace where at a formal *diwan** were received all *ulema*, consuls and senior officials. After sherbet and coffee, the *firman* of appointment was read aloud. Gordon then made a speech. 'I have no doubt that God will help us and guide us in restoring the present critical position. I could have brought an army with us, but did not do so because I have perfect confidence in the troops here now.' He introduced Stewart as his 'brother' and *vakil†*, to be obeyed like himself, although he had come in such a hurry that he had no uniform. Then came the words everyone wanted to hear: 'No man shall be answerable for any arrears of taxation up to the end of 1883, and all the old registers will be burnt. Taxes for 1884 are halved. I allow slave-dealing [sic] in the Sudan just as it used to be in former days.'[1]

Always a showman, he added to the illuminations by making a huge bonfire of the tax records, *courbaches*, stocks and instruments of official torture. While he and a team of clerks started work on scores of petitions, Stewart went to the gaol where the prisoners were packed like sardines, chained two-by-two, and began an inquiry which resulted that afternoon in the release of twenty who were held without trial, or after the expiry of their sentences, or on insufficient evidence. Gordon felt 'quite left-handed' without Barzati Bey, killed with Hicks. He visited the bereaved

* Reception.
† Deputy or prime minister.

family, promised to be a father to the children and gave £100 to the widow. He could not have had much time for the feast of turkey, lager and Bass's pale ale which Power had prepared.

Next day Stewart continued his gaol-delivery; Gordon visited the schools where pupils and staff, all in school uniforms, sang songs in his praise: 'I like the delight of the small black boys who were yelling about the remission of taxes when the little chaps had never paid a sou.' He did not feel the need, like de Coetlogon, to hold camphor to his nose as an antidote to Khartoum's stink, but the smell of official corruption was powerful, for a spot-check of stores resulted in angry words and dismissals.

He formally announced the Mahdi's 'appointment' as Sultan of Kordofan. He set up a council of notables, nominated by himself. He inspected the garrison deployed in action stations. The troops had improved since Stewart had last seen them, more blacks and more experienced officers having come in from out-stations. Some of the senior officers had fought in the Sudanese contingent which had performed well in the French expedition to Mexico. Gordon approved the defences built by Abdul Qadir, including thousands of broken bottles, 'crows' feet' and electrically-operated biscuit-tin mines, guaranteed to give 'a *mauvais quart d'heure*' to a barefoot enemy rushing the defences. To promote an air of normality, he ordered three of the gates, blocked on de Coetlogon's orders, to be opened, and the pass-system for controlling ingress and egress to be suspended. To encourage the villagers to bring produce to market, he abolished the *octroi* duty on merchandise brought into the town.

The garrison was re-deployed, with the blacks, as the most reliable troops, brought into Khartoum under Faragh Bey ez Zeini, a tough Mexico veteran. The white (i.e. Egyptian) troops and Bashi-Bazouks, due for repatriation, were sent across the White Nile to hold Omdurman. 'The problem of evacuating the Sudan,' Stewart had written on 17 February, 'is continually on our minds. I must confess that the more one looks at it, the more difficult it becomes. However, perhaps when it is eventually tackled, it will resolve itself somehow or other . . . Gordon's idea is to get out the white element and the whitey-brown or Bashi-Bazouks, and to leave the pure black or Sudanese to manage their own affairs.' Although Gordon's heart was not in a programme of scuttle, he accepted it as inevitable. When Faragh Bey and the *ulema* suggested that the Egyptian troops should be retained a little longer, he choked them off, calling Faragh an old woman and treating the *ulema* to a sermon on Trust in God.

Evacuation of the Egyptians was his first job; and it can be taken for granted that he and Stewart methodically set about making, in modern military terms, 'an appreciation of the situation'. So let us now examine the problem as it appeared to them on 20 February 1884.

Gordon's object was to evacuate (in order of priority) non-Sudanese troops and civilian government employees, foreign consuls, and as many others as wished to go, all with their families, to Korosko, about 600 miles away by the shortest route (river to Abu Hamed, thence across the Nubian Desert).

The garrisons in Bahr-el-Ghazal and Equatoria could best get out via Uganda; those along the Abyssinian border by agreement with King Johannes who was no friend of the Mahdi; and those in eastern Sudan via Suakim. Berber must be held until the operation was complete. So he was concerned only with Khartoum and Sennaar, 200 miles up the Blue Nile, loosely invested but still accessible by steamer.

Of the Khartoum garrison about 2,000 were 'white' and 1,900 were Bashi-Bazouks. In Sennaar there were probably about 700 'white' soldiers. A few officers had families with them: the rank-and-file made temporary arrangements with Sudanese women who would prefer to stay behind, so military dependants posed no great problem. Of civilian government employees there were about 200 in Khartoum, of whom perhaps half were Egyptian. Many would have families. The Corps Diplomatique consisted of Power; Herbin, the French Consul; Leontides, the Greek Consul; and old Hansal who still represented the Dual Monarchy. It is impossible to make any accurate estimate of non-Sudanese citizens – an Austrian tailor, some Greek cotton-planters, Copt, Greek, Syrian and Egyptian traders, their wives and families – who might wish to go: no doubt their numbers fluctuated with their confidence. Baring's estimate on 21 January of 10,000–15,000, out of a total Khartoum population of about 24,000, seems rather high.* The Egyptian Government was under no such obligation to private citizens as to its own employees, but Gordon felt responsible for them too. So for the numbers involved we arrive at the following very rough figures:

Military	4,600
Civil Servants	100
Families	800
Others	10,000–15,000
	15,500–20,500

Factors affecting the operation were:

(a) *Transport.* We do not know how many camels could be hired at short notice from tribes who, if not actually hostile, would be more interested in

* On 11 January Baring had given an estimate of 6,000.

robbing the fugitives than in facilitating their escape; clearly the number was limited. The ineffable Hussein Pasha Serri demanded fifty for his personal baggage, but had to make do with fifteen.

The principal transport would be by river. There were seven steamers available at Khartoum, plus two between Berber and the Sixth Cataract, and one bottled up at Sennaar. (There were two more in sections in Khartoum dockyard, but it would take weeks to assemble these.) Some would be required for the mobile defence of Khartoum and for operations towards Sennaar. Perhaps four, plus the two below the Sixth Cataract, would be available for the evacuation. The four largest were 140–150 feet long, each holding up to 500 men. But the larger they were, the slower and the less suitable for passing the cataracts. So perhaps we can guess that the steamers used for the evacuation would carry an average of 300 passengers each, tight-packed. There were also at Khartoum about 120 native sailing-boats, holding up to 60 passengers each. Two could be towed behind each steamer. So a single lift by four steamers and eight native boats could carry about 1,700 passengers.

(b) *The state of the river*. Of the cataracts between Khartoum and Korosko, the Sixth, between Khartoum and Berber, and the Fifth, between Berber and Abu Hamid, were passable in both directions by small steamers from about April to September, depending on the height of the Nile. The Fourth, Third and Second, between Abu Hamid and Korosko, were serious obstacles to upstream traffic, negotiable only with the aid of hundreds of men on tow-ropes. The Fourth was particularly dangerous.

(c) *The attitude of the tribes along the evacuation-route*. On the east bank of the Nile, between Khartoum and the Atbara river junction, the most powerful tribe was the Shagiya, controlled largely by the Mirghani family and its associated Khatmiya religious brotherhood, who were hostile to the Mahdi. The Shagiya were the 'trusties' of the Egyptian occupation, providing many irregular troops. The desert to the west of the Nile was the territory of the Kababish Bedouin, also antipathetic to the Mahdi because of their trading connection with Egypt and their addiction to tobacco and native beer, which he condemned. These two tribes were more or less for the Government, though their loyalty was shaky. But from Berber to Dongola the river was dominated by the Jaalin and Dongolawi whose way of life had been disrupted by Gordon's attacks on the slave-trade and in particular his harrying of the Jalaba. These must be considered as potentially hostile.

These factors indicated that the only practicable method of evacuation was by river to Abu Hamid and thence across the desert to Korosko. The operation should if possible be completed before the level of the Nile dropped in October. The round-trip from Khartoum to Abu Hamid would take about fifteen days.

Purely as an administrative exercise, provided there were no ship-wrecks nor engine failures, the operation could just be completed in about eleven lifts between March and the end of September. But if the Ansar were to invest Khartoum or the riverine tribes rise, and the vessels, packed with refugees, had repeatedly to run the gauntlet down to Abu Hamid, and slowly back against the current, then it would be obviously impossible.

However on 20 February Gordon asked Baring to make arrangements at Korosko to receive 1,800 evacuees and forward them onto Lower Egypt; and on the 26th the first party of sick Egyptians were sent down, to be followed shortly by a second, and by a consignment of civilian officials, women and children. It was no *sauve qui peut*; every detail was arranged by Stewart. Soldiers' kit, pay and allowances were checked and issued up-to-date; biscuits were issued for forty-five days; those to be invalided out were given discharge certificates; gratuities were paid to deceased soldiers' dependants. All were provided with passes to their villages in Egypt. The move went like clockwork: with only two deaths *en route*, 1,798 civilians and 340 Egyptian troops arrived safely at Korosko. With them went de Coetlogon, his departure widely unlamented for he was a Job's comforter, full of gloom. He must have been embarrassed at being entrusted by Gordon with a letter, intended for publication, describing Khartoum as safe as Kensington Park.

It was of the utmost importance that the tribes between Khartoum and the Egyptian border be kept quiet until the evacuation was completed. The idea of handing over to a confederacy of petty sultans was by now clearly a non-starter: either the sultans were so petty as to have lost all prestige; or, like Abdul Shakur, they were broken reeds; or, like the Baggara sheikhs, they had joined the Mahdi. So Gordon believed that the only man capable of keeping the northern tribes quiet was Zebeyr. Besides the fear that he inspired, he was a member of the Jaalin tribe and a close friend of the *Mudir* of Berber, which would give him a power-base just where one was most needed. The slave-trading tribes would be far better disposed to him than to Gordon. No one but he could measure up to the job. Whether he would accept it, if offered, was a question Gordon never considered.

So on the very day he arrived in Khartoum Gordon sent a long telegram to Baring. Withdrawing his suggestion (which Baring had not yet received) that the Khedive's sovereignty continue, he now made the even more startling recommendation that Britain assume sovereignty over the Sudan, selecting a ruler and promising him moral support but no more. 'As for the man, H.M.G. (not the Khedive) should select one above all others, namely Zebeyr.' He should be given the K.C.M.G., and a small subsidy provided he stayed out of Darfur, Bahr-el-Ghazal and Equatoria, continued the payment of government pensions, refrained from taking vengeance on those who had suppressed his son's revolt, kept import and export duties below four per cent, and informed Cairo regularly of the height of the Nile.[2] Stewart cautiously supported the idea, while doubting if they had been long enough in the country to make a firm recommendation. On the previous day he had written, 'The only candidate we can think of is Zebeyr . . . Whoever is selected will have to hold his own by fighting. I should recommend leaving him the black troops to give him a fair start.'

Baring, true to his word, recommended to Granville that Zebeyr be sent, but not until Gordon had left the country. This was an error; the whole point of sending Zebeyr was that he should keep the northern tribes quiet during the evacuation. Anticipating ructions at home, Baring pointed out that slavery would continue in the Sudan, whoever ruled it; and expressed the hope that the refining influence of several years' residence in Cairo might have implanted in Zebeyr a small seed of humanity. 'You must take Gordon as he is,' he wrote privately to Granville, 'for better or for worse, and on the whole the better predominates over the worse . . . As to his telegram, there is a good deal of nonsense in it; but as is always the case with Gordon's utterances, at the bottom of what he says there is a good deal of sense.'[3]

The recommendation reached Granville just as the anti-slavery lobby was seething with indignation at Gordon's proclamation that slavery, and indeed the slave-trade, would continue. There were the gravest objections, Granville replied on 23 February, to H.M.G. appointing anyone as Gordon's successor, and 'public opinion here would not tolerate the appointment of Zebeyr'. Could Gordon recommend anyone else?

Of course he couldn't and wouldn't. Moreover he already had doubts about the whole policy of evacuation, which he expressed that day to Lady Cardwell, wife of the Secretary at War in the late Conservative Government. He can hardly have expected Lady Cardwell to keep his views to herself, and never asked her to do so. 'It is a sad affair, and not understood by our Government who think that we can withdraw the garrisons from the well-affected people; the two are however inseparable, and this makes great difficulty, for I cannot leave the defenceless exposed to danger or take away the troops.'[4]

Nevertheless, despite these doubts expressed in what one cannot regard wholly as a private letter, he continued to obey orders; but to Baring's inquiry he dashed off an impulsive reply which was to destroy all that was left of the Cabinet's faith in him. Even if Zebeyr were sent, there would still remain the problem of extricating a steadily diminishing rearguard in the face of overwhelming numbers. Gordon had been forbidden to go to the Mahdi; his friendly letter had drawn no response. Withdrawal, therefore, must be treated as a military operation; and the essence of making a clean getaway is to give the enemy 'a bloody nose' before pulling out. That was the real justification for the recommendation he now made. Unfortunately he gave a spurious reason for it, perhaps because he thought a bunch of politicians would find a political calculation more convincing than straight military advice.

He telegraphed, on the evening of 26 February:

When evacuation is carried out Mahdi will come down here and by agents will not let Egypt be quiet. Of course my duty is evacuation and the best I can do for establishing a quiet government. The first I hope to accomplish. The second is a difficult task and concerns Egypt more than me. If Egypt is to be quiet Mahdi must be smashed up. Mahdi is most unpopular and with care and time could be smashed ... If you decide on smashing Mahdi then send another £100,000 and send up 200 Indian troops to Wadi Halfa and send officer up to Dongola under pretence to look out for quarters for troops ...[5]

The Cabinet was appalled. *Smash up the Mahdi!* It was not for this that Gordon had been sent on a peaceful mission to withdraw – or advise how to withdraw – the garrisons. Thereafter they regarded his every suggestion with deep suspicion, convinced that he was trying to bounce them into reversing their policy and embarking on military operations which they were determined to avoid. Yet Gordon's advice was perfectly consistent with the policy of withdrawal; and on the very day he sent off that fatal telegram, the first party of Egyptians set off down-river. The misunderstandings might have been cleared by Stewart, but on the 26th he was busy all day on the evacuation, and on the 27th he departed with two steamers on a five-days' reconnaissance up the White Nile. During those days irretrievable damage was done.

Gordon on the 26th had also proclaimed that, since some people still continued in rebellion, he was obliged to 'have recourse to severe measures'; he added that British troops were on their way 'and in a few days will reach Khartoum. Whoever persists in wicked conduct will receive the treatment he deserves.' The reference to British troops is inexplicable except as an unhappy inspiration by an Arabic scribe who had heard rumours of operations around Suakim; Gordon could not at this time have intended to raise hopes of British intervention. The 'severe measures' consisted of Stewart's reconnaissance up the White Nile, which never fired a shot, for Stewart contented himself with distributing

Gordon's proclamation on taxes and slavery to those who seemed friendly, and reporting the number and demeanour of those who did not. Unfortunately Gordon had described this peaceful outing as an expedition 'to attack rebels in the vicinity', and in passing on this telegram, Baring had omitted the next sentence, that evacuation had started. Moreover he sent the text of Gordon's second proclamation, promising 'severe measures' and the imminent arrival of British troops. The result of all this, said Dilke, was to frighten the Cabinet out of their wits.

In thirty-one days, Baring noted, Gordon had drifted through five successive proposals, from reporting on the Sudan to smashing up the Mahdi. By no means clear himself as to what Gordon wanted, he did his best to enlighten Granville, explaining on the 29 February that the alternatives were: (a) simply to evacuate the country, or (b) to evacuate while leaving behind some sort of government. Gordon was evidently in favour of (b). 'I entirely agree with him: from every point of view, whether political, military or financial, it will be a most serious matter if complete anarchy is allowed to reign south of Wadi Halfa.' He and Nubar considered that the only answer was Zebeyr with £50,000 a year payable while he behaved himself. With an eye to the Anti-Slavery Society Baring added, 'Any attempt to settle the Egyptian question by the light of English public opinion is sure to be productive of harm, and in this as in other cases it would be preferable to follow the advice of the responsible authorities on the spot.' Vain hope!

Granville's reply was a masterpiece of procrastination. 'Can you guarantee that his official income will be a sufficient bribe to prevent his embarking on his former lucrative pursuits or even of his not going over to the Mahdi?' The Government was not convinced of the urgency of appointing any successor to Gordon 'who, they trust, will remain some time longer in Khartoum'.

During the five days of Stewart's absence Gordon clouded every issue by sending no less than thirty telegrams, some of great length. Unable to cope with these *seriatim*, Baring posted the more lucid in batches to Granville. 'His statements and proposals are hopelessly bewildering and contradictory. I attribute a good deal of this to the fact that Stewart has left him to go up the White Nile. I do not mean to say I have lost confidence in Gordon. Such is not the case – but in dealing with his proposals it is often difficult to know what he means, and still more difficult to judge what is really worthy of attention and what is more or less nonsense.' Among Gordon's telegrams were: 'There is just the chance that the Mahdi's troops might be enticed over with money. Shall I try it?'; 'the Mahdi has no power outside El Obeid and would never advance from there'; the Mahdi would probably be pulled down by a slave revolt, 'what a wonderful *dénouement* that would be'; the situation was 'ticklish but we will pull through'; some influential men would not accept appointments 'and I don't blame them'; the choice was between the Mahdi, Zebeyr with £100,000, and 200 British troops to Wadi Halfa ('who would run no more risks than Nile tourists') while Indian troops opened up the Suakim–Berber road 'at which the rebellion would immediately collapse'; 'Is it justifiable to send troops to fight rebellion in the entanglement we are? Yet if I do not, many loyal people will join the Mahdi'; evacuation was impossible without help, 'they refused Zebeyr and were quite right (may be) to do so but it was the only chance. It is scarcely worth saying more on the subject. I feel a conviction that I will be caught in Khartoum'; 'the combination of Zebeyr and myself at Khartoum is absolutely essential'. He also, for good measure, wrote to Baker on 26 February, 'Heads or tails, but will trust'; and on the 29th, 'We are all right up here for the present. You and Lady Baker would enjoy the excitement.'

The Cabinet, wrote Dilke, 'were evidently dealing with a wild man under the influence of that climate of Central Africa which acts upon the sanest man like strong drink'. In Baring's telegram to Gordon restraint and asperity were nicely blended. 'I am most anxious to help and support you in every way, but I find it very difficult to understand what it is you want. I think your best plan will be to reconsider the whole question carefully, and then state to me in one telegram what it is you recommend.' To Stewart on the same day he wired, 'Pray make him understand that my sole object is to help him . . . but it adds immensely to my difficulties to receive constant and sometimes contradictory telegrams, apparently written on the spur of the moment . . . I really can do little to help him for I cannot understand what he wants.'[6]

Stewart on 4 March sent a long telegram explaining and summarizing Gordon's considered recommendations with which this level-headed, astute man had now come to agree:

The principal desire of Gordon is to have Zebeyr as soon as possible. His reasons are: Zebeyr is the only man with sufficient prestige to hold the country together, at any rate for a time, after the evacuation . . . Among the Shagiya irregulars he will be able to get at sources of action and information now closed to us. He will be opposed to the Mahdi. I agree with Gordon . . . I assure you none are more anxious to leave this country than myself and General Gordon, and none more heartily approve of the policy of evacuation. Unless, however, Zebeyr is sent here I can see little probability of this policy being carried out. Zebeyr's subsidy should be payable, a precaution against treachery, through Gordon.

On 29 February Graham had defeated Osman Digna at El Tib, and Gordon assumed that the Suakim–Berber road would soon be open. A small force of cavalry should then be sent to Berber, another to Wadi Halfa, which would keep the local tribes quiet and greatly help the evacuation. Stewart, as a hussar, took a more realistic view of what a few cavalry, unsupported, could accomplish, and wrote, 'Notwithstanding our telegrams, I really fail to see how you can at this season of the year send an expedition from Suakim to Berber . . . over that awful plain.'

He amplified his telegram of the 4th by a letter of the same date:

As regards Zebeyr, I think you have no option . . . Even if we could sneak away, I am convinced Gordon is the last man in the world who would do so . . . How far Gordon and Zebeyr will be able to work together, only time can show. I apprehend, however, that Zebeyr, like the rest of the world, knows what is to his own advantage. I fully sympathize with you about the many and divergent telegrams you get. Gordon telegraphs directly an idea strikes him. There is no use trying to stop it. Were I you, I should always wait for a few days before acting unless the subject is so evident that there can be no doubt about it . . . I fancy all we can really do is to hang on till the rivers rise and then get away as soon as possible . . . The Government having sent Gordon up here will have to support him, and I am convinced from what I know of him that he will never leave the Sudan until he has established some form of tolerably stable government. I must also add that I think he is perfectly right.

Nothing in the whole drama is more remarkable than the way in which Gordon's extraordinary personality gradually won over the hard-headed Stewart to his views. Three weeks ago Stewart had been 'convinced no effort of his will prevent the reign of anarchy'. Only three days ago Stewart had written to his sister, 'I cannot say . . . that I care very much what happens to the Sudan once I have left. All this humanitarianism is folly. If people like to fly at each other's throats, why should we interfere with them, as long as they do not annoy us?' Now, exposed to Gordon's persuasive charm, 'I think he is perfectly right.'

Gordon, meanwhile, Stewart wrote to his mother, 'is always asking for children's prayers. Little innocents he calls them.' And to Capsune Gordon wrote with transparent sincerity, 'I am back among my black lambs and they show their white teeth when I speak to them. I am glad you are a good boy and pray for me, for you can help me more than a million soldiers.'

To Baring on 3 March he sent a telegram in which he made clear for the first time that his honour and conscience committed him. 'You must see that you could not recall me nor could I possibly obey until the Cairo employees get out. How could I look the world in the face if I abandoned them and fled? Would you do so?' Baring replied, 'There is not the smallest idea of recalling you. On the contrary, the Government is anxious that you should remain.'¹

On receiving Stewart's telegram of 4 March, Baring besought Her Majesty's Government to allow Zebeyr to be sent without delay. In reply Granville, on the 5th, sent a flat refusal, coupled with a fatuous inquiry about how Baring reconciled his recommendation of Zebeyr with the prevention of slave-hunting, the evacuation of the Sudan and the security of Egypt. He also asked for a statement of the strength of every garrison, which had been on his file since December. 'Your report should be full and be sent by mail.' It was a response which reduced Baring to despair.

So the ball was passed back to Gordon, who replied with all the stale old arguments: 'Zebeyr is fifty times the Mahdi's match', and would 'make short work of the Mahdi . . . If you do not send Zebeyr you have no chance of getting the garrisons away.' This was the essential point which had been lost sight of, not least through Gordon's incurable verbosity, his undigested inspirations, his addiction to changing his mind and committing every change of mind to a fresh telegram. Stewart asked for a little time to think it over: it was, he suggested, no use badgering Baring 'as the difficulty was not at Cairo but at London . . . Gordon got very annoyed and left the table. Seeing he was annoyed, I got up and wrote the telegram as he desired.'

At this point Gordon committed one of his appalling indiscretions, which demolished any chance there might have been of the Cabinet letting him have Zebeyr. It arose out of his addiction to calling in the aid of the press, his liking for Frank Power and the young man's hero-worship. ('Gordon is the most lovable character – quiet, mild, gentle and strong; he is so humble, too. The way he pats you on the shoulder when he says, "Look here, dear fellow, now what would you advise?" would make you love him . . . He appears to like me and already calls me Frank . . . He is indeed, I believe, the greatest and best man of the century.')

On that day Gordon was in a thoroughly difficult mood. He was annoyed because his name had been omitted from a proclamation made at Suakim. Stewart had tried to calm him down, 'but it was no go'. In his irritation he now made the lamentable decision to secure press support for his views. On returning from writing Gordon's telegram, Stewart found him with *The Times*' correspondent. There followed a discussion on the propriety of a serving officer writing to the press, with Stewart arguing that it was highly improper. But Gordon insisted, and Power was briefed at length on the necessity of Zebeyr and a small cavalry force at Berber to prevent the northern tribes rising: 'This would settle the question.' Gordon warned Power that the interview must not be published without Baring's concurrence: Power must send it to Moberley Bell, *Times* correspondent in Cairo, who would show it to Baring. But he held to Baring's head the pistol of resignation, telegraphing, '*Times* correspondent interviewed me tonight. I gave him my views . . . If you disapprove of publication, then make Stewart my successor and ask Moberley Bell to cancel telegram.' This explosive message would have been sent *en clair*, had not Stewart succeeded in getting it encyphered. Nevertheless, though furious, Stewart could still write, 'The affair is very annoying, but I think the Ministry and people at home ought to . . . give him Zebeyr.' In a telegram he added, 'Home Government should not delay in sending Zebeyr. He has great influence with his tribe between Berber and Khartoum.'

Baring had recently been reproved by Granville over leaks to the press. 'I despair of doing anything about leakages,' he replied. 'In addition to the usual causes, it is most difficult to get Gordon to use cyphers. In matters of this sort his character makes him most difficult to control.' But, faced by Gordon's threat of resignation, he let Power's piece through after persuading Moberley Bell to expunge Gordon's 'foolish abuse' of the Khedive. 'I think Zebeyr had better be sent,' he advised.

When a man like Zebeyr is let loose, no one can guarantee what he will do. All that can be said is that it is impossible that Zebeyr will turn against Egypt, that it will not be in his own interest to do so . . . A good many of the difficulties have been raised mainly by the actions of Gordon himself. First he abuses Zebeyr violently and excites public opinion in England against him. Then he sends a number of wild contradictory telegrams which necessarily shake your confidence in his judgement. Lastly he communicates everything he has to say to the Press. I do not regret having sent Gordon, but it will be a great relief to me when he comes back . . . The only way I can read the facts is that Gordon's influence does not extend outside the walls of Khartoum, and his influence is sure to wane as time goes on.[8]

Power's despatch was published in *The Times* of 10 March. It could hardly have appeared at a more inopportune time, for the British public – at least that part of it from which a Liberal Government drew its support – was in a mood of sympathy with oppressed people. The Anti-Slavery Society was still seething at Gordon's condonation of the slave-trade. A week earlier *The Times* had published a highly emotive report from Moberley Bell that 'Colonel Stewart will return to the White Nile at the head of 2,000 Bashi-Bazouks to overawe the natives'. *Bashi-Bazouks!* Visions of Bulgarian atrocities at once roused the Liberal conscience. It seemed that, not content with conniving at the infamous slave-trade, Gordon was calling for the greatest slaver of all to preside over its revival; and the storm broke over the Cabinet's head. The committee of the Anti-Slavery Society warned Granville on 10 March that the appointment of

Zebeyr would be a 'degradation to England and a scandal to Europe'. W. E. Forster, infallible barometer of the Liberal conscience, sounded off in the Commons: 'If Gordon has given this advice . . . I am not prepared to follow him.' Practically every contribution to the debate, especially by Government backbenchers, was in the same sense.

The next day the Cabinet met to consider the matter. They had before them the latest telegram from Baring, dated 9 March. In it Baring stressed that the slave-trade would continue after evacuation whether Zebeyr was there or not, and that a refusal to send him would make it impossible to implement the policy of evacuation. The matter must be settled without delay as Gordon 'thinks there is a considerable danger of his being hemmed in'.

But Baring was 2,000 miles away, and the Anti-Slavery Society was next door. This might bring the Government down, with Liberal dissidents, the Conservative Opposition and the Irish all, for different reasons, uniting against it.

Nevertheless it seemed as though Gordon would have his way. An unsigned note in Gladstone's writing dated 15 March says, 'If Baring . . . thinks it best to send Zebeyr and can make what he may think a proper arrangement with him, we will support him. I much regret that we have been so frightened about Zebeyr.' He made the ingenious suggestion that Gordon should simply be authorized, as governor-general, to appoint whomsoever he pleased as his deputy, 'which would mean Zebeyr', but Her Majesty's Government would be free of blame. Baring was told, 'Cabinet ready to approve choice of Zebeyr . . . but not to make appointment. This should be by Egyptian Government.' But while Gladstone was on the whole for sending for Zebeyr, other ministers were evenly divided, and at the time of the crucial meeting he was again ill. Hartington went to consult him, returning to report, 'He thinks it very likely that we cannot make the House swallow Zebeyr, but he thinks he could.' Gladstone, however, was forbidden by the doctor to leave his bed. Another note in his handwriting completes the story: 'On Saturday 15th it seemed as if by my casting vote Zebeyr was to be sent to Gordon. But on Sunday the Chancellor and Chamberlain receded from their ground and I gave way.' So Gordon's recommendation was turned down after all.[9]

No one can say whether Zebeyr could or would have stood up to the Mahdi. He himself believed, or said he believed, that the Mahdi could not be defeated, but could be persuaded to make an acceptable peace.[10] He might have defected, and there were several unsubstantiated reports that he was in communication with the rebels. He might have proved a back-number, discredited by too long a sojourn in Cairo, with nothing but the remains of a prestige which had no relevance to the Sudan of 1884. But short of full-scale British military intervention, evacuation was possible only if the northern tribes were kept quiet for the vital months of high Nile, and Zebeyr was the only man who might have kept them quiet. The Cabinet, however, would not risk the wrath of the Anti-Slavery Society and a motion of No Confidence in the House of Commons.

But by the time they made their final decision, it was already too late. The moment for Zebeyr was past, for that had happened which Gordon had believed only Zebeyr could prevent. The situation was deteriorating. To the Mahdi's commander in the Gezira Gordon wrote a friendly letter listing reduced taxation, slave-holding and all the goodies he had to offer, but received a dusty answer. Stewart found that up the White Nile the Mahdi's officers were organizing the collection of grain and 'the Arabs were greatly embittered against anyone with a white face'. Of the Sheikh el Obeid, 'a very holy man but a decided trimmer', Gordon had hopes; but when he heard that Gordon had come without troops, the Sheikh seemed inclined to commit himself to the rebels. The Shagiya irregulars (of whom there were 2,000 in the Khartoum garrison) were threatening to change sides unless they got more pay. The Khartoum notables, fearing a servile revolt, refused to allow their slaves to be armed. From Shendy (half-way between Khartoum and Berber) came reports of the Mahdi's agents among the tribes. By 9 March the situation north of Khartoum was so ominous that Stewart noted in his journal, 'Telegraph working.' On that day another lift of civilians to Berber was organized.

On the 9th the telegraph line to Berber was cut, but apparently only by local scallywags, for it was repaired next day. The Sheikh el Obeid's village was reported to be full of rebels with banners, and there were rumours of a rebel advance on Berber. Anticipating a break in the line, Gordon on the 9th and 10th sent Baring a bewildering series of telegrams. Utterly unable to take 'no' for an answer, he first telegraphed, 'If the wire is cut, I shall consider your silence is consent to my propositions and shall hold on to Khartoum and await Zebeyr and British diversion at Berber.' Next he wired, 'I have the written authority of the King of the Belgians to take over the province of Equatoria and Bahr-el-Ghazal and all money responsibilities'; meanwhile Stewart would take the Cairo employees down to Berber, and to facilitate their exodus the Berber-Suakim route should be opened. Half an hour later he wired, 'There is no possibility of the people rallying round me. If you mean to make the proposed diversion to Berber of British troops and to accept my proposal re. Zebeyr, it is worth while to hold on to Khartoum. If you decide on neither of these steps . . . your instructions had better be that I shall evacuate Khartoum with all the employees and troops and move the seat of government to Berber . . . You must give me a prompt reply.' Ten minutes later, 'If the immediate evacuation of Khartoum is determined in spite of outlying towns, propose to send down all Cairo employees and white troops with Stewart to Berber . . . I would also ask H.M.G. to accept the resignation of my commission and I would take all steamers and stores up to the Equatorial and Bahr-al-Ghazal provinces, and consider the provinces as under the King of the Belgians . . . If you object, tell me.'[11] Lest he be under any misapprehension, Baring replied, 'There is no intention on the part of the Government to send an English force to Berber.' But it was not until 9 April that Gordon received this telegram, smuggled through by hand. For on 10 March the telegraph line linking Khartoum and Berber was again, and finally, cut.

Stewart, sending down by steamer his journal and last batch of letters, congratulated Baring on the interruption in the telegraph communication:

The shower of telegrams we have been sending you of late must have acted somewhat like a cold douche. Yesterday I told Gordon that his numerous communications might tend to confuse you, but he replied he was merely giving you different aspects of the same question . . . Unless we evacuate immediately, which would entail the loss of the Sennaar garrison, I can see nothing for it but to hold on here as best we can till the Blue Nile rises . . . We can decide on nothing till we know the intention of H.M. Government:

1. Do they decide on immediate evacuation?
2. Are we to hold on till we can attempt the relief of Sennaar?
3. Will H.M. Government send an expedition to our assistance?

You will of course understand that in the two former cases all may not go well.

I never met anyone whose mind and imagination are so constantly active as Gordon's. For him to grasp an idea is to act on it at once. Hence his numerous telegrams. He dreams and thinks of nothing now but this awful Sudan, so that I assure we get our fill of it.

There was a postscript: 'A considerable body of Arabs has appeared within sight of Khartoum on the right bank of the Blue Nile. We are throwing up a fort on the right bank. The Bashi-Bazouks will form the garrison.' It was the last word Baring was to receive from 'this cool, sagacious and courageous officer'. To Augusta, Gordon wrote, 'The tribes have risen between here and Berber and cut our route.'

The siege of Khartoum had begun.

19

THE DEFENCE OF KHARTOUM

It was not at first a very close siege. There were rebel camps to the north, south-west and south-east, but no ring round the city. With Halfaya, eight miles downstream and held by the Shagiya, there was free communication by steamer. Messages could be smuggled in and out, private letters, despatches to Baring and to *The Times*; but one never knew whether they would get through. Steamers could use the White Nile at any time, the Blue Nile when it rose in June and the Nile down to Berber more hazardously. There was no great shortage of food; the country people brought it in more freely than before Gordon's arrival, and as soon as the Blue Nile rose, grain could be brought from the Sennaar area.

Probably the first six months of the siege were a happy period in Gordon's life. Although sometimes conscience-stricken because 'killing people or devising means to do so has been my lot', he was by temperament a terrific fighter who believed that 'there is no earthly success except in war when you beat your enemy.' As a higher commander he made the fundamental error of underestimating the enemy, from which many ill consequences were to follow. But when it came to fighting, he was in his element. Baker realized it: 'As soon as I heard Gordon was to go to the Sudan, I knew there would be a fight.' With no bureaucratic distractions, no worries about revenue and expenditure, no demands from Cairo for reports and returns, he could concentrate on a job at which he was supremely competent, the defence against odds of a beleaguered town. With the cutting of the telegraph line he was freed from his greatest temptation; with the escape-route cut, evacuation was so obviously impossible without a relief force that he could leave the whole matter to Providence (improbably personified by Mr Gladstone), cease trying to be a politician and just be a soldier. To this he brought immense reserves of courage, determination and faith, and an extraordinary fertility of invention and resource.

Khartoum was an open town with no permanent fortifications. The defended area was roughly triangular in shape, bounded by the Blue Nile, the White Nile and an eight-foot ditch and rampart, built by Abdul Qadir, from 5,900 to 6,700 yards long according to the height of the rivers at each end. In front of this, crows' feet, broken bottles and electrically-detonated land-mines were laid in profusion. Gordon, always the sapper, supplemented these by wire entanglements and small mines actuated by a match if trodden upon. These were somewhat unpredictable: one, exploding prematurely, killed six soldiers and the officer laying it, another merely gave a donkey a fright; but 'we covered the works with them and they have deterred all attacks.' At first the wire was presumably barbed*; but later they had to use telegraph wire for this purpose. 'Land mines are the things for the defence in future,' wrote Gordon; and 'I think good wire entanglements with mines will defend any place if one has anything like moderate troops behind the parapet . . . No field artillery will neutralize their effects, and only a continuous bombardment of days could destroy them.' There were two outworks, Omdurman across the White Nile and North Fort on the right bank of the Blue Nile. Gordon's command-post was at his official residence, the palace or *hukumdariya*, linked by field telegraph to the outer defences which he could watch through a telescope on the roof. The fifteen-mile perimeter, plus outlying forts, although much of it was river-frontage, was too long for 9,000 defenders including volunteers and irregulars; but it had to enclose grazing for the Bashi-Bazouk horses and for cattle, sheep and goats. (In the first months of the siege fresh meat was on the ration, and hospital patients had milk too.)

The steamers were Gordon's greatest asset; each one, he thought, worth 2,000 men. Under Stewart's supervision, the dockyard artificers converted them into miniature warships, armed with Krupp breech-loading cannon and *miltrailleuses*. One of the best was the *Bordein*:

At the bow [was] a rude turret of baulks of wood, fastened together with iron pins, and built up from the deck so as to give a gun-platform, to fire over the bulwarks. The turret was bullet-proof, but not shot- or shell-proof. In this turret there was one gun firing right ahead through a port-hole. At the foot of the turret was the cooking place, where all day long the slave girls were baking *dhoora* cakes for the soldiers and sailors. How they never set the ship on fire was always a mystery. Behind this was the hatchway of the fore-hold; then the fore-mast, to which a bird-cage was slung for a look-out man, a sort of iron bucket; next followed on each side small dirty cabins at either end of the paddle boxes, and between the paddle boxes the midship-turret – a square box built like the other of baulks of wood pinned together. The floor

* Barbed wire had been in mass-production since about 1874.

of the turret was just high enough to enable the one gun in it to fire well over the top of the paddle boxes. Within the turret, shot, shell, and cartridges were lying about in a way that would soon have put an end to a boat not manned by orientals. After the turret came the funnel, with many a bullet hole through it, and the boiler, partly above deck, but protected by logs of wood placed over it. Then came the hatchway of the main-hold, and, just behind it, a saloon or deck-house ... On the top of the saloon a place had been prepared for infantry by making walls of boiler-plate iron. The wheel was on the top of this deck-house, and particular care had been taken to protect the helmsman. Round the sides of the ship the bulwarks and deck-house were protected by sheets of boiler-plate iron fixed to wooden stanchions. Besides the crew, the steamer carried about fifty infantry and artillery men.

Commanded by some of his best officers, the steamers were used for close protection, sorties to break up enemy concentrations, raids to capture cattle and excursions to buy grain. They stank, said Gordon, like badgers.

Gordon's defence was active and aggressive, but the first sortie was a disaster. On 13 March the Ansar had driven the Shagiya irregulars from Halfaya, so on the 16th a force of 4,000 troops was sent to recover the village. With it were two senior black officers. These, it was alleged, first parleyed with the rebels; then, when the fighting started, killed an artillery officer who refused to cease fire and a bugler who refused to sound the retreat. The sortie was defeated; and the two pashas were court-martialled for murder and treason and executed by firing squad. Later Gordon came to believe (though no one else did) that their conviction was unjust, and compensated their families; but this stern action, combined with a curfew and frequent township patrols, put a stop to sniping and other manifestations of Mahdism in Khartoum.

On 22 March there arrived three emissaries with the Mahdi's reply to the letter Gordon had sent from Berber. Its pride, politeness and dignity would have made Gordon realize – had he been able to understand it – how he had underrated his enemy. 'Know that I am the Expected Mahdi, the Successor of the Apostle of God. Thus I have no need of the sultanate, nor of the kingdom of Kordofan or elsewhere, nor of the wealth of this world and its vanity. I am but the slave of God, guiding unto God and to what is with Him . . . and God has succoured me with the prophets and the apostles and the cherubim and all the saints and pious men to revive His Faith . . .' The Turks had misunderstood him, because their concern was for this world, not for the hereafter. His prisoners-of-war could not be sent back, for they had all professed Islam. 'As for the gift which you have sent Us, may God reward you well for your good-will and guide you to the right . . . It is returned to you herewith with the clothing We wish for Ourself and our Companions who desires the world to come.'

In return for the Robe of Honour and *tarbush*, the Mahdi sent a patched *jibbah*, a turban and a rosary. He was not devoid of humour, but Gordon did not see the joke, throwing the gifts angrily away. In a curt reply he addressed the Mahdi as 'Sheikh', thus implying that the grant of the Sultanate of Kordofan was cancelled, and declined further communication.[1]

Along the White Nile, the Blue Nile, and on the west bank downstream of Khartoum the advance guard of the Ansar, some 9,000 men, with thousands of rifles and artillery captured in El Obeid, drew closer. Their chiefs, who included a former judge of the Khartoum Court of Appeal, wrote Gordon an *apologia* for their defection. 'We have no doubt that Mohamad Ahmed is the Mahdi, and we believe in his divine mission. We have been ordered by him to lay siege to you and attack you. If you surrender you will be safe, and bloodshed will be prevented.' Gordon sent a defiant reply. He ordered a steamer to be assembled from pre-fabricated parts which had lain rusting in the dockyard for years; and five steamers to be positioned for close defence – two on the White Nile, two on the Blue Nile and one at the junction.

There was a troublesome shortage of cash, due largely to hoarding, and the money sent from Cairo had not arrived. The troops, if they were to remain loyal, must be paid. So Gordon established a lithographic press for printing serially numbered currency notes of denominations running from 1 to 5,000 piastres, and some of £50. In all, some 91,700 notes, worth £168,500, were printed. At least 50,000 of these were signed by Gordon's own hand, a prodigious labour in the heat and dust of a Khartoum April: thereafter they were signed by an improvised hecto-graph process. At first there was difficulty in getting troops and merchants to accept them, but soon they were so acceptable that many were forged.[2]

The Mahdi appointed a Dongolawi, Abu Girga, as overall commander of the siege. At Messalimieh a government force surrendered, with over 2,000 rifles, and the rebels captured their first steamer. The capture by the Ansar of Shendy tightened the noose, but Gordon was sure that relief was on its way.

His confidence was unfounded. On 13 March Graham had defeated Osman Digna at Tamai, and wished to push on across the desert to Berber. In this he was supported by military authorities in Cairo and by Baring who on 16 March warned Granville that if this was not done, 'the question will very likely arise of sending an expeditionary force to Khartoum to bring away Gordon'. But military advice was conflicting: Wolseley had a keen appreciation, based on his experience in Canada and Ashanti, of the advantages of a river as a main line of communication: he was already thinking in terms of a methodical advance up the Nile from Egypt, and advised against the Suakim–Berber route. This advice the Cabinet gladly accepted, as an advance across the desert was associated with a project dear to certain British commercial interests, of constructing a Suakim–Berber railway, which smacked of imperialism and was hardly compatible with evacuation. So, instead of any military operation, Granville suggested negotiations with Osman Digna ('useless' wired Graham) or sending two Arabic-speaking British officers to Berber.

The two selected were Majors Kitchener, R.E., and Rundle. They were ordered to help Hussein Pasha Khalifa open the route to Suakim, keep contact with Gordon and take their orders from him. In the event the situation was to deteriorate too quickly for this programme to be followed; but Kitchener did good work in strengthening the wavering loyalty of the Kababish tribe, and in supporting Mahmoud el Haj Mohamad, the *Mudir* of Dongola. The latter was a very remarkable man: a Turk, a fanatical Moslem who affected the life-style and even the weapons of a dervish, he was nevertheless loyal to the Khedive, and for several months led his irregulars against the rebels; he was not strong enough to restore the situation, but prevented it from getting worse.

On 24 March Baring tried again. 'The question now is how to get General Gordon and Colonel Stewart away from Khartoum', bearing in mind that 'they would not willingly come back without bringing with them the garrison of Khartoum and the Khartoum officials.'* Either the Suakim–Berber route must be opened immediately, or Gordon must hold on until the autumn when the desert crossing would be easier. He, Stephenson, Wood and Graham all agreed that this route, though risky, was far more promising than the Nile. In a private letter to Granville he said that he blamed himself for letting Gordon go, 'but I do not think we can leave him stranded'.

Nor did the Queen. 'Gordon is in danger,' she telegraphed to Hartington, 'you are bound to try to save him.' Gladstone did not agree. He had before him not only Wolseley's advice against a dash from Suakim, but a telegram from Gordon himself, dated 8 March, saying that he had supplies for six months and that the rebels would probably not venture to attack Khartoum directly.[3] So why all this hurry?

The case for procrastination was put in Gladstone's letter to the Queen on 28 March. In principle he confirmed his verbal assurances that Gordon would be supported:

On the other hand he believes he also indicated to Your Majesty a sense of the difficulties which attach to any full action ... from the number and rapidity of his various declarations, in some instances from their want of

---

* He might have added the Sennaar garrison and the 12,000–15,000 non-officials.

consistency, and from his too free communications with persons who act as correspondents of the public journals. It would not be fair to this remarkable man to omit a reference to the most serious item of all, namely the very imperfect knowledge with which the government are required at the shortest notice to form conclusions in respect of a peculiar, remote and more than half-barbarous region . . . Sir Evelyn Baring . . . makes a declaration which amounts to a reversal of policy; he over-rides the most serious military difficulties; he acts, so far as it appears, alone; he proposes to provide for dangers to General Gordon of the existence of which Your Majesty's Government do not possess evidence; and he does this in ignorance of what are at the time General Gordon's circumstances, opinions and desires. In conversation here yesterday the joint opinion was that an effort be made to ascertain these.[4]

Already on 25 March Granville had acted on this collective indecision. From behind the cover provided by Wolseley and, indeed, Gordon himself, he had in a telegram to Baring finally rejected the Suakim-Berber project and asked what aid Gordon required. 'Her Majesty's Government,' he added, 'desire to leave full discretion to General Gordon to remain in Khartoum if he thinks necessary or to retire by southern or any other route.' Gordon got this helpful message, smuggled through by Cuzzi, two weeks later.

Baring continued loyally to support a man in whose judgement he had little confidence. On 26 March he invited the Cabinet to

place themselves in the position of Gordon and Stewart. They have been sent on a most difficult and dangerous mission by the English Government. Their proposal to send Zebeyr was rejected. The consequences they saw have occurred . . . If it be decided to make no attempt to provide present help, then I would urge that Gordon be told to try and maintain his position during the summer and that then, if he is still beleaguered, an expedition will be sent as early as possible in the autumn to relieve him . . . Having sent Gordon to Khartoum, it appears to me that it is our bounden duty not to abandon him.

Gladstone was unmoved. The Government, Granville telegraphed on 28 March, were unable to agree to send a force in the autumn: Gordon had full discretion to leave Khartoum whenever and by whatever route he wished. They could not add to his instructions until they received 'further information as to General Gordon's condition and prospects as to security, and also if possible his plans of proceeding and his wishes in the present position of affairs in the Sudan.'[5]

The subject of this agonized indecision was now looking elsewhere for succour. To Wood he wrote, 'Turks should be aided and subsidized to put down this trumpery revolt . . . I hear you are forming a black brigade and a Turkish brigade; what possible use can they be except for parade purposes at Cairo? . . . If sent up here they would settle the question of the Sudan and enable us to put down the Mahdi and then, after forming some government, evacuate.'

Sir Samuel Baker, whom Baring found quite insufferable and 'hanging about Cairo waiting for some appointment which he won't get', telegraphed to Gordon, 'Hold Khartoum. England moving.' To him Gordon wrote, 'We are hemmed in by some 500 determined men and some 2,000 rag-bag Arabs.* He asked Baker to sponsor an appeal to British and American millionaires who might pay for 2,000 or 3,000 Turkish troops with Zebeyr in command: 'That would settle the Sudan and the Mahdi for ever.' Another appeal for Turkish troops was sent to the Sultan. They could be financed by mortgaging the customs revenues of Suakim and Massawa. 'If Your Majesty sends these men, they will not have to fire a shot, the rebels will dissolve as ice before them.'

On 9 April Gordon received the month-old warning from Baring. 'So far as I know there is no intention on the part of the Government to send an English force to Berber.' All his suspicion and prejudices revived: Baring, he decided, was responsible for the British Government's pusillanimity. To Baring he telegraphed angrily:

As far as I can understand, the situation is this: you state your intention of not sending any relief force up here to Berber, and you refuse me Zebeyr. I consider myself free to act according to circumstances. I shall hold on here as long as I can, and if I can suppress the rebellion, I shall do so. If I cannot, I shall retire to the Equator and leave you with the indelible disgrace of abandoning the garrisons ... with the certainty that you will eventually be forced to smash up the Mahdi under greater difficulties if you would retain peace in Egypt.

He informed Baring of his appeal to Baker.

I do not see the fun of being caught here to walk about the streets for years as a dervish with sandalled feet; not that, D.V., I will ever be taken alive. It would be the climax of meanness, after I had borrowed money from the people here, had called up them to sell their grain at a low price, etc. to go and abandon them ... and I feel sure that, whatever you may feel diplomatically, I have your support – and that of any man professing himself a gentleman – in private.[6]

Here is Gordon's reason for not making his own getaway with the Egyptian troops and officials, as he could at any time have done. Orders or no orders – and he was never positively commanded to do so – he would never desert thousands of people who, he believed, would be slaughtered by the triumphant dervishes, and to whom he had put himself under an

---

* In Equatoria Gordon had applied the term 'Arab' to almost all non-Sudanese officials and soldiers. But in 1884 it was the term he generally used for the Mahdi's Sudanese rebels.

obligation of honour by calling on them to resist the Mahdi. It is hard to see how anyone can dispute that Gordon – whatever his errors in judgement and his numerous changes of mind – was in this absolutely right. As for his scheme to bring in Turkish troops, Baring and others believed this to be counter-productive, since the revolt was essentially against Turkish misrule.

In mid-April Gordon for the first time flagrantly disobeyed orders: he sent to Berber, to be telegraphed onto Cairo, a message to Zebeyr appointing him Deputy Governor-General of the Sudan and ordering him to proceed to Berber and armour the steamer there. Baring intercepted the message and telegraphed to Granville, 'Zebeyr is being watched and his escape will be prevented.' But these precautions were hardly necessary: Zebeyr had learned from Gordon's press campaign to place a high value on his services. First he refused to go to the Sudan so long as Gordon was there, 'for if anything happened to him it would be on my shoulders.' Then he refused to go so long as he had creditors at his heels, 'it would not be dignified.' The bankrupt Egyptian Government must compensate him to the tune of £947,067 for his confiscated property, or at least let him have £20,000 cash down to settle his more pressing debts, before he would go.[7]

The Cabinet was divided about Gordon. Their confidence in him had completely evaporated. 'A wild man' and 'quite mad', noted Dilke in his diary. Nor did the publication of *Reflections in Palestine* reassure them: Northbrook said that, if he had previously read this, nothing would have induced him to consent to Gordon going anywhere: 'It was the book of a madman.' A year later Gladstone wrote two notes which explain his attitude in the spring of 1884:

I had from the first regarded the revolt of the Sudanese as a justifiable and honourable revolt. We sent Gordon on a mission of peace and liberation . . . I have never understood how this mission of peace became one of war. But we knew the nobleness of his philanthropy, and we trusted him to the utmost . . . He never informed us that he had himself changed the character of his mission . . . Gordon, perhaps insensibly to himself, and certainly without our concurrence, altered the character of his mission and worked in a considerable degree against our intentions and instructions.

On the question of evacuation Gladstone noted that de Coetlogon had in 1883 considered the operation perfectly feasible. 'Why Gordon did not prosecute it is a mystery.' (In de Coetlogon's time the northern tribes had not risen.) 'I incline myself to the belief that, while Gordon's extraordinary gifts exercized a powerful, fascinating influence over those near him, he was quite mistaken in supposing that he had the attachment of a large body of population whom he could not remove and whom we were therefore bound to succour.'[8] Granville, who in the Cabinet was closest to the Prime Minister, could not accept 'that either generals or statesmen who have accepted the offer of a man to lead a forlorn hope are in the least bound to risk the lives of thousands for the uncertain chance of saving the forlorn hope.' He thought that Gordon should have been recalled, but failed to press the view strongly enough to gain support in the Cabinet.[9] Anyhow, if Gordon had been sent a recall-order, could he – and, if so, would he – have obeyed it? Brett, Stephenson and, indeed, Gordon's own communications with Baring gave the Cabinet fair warning that he would not, but Gladstone and Granville never really took cognizance of this.

But although Gordon's advice had often been wild and conflicting and his judgement open to criticism, he had in fact evacuated 2,140 Egyptians in three weeks. If, since 11 March, he had suspended the evacuation, the reason was obvious to all save Mr Gladstone and Lord Granville. Nevertheless there was a growing belief in the Cabinet – not entirely without foundation – that Gordon was now trying to make them change their policy of scuttle into one of conquest. Gladstone, therefore, imperfectly informed by Hartington on the flexibility of Gordon's instructions, was convinced that he had thrown these to the winds and should be left to his fate. Instinctively he believed that if an expedition reached Khartoum to bring him away, Gordon would refuse to leave. Moreover there was trouble brewing in Afghanistan, so he did not wish to commit troops to the Sudan.

Six ministers, while believing in varying degrees that Gordon was disobedient, deceitful and demented, still did not think he should be thrown to the Mahdi. But although they agreed in principle to an expedition, they were at odds about its scope, route and timing. Hartington, briefed by Wolseley, wanted a large expeditionary force and a prolonged occupation of the Sudan for which preparations should start at once. As early as 6 February he had warned Granville:

The Duke of Cambridge has been with me saying what will be said by a great many people, 'that something should be done' . . . If Gordon is shut up there surrounded by infuriated fanatics, what are we going to do about it? Gordon is our officer etc. I know that the Cabinet would not agree to any effectual measures for the support of Gordon . . . but it would be as well to settle what line we are going to take in the event of Gordon coming to grief . . . If he is shut up in Khartoum, can we sit still and do nothing?[10]

Dilke, the wenching, fencing, Browningesque republican romantic, was as angry as any at Gordon's conduct, but saw what Gladstone and

Granville refused to see – that he was in mortal danger and that ordinary schoolboy honour (and the electorate) would demand his rescue. Dilke believed, however, that 'high Nile' would be soon enough; and he shared with Joseph Chamberlain the minimum of military knowledge and the fantasy that 1,000 picked, swiftly moving men could snatch Gordon out of danger. The Lord Chancellor threatened to resign if an expeditionary force was not sent in the autumn, and the Home Secretary if it was. From the wings Baker thundered advice of the most bellicose nature: 'Sir Samuel,' observed Granville, 'has much knowledge of the Sudan (and of the £40,000 which he brought away from it) but is not to be relied upon.'

The 'hawks' outnumbered by six to five the ministers who would have nothing to do with a relief force in any circumstances; but the latter included Granville, the minister most immediately responsible, and Gladstone, aged seventy-five, more obstinate, more unscrupulous and more formidable than the rest of the Cabinet put together. To get his way he used all his political skill – oratory, sophistry, invective and, above all, procrastination, an art in which he excelled. So the Cabinet postponed a decision from week to week, hoping that the problem would solve itself. Had not Gordon himself written, as late as 28 March, 'I think we are now safe, and when the Nile rises, we shall account for the rebels.'? Anyway, the best military advice (Wolseley's) was that no advance was possible until July, so why the hurry?

There were more urgent and interesting matters – notably the preparation of a Franchise Bill – in Westminster than in Khartoum; *The Times* and the Tories were foes more menacing than the Mahdi. As though to emphasize the Cabinet's scale of priorities, Baring was summoned to London to attend a conference on the perennial problem of Egyptian finances. He was replaced in Cairo by Mr Edwin Egerton, who lacked Baring's forceful personality and was even less compatible with Gordon. 'How fatal of Gordon,' he wrote, 'to have made so many statements which were not true to the natives. It lowers trust in our word . . . The second time he went to the Sudan as Governor, his brain was much wilder than the first time; and now the third time it seems to be beyond control.'

In the most narrow sense, Gordon had never asked for a relief force, and ministers in debate made the most of this. But as Hartington wrote to Granville on 15 March, 'I think it is now clear enough that whether he has a right to it or not, he expects help; and it is also I think clear that he will not be able to leave Khartoum without some such help.'[11] On 1 April *The Times* published a week-old despatch from Power, smuggled out to Berber and thence telegraphed. 'We are daily expecting the British troops. We cannot bring ourselves to believe that we are to be abandoned.' Two days later in the Commons, Gladstone, blandly ignoring the realities of power in Cairo and the part played by Her Majesty's Agent-General, drew a specious distinction between Gordon's reporting duties as British commissioner and his executive duties as the Khedive's governor-general. With the latter, he said, Her Majesty's Government could not interfere save in 'a clear necessity'. And, pray, what was the necessity? Gordon was authorized to withdraw whenever he thought proper; 'neither is he under any inability to leave the Sudan at the moment of his choice . . . We gather quite definitely that Gordon believes himself to be safe in Khartoum . . . There is no necessity for our intervention.' Fiercely he rounded on the Opposition who had spoken of the 'failure' of the Government's plan. 'Is that the way those who claim to themselves a monopoly of the terms "loyal", "constitutional" and "patriotic" justify their claims?' As for Mr Power, he was a mere newspaper correspondent, appointed temporary consular agent. 'And yet the right honourable gentlemen take an opinion of Mr Power, transmitted to *The Times*, as virtually equivalent to an official declaration of policy conveying the mature conviction of General Gordon. Really, sir, it is a farce to treat it in such a spirit.' It was a thoroughly dishonest performance, but it routed the Opposition.

The problem of Gordon, however, could not be solved by oratory or political manoeuvring, and the Mahdi was insensitive to resolutions of the House of Commons. On 11 and 13 April, in two powerful memoranda, Wolseley impressed upon Hartington that the Government really 'must at once determine on the line of action or inaction it means to pursue', and let Gordon know. His own opinion was that preparations should start now and that Gordon be informed in clear that help was on its way, and in cypher that it would arrive by mid-November. 'A garrison which knows an English force will come to its relief within a certain time will eat its boots rather than surrender'; 'The English people will force you to do this, whether you like it or not.'[12]

Hartington forwarded this to Granville with a covering note:

We can hardly say any longer that he does not want troops . . . It is nearly time for us to make up our minds what we are to do . . . We are now waiting in hopes that Gordon will send us a message to say that he does not want British troops and that he is going to effect the evacuation of the Sudan without them. It seems rather a broken reed to lean on . . . I do not agree with Northbrook that it would be of any use to send Gordon the most positive orders to come away, leaving the main part of the garrison behind. I do not think he would obey . . . The first thing we have to decide is whether we intend to leave Gordon to his fate, because, if we do not, the sooner we begin preparation the better.[13]

But that was precisely what they could not decide. On 23 April the Cabinet met to consider Wolseley's memorandum; alternative plans for an advance up the Nile or from Suakim; a telegram from Baring saying that they must start preparations at once to take advantage of 'high Nile'; Gordon's proposal to retire to the Equator; and his alternative proposal to bring in a private army of Turks financed by millionaires.

Gladstone cannot be charged with failing to apply his mind to the problem. In preparation for the Cabinet meeting he had jotted down most of the pertinent questions, but supplied answers which confirmed his preconceived notions. Gordon, he noted, 'apparently thinks [Khartoum safe against all attacks] for many months. Has never asked for a British soldier at Khartoum. Has never intimated that he cannot get away, but rather the contrary. Has shown no sign of being ready to retreat now. Nor of being hard-pressed by tribes in the vicinity.' From these reflections he drafted some notes for his colleagues:

1. We ought not to act in the Sudan otherwise than by pacific means except for the safety of Gordon and his party. 2. If in consequence of his being in danger we have to act by military means, the object of our action ought to be, and to be known to him to be, to bring him away at once from Khartoum. 3. Gordon should be informed that we can be no parties to supplying him with Turkish or other forces for the purpose of undertaking military operations, and that such proceedings are not within the scope of any commission which he holds, and are at entire variance with the pacific policy which was the purpose of his mission to the Sudan.

It followed that the only action necessary was to ask Gordon if he was in danger and what help he required. After four hours' discussion Gladstone as usual had his way. Gordon was asked what he intended to do, and what force, advancing by what route, would suffice to rescue him – an inquiry which took three months to reach him.[14]

A vast gulf of misunderstanding separated the soldier in Khartoum from the politicians in Westminster. They could not begin to visualize the problems in withdrawing thousands of terrified Egyptians, men, women and children, through hundreds of miles of hostile territory. Even to communicate with Gordon required that a message be written in minute handwriting on a piece of fine parchment, which was rolled up and inserted into a quill for secretion in the traditional hiding-place in the courier's body. Her Majesty's Government was willing to pay £800 to anyone who would take a message to Khartoum and return with an answer in thirty days, but there were no takers.[15] How could enlightened Liberal statesmen in the age of Darwin, steam-engines and gas-lighting grasp so bizarre a situation? It escaped their comprehension (and, to be fair, Gordon's) that it is far easier to find people to carry messages out of than into a besieged town; because some of Gordon's messages eventually reached them, they assumed that theirs reached him; and, receiving no reply to their fatuous questions, concluded that he was deliberately ignoring them: 'If,' complained Granville, 'Gordon can communicate with the outer world, it is monstrous his not doing so with us.'[16] As in great issues, so in small. Baring had passed on an earlier proposal by Gordon to retain 3,000 'black' soldiers to establish Zebeyr. No one but Liberal politicians could have equated 'black' with 'Egyptian', but they saw this as evidence that Gordon was deliberately defying instructions to evacuate Egyptian troops.

On 25 April Parliament reassembled after the Easter recess and the Opposition tabled a Censure Motion, 'That this House regrets that the course pursued by Her Majesty's Government has not tended to promote the success of General Gordon's mission, and that even such steps as are necessary to promote his personal safety are still delayed.'

The motion was down for debate on 12 May, the very day on which the difficulties of communicating with Khartoum were much increased by the rebels surrounding Berber. This made a relief expedition more difficult and more urgent, but it did not weaken the Prime Minister's determination not to send one. Rather than resort to the hateful use of military force, the campaigner of Midlothian was even 'inclined, if Gordon agrees, to make him over to the Turk'.[17] The Cabinet, Morley told Blunt, 'were ready to bite their tongues out' for having sent Gordon, who 'had done everything he said he wouldn't do and nothing that they told him to do'. Gladstone could not express himself quite so freely in the House: he insisted that Gordon had been sent solely on a peaceful, reporting mission; had never asked for British soldiers to relieve him; and had never said he was prevented from leaving Khartoum. What about the other garrisons? Were the Conservatives prepared to send expeditions to relieve them all? Would they say, here and now, that they would send one to Khartoum? Glaring at the Opposition, stabbing his finger at them, he screamed, 'Look! Dumb!' The Censure Motion was defeated.

It was in this debate that Gladstone used words often to be quoted against him. A relief expedition, he said, would be a 'war of conquest against a people struggling to be free. [Oh! Oh!] Yes, these are people struggling to be free, and rightly struggling to be free.' It was a view that Gordon in the past had frequently expressed, but his mood was now very different. Having inspected the hospitals, schools, workshops and steam-driven dockyards of Khartoum, he wrote angrily to Baring, 'It is deplorable to think of their destruction by a feeble lot of stinking dervishes.' Similar sentiments stimulated private enterprise in Britain.

There was a scheme to send to the hero's rescue a private army, financed by Baroness Burdett-Coutts, of big-game hunters, 'men who would go a thousand miles to shoot a lion'. Or perhaps a single lion-hunter named 'Curly' Knox should travel to Khartoum in disguise and carry Gordon away with him. Gordon's admirer, Mrs Surtees-Allnatt, started raising £80,000 to buy his way out through the tribes. Blunt offered to go alone to Kordofan and negotiate with the Mahdi. Short of a proper relief force, this was perhaps the most promising suggestion; Gladstone's Private Secretary, who rather fancied it, minuted that Blunt 'is not as cracked as Gordon and is as well acquainted with Arabs and their ways'; but Granville preferred 'Gordon's madness to Blunt's' and the spirited offer was refused.

It is difficult for us to appreciate the vehemence of the public demand for Gordon's relief. No modern government would dream of sending even a helicopter to rescue its officer threatened by an anti-colonialist rebellion; they would be far too scared of progressive protest. But the progressive establishment of 1884 was generally for a rescue. As Forster pointed out of the Commons, hitherto the Government had done little but ask Gordon if he was in danger: 'I believe everyone but the Prime Minister is convinced of that danger.' Since Britain's hero was imperilled, Britain must rescue him. This instinctive reaction, extending far beyond the Conservative Opposition and the anti-slavery lobby which by rejecting Zebeyr had virtually condemned Gordon to death, was made up of many disparate elements: admiration for Gordon's achievements and image as warrior-saint; jingoism; racial arrogance and shame at being beaten by the dervishes; hatred of the slave-trade; humanitarianism; commercial and capitalist ambitions; the spirit of evangelical missionary endeavour. Early in May there were mass meetings in Hyde Park and Manchester to protest against Gordon's abandonment. Subscriptions towards the cost of a relief force (including £5,000 from 'a well-known lady') poured into the editorial office of *The Times* and were all returned because it was 'impossible to relieve the Government of its responsibility'. Editorials denounced the Government's evasiveness and dishonesty; *The Times* called for prayers 'for General Gordon in imminent peril at Khartoum'; and the Prime Minister was publicly hissed.

Not that he cared a rap for the public when he thought it was misguided. As a result of the censure debate Gordon was again 'enjoined to consider and either report on, or if possible, to adopt at the first proper moment measures for his own removal and for that of the Egyptians in Khartoum . . . by whatever route he may consider best.' He received this message in August.[18]

After a week's siege Berber was surrendered by Hussein Pasha Khalifa who forthwith joined the Mahdi. Nor was Cuzzi more heroic, preferring apostasy to martyrdom. A serious loss was of the small steamers, *Fasher* and *Musselemieh*, captured by the dervishes when the town fell. Included in the loot was £60,000 on its way from Cairo to Khartoum, Gordon's medals and Stewart's uniform. Cuzzi, renamed Mohamad Yusuf and dressed as a dervish, was sent to Khartoum with a summons to surrender. Gordon had no use for Christians who 'denied their Lord' and curtly requested the Mahdi, if he sent any more emissaries, not to send a European.

The fall of Berber had no immediate effect on Khartoum. Indeed during the following weeks the defence prospered. Heavy rains in April raised the level of the Nile abnormally early, giving the steamers more freedom of action. Sorties brought in sheep, cattle and corn. Stewart, by 'two splendidly directed shots from a 20-pounder at the Palace', demolished the most dangerous of the enemy gun-positions. He, Power and Ibrahim Fauzi formed Gordon's staff. The steamers were commanded by two first-class Egyptian officers, Mohamad Nushi Pasha and Saati Bey; the land-sorties by an equally good man, Mohamad Ali, 'the fighting Pasha'; the garrison as a whole by the Mexican veteran, Faragh ez Zeini, now general and pasha.

Gordon himself, as governor-general, took no part in the sorties, though he was often under fire; sometimes he amused himself by taking a rifle and spending an hour sniping; he nearly lost an eye when the base of a cartridge blew back. But he was the brain and heart of the defence – supervising the training of citizen volunteers and Shagiya levies; making the rounds of the sentries by day and night; strengthening the defences by mine-fields and wire-entanglements; organizing the fitting out of his flotilla; boosting the arsenal's weekly output to 40,000 rounds of Remington ammunition; bullying and jollying traders into selling their hidden grain reserves; ensuring that the *ulema* stressed the falsity of the Mahdi's pretensions; keeping up everyone's spirits by the extraordinary magnetism which he exercised over all in contact with him. In all major decisions he consulted the council of notables, associating them with the defence.

A feature of his public image was a disdain for the honours of this world. To Baring he wrote, 'It may be bad taste to say, but if we get out of this, give Stewart the K.C.M.G. but spare me the disagreeableness of having to refuse it.' He was, however, alive to the importance of medals to soldiers' morale, and in the past had gone to considerable pains to ensure that veterans of the Ever Victorious Army and of the Sudanese contingent in Mexico received the campaign-medals due to them, and that there was new *Légion d'Honneur* ribbon for the handful of black officers entitled to wear it. Now, assuring Baring 'you will not be asked to pay for it', he instituted a Khartoum siege medal in silver-gilt, silver and copper, which proved enormously popular, changing hands at high black-market prices; he also made a liberal distribution of bey and pasha titles to deserving (and in some cases undeserving) officers and civilians. Less efficacious were his direct appeals for intervention by the Sultan of Turkey and the Pope; nor did he succeed with his attempts to win over the Mahdi's adherents. But he never rested, never despaired; and if from time to time he sought relief in the brandy-bottle, there is no evidence of this. He smoked incessantly.

At home the ground-swell of public opinion became more disturbing. Hartington's attitude was crucial. He was widely respected for integrity, if not for intellectual eminence, and as heir to the Duke of Devonshire he headed the aristocratic Whig element in the Liberal Party. His resignation could bring down the Government, and he was much influenced by Wolseley. The latter protested that he wished to avoid the bloodshed and expense of a relief expedition. It might have been avoided by sending Zebeyr, 'the ablest ruffian in all Egypt', but that chance had been lost. Now he hoped that active and obvious preparations, 'like building boats, providing transport etc.', would weaken the Mahdi's resolution; but this was not done either. Wolseley was getting restive; so, therefore, was Hartington.

Gladstone's opposition to any relief expedition in any circumstances was weakening. On 13 May he told Dilke that he intended to raise the question of Gordon's rescue at the proper time. But political rather than military considerations still dictated the route it should take: the Suakim-Berber route, with its implication of a railway, he ruled out because 'it would be to our immense advantage that the expedition (should one be needed) should be . . . *leaving no* trace behind it.'[19] Throughout June he was still hoping that no expedition would be necessary, and was encouraged by a rumour of 'Garibaldi [sic] quitting Khartoum'. This proved to be false, but Sir Henry Gordon assured him that his brother did not want any English relief force. Henry's interventions were unhelpful. 'Do you still wish to have Zebeyr up?' he telegraphed to Gordon on 27 July. 'If so, I will manage it provided I have the request under your hand . . . Do not write to Government.' He followed this up by a most injudicious letter to Zebeyr which caused Baring to infer that 'we have to deal with two lunatics in the Gordon family.'[20]

On 20 July there was telegraphed from Dongola a message from Gordon that Khartoum and Sennaar were '*en bonne défence*' and asking for news of the relief expedition. He was again informed that 'the Government continue to be anxious to learn from himself his views and position, so that if danger has arisen or is likely to arise . . . they may be in a position to take measures accordingly.' This helpful message took four months to reach him.

But Khartoum, Wolseley pointed out, must sooner or later run out of food and ammunition; 'poor Gordon will have his throat cut', and he himself did 'not wish to share the responsibility of leaving Charley Gordon to his fate'. A brigade must be sent out now, if it was to reach Khartoum by mid-October. He warned the Duke of Cambridge that 'Gordon must be relieved before his Krupp ammunition runs out (as it must very soon).' The Duke suggested that at least Krupp ammunition be sent to Dongola, though how this would help Khartoum was not very clear. But Gladstone was unmoved: 'The ammunition is to be sent to enable Gordon to work out a policy opposite to ours.'[21]

In vain Hartington pressed Gladstone for a Cabinet decision, writing, 'I really do not feel I know the mind or intention of the Government . . . We may at any time receive news from Khartoum which may show the necessity for an expedition for Gordon's release. The time is approaching when military operations may be possible as regards climate, but I may have to tell the Cabinet that for want of preparations nothing can be done.' He was the minister most troubled in his conscience, but he had not the personality to insist on his colleagues grappling with the problem, which was put off from week to week. 'At the last Cabinet,' he complained to Granville on 15 July, 'summoned, as I hoped, to decide on [the expedition], I got five minutes at the fag-end, and was as usual put off.'[22] Selborne, the Lord Chancellor, was also troubled, and argued, that Her Majesty's Government really could not act towards its own servant, 'who has accepted at our instance a mission of extraordinary difficulty', as if it had no responsibility towards him. Gladstone disagreed: 'To send an expedition at the present time would be to act in the teeth of the evidence as to Gordon . . . and would be a grave and dangerous error.' On his instructions, Egerton again, on 31 July, wrote asking Gordon, 'if you are in prospect of danger. If so, advise us as to force necessary for your removal . . . You are free to promise money rewards.' But Hartington's attitude was crucial, and on 31 July he at last threatened resignation if no expedition were sent. In a letter written to Granville for circulation to other ministers he wrote, 'It is a question of personal honour and good faith, and I do not see how I can yield upon it.'[23]

Gladstone realized he was almost cornered. 'Hartington's letter,' he wrote to Granville, 'creates a very formidable state of things.' Whatever the fate of Khartoum, the Government would fall if no expedition were sent or, at least, more or less promised. On 5 August Gladstone himself moved in the Commons for a sum 'not exceeding £300,000 to enable Her Majesty to undertake operations for the relief of General Gordon, should they become necessary'. To his accomplice, Granville, he pointed out that this in itself did not commit the Government to anything; however, Wolseley could at last start ordering boats. On 8 August General Stephenson was sent orders to assemble transport and supplies, concentrate a British brigade at Wadi Halfa, and make other contingent preparations.[24]

It might have been thought that the Prime Minister would now wish to send the relief force without further delay. Such was not his intention: as he saw it, the longer the delay, the better, for there was always the chance that the expedition might prove unnecessary. To this straw he clung throughout August. Could not the *Mudir* of Dongola 'play the part so unhappily projected by Gordon for Zebeyr?' Kitchener, the man on the spot, had reported that the Kababish tribe might be bribed to rescue Gordon, though he added ominously, 'Who will guarantee, if they do go to Khartoum, that Gordon will come out?' On 19 August Gladstone was convinced that Gordon, despite his 'wild telegrams', 'if he thinks fit can make his way to Dongola'. The Government, therefore, was 'not at present convinced that it will be impossible for General Gordon . . . to secure the withdrawal from Khartoum by the employment of force or by pacific means of the Egyptian garrisons and of such of the inhabitants as wish to leave.'[25]

Deftly withdrawing the last ace from his sleeve, Gladstone ruled that the final decision could not be made without consulting every member of the Cabinet who must not 'become unawares the slaves of Gordon's (probably) rebellious ideas'. As ministers were now dispersed from the Highlands to the Riviera, such consultation could not be hurried. Hartington did not believe that Gordon could send out messages: if it were possible, Power would have sent one to *The Times*, for such a message would be worth thousands of pounds. 'There is no proof,' he protested, 'that Gordon is ignoring or acting in opposition to our instructions'; and in any case public opinion 'would not be satisfied if our action is in any degree based on that supposition . . . If when the Cabinet is scattered all over the country . . . I have to wait to collect the opinions of Ministers . . . I despair of acquitting myself of the responsibility that will be placed on me.' Gladstone, however, insisted on this last delay, and even deluded himself that a small force of 'a few hundreds' would suffice. 'I am very glad,' he congratulated Granville, 'that your consent was limited to this minor effort.'[26]

Nevertheless matters were now out of the hands of the politicians: military preparations proceeded at their own sluggish momentum, if only because by 15 August already £750,000 had been spent on Parliament's authority to spend £300,000. It was decided that Wolseley should command. He arrived in Cairo on 9 September, accompanied by Baring. The latest news from the Sudan was reassuring, Kitchener telegraphing from Dongola on 2 September that letters passed into Khartoum fairly easily. 'There is no doubt,' he reported on receiving a somewhat garbled message from Khartoum, 'that Gordon means he can hold out till the middle of November. From conversations with his messengers I think he can hold out longer, and when he knows English troops are coming, everything will be easier for him.'

As late as 16 September Wolseley was warned not to move unless it was absolutely necessary; and it was not until the 25th that he was given formal orders to go ahead. 'The primary object of the expedition is to bring away General Gordon and Colonel Stewart from Khartoum . . . Supreme military and civil power will be conferred on you . . . General Gordon and Colonel Stewart are placed under your instructions.' He was also to use 'his best endeavour' to evacuate the Egyptian soldiers and civilians; and was given a wide discretion in the selection of a successor government, provided he did not select Zebeyr. He was armed with the Khedive's *firman* too, just in case he needed it with Gordon.[27]

Khartoum's aggressive defence still prospered, despite a 3,000 per cent inflation aggravated by the hoarding of food. The municipal authorities carried out a search which disclosed large quantities of grain buried in merchants' houses. This was confiscated and sold at a reasonable price or distributed as rations to some 3,000 people too poor to buy. Hospital patients still had fresh bread, butter and meat, and Gordon organized backgammon and dominoes for them. By fierce sorties the dervishes were driven back some miles, which enabled the peasants to bring in more produce for sale; and the steamers under Saati Bey made almost daily raids, shooting up rebel positions, destroying the irrigation works of hostile tribes, bringing in corn, sheep and in a single raid as much as 1,000 cattle.

On 10 July, however, there was a set-back. Saati Bey, having burnt a rebel camp on the Blue Nile, attacked another position. There a square of 200 *fellahin* troops was broken by a charge of only eight dervish horsemen, and Saati was killed. But the blacks under Mohamad Ali had a brilliant success on 28 July at Buri on the Blue Nile, capturing seventy-eight Remingtons besides a large quantity of other arms, ammunition and horses. Gordon had forbidden the practice of bringing in the heads of dead rebels, so no accurate count of enemy casualties could be made. The following day the steamers and armoured barges cleared thirteen small and two large rebel forts, demolishing two artillery pieces. Resorting to his favourite tricks of psychological warfare, Gordon sent black soldiers to entice over, with promises of clothes, food and pay, the Ansar's slaves and *Jihadiya*: 'The general opinion is that the rebels will leave dangerous vicinity, not for fear of bullets, but for fear of losing their live chattels.' This did not happen, but at least, thanks to Gordon's initiative, desertion was a two-way traffic. When blacks came over, he gave them a dollar and showed them their 'black pug faces' in a mirror . . . 'they have never seen themselves before. They generally approve of the reflection, especially the black sluts who think themselves Venuses.'

A more questionable psychological tactic was the frequent publication of news of English and Turkish troops, 20,000 or 30,000 advancing on Khartoum from Dongola and Kassala. Gordon used to draw pictures of these phantom soldiers, saying he had received them by smuggled post. At first this had a good effect on morale; but eventually, when no relief came, it became counter-productive. Military bands were kept hard at work, playing cheerful music on Fridays and Sundays.

On the night of 29 July Gladstone's questionnaire of 23 April was smuggled in. Gordon replied with gusto:

> You ask me 'to state cause and intention in staying in Khartoum, knowing Government means to abandon Sudan', and in reply I say, 'I stay at Khartoum because the Arabs have shut us up, and will not let us out.' I also add that even if the road was open, the people would not let me go, unless I gave them some government or took them with me, which I could not do. No one would leave more willingly than I would, if it was possible.

He further assured Baring (not, perhaps, with absolute truth) that 'if there was any way of avoiding this wretched fighting, I would avoid it, for the whole war is hateful to me. The people refuse to let me go out on expeditions for fear of the bother that would arise if anything happened, so I sit on tenterhooks of anxiety.' But 'the troops and people are full of heart. The Arabs are in poor heart.' Since 16 March the garrison had lost only 30 killed, 50 or 60 wounded. 'The only reinforcements the Sudan has received since 27 Nov. 83 . . . is seven persons, including myself! And we have sent down over 600 soldiers and 2,000 people. The people here and the Arabs laugh over it.' He hoped soon to open the Blue Nile, relieve Sennaar and then retake Berber. 'I will conclude by saying that we will defend ourselves to the last, that I will not leave Khartoum, that I will try to persuade all Europeans to escape, and that I am still sanguine that, by some means not clear, God will give us the issue.'[28] Baring received this letter, dated 30-31 July, two months later.

It was not difficult to get messages out of Khartoum, the safest way being to Kassala whence a Seyid of the Khatmiya religious brotherhood, hostile to the Mahdi, forwarded them to Suakim. ('You ought to give him a present of £500.') It was very difficult to pass them in. One of

Augusta's letters was photographed, reduced to a size so small that it can hardly be read with even the most powerful magnifying-glass, rolled up and hidden in a cartridge-case.

On 18 September there arrived in Cairo three long messages from Gordon, addressed to the Khedive, Baring and Nubar, one dated 23 August, the other apparently written earlier. He stressed again that evacuation was impossible without a British relief expedition, and that Zebeyr with a Turkish force must be sent up to hold the Sudan. 'Gordon's letters,' wrote Baring, 'appear more rational than anything he has written since his arrival in Khartoum.' But the Cabinet still thought them 'wild'. Hartington suggested that Wolseley be consulted: 'He knows Gordon and is more likely to be able to interpret his dark sayings . . . Gordon has never understood us nor we him.'[29]

What particularly upset them was a sentence in Gordon's letter that he was sending Stewart with the steamers to take and burn Berber, the steamers returning and Stewart then going onto Dongola to open communication with the relief force. The gist of these messages was leaked to the press, and when Gladstone read of this satanic plot to incinerate the very homes of freedom-fighters (mud huts which could be rebuilt in a day) 'his face hardened and whitened, his eyes burnt . . . with a deep fire as if they would have consumed the paper.' That man was not merely a lunatic, but was palpably trying to bully Her Majesty's Government into a policy of conquest to which it was adamantly opposed. With a brow like thunder he strode from the room, and a few hours later Baring was instructed that the delinquent be downgraded from Governor-General of the Sudan to Governor of Khartoum, and placed unequivocally under Wolseley's orders. Stewart was sent repeated orders *not* to burn Berber. 'We must get at Gordon,' wrote the Prime Minister to Hartington, 'and bring to issue his future conduct and position. I do not see that we have much misjudged him . . . I feel we shall have trouble with him yet.' Wolseley, too, foresaw trouble, but warned Hartington, 'Do what any government may like to discredit him, Gordon will always be a favourite with the English people . . . a dangerous man for any government to abandon and throw over.'[30]

Gordon never heard of his demotion; though perhaps it was in anticipation of something of the kind that (not for the first time) he resigned his commission in Her Majesty's service and informed the Chief of Staff of the expeditionary force that, 'appointed by Tewfik Pasha (the *soi-disant* ruler of this land), it is in my limits to appoint any other person I may select as provisional Governor-General . . . and to hand over the government to him.' He sent Mohamad Ali on another successful raid up the Blue Nile, and wrote on 24 August, 'We are going to hold out here forever.' But his luck was running out. He decided to break up a rebel concentration at El Foun, twenty-five miles up the Blue Nile. On 4 September Mohamad Ali dispersed it; but next day, pressing the pursuit beyond range of the steamers' guns, he fell into an ambush and was killed with over 1,000 of Gordon's best infantry.

This was unmitigated disaster: in a couple of hours Gordon had lost the pick of his striking force. The Ansar now closed in and the peasants ceased bringing supplies to market. No longer could he think of capturing Berber; the best he could do was to send down to Dongola not another message, written on cigarette-paper and carried in the fundament of a native who might or might not get through and could not influence the authorities if he did, but his Chief of Staff, who could describe exactly the plight of Khartoum and whose words would carry weight. The precise circumstances of Stewart's departure are not known. In three letters written to Baring in July and August Gordon had said he would *send* Stewart, 'if he will consent to go'. But in his journal of 3 and 5 November he says that Stewart, when he heard that the *Abbas* was going down with despatches,

said he would go, if I would exonerate him for deserting me. I said, 'You do not desert me. *I* cannot go, but if you go, you do great service.' I then wrote him an official; he wanted me to write him an order. I said, 'No, for though I fear not responsibility, I will not put you in any danger in which I am not myself.' I wrote a letter, couched thus: '*Abbas* is going down; you say you are willing to go in her, if I think you can do so in honour. You can go in honour, for you can do nothing here, and if you go, you will do me a service in telegraphing my views.'

'This,' Gordon said, he did 'on account of eventualities which might arise'; that is to say, he did not want to be accused of sending Stewart to his death. Gordon's description of Stewart as 'a brave, just, upright gentleman', and Stewart's letters written to Gordon on his way downstream, indicate that they parted in complete accord. With Stewart went Power and Herbin, the French Consul, who had taken a vigorous part in the defence.

Gordon planned their expedition with care. He had the *Abbas* fitted with buffers to protect its bottom against submerged rocks; he sent the steamers *Safia* and the *Mansurah* to escort them past Berber; he instructed them never to land except to collect fuel from some lonely spot; and he sent also two sailing-boats containing nineteen heavily-armed Greeks. With them went private letters, despatches, Stewart's journal and, inexplicably, Gordon's cypher-books. They carried a reproachful letter to Baring:

How many times have we written asking for reinforcements? No answer at all has come to us ... and the hearts of men have become weary at this delay. While you are eating and drinking and resting on good beds, we ... are watching night and day, endeavouring to quell the movements of this false Mahdi ... The reason why I have now sent Colonel Stewart is because you have been silent all this while and neglected us, and lost time without doing any good. If troops were sent, as soon as they reach Berber this rebellion will cease.

They left Khartoum on 8 September. On the same day the *Bordein* and the *Tel el Hawein* with a strong force under Mohamad Nushi were sent up the Blue Nile to collect supplies, replenish the Sennaar garrison and bring back the *Ismailia*.

20

♠ THE DEFENDER OF KHARTOUM

Gordon was now on his own, and very lonely. His ignorance of their language was a barrier to friendship with Egyptians and Arabs; poor old sozzled Hansal, with his seven 'female attendants', was no great social asset, nor was the Austrian tailor. Among the remaining Greeks the only one he found congenial was George Stamboulieh, an old friend from his former days in Khartoum, though Stamboulieh was frankly a defeatist who advised surrender. Every day Gordon spent hours writing up his journal – a mixture of war-diary, reminiscence, religious soliloquy and political reflection. Much of it was devoted to the turkey-cock who tyrannized over his backyard until tucked under the Governor-General's arm and rocked to sleep. ('I am one of those who believe in the fore and future existence of what we call animals.') There were digressions into subjects so diverse as the award of the Victoria Cross; the Army Medical Department ('bores and croakers'); Indian soldiers (of which he knew nothing); human glory ('nine-tenths twaddle, perhaps ninety-nine hundredths twaddle'); nepotism (he was against it), and voluntary euthanasia (he was for it).

Sandwiched between all this irrelevant matter – sometimes four or five thousand words a day – were advice, protests and admonition for Baring, Her Majesty's Government and the commander of the relief force. It was as discursive as his private correspondence from Equatoria and Kordofan, but at first ironic rather than cross, humorous – even flippant – and at times almost serene. It does not suggest that he was generally unhappy, though he was at times under pressure from a growing persecution-complex.

The journal was in six volumes, early volumes being endorsed, 'To be read and copied by Colonel Stewart, and extracts given Mr Power (as by promise). Afterwards to be given to Miss Gordon, Southampton, if not wanted by Foreign Office.' As it was to have a wide official and private circulation, it was also endorsed, 'No secrets so far as I am concerned' and, 'To be pruned down if published.' None of those for whom it was written were to see it before mid-January.

Cuzzi – Mohamad Yusuf – brought more messages from the besiegers. 'He looked pretty miserable' and was made to crawl on hands and knees along a zigzag path through the mine-fields, well primed with tales of this frightful new weapon. He brought a lot of information, some perhaps true, about the Mahdi, and returned with a headstall which an Ansar emir had lost in the last battle ('at which they were amused'). His arrival led Gordon to reflect on the phenomenon of apostasy. 'If the Christian faith is a myth, then let men throw it off; but it is mean and dishonourable to do so merely to save one's life if one believes it is the true faith. What can be more strong than the words, "He who denies me on earth, I will deny in Heaven".' At El Obeid, he was told, all the priests and nuns, except the Superior, Don Luigi Bononi, had apostasized, and the nuns had married Greeks to save themselves from outrage. ('What a row the Pope will make! . . . It is the union of the Greek and Latin churches.') Moslems' apostasy was no less deplorable: 'There is scarcely a great family in the Sudan who have not accepted Mohamad Ahmed as Mahdi to save their property.' He lectured the *ulema* on the degeneracy of modern religion, and to Cuzzi's grovelling request for an interview he replied, 'I do not want to see you.'

In mid-September the main army of the Ansar arrived at Omdurman. It was led by the Mahdi's Field Commander, a man of the Jaalin tribe named Abdur Rahman el Nejumi (or Wad-el-Nejumi). Although without formal military training, he was a very able general, and he brought with him a number of artillery pieces captured in El Obeid and served by Egyptian deserters. These included modern mountain guns, a serious danger to Gordon's steamers.

With Wad-el-Nejumi and Ibrahim Abd el Qadir, Gordon conducted a lengthy and fruitless correspondence, using George Stamboulieh as his go-between. Making a particular set at Ibrahim, a highly atypical dervish whom he remembered as a Khartoum judge, he sought to win him over by gifts of soap (a commodity in short supply among the rebels) and arguments from the *ulema* discrediting the Mahdi's claims. He got no change, only profuse compliments:

Your mercy and kindness to the natives in general and to us in particular are admitted by all . . . but the truth of this Imam, the Expected Mahdi, peace be on him, does not allow us to accept your instructions. We cannot ignore God's orders and his Prophet's . . . We have warned you three times because of your love to us . . . our aim was your safety and the safety of the citizens, but our warnings were without avail: flattered by the hypocritical words of the useless *Ulema* you have with you, you deny the truth of the Mahdiya of this Imam.[1]

Calling on Gordon to surrender, Wad-el-Nejumi warned him that the Mahdi had

supplied us with trusty men from among his companions, men who love death as ye love life, and who count on fighting you as the great reward ... He has provided us with weapons of war in which thou thinkest is the victory – with Krupp cannon and mountain guns ... And know, Oh Honourable Pasha ... that if thou dost submit to the command of God and His Prophet, thou shalt save thyself and ... those who are with thee. Otherwise do not doubt that ye will be destroyed.

If Gordon's temper was short – on one occasion it was so short that he thrashed his cook for failing to buy some tea-cups – it was largely due to the intrigues of the Shagiya tribe. The two most effective loyalists were the formidable Mirghani sisters, Fatmeh and Nefiseh, who bullied the Shagiya elders into taking an oath of loyalty to the Government but could not make them keep it. The Shagiya deserted, they thieved, they bore false witness – yet they and the Kababish were the only tribes north of Khartoum who had not gone over wholly to the Mahdi; they held the isolated outpost of Halfaya; and they provided some 2,300 levies of dubious quality for the Khartoum garrison. Those who joined the Mahdi – and Gordon very sensibly allowed the disaffected to do so – complained that the loyalists were unlawfully holding back their slaves, so Gordon had to make a special trip downriver to Halfaya and ask 'each pug-face' whether he wished to remain with the Government or join his master with the rebels. 'The Shagiya know no shame; it is an unknown quantity with them. I wish I commanded the Arabs professionally speaking.' As soldiers the Shagiya were on a par with the Bashi-Bazouks and *fellahin* troops: dispraise could go no further. The only soldiers in Khartoum worth the name were the Negroes – 'as cocky as possible' and 'wonderfully clean ... with the gloss of a well-cleaned and polished boot, such as the little London shoeblack loves to turn out for a penny'.

At least one of Gordon's clerks was heart and soul for the Mahdi, and let out that it was he who invented reports of English troops advancing; but Gordon could not send him to the Mahdi because he knew too many secrets. His Chief Clerk, Ibrahim Rushdi, was venal, impertinent and malingering. The postal clerks, who had nothing to do, demanded a rise in pay (inflation, they said). 'One comes on a group of clerks, heads all together, in the chief clerk's room; one sees disturbed countenances. I cannot help thinking, "You are concocting some devilry".'

As for his innumerable servants! 'If these are not *eating*, they are *saying* their *prayers*; if not *saying their prayers*, they are *sick*. One snatches at them at intervals ... You want to send an immediate order, and there is your servant, bobbing up and down, and you cannot disturb him ... If I am in a bad temper, which I fear is often the case, my servants will be always at their prayers.'

If the servants were abominable, Her Majesty's diplomats – Egerton, Baring and Co. – were worse: 'I hate our diplomats ... They are arrant humbugs'; 'Baring deigned to say he would support me. Of course, that was of enormous importance, to have his approbation!' Indeed he had convinced himself that they positively *wanted* him to fail. When Stewart, Power and Herbin arrived at Dongola, Her Majesty's Government would be 'most disagreeably surprised by their emerging. "Why could not these fellows wrap their togas around them and disappear and not bother us?" '

His capacity for self-delusion was further illustrated by a passage in his journal for 18 September which he deleted but left legible: 'My whole efforts have been directed to carry out my instructions, viz the withdrawal of the garrison and the refugees; and had it not been for the defeat of Mohamad Ali Pasha, I should have got them out, at least two-thirds of them at Khartoum and Sennaar.'[2] This is just not true. Mohamad Ali was killed on 5 September: no effort at evacuation was made after the rebels cut the escape route to the north on 10 March, since this obviously made the operation quite impossible without a relief force.

As before, his ignorance of Arabic was a terrible drawback. Spies and deserters brought him rumours of all kinds, and because he could not cross-examine them, he swallowed the most ridiculous stories: the Mahdi, he was told, induced crocodile tears at appropriate moments with pepper carried under his fingernails; the Mahdi was dead; the Mahdi was advancing on Omdurman – no, he had been recalled by a rebellion in Kordofan. The Mahdi's black *Jihadiya* had been disarmed – would at the first battle turn against the Ansar – would come over in droves. A heroic little rebel had been shot for declaring that he believed Mohamad Ahmed was the Mahdi and his opponents were all dogs; a loyalist lad had been spared by the rebels although the little chap had shouted that he was as much the Mahdi as Mohamad Ahmed, they might kill him if they liked, but he was going to stay with the Government and Gordon Pasha. All was grist to his journal, alongside strength- and ammunition-returns, reports on raids and political events, imaginary descriptions of deplorable scenes in Baring's office and the United Services Club. 'I am ignorant of all that goes on, ignorant of the Arabic language except in my style, ignorant of the Arab customs, etc.' Yet when he asked their advice, his counsellors invariably replied, 'Do what you think right ... you will do better than we do.' They probably knew it was a waste of time to offer him advice, since he would never take it.

He spent much of the day on his roof, with a high-powered telescope, watching the enemy and (equally important) the garrison sentries to see if they were alert. If they were not in position, or dropped off to sleep ('These people are enough to break anyone's heart'), someone was for a flogging.

Inevitably there was a fifth column. On the night of 12 October he made 'a sort of general arrest of all who are supposed to be in communication with the Mahdi. I shall not hurt them, but shall send them out to the Mahdi.' He hated the necessity: 'When once one begins this detestable practice, one can never stop . . . Wilfrid Blunt will make a nice row about it.' But it had a good effect on the town. The Mahdi's principal propagandist Gordon had interned, then released, then put on the government pay-roll. But he persisted in his evil ways, and even organized an attempt to blow up the cartridge factory, so in the end he was court-martialled and shot.

Again the besieging forces were pushed back; quantities of *dhoora* were brought in, and the price of meat actually fell from 10s. to 2s. a pound. But in the long run, unless relief came, Khartoum would be starved into surrender. 'I toss up in my mind whether, if the place is taken, to blow up the palace and all in it, or else to be taken, and with God's help to maintain the faith, and if necessary to suffer for it . . . The blowing up of the palace is simplest, while the other means long and weary suffering and humiliation. I think I shall elect the last . . . because the former has more or less the taint of suicide.' All day hawks hovered overhead: 'I often wonder whether they are destined to pick my eyes, for I fear I was not the best of sons.'*

Rumours filtered through of the relief expedition at Dongola, but Gordon suspected that it had got no further than Shepheard's Hotel. He put more faith in Stewart, who, he calculated on 17 October, should be in communication with Europe in five days' time, with Power's telegrams appearing in *The Times* on the 23rd: 'It makes me laugh to think of the flutter in the dovecot which will follow. "That beastly Sudan again."' Another thing which made him laugh was a message authorizing him to buy his way out ('and be sure to look after yourself'!):

The pomp of Egerton's telegram informing me that Her Majesty's Government would (really!) pay on delivery so much a head for all refugees *delivered* on the Egyptian frontier, and would (*positively*, it is incredible!) *reward* tribes with whom I might contract to escort me down. It was too generous for one

* Proverbs xxx, 17.

to believe! Egerton's chivalrous nature must have got the better of his diplomatic training . . . The clerks . . . to whom I disclosed it are full of exclamations of wonder at his generosity![3]

In a passage which he crossed out but still left plainly legible, he added, 'One can imagine him sitting down to his dinner after despatching that telegram with the consolation that, if he was not Talleyrand, he was, at any rate, closely related to him.' Yet Gordon could admit that he was not entirely without blame. 'I own to having been very insubordinate to Her Majesty's Government . . . but it is my nature, and I cannot help it . . . If I was chief, I would never employ myself . . . To men like Dilke, who weigh every word, I must be *perfect poison*.'

Many rumours came in of Stewart's progress, and on 21 September came two telegrams which Gordon could not read because he had sent away his cypher-books. There were also some 'photograph letters' which he could only partially make out; month-old letters, listing the regiments and senior officers on their way to Wadi Halfa but omitting to mention how far they had progressed; and one addressed to Stewart from his friend, Kitchener, who knew neither the route the expedition would take nor how far it had reached, but asked, 'Is there anything I can do for you or General Gordon?' On 22 September the *Safia* and the *Mansureh* arrived with a little more news from Kitchener, who was at El Debbeh. Wolseley was to command the expedition, and the 35th Regiment had been ordered to advance from Wadi Halfa to Dongola: 'A few words about what you wish would be very acceptable.'

These communications enraged the man they were intended to reassure. Why tell him the names of the generals and regiments when all he wanted to know was when to expect them. The truth dawned upon him: they all wanted to see him dead, captive or disgraced! More and more a persecution complex embittered his official journal, expressed often in imaginary monologues and dialogues by Kitchener, Baring, Egerton and others:

Well, he pitched into me for asking Stewart if I could do anything for him (the communications being so easy) and for telling him the names of the generals (to my mind a most important matter, for it would strike terror among the Arabs). *He* says *he* does not care who the generals are (which is sheer heresy and most sickening). It is very clear his liver is out of order, to go and attack officers in his own corps like that.

Egerton had asked to be informed 'exactly' when the garrison expected to be in difficulties.

I am sure I should like that fellow Egerton. There is a light-hearted jocularity about his communications and I should think the cares of office sat easily on him ... It is as if a man on the bank, having seen his friend in the river has already bobbed up two or three times, hails, 'I say, old fellow, let me know when we are to throw you the lifebouy ... It is a pity to throw you the lifebuoy until you are really *in extremis*, and I want to know *exactly*, for I am a man brought up in a school of exactitude.'

Lord Granville was another target for Gordon's schoolboy humour:

Whaaaat! *Positive information from Dongola, Khartoum holds out!* ... Why, he ought to have given in. They will be howling for an expedition ... *That abominable Mahdi!* Why on earth does he not guard his roads better? *What is to be done?* Ask him more questions and trust to time? Well, not a bad idea. Telegraph out to say Government cannot act until they know exact state of affairs as to provisions etc.

Three days later he was at Granville again. 'Bother them! They have got in more *dhoora*, that is another two months they will hold out. What that Mahdi is about I cannot make out.'[4]

He was delighted to discover from an old Army List that Baring, as a young officer, had written training manuals on 'Peace Manoeuvres' and 'Rules for the Conduct of War Games ... The Box of Men can be had for £6.6.0.' This inspired, 'Splendid! A nice way he has manoeuvred us and carried on his *war-games*! Note. *Baring on the Conduct of War Games* is out of print. That will be a loss! But I expect the *box of men* can still be had.'[5]

Although the more offensive passages in his journal are crossed out (and have been omitted from published editions) all could be read, and were intended to be read, by those whom he accused of deliberately betraying him, and by scores of other people.

Of far more interest than the fatuous messages from Egerton and Kitchener, the *Safia* and the *Mansureh* brought letters from Stewart. The news was good. The Shagiya on the right bank were still mainly pro-government, though some left-bank tribes had declared for the Mahdi. Stewart had destroyed several enemy camps, which gave them a good supply of firewood for the steamers. They were quite confident they would get through.

Four days later, on 26 September, at 4 p.m., 'Steamers from Sennaar in sight. Now we shall be all together again, thank God!' Mohamad Nushi returned in triumph, having replenished the Sennaar garrison; stocked up his steamers with corn, oil, cattle, sheep and coffee; fortified the loyalty of the local tribes; and shot up several rebel camps. Gordon made him a pasha. His steamer was shot through and through by shell-fire, the holes near the water-line patched with old sails. With him came the *Ismailia*, which had been bottled up for months at Sennaar. The pride of Baker's navy stank like a cesspit. Gordon was in mellow mood as he wrote another Granville soliloquy that evening. 'I declare I am going to have an attack of gout. *It is really enough to make a saint swear* . . . Baring said he was safely netted . . . That tinkering idiot of a Mahdi! One can depend on no one nowadays. Had Egerton been in charge, he would have so managed affairs as to repair all the mistakes of the Mahdi.'[6]

They were not together again for long. Gordon calculated that the relief force would reach Debbeh by 24 October, so on 30 September he sent Mohamad Nushi Pasha with the *Tel-el-Hawein*, *Mansureh* and *Safia*, each carrying 300 soldiers, to await them at Shendy or across the river at Metemeh. Imagining the relief force streaking across the desert unimpeded by artillery, he sent down field-guns for them. In the event Mohamad Nushi and his soldiers, all Egyptians, with the help of the Shagiya loyalists whipped in by the redoubtable Mirghani ladies, fought a heroic campaign not for a mere three weeks but for nearly four months.

Gordon was (or pretended to be) so sure of the relief force that he rented houses, engaged servants, hired furniture and arranged contracts for their bread, meat and vegetables. He only hoped the General would not invite him to dinner. Never a great admirer of British infantrymen, he amused himself by forecasting their vicissitudes as they bumped across the desert:

'See-saw, see-saw, why, it is enough to kill a fellow . . . I would give a shilling to have an hour's sleep . . . Give you the water-bottle? I can't. I don't dare touch the rope of this long-necked brute. Hullo: there is someone come a cropper. Rifle broken of course.' They *will* drop vesuvians* on camels who will not like it; they *will* get galled, and not have glycerine; they *will* drop their pipes and not dare descend for them . . . as they mount, they *will* go over the other side and swear – oh how they will swear! . . . aches and pains in every part of the body.

Meanwhile Kitchener is depicted as expressing mild satisfaction that the Mahdi was doing better, otherwise no particular news from Gordon. 'Abuse as usual of Intelligence Department . . . He finds it much more difficult to get letters through and will have time to get over his liver-complaint . . . Stewart says it was a perfect pandemonium to be boxed up with him in one of his tantrums.'

Gordon sent with Mohamad Nushi the first two volumes of his journal, others following whenever a steamer went down to Shendy. Every volume bombarded Kitchener, Baring and officers of the relief force with advice and reproaches. Long deleted passages are headed 'Abuse of Baring'.

* Lighted matches.

Time and again he insisted that the expedition was not coming out to save *him*. 'I altogether *decline* the imputation that the projected expedition has come to *relieve me*. It has come *to save our national honour in extricating the garrisons etc. from a position our action in Egypt has placed the garrisons . . . I came up to extricate the garrisons and failed. Earle* comes up to extricate garrisons and (I hope) succeeds. Earle does not come up to extricate me* . . . I am not the *rescued lamb* and will not be.' They had better understand that nothing would induce him to leave his troops. 'It would be mean . . . to leave men who . . . have stuck to me, though a *Christian dog in their eyes*, and force them to surrender to those who have not conquered them . . . to save one's own skin. Why, the black sluts would stone me if they thought I meditated such action.' If, in March, he had been told to shift for himself, he could and would have done so, by the Equatoria route. (Or so he said.) But H.M.G. had not given him that order, indeed Baring had 'put a veto' on his going south. Now, six months later, having committed the loyalists against the Mahdi, he could not desert them.

It has been suggested that in his refusal to leave Khartoum Gordon was deliberately seeking death. Those who put this point rely on numerous letters, mainly to Mrs Freese, in which he enlarges on his longing to die. But most of these letters were written from Gravesend, Galatz and Mauritius, when he was bored and depressed by the futility of his work. No middle-aged man with a death-wish could have survived three years of Equatoria or the rigours of his safaris in Kordofan and Darfur. Gordon stayed in Khartoum because he could not leave it in honour. How could he return to England as the discredited hero who had saved his own skin and left those who trusted and followed him to be chopped up by the dervishes?

The best plan now, he advised through his journal, the only way to 'avoid a skedaddle programme', was to send up Zebeyr with enough Turkish troops to smash up the Mahdi and govern the country. Failing that he should be sacked and replaced by Abdul Qadir Pasha who, with no personal obligations to the people, could put the best face on an ignominious scuttle. Only then could he leave, and be in Brussels by December.

His journal is full of bitter complaints about the failure of Kitchener and the Intelligence Department to send him news. 'If I had not exerted myself in the spy business, we should never have had a word . . . I never saw such a poor lot as these outsiders. Even if they had to pay £20 out of their own pockets, one might have expected them to do it, considering the circumstances. They might have been paid back. I never saw such

* General Earle, whom Gordon believed to be in command of the relief force.

a feeble lot in my life!' The explanation was obvious: he was an embarrassment to them; Kitchener & Co. did not *want* him to be rescued. 'Kitchener: "Hurrah! Capital news! The Mahdi has *him* on the hip! . . . Bottled *him* up now!" . . . Granville: "Well, this is somewhat better news . . . One must not be ungrateful, but one must be permitted the remark, why that Mahdi did not move before he has spoilt my holiday?" ' So Gordon's growing persecution complex led him into ever greater delusions and absurdities.

On 16 October two unhappy letters were brought from Slatin. One offered Gordon his services, the other sought to excuse his surrender in Darfur and his apostasy. The surrender needed no excuse, since it came at the end of a long struggle against odds which, after the defeat of Hicks, were overwhelming. The apostasy was not the act of a coward, but was intended, while the campaign was still in progress, to secure the loyalty of his troops. 'Whether by my conversion I committed a dishonourable act is a matter of opinion – it was made more easy for me because I had, *perhaps unhappily*, not received a religious education.' He begged Gordon to accept him back, and as a ruse to ask for him to be sent as an emissary to discuss terms of surrender. Gordon would have nothing to do with a renegade. He sent no reply to Slatin, and he would certainly not connive at Slatin coming over by a ruse and thus 'breaking his parole, which should be as sacred when given to the Mahdi as to any other power'. However, if they both survived the siege, 'I shall take him to the Congo with me, he will want some *quarantine*; one feels sorry for him.'

On 21 October there arrived before Omdurman the Mahdi himself with reinforcements of tribal levies, regular black *Jihadiya* and all his European captives – 'nuns, priests, Greeks, Austrian officers – what a medley!' Gordon at first thought he had come to sue for peace, but the Mahdi ordered the siege to be pressed and brought more modern artillery, to the peril of Gordon's precious gun-boats which were really no more than converted 'Thames penny paddle-steamers'.

On 19 October Gordon carried out a stock-taking of his resources. These consisted of:

Regular black troops	2,316
Regular Egyptian troops	1,421
Bashi-Bazouks	1,906
Shagiya	2,330
Town militia	692
	8,665

He had twelve artillery pieces in the lines and eleven in the seven steamers, with 21,141 rounds of ammunition for them. He had 2,165,000 rounds of Remington ammunition in reserve, and the arsenal was turning out 40,000 weekly. His only serious shortage was of food: he had no more than nine weeks' supply of grain and biscuits, plus his remaining live-stock and any which could be taken from the enemy.[7] The civilian population, some 35,000, was a millstone round his neck, and his greatest trial was 'the way that one is waylaid as one goes out with petitions for *dhoora*, and howled at. These are the times when one feels *amiably* disposed towards the gentlemen who have ruled in Cairo for the last seven years.'

The relief force, Gordon advised its commander, should be divided into three detachments – one to secure a firm base at Debbeh; one to move upriver and recapture Berber; and a mobile column to cross the desert, meet steamers at Metemeh and push on to Khartoum. For the desert-crossing they need not burden themselves with artillery: Mohamad Nushi would supply it. In no circumstances should they send back to him Mohamad Nushi's *fellahin* troops and Bashi-Bazouks. 'I nobly present you with them all.' As for the fighting column, its task was child's play:

I cannot too much impress upon you that this expedition will not encounter any enemy worth the name, the struggle is with the climate and the destitution of the country. It is one of time and patience, and of small parties of determined men, backed by native allies which are got by policy and money. A heavy lumbering column, however strong, is nowhere in this land. Parties of forty or sixty men, swiftly moving about, will do more than any column. Native allies above all things, at whatever cost ... I do hope you will not drag on that artillery. If you let detached parties dash out here and there you will spread dismay in the Arab ranks.

Native allies at any cost (like the Shagiya?) – 'detached parties' of forty and sixty 'dashing out here and there' – one reads with incredulity Gordon's advice on fighting the Ansar, as ferocious, swift-moving, brave and aggressive as any enemy the British soldier had met. Can he have meant it seriously? Or was he trying to instil a sense of urgency into the relief force? Perhaps he was indulging the habit which Reinach had noticed, of startling people by saying what he did not really believe. (He recommended precisely the same tactics, 'little biting expeditions', for opposing a Russian advance on India.) One should remember that Gordon never saw a dervish charge. Indeed, until he arrived at Khartoum in February 1884, he had probably never even met anyone who had seen a dervish charge; and he would not then have been impressed by the warnings of those who had run away. So he thought the Ansar were like the tribal bands he had beaten in Darfur and Kordofan, and recommended the methods he had followed with such success. Graham, who in March had seen a British square broken by the dervishes, could have told him he was talking nonsense and Gordon would have taken it from Graham; but there was no one in Khartoum to tell him so. Wolseley wrote, 'I am a great believer in Gordon, and his views, which some scoff at, are always to me full of sound commonsense unfettered by routine or red-tape.'[8] But he did not take Gordon's advice.

Gordon drew up, on 3 October, a detailed programme for the relief force:

28th October. Berber occupied.

5th November. 10,000 troops at Khartoum. 6,000 Turks land at Suakim and march to Berber. 4,000 Turks land at Massawa and march to Kassala.

8th November. Defeat of Arabs on south lines* – unless they have bolted.

12th November. Defeat of Arabs near El Foun,† unless they have submitted.

15th November. Despatch of force to Sennaar.

1st to 10th December. Arrival of Turks at Berber and Khartoum, and at Kassala

20th December. Return of Her Majesty's forces to Wadi Halfa.

The frontier to be at Wadi Halfa ... All steamers etc. to be handed over to the Turks ... I see nothing to prevent the whole affair being settled by the end of January ...

As for the slave-trade, one cannot help it.

Humanly speaking, there will probably be three fights, costing each fight *eight* killed and *fifteen* wounded.

The whole affair was indeed to be settled by the end of January, but not in the way he envisaged. For no one had the smallest intention of sending any Turks; when Gordon drew up his programme, the first of the 800 boats, ordered in August, had not yet arrived at Assouan; and Wolseley, still in Cairo, complaining that Gordon 'inundates us with telegrams without giving us any satisfactory intelligence', was hoping to be at Debbeh, where the telegraph line ended, early in December and to be 'shaking hands with Gordon' about 31 January.[9]

This methodical advance was to be further delayed by Wolseley's refusal to use native boats, of which there were plenty available, and boatmen accustomed to local conditions. He had insisted on ordering from Canada specially-built boats such as he had used on the Red River expedition, with Canadian crews. By the time these began to arrive in October, the Nile was falling, and it was becoming every day more difficult to pass the cataracts. Moreover the crews, instead of the skilled

---

* South lines: the southern defences of Khartoum, between White and Blue Niles.

† El Foun: sixty miles up the Blue Nile, where Mohamad Ali Pasha had been killed.

voyageurs whom he had expected, were a mixed bag of lumberjacks, storekeepers and lawyers commanded by a Toronto alderman. Furthermore Wolseley's Chief of Staff, General Buller, had failed to arrange a supply of coal for Messrs Thomas Cook's tourist steamers by which the expedition was to travel up to the Second cataract.[10]

Gordon, however, continued to be buoyed up by positive, eye-witness accounts of spies and deserters who had themselves *seen* British troops and eight steamers only a day and a half's march below Berber, or at the worst at Debbeh, on 22 October. 'If they do not come before the 30th November, the game is up, and Rule Britannia!' But he was confident that they would attack Berber at the latest by 10 November. Meanwhile another force would move rapidly across the desert from Korti to Metemeh, so 'the relief of the garrisons is only a question of crossing a *well-surveyed road* of 150 miles, at the end of which are found *five steamers* and *nine guns.*' There would be no danger, and few administrative problems since he sent a map showing the wells *en route*. So 'on the 15th November I ought to see Her Majesty's uniform.' So wrote Gordon between 28 and 30 October. On the 23rd at Wadi Halfa, 600 miles downstream of Berber, an officer of the relief force wrote, 'The expedition is planted and taking root here.' Still at Wadi Halfa on 9 November (the day Gordon counted on them arriving at Berber) he wrote of 'orders, counter-orders, muddles . . . no sign of an advance from here'. The nearest British troops, only 250 mounted infantry, were at Dongola.[11]

Gordon had entrusted Stewart to inject into the relief force a greater sense of urgency. But on 22 October he received from the Mahdi a letter claiming that, 'by the Will of God', the *Abbas* had been taken and Stewart, Herbin and Power slain, 'whose souls God had condemned to the fire and to eternal misery'. The Mahdi enclosed, moreover, a detailed list of all the captured papers, which gave him priceless information. 'We never miss any of your news, nor what is in your inmost thoughts, and about the strength and support – not of God – on which you rely. We have now understood it all. Tricks in making cyphers and in using so many languages are of no avail.' He added that the troops in Bahr-el-Ghazal had surrendered.

Gordon's defiant reply was that he did not care who had surrendered or who had been captured. 'As for the letters,' he noted in his journal, 'I cannot make head or tail of them, so I leave them to the Arabic scholars of the Universities.' Next day he recorded, with more optimism than veracity, 'I have sifted out the Mahdi's letter respecting the capture of the *Abbas* and do not believe it; the papers . . . were never in the *Abbas*, they were taken from a spy I sent out from here.'

But on 3 November there arrived the *Bordein*, back from a mission to Mohamad Nushi and carrying a letter from Kitchener confirming the disaster. Stewart, having run the gauntlet of Berber, had sent back his escorting steamers, and on reaching the most dangerous cataract he had cut loose the towed boats for their own safety. A few hours short of Kitchener's camp, the *Abbas* struck a rock at full speed and foundered. There then arrived the local sheikh, reassuringly garbed in *tarbush*, trousers and Stamboulieh coat, who invited Stewart and his party to his house – unarmed lest they frighten the locals. While they were waiting for a meal, armed men burst in and butchered them all. Gordon was deeply distressed. He felt responsible for their deaths, and again and again in his journal he reverted to the subject, writing accounts of their departure not at his orders, but by their own free-will. It was a terrible blow.

Kitchener added that Wolseley was at Wadi Halfa and that at Dongola was a 'considerable number' of English troops who would 'definitely' advance 'on or about the 1st November'. But Kitchener was wrong: he was an intelligence officer, unfamiliar with operational plans. Unforeseen delays – the inexperience of the boat-crews, the overloading of boats and camels, the muddle over the coal contract – had forced Wolseley to postpone his forward concentration from early December to Christmas.[12] Gordon reflected, 'It is not easy to get over the feeling that a hope existed of no expedition being necessary, owing to our having fallen . . . If a boy at Eton or Harrow acted . . . in a similar way, I *think* he would be kicked, and *I am sure* he would deserve it.'

21

⌂ THE FALL OF KHARTOUM

⌂ On 2 November, after discovering the theft of a large quantity of
biscuits, Gordon calculated that he had food for six weeks, 'and
then the sponge must be thrown up'. He decided not to put the troops on
half-rations, lest they mutiny or desert *en masse*. 'I should be an angel if I
were not rabid with Her Majesty's Government . . . to lose all my
beautiful black soldiers is enough to make anyone angry.' Two days later
he sent Wolseley a long letter, which got through to Dongola in ten days,
giving all his views about Stewart ('his journal was a gem'), the best
tactics for the relief force, the apostasy of the Mahdi's European captives,
events in Khartoum, payment of messengers, and the advisability of
handing over the Sudan to the Sultan of Turkey with £2 million a year
to run it. In it he wrote, 'We can hold out for 40 days with ease; after
that it will be difficult.' Wolseley, knowing his Gordon, was sure he
would hold out for longer, and saw no need to change the plan which was
to concentrate 9,500 men, forward of Debbeh, by Christmas, and advance
through Metemeh to reach Khartoum by 31 January. He was forming a
mobile column of 1,500 picked men, all mounted on camels, to push on
rapidly if the garrison was *in extremis*.

On 5 November there was discovered a bundle of English newspapers
in which Kitchener had wrapped his last batch of letters. They were
dated 15 September 'and are like gold . . . We have had no news since
the 24th February.' They reported the departure of Wolseley from
Victoria Station 'for the *Gordon relief expedition*!! NO! For the relief of
Sudan garrisons.' But there was still no clue to when it would arrive.

This Gordon could have learned from messages sent by Wolseley on
20 September and 26 October. He had received at least the first of these,
but could not read it because he had sent away his cypher-books.
Wolseley was furious when he learned of this. 'That any man can have
been so idiotic is to me a puzzle . . . I have sent any number of copies
of this letter which must now be with the Mahdi, and it is extremely
provoking that when I do get a copy in, the answer is that he cannot make

it out having no longer any cypher.' So Wolseley was obliged to write obscurely, on 17 November:

> Will have an army between Debbeh and Ambukol on a day you can fix by counting 283 days on from this day's anniversary of your commission as Major General ... I send you a printed paper containing two cyphers. If you use the former, key-word will be Christian name of your mother's father. If you use the latter, they will be number of cash in 31451 taels with the day of the month in which you were born added to that number ... Can you recommend a good man of the Sudan to rule in Khartoum? No use recommending black gentleman in Cairo.

It does not seem that Gordon ever received this, or another in improvised cypher sent a month later.[1]

Gordon was 'worn to a shadow by this food question'. Having lost one steamer with Stewart and sent three more down with Mohamad Nushi, he could risk no more on foraging expeditions. On 2 November he had enough food for six weeks only. But this was eked out by corn disclosed in house-to-house searches, and by forty-one cattle captured by the garrison of Omdurman when the dervishes drove the beasts forward to explode the land-mines. By dint of such windfalls he always did a little better than his calculations. Thus by 14 November there was still enough for five weeks; by 28 November for three and a half to four weeks; and the final two weeks' supply, checked on 14 December, lasted in fact for nearly six. The daily ration for each of the 8,600 soldiers was 200 *dirrhems* (1⅛ lbs) of biscuit and 400 *dirrhems* of *dhoora*. Four pounds a day sounds adequate, but most soldiers had to share this with their women and children. There were about 34,000 civilians who had to be fed – soldiers' dependants from their men's rations, the well-to-do on payment, the poor free. Everyone was hungry most of the time, except perhaps for the black officers who stole their men's rations. (Egyptian officers behaved better in this respect.) But by 21 November no one had died of hunger.[2]

The Mahdi, well informed by deserters and so short of ammunition that some of his guns were firing stones, decided to capture the town by starvation rather than by assault. The defenders had enough rifle- and artillery-ammunition to last at least until their food ran out: they even had enough for their *mitrailleuses*, which were very effective against the enemy artillery: 'With a good *mitrailleuse* and a sharp operator, with *telescope sight*, no gun should be served with impunity at 2,000 yards range.' Gordon was so well off for rifle-ammunition that he encouraged harassing fire at extreme range, up to 3,000 yards.

Battle casualties were light so long as his troops were on the defensive, dug in or on the armoured steamers. They had lost nearly 1,900 killed and

242 wounded between 17 March and 22 November, but most of these had been in the summer sorties, especially Mohamad Ali's disastrous defeat. The enemy rifle-fire was wildly inaccurate and even the *fellahin* troops fought quite well behind cover. But Gordon could not risk the sorties and counter-attacks which had been so successful before the loss of the 'Fighting Pasha' and the best of the blacks.

The steamers were targets which even the dervishes could hardly miss with modern artillery and a quick-firing Nordenfeldt; the armour was not proof against direct shell-hits and the Krupp mountain-guns made holes in it two foot in diameter. Whenever they were under fire Gordon was on tenterhooks. On 12 November the *Ismailia* was hit again and again; and the little *Husseinyeh*, repeatedly holed below the water-line, grounded in midstream just below Omdurman. 'I have lived *years* in these last hours! The enemy brought up three guns to fire on her at not more than 1,200 yards, and showed the greatest pluck . . . though overwhelmed with the musketry fire of the castellated *Ismailia* . . . No Royal Navy vessels would have behaved better than the *Ismailia* today; she passed and re-passed the Arab guns upwards of twenty times, when any one well-placed shell would have sunk her.' But despite desperate efforts, the *Husseinyeh* had next day to be stripped of her guns and abandoned.

The Mahdi had his camp just west of Omdurman; the Sheikh el Obeid's camp was north of the town, beyond the Blue Nile; Abu Girga's on the near bank of the Blue Nile, south-east of the defences; and Wad-el-Nejumi's, to the south. Their main effort was against Omdurman, for which they used the best of the *Jihadiya* who had been trained by Zebeyr and Gordon. The fort was badly placed, 1,200 yards from the river, so that steamers could neither provision nor properly support it. But it had to be held: otherwise the enemy, holding the left bank in force, could deny the White Nile to the *Ismailia*. Communication with Omdurman was, until 13 November, by telegraph: but on that day the enemy, infiltrating between the fort and the river, cut the line. Thereafter they had to communicate by bugle signals. But Faragh Allah Bey had a stout heart, enough food, and a quarter of a million rifle-cartridges, so Gordon was on the whole not unduly worried about Omdurman. He could not risk a disaster by sending out a force to relieve it.

The whole town was continually under long-range fire, not very dangerous, but wearing on the nerves. To show his contempt for it, Gordon used to sit at the open window of his palace, silhouetted by a strong light at night. Bordeini Bey, a trader on the committee of notables, tells of Gordon boasting that God in creating men had run out of fear when it came to his turn, so he was created without it: but the story is a chestnut, told of several others. When the firing became a nuisance,

Gordon used to post on his roof a squad of boy-buglers, enthusiastic snipers though so small that they had to stand on boxes to shoot over the parapet. They were always claiming to have done fearful execution (at a range of at least 2,000 yards). Gordon was sceptical, but there was plenty of ammunition, and they enjoyed it. When not sniping, they taunted the enemy by playing battle-signals such as 'We are strong, We are strong' or 'Come to us! Come to us!' The buglers with the Mahdi's *Jihadiya* responded in kind.*

Gordon continued to 'declare *positively* and *once for all, that I will not leave the Sudan until everyone who wants to go down is given the chance to do so*, unless a government is established that relieves me of the charge; therefore if any emissary or letter comes up here ordering me to come down, I WILL NOT OBEY IT, BUT WILL STAY HERE, AND FALL WITH THE TOWN, AND RUN ALL RISKS.' At least Gordon was safeguarded against the uttermost horror: 'He will enable me to keep my faith and not deny Him.'

Next to food, the garrison's worst deprivation was of reliable news: they fed on rumours. It was positively reported on 23 November that British troops were at Metemeh; and there was great jubilation when the smoke of a steamer was seen in the distance on the 25th. Bitter was the disappointment when it turned out to be the *Bordein*, sent up by Mohamad Nushi with letters and telegrams brought across the desert from Debbeh. The leading elements of the expeditionary force had only just reached Korti and Ambukol ('which is LIVELY'). Thereafter there were reports of Berber falling to British troops on 28 November and 4 December, of four steamers surging up to Khartoum towing boats full of soldiers. But in fact not a single British soldier was to advance beyond Ambukol before 30 December.

What the *Bordein* did bring was a letter from Watson, to which Gordon replied, 'I will accept *nothing whatever* from Gladstone's Government. I will not even let them pay my expenses . . . I will never set foot in England again – but will (D.V. if I get out) go to Brussels and so on to Congo.' There were telegrams from the Khedive, Baring and Wolseley. 'I am sure,' Gordon wrote, 'we are deprived of a treat by not being able to decipher the long telegrams'; but he had, in fact, deprived himself of what he most needed – news. There was a telegram in clear from the Khedive cancelling his secret *firman* to evacuate the Sudan, which Gordon had already torn up. And there was a rather obscure message from the Khedive to the *ulema*, implying that Baring and Wolseley were on their way up.

* The Egyptian Army had adopted from the French a very complex system of battle-signals by bugle-call.

Gordon was delighted by the thought of the portentous Baring bumping along on a camel: if he did so, 'I shall consider he has expiated his faults and forgive him.' How the ex-Khedive would chuckle at the news! 'I can see him twinkling his little eyes over it.' Less pleasing was the implication that he might have to share with them responsibility for a 'policy of skedaddle'. He would have no part in this: 'Whoever comes up here had better appoint Major Kitchener Governor-General, for . . . *I am impossible* (what a comfort!).'

Then a better idea occurred to him. The Sudan was still part of the Khedive's dominions; he held the Khedive's *firman* to govern it; unless Baring and Wolseley had also obtained a *firman* (and he was sure they would not have deigned to do so) they had no *locus standi*. So, *he* was empowered to appoint anyone as his successor, subject to the Khedive's approval. 'I shall perhaps appoint Baring . . . and shall bolt' – as he could then do in honour, leaving to others the choice of scuttling out, evacuating the Egyptians, setting up a successor government, or anything else they fancied. Or perhaps he would make Kitchener his successor. 'I would much like to know the contents of Lord W's telegram to me, also the telegrams in cypher from Nubar and Baring; but I never shall have that pleasure.'

Two days later he devised another scenario for the relief:

British expedition comes up to relieve British subjects in distress; it finds one of its subjects acting as ruler; it takes him away, and he, on going, appoints Zebeyr as ruler . . . Now who can say anything to the British Government? It had nothing to do with the appointment of Zebeyr . . . This will be a splendid dodge; it first clears H.M.G. of any blame, it puts the blame on me, and in the storm that is caused, I shall have been so effectually blackened that everyone will forget the – well, we will not say it in direct words (count the months), we will call it the DELAY . . . The Opposition will be perfectly wild at seeing the Ministry get out of the mess . . . while the Anti-Slavery Society will empty the vials of their wrath on me . . . Baring will get such kudos! For my part I shall get out of any of those wretched honours, for the Ministry will be only too glad to say, 'We could not, you know, confer any honours on him after such disreputable conduct' . . . I think it is a splendid programme.

It was not, however, a programme which he could ever have followed; for Wolseley had the Khedive's *firman*, overriding Gordon's, to hold in reserve in case Gordon should be disposed to disobey him.

On 13 and 14 December, with food in store for only two weeks, Gordon wrote his farewell letters. One was to Augusta:

This may be the last letter you will receive from me, for we are on our last legs owing to the delay in the expedition. However, God rules all, and as He will rule to His glory and our welfare, His will be done. I fear, owing to circumstances, that my affairs pecuniary are not over-bright . . . Your affectionate brother, C. G. Gordon. P.S. I am quite happy, thank God, and like Lawrence, I have '*tried* to do my duty'.

To Watson he wrote:

I think the game is up, and send Mrs Watson, you and Graham my adieux. We may expect a catastrophe in the town on or after ten days' time; this would not have happened (if it does happen) if our people had taken better precautions as to informing us of their movements, but this is 'spilt milk'. Good-bye. Mind and let my brother (68 Elm Park Road, Chelsea) know what I owe you.

On the 13th he decided to close his journal and send down the last volume, with his letters, by the *Bordein* in two days' time.

If some effort is not made in ten days, the town will fall. It is inexplicable, this delay. If the Expeditionary Forces have reached the river and met my steamers, one hundred men are all that we require, just to show themselves . . . All that is absolutely necessary is for fifty of the Expeditionary Force to get on board a steamer and come up to Halfaya, and thus let their presence be felt; this is not asking much, but it must happen *at once* or it will, as usual, be too late.

He concluded his journal on the following day, 14 December. 'Now MARK THIS, if the Expeditionary Force, and I ask for no more than two hundred men, does not come in ten days, *the town may fall*; and I have done my best for the honour of our country. Good-bye. C. G. Gordon. You send me no information, though you have lots of money. C. G. G.'

If Gordon was anxious for information about the relief force, Wolseley was no less in need of information from Gordon. On 14 November he had received Gordon's message of 4 November, 'We can hold out 40 days with ease, after that it will be difficult.' Thereafter was silence until 31 December when he received a piece of paper the size of a postage-stamp on which was written, 'Khartoum all right 14.12.84. C. G. Gordon.' The messenger brought a rambling verbal message to the effect that he must come quickly, with a large force as the enemy was very numerous; that he must not leave Berber behind him in enemy hands; and that Khartoum could be taken only by starvation. 'Altogether,' wrote Wolseley in his journal,

this is most unsatisfactory and unsettles my plans without giving me any information that is worth having . . . Gordon's nerve cannot be as fresh and vigorous after all he has gone through . . . as when he and I last met . . . Gordon, who is one of the greatest smokers I have ever known, still has cigarettes, as he offered the messenger one . . . I am delighted to know that the gallant soul has at least this one earthly pleasure left him.[3]

Wolseley was aware of Gordon's general views on colonial warfare. He took with a pinch of salt the fantasy of detached parties, forty or sixty men, dashing about the desert and confusing the dervishes by the rapidity of their movements; but he was prepared to take 'a great leap in the dark' by pushing the desert column to Metemeh and straight onto Khartoum without waiting for Berber to be taken; and possibly in sending ahead of the main column a picked force of 1,500 camel-mounted men if the fall of the town seemed imminent. But transport difficulties had put him badly behind schedule: the full concentration at Korti and Ambukol, planned for Christmas Day, could not now take place until 22 January; and there were insufficient camels for the desert column to reach Metemeh with a single lift. However on 30 December that column under General Sir Herbert Stewart set off from Korti to establish an intermediate supply depot half-way to Metemeh. Then came Gordon's message; the very apostle of '*l'audace, toujours l'audace*' was now preaching caution; Wolseley over-reacted: 'Gordon's message,' he telegraphed Baring,

compels measures that will postpone my arrival at Khartoum. He warns us not to leave Berber in my rear, so that I must move by water and take it before I march on Khartoum. Meanwhile I shall have established post at Metemeh by men and stores sent across the desert. I shall be able to communicate with Gordon by steamer, learn exact position, and if he is *in extremis* before infantry arrive by river, to push forward by camel corps to help him at all hazards.

In his diary he elaborated:

All along I have been counting on an expression which occurs more than once in Gordon's letters, that the whole attack on Khartoum would collapse if he had only a few hundred determined soldiers on whom he could depend. I have been basing my calculations on this view of the position and had therefore determined forcing my way into Khartoum with about 1,500 of the finest men in our or any other army. Now this message from him tells me not to advance unless I am strong.

The essential point was that in the new plan the desert column was to be strengthened (entailing more delay) and it was not to advance to Khartoum until Berber was taken. Indeed it would not reach the town in force until March.[4]

Wolseley was arguably at fault in changing his plan on the strength of a rambling verbal report by a Bedu letter-smuggler; but in view of Gordon's note which the man brought, 'Khartoum all right 14.12.84', he cannot be greatly blamed. Why Gordon sent this misleading note is a mystery: why he did not send a full report of his situation, using the sort of improvised code which Wolseley but not the Mahdi would understand, is another. It has been suggested that the note was intended to be intercepted and to mislead the enemy: instead, it misled Wolseley. Moreover Wolseley himself was given a direct order by Hartington not to go on with the desert column but to remain at Korti co-ordinating the movements of both columns: partly because he was not on the spot, the 1,500 strong camel corps, which might perhaps have reached Khartoum in time, was never used for the purpose for which it was intended.[5]

Nevertheless Wolseley was still confident of success, and warned Hartington that Gordon would probably try to embarrass the Government by refusing the G.C.B. or any other award. As soon as he was relieved, Gordon had better be promoted to lieutenant-general in recognition of his gallant defence. This he could not refuse, and 'he could not then pose before the public as a man who had rendered you great service but who refused your rewards because he disliked your Government.'[6]

Of the last weeks of the siege we know little. On 29th December Gordon is alleged to have sent out one message rolled up in a cartridge case:

> To all the Confederate Powers from Gordon Pasha – I beg to offer you my salutations, and beg to inform you that I am, by God's help, well ... Admire, O ye kings, the British and the Ottoman Governments, who summoned me to be Governor-General of the Sudan, to put down the revolt. I have now been here for one year, during which period they have not inquired after me; while one kingdom is celebrated for its wealth and the other for its power. I say this, therefore, that although I am of no importance, yet these two Governments should have fulfilled the conditions under which I was sent here, viz to uphold the honour of the Government ... God is with me, and God is all-powerful.

The letter never reached its royal addressees, but the clerk to whom it was dictated kept (he said) an Arabic copy.

On the same day Gordon scrawled on a scrap of paper, signed and sealed, 'Khartoum all right, could hold out for years.' This message, highly misleading, did reach Metemeh.

All we know of the last six weeks comes from Bordeini Bey, not perhaps wholly reliable;* from the reports of spies and refugees collected by Kitchener; from evidence given at various Courts Martial and Courts of Inquiry in Cairo; and from the fragmentary recollections, many years later, of veterans who had fought on either side. These sources differ considerably, particularly on numbers and dates.

Gordon slept much of the day, in order to make the rounds at night,

---

* He describes scenes in the palace which, according to two of Gordon's servants, he never entered in these last weeks: and Gordon is said to have threatened to cut out his tongue as the only cure for his mendacity.[7]

essential if the sentries, starving, exhausted and increasingly despondent, were to be kept awake. He spent hours on the palace roof watching through his telescope the enemy, his own defences and, of course, the northern horizon for the smoke or dust-cloud which would be the first sign of relief. It can be assumed that he shared his men's hunger, which to him would be little hardship. For clothes he was reduced to a roughly-made uniform of undyed local cotton. But he had his cigarettes.

At the end of December, with the food in store almost finished, there was a last search through the town for hidden grain and a little was discovered; the last skinny milch-cows were slaughtered; and the crops on Tuti Island were harvested under fire. These measures produced enough food for about one week on the full scale: but a committee of officers and civilians, on which Gordon greatly relied, cut the regular soldiers' daily ration from 200 *dirrhems* of biscuit and 400 of *dhoora* to 100 *dirrhems* (11 oz.) of any grain which could be found: the Shagiya, Bashi-Bazouks and volunteers were given slightly more, lest they mutiny. Civilians were dying of starvation and special rewards had to be given for burying them. So weak were the soldiers that Gordon ordered them not to stand up to salute. The greatest relief to the food supplies was on 6 January, when most of the civilians went over to the Mahdi. Gordon wrote asking him to feed these poor people. After this exodus only about 14,000 civilians remained.[8]

If Khartoum was short of food, Omdurman was even shorter. Gordon made two attempts to draw the Ansar away from it by diversionary sorties elsewhere: despite local success, both failed in their main object. At a council of war, he proposed to lead a last sortie across the river to link up with the garrison which would fight their way to the river-bank. Said Lieutenant-General Faragh Pasha ez Zeini, the Mexico veteran, 'I redeem you with my soul and will save you this trouble. I will relieve the fort myself.' The attempt was made on 4 January, but by then the enemy were in force between Omdurman and the river, with rifles, a *mitrailleuse* and a quick-firing Nordenfeldt. Despite desperate fighting, the half-starved troops were unable to break through. On or about 12 January Faragh Allah signalled that he had not a scrap of food left, and Gordon authorized surrender. It was with sadness and sympathy that he watched the valiant garrison march out of Omdurman – not into captivity but to join the Mahdi's *Jihadiya*. The surprising thing is that more did not do so in those last hopeless weeks. Indeed the balance of desertions was the other way, several hundred* of the Mahdi's black soldiers coming over to join the starving garrison – an extraordinary proof of the devotion

* The Court of Inquiry put the total at 1,200: Bordeini Bey at 200–300.

Gordon inspired among those who served under him, especially his beloved blacks.

With the fall of Omdurman the White Nile was denied to the steamers. Gordon tried to boost morale by enormous pay-bonuses (in promises or paper). But of what avail were these when there was nothing but an occasional fish, caught at night, to buy? Dogs, cats, rats, donkeys, gum and goatskin water-bags were all eaten; and a horrible bread was made by pounding up a little *dhoora* with the heart of date-palm trees.

All the reserve ammunition was collected in the Catholic church, a stone building near the palace, and a mine laid so that it could be blown up lest it fall into enemy hands. A small steamer was provisioned and moored just by the palace gardens, for the town notables and Europeans to make their escape when the dervishes burst in. Some thought that Gordon Pasha would escape in it at the last moment, but he had no such intention.

Gordon had for months been in intermittent communication with the Mahdi, who had extolled his good deeds but insisted that these counted for nothing until he accepted Islam – an essential condition of a peace settlement. But he had no wish for Gordon's blood: he would far rather the English Pasha simply departed and left Khartoum to fall into his hands with no further loss or effort. On 12 January he must have been aware that the relief expedition was approaching; using as envoy a man disguised as a woman (since his last envoy had been shot on approaching the walls), he sent his final, and generous, terms for an honourable surrender:

In the name of God the merciful, the compassionate.
Praise be to God the kind guardian.
May God's blessings and peace be upon our Lord Mohamad and his household. Greetings.
From: The Servant dependent upon God, Mohamad el-Mahdi Ibn Abdullahi.
To: Gordon Pasha, may God protect him from every evil He did not will.
If God wills your happiness and you accept our advice and enter into our security and guarantee – that is what we wish. If, however, you would rather rejoin the English we will send you to them.
Having seen what you have seen, how long are you going to disbelieve us? We have been told by God's Apostle, may God's blessings and peace be upon him, of the imminent destruction of all those in Khartoum, save those who believe and surrender; them God will save. We do not wish you to perish with those doomed to perish because we have frequently heard good of you. Yet often as we have written to you about your regeneration and felicity, you have not returned to us an answer that will lead to your good, as we hear from those who come to us from your place. However, we have not yet despaired of your regeneration and felicity, and because of the virtue we hear

is in you we will write you a single text from God's book in the hope that by it God will facilitate your regeneration since He has made us the doorway to his mercy and guidance. For this reason we have repeatedly written to you urging you to return to your own country where your virtue will achieve the highest honour. In order that you should not abandon hope of God's mercy I say to you that God has said, 'Kill not thyself for God is merciful to thee.' Peace be upon you. 25th Rabi Awwal, 1302 [12 January 1885].

It was reported to me in the reply you sent us that you had said that the English wished to ransom you alone from us for £20,000. We know that people say many bad things about us which are not in us, in order that those shall be misled whom God has condemned to perdition. The falsehood of these allegations can only be known to those who meet us. As for you, if you accept our advice you will be thereby blessed: but if you wish to rejoin the English we will send you to them without claiming a farthing. Peace be upon you.[9]

There is no doubt of the Mahdi's *bona fides*. His was a noble character, and in his faith he was no less sincere and single-minded than Gordon. Before anything else he wanted to save the English Pasha's soul: if that were denied him, he would be glad to save the body. But Gordon, of course, could not possibly accept the offer.

Gordon had never ceased to proclaim that help was on its way; and on 20 January it seemed that he might be vindicated. There was from the Mahdi's camp a salute of 101 guns, as though to celebrate a victory. But Gordon had seen through his powerful telescope crowds of women wailing. From this, and from the reports of his best spy, a Shagiya woman who crossed the river every night to talk to the rebels, he drew the opposite conclusion – that the Ansar had been defeated, and that the gun-salute was a ruse.

He was right. On 8 January, having established his supply depot at Jakdul, Sir Herbert Stewart had set off a second time from Korti, intending to march through to Metemeh. But on the 17th, two days beyond Jakdul, he encountered at Abu Klea a force of 10,000 dervishes who in their first wild charge broke into a square. After a bloody battle, the dervishes were defeated; but among the dead was Colonel Burnaby, a cavalry thruster who had been picked to lead the advance from Metemeh. Two days later, in another successful engagement on the banks of the Nile, General Stewart was mortally wounded. Command then devolved on Sir Charles Wilson, an intelligence expert with no previous operational experience.

His orders were to establish a base at Metemeh, join up with Mohamad Nushi's flotilla; make contact with Gordon by steamer to ascertain his situation; and leave three officers in Khartoum to assist in the defence. He had no orders to relieve the town; that was scheduled for the first week in March – unless in the meanwhile the situation was so desperate as to warrant the risk of sending in, unsupported, the camel corps, who had suffered considerable casualties and whose camels were in need of rest.

At Metemeh on 21 January Wilson met the steamers and received Gordon's journal and letters. Burnaby, Stewart, or Wolseley might have been so moved by the last entries in the journal as to send on the camel corps and all the steamers at once, with what result none can say. But the carnage at Abu Klea had convinced Wilson that the dervishes were a most formidable enemy, in whose presence it was madness to take risks. Moreover there was Gordon's last, indubitable message, dated 29 December: 'Khartoum all right, could hold out for years.' For the second time, in sending an over-optimistic message, Gordon may have intended to mislead the enemy: instead, he again misled his friends. Wilson saw no reason to do anything more than obey orders, without marked sense of urgency. It was not until the morning of 24 January that, with two steamers, he set off upstream. Many people, starting with Wolseley, who was himself not free from blame, have blamed Wilson for the delay. It is not given to every commander to be a Nelson.

When the garrison heard for certain of British troops at Metemeh, they were overjoyed. The siege now seemed virtually over: at any moment they might see the smoke on the horizon, hear the thud of guns battering the enemy at Halfaya: their sufferings were at an end, soon they would receive the rewards of their steadfastness. But as the days passed they again lost heart, their disappointment all the more bitter for their momentary exhilaration. They were not moved by Gordon's promise on the 24th that every subsequent day they held out would count as a month for pay, seniority and pensions. The soldiers were at last saying openly that he had deceived them. Even the stout-hearted Faragh Pasha ez Zeini on the 23rd advised capitulation: there was a violent row, Gordon is said to have struck him and he left the palace in a rage. On the following day another council-of-war was held: some took Faragh Pasha's line, but none could stand up against Gordon's inflexible resolve. Tomorrow, he assured them, the steamers could not fail to arrive: he himself would not go aboard, lest he be outranked by the newcomers and ordered to leave Khartoum: but all the senior officers should put on full-dress uniform to give a real welcome. They did not believe him.

Meanwhile, the enemy was disconcerted. After their unbroken run of victories, the Mahdi and his emirs had not believed that the British and Egyptian Governments would dare send another army against them. But here was one on its way, defeating God's warriors with terrible slaughter at Abu Klea. It seemed as though they had failed to reduce Khartoum by starvation: should they assault it, or should they withdraw? On the

20th the Mahdi held a council-of-war. Only one emir advised the bolder course. But the case for this had been strengthened by an officer of Bashi-Bazouks who on the previous day had deserted with information not only of the garrison's desperate plight, but of a weakness in the defences. On the western end of the south lines the White Nile in flood had filled the ditch, levelled the rampart and rendered innocuous the dreaded land-mines. The flood had now receded, leaving a 1,500-yard stretch of gleaming mud covered in places with shallow water. The garrison had not the strength to make good all the damage: there was a 500-yard gap between the end of the defences and the river, soft mud but passable.

So irresolute were the emirs that if only two steamers and a couple of hundred British troops had arrived at Halfaya on the 24th or 25th, the entire Ansar might have withdrawn to Kordofan: on the other hand they might have turned on such a small force and annihilated it, or simply ignored it and continued the siege. Even in 1885 expert opinion on this point, among British, Egyptian and Sudanese officers, was divided. But the Mahdi himself was not irresolute. Putting his trust in God and with a shrewd eye for the fleeting military opportunity, he determined to attack before the relief force arrived. He even sent Gordon a warning of his intention.

On the morning of 25 January Gordon watched the enemy in the Mahdi's camp loading up their camels and moving towards the river. Thinking that this indicated an attack, he sent out warning orders that everyone who could carry arms, from eight years old to eighty, man the defences: in twenty-four hours, he promised, the English were sure to come. Bordeini Bey claims to have entered the palace and found the Pasha feeling ill and at the end of his resources not only of food but of health, courage and confidence. His hair had turned white with the strain. 'I have nothing to say,' he exclaimed, 'the people will no longer believe me. I have told them over and over again that help will come, but it has never come and now they must see I tell them lies . . . Go and collect all the people you can on the lines and make a good stand. Now leave me to smoke these cigarettes.' It was impossible to get all the soldiers and male civilians into the defences: they were too weak to move; many of the famished soldiers left their posts, in search of food; despair was on every face. Gordon remained all day in his palace, smoking, and sat up till midnight, when he dropped into an exhausted sleep.

After dark the dervishes assembled in great numbers at Wad-el-Nejumi's camp, and the Mahdi crossed over from Omdurman to address them. Seated on his camel so that all might see him, he harangued the multitude on the battle before them. Apart from Gordon and three others, whom they must on no account slay, 'Whomsoever you encounter in battle, kill him. God has said, "Their belief in Me only after they have seen my might profiteth them nothing."'

He asked, 'Do you intend to attack Khartoum tomorrow morning?'

They shouted in reply, 'Yes, Lord of All!'

'Will you advance with pure hearts and full determination to fight in God's cause?'

'Yes!'

'Even if two-thirds of you should perish?'

'Yes!'

They then repeated with him the Fatha, the first chapter of the Koran, and marched off to their battle-stations.

Forty-three minutes after midnight the Ansar advanced against the south front. Wad-el-Nejumi directed the operation with great skill, using some 20,000 men under Abu Girga for diversionary attacks along five miles of the front, while a massive Napoleonic column of some 40,000 men, under his personal command, broke through the single battalion holding the sector where the flood-water had levelled the defences. Some units behaved well, forming square when surrounded and fighting to the last; but most were too weak. The *fellahin*, Shagiya and Bashi-Bazouks were slaughtered to a man, most of the blacks were spared to join the *Jihadiya*.

No one had roused Gordon when the attack started, and he was awakened by the din of drums, shouting, screaming and rifle-fire as the dervishes charged through the narrow streets. He put on his uniform, sword and revolver to meet the fate for which he was well prepared.

There are many accounts of Gordon's end, which fall into two main categories – those who plagiarize the first account to reach Cairo, by Bordeini Bey, who does not claim to be an eye-witness and whose veracity is suspect; and three eye-witness accounts which differ considerably from this. Bordeini Bey's is the accepted version because it was first in the field and has been made the subject of a famous picture. According to this, Gordon and his cavasses and bodyguard kept up a hot fire on the rebels from the roof but could not prevent them swarming into the palace garden. Gordon then, carrying his revolver, his left hand resting on the hilt of his sheathed sword, walked to the head of an outside staircase. Four men rushed up the steps and one, a Dongolawi named Taha Shahin, with a shout of 'Oh cursed one, your hour has come!' plunged his great broad-bladed spear into Gordon's breast. Gordon made a gesture of scorn and turned round, to receive another spear in his back. They then hacked at his body with their swords, killing him in a few seconds.[10]

There is an East Coast Arab proverb, 'To die like a sheep is to die like a gentleman.' It is not one to which Gordon would have subscribed. All his life he was a fighter. The story that he died unresisting is not supported by eye-witnesses. Kitchener, carrying out a full investigation seven months later, was able to find only one man, the servant of the Head Clerk, who claimed to have seen Gordon die. According to this man, Gordon was shot while leading a party of soldiers and armed *cavasses* from the palace towards Hansal's house.[11] As this was near the church where the reserve ammunition was stored, it is likely enough that Gordon was fighting his way there either to blow up the magazine or to obtain more rifle-cartridges.

By far the most circumstantial account of Gordon's death is by his bodyguard, Khalil Agha Orphali, who was fighting beside him when he fell. It tallies significantly with that of an eye-witness fighting on the other side: both say Gordon was shot on the palace stairs by a black dervish. It is not inconsistent with Gordon being killed on his way to the church. It also tallies with the story told by Charles Neufeldt who was not himself an eye-witness, but who as prisoner of the Mahdi was able to speak with many who were. Khalil stated that the enemy, in spite of rifle-fire by the defenders, broke open with axes the southern gate of the palace garden and rushed up the stairs where he himself, struggling with them, was speared in the right hand. Gordon stopped the rush with revolver-fire, and as the dervishes withdrew, went to Khalil's help. He was wounded in the shoulder by a thrown spear, and the enemy came on again. Again he stopped them with rapid revolver-fire, and when his revolver was empty, went for them with his sword. A black dervish, standing in the courtyard below, took careful aim and shot Gordon in the chest, knocking him back against the wall. But he recovered and once again, with Khalil, beat the enemy down the stairs. At the bottom he was felled by a spear-thrust in his right side, and at the same time Khalil was knocked senseless among the bodies so did not actually see Gordon die.[12]

The reader may take his choice. The story that Gordon was speared, unresisting, his revolver unfired, his sword undrawn, accorded with his contemporary image as a Christian martyr. But the weight of eye-witness evidence is that he was shot and that he went to his God not as a sheep, but as a soldier. So angry was the Mahdi when he heard of his death that the killer never owned up to the deed.[13]

The head was cut off and carried in a leather bag to the Mahdi's camp. There it was displayed exultantly to Slatin. 'Is not this the head of your uncle, the unbeliever?'

'What of it?' replied Slatin. 'A brave soldier, who fell at his post. Happy is he to have fallen. His sufferings are over.'

Two days later Wilson's steamers arrived within sight of Khartoum.

EPILOGUE

From the Queen, who sent her Prime Minister a furious telegram *en clair*, to the wit who renamed him the M.O.G. (Murderer of Gordon), the British public reacted with rage to the news from Khartoum. England's hero slain and England's finest general frustrated in his noble purpose by a horde of Fuzzy-Wuzzies! It was incredible! It was unimaginable disgrace! From end to end of the country Gordon memorials of all kinds were unveiled, Gordon Boys' Clubs opened, Gordon songs and poems poured from the printing presses. Over the next ten years at least twenty-five books and innumerable pamphlets were written in his praise.

The Government kept its head. Through no fault (Mr Gladstone explained) of theirs, the expedition which they had so reluctantly launched had failed in its purpose. Briefly it was intended to press on to Khartoum and re-establish British prestige, but Gladstone's innate pacifism, confirmed by Wolseley's new pessimism, reasserted itself; all British and Egyptian troops were withdrawn from the Sudan, except for a garrison left in Suakim.

A strong British contingent remained in Egypt to defend it against Mahdist invasion, together with a Military Mission to reform the Egyptian Army. Whatever Mr Gladstone might say, not a man of that contingent or that mission doubted for one moment that the real object of his presence was to avenge Gordon.

Six months after Gordon, the Mahdi died, and was succeeded by his Deputy, the Khalifa Abdullah al Taashi, a far less able man. A succession of poor harvests, with sundry epidemics and tribal rebellions, brought the Sudan to a sorry condition – though perhaps not as miserable as was made out by Slatin and other Europeans who escaped from captivity and wrote highly emotive books on their experiences. After many frontier raids and skirmishes, in 1891 Wad-el-Nejumi led the Ansar into Egypt. He was soundly defeated and killed.

In due course, with a Conservative Government in power, the time was thought ripe to avenge Gordon. Under General Sir Herbert Kitchener an Anglo–Egyptian army – far more formidable than that envisaged by Gordon or led by Wolseley – advanced with ponderous deliberation up the Nile and smashed the Ansar outside Omdurman. Its victory was celebrated by a service held in the ruins of the palace where Gordon had died. Very soon, as a fitting memorial, the Gordon College was founded in Khartoum. Of that at least he would have strongly approved.

The Sudan was conquered and ruled as an Anglo-Egyptian Con-dominium, with the accent on Anglo. On the whole it was the most successful and altruistic of all Britain's colonial ventures, from which Britain gained very little and the Sudanese people a great deal. Half a century later, without much of the bitterness attendant on the withdrawal from Empire, Britain and Egypt both pulled out, leaving the Sudanese to rule themselves, as they have done (after some initial troubles) with increasing assurance and good sense. Of that, too, Gordon would have approved.

SOURCES AND REFERENCES

I have given detailed, specific references only for matters which are contro-versial, hitherto unpublished or of particular interest.

There are scores of books about Gordon, and four volumes of his corres-pondence at different stages of his career, selective, somewhat over-edited, and in some cases bowdlerized for evangelical consumption. The books which I have found most useful are listed in the sources which I give for each chapter.

There are hundreds of manuscript letters written by Gordon, and a few to him. Only a small proportion of these have been published. The principal collections are:

British Museum Manuscripts Room. Gordon's letters to his sister, Augusta, and other relatives. Also letters to Baker, Watson, Rivers Wilson, the Secre-tary of the Anti-Slavery Society, Gessi and others. The original manuscript of Gordon's Khartoum Journal.

Middle East Centre, St Anthony's College, Oxford. Gordon's Crimean Diary and most of his letters to Mrs Freese.

Rhodes House, Oxford. Gordon's letters to the Revd Horace Waller and the Secretary of the Anti-Slavery Society.

Boston Public Library (U.S.A.). Gordon's letters to the Revd R. H. Barnes.

Smaller collections are in: *National Library of Scotland* (Mackinnon papers); *National Army Museum; Museum of the Royal Engineers, Chatham; Gordon Boys' School, Woking; Church Missionary Society; Royal Geographical Society; Cape Colony Archives, Cape Town.*

There are at least five private collections of Gordon's correspondence – two in Britain, two in the United States and one in Ireland.

Abdin Palace, Cairo. The Egyptian Government Archives contain many letters between Gordon and ministers in Cairo. This is probably the largest and most interesting quarry of Gordoniana still to be exploited. I do not believe any recent biographers have had access to it, but many of the letters have been published in Georges Douin, *Règne de Khedive Ismail*, 1938 and M. H. Shukry, *Equatoria under Egyptian Rule*, Cairo, 1953.

Museo dell' Africa Italiana, Rome, contains Gessi's letters to Gordon.

Public Record Office contains much material relating to Gordon's last mission to Khartoum, and a little relating to his service in China. Not all of it has been reproduced in Blue Books.

British Museum Manuscripts Room has material about Gordon in the Gladstone and Dilke papers.

Chatsworth Library contains much correspondence about Gordon between Lord Hartington, Lord Granville and Lord Wolseley.

University of Durham Library, Oriental Section, contains Col. Stewart's corres-pondence and the journals of his missions to Khartoum in 1882-3 and

1884. Also unpublished papers by Sir Reginald Wingate, Baron Malortie and others; and Cairo Intelligence Reports concerning Gordon's last mission and death in Khartoum.

1. CHARLEY GORDON

Principal Sources

H. W. Gordon, *Events in the Life of Charles George Gordon*, 1886.
Dr James Macaulay, *Gordon Anecdotes*, 1885.
General Gordon's Letters from the Crimea, the Danube and Armenia, 1884.
General Gordon, *Letters to His Sister*, 1888.

Particular References
1. B. M. Add. MS. 51294, 20 and 23 Nov. 1877; Add. MS. 51295, 5 Mar. 1879.

2. THE CRIMEA

Principal Sources

As for Chapter 1. plus:
Gordon's Crimea Diary, in Freese MSS. in St Anthony's College, Oxford.
Sir Harry Jones, *Operations connected with the Corps of Royal Engineers*, 1859.
Royal Engineers Journal, Vol. XXV, No. 4, April 1917.
A. W. Kinglake, *The Invasion of the Crimea*, Vol. VII, 1887.
Cecil Woodham-Smith, *Florence Nightingale*, 1952.

Particular References
1. B.M. Add. MSS. 52389, f. 14.
2. Barnes MSS. in Boston Public Library, 26 Sept. 1883.
3. B.M. Add. MS. 51291, 10 July 1855.
4. ibid., 30 June 1855.
5. *More about Gordon*, by One who knew him well (Mrs Freese), 1894, pp. 4–5, 12; W. E. Lilley, *Gordon at Gravesend*, 1885, pp. 21–2; *Letters to His Sister*, p. 253, footnote; Sir Gerald Graham, *Last Words with Gordon*, 1887, p. 16; F. D. Maurice and C. C. A. Arthur, *Lord Wolseley*, 1924, I, pp. 147–8; II, p. 90.
6. Gordon to Charles Harvey, 21 Sept. 1859 and 27 May 1860.

3. THE TAIPING REBELLION

Principal Sources

Gordon's correspondence with his family in B.M. Add. MSS. 52386, 52389, 51291.

P.R.O., F.O. 17, Nos. 353, 371, 374, 391.
H. W. Gordon, *Events in the Life of Charles George Gordon*, 1886.
S. Y. Tseng, *The Taiping Rebellion and the Western Powers*, 1971.
Stanley Lane Poole, *Life of Sir Harry Parkes*, 1894.
J. W. Foster (tr. and ed.), *Memoirs of Li Hung Chang*, 1913.
Thomas Lyster, Letters from, *With Gordon in China*, 1891.
A. Wilson, *The Ever Victorious Army*, 1868.
A. E. Hake, *Chinese Gordon*, 1884.
A. E. Hake, *Events in the Taiping Rebellion*, 1891.
S. Mossman, *Gordon in China*, 1875.

Particular References

1. Gordon to Charles Harvey, 25 Oct. and 13 Dec. 1860; B.M. Add. MS. 52389, ff. 218, 233.
2. Gordon to Charles Harvey, 20 Oct. and 13 Dec. 1860, 5 Feb. 1861.
3. P.R.O., F.O. 17, 371, f. 280.
4. P.R.O., F.O. 353, ff. 26–40; P.R.O., F.O. 17, 371, ff. 61–71.
5. P.R.O., F.O. 17, 391, ff. 236–9, 244–5.
6. B.M. Add. MS. 52389, f. 279.

4. THE EVER VICTORIOUS ARMY

Principal Sources

As for Chapter 3, plus:
B.M. Add. MS. 52393 for particulars of the establishment etc. of the E.V.A.
P.R.O., F.O. 17, Nos. 393, 396.
Blue Book, China, No. 3, 1864.

Particular References

1. Barnes MSS. in Boston Public Library, 26 Sept. 1883.
2. B.M. Add. MS. 52386, ff. 37–42.

5. THE GREAT GENERAL KO

Principal Sources

As for Chapter 4, plus:
B.M. Add. MS. 52387.
P.R.O., F.O. 17, No. 407.
D. C. Boulger, *The Life of Sir Halliday Macartney*, 1908.

Particular References

1. B.M. Add. MS. 52386, f. 90; Add. MS. 52389, ff. 365, 367.

2. Gordon's account of events in Soochow are in Blue Book, China, No. 3, 1864. There are further details in Boulger, op. cit., pp. 102–5.
3. B.M. Add. MS. 52386, ff. 143–7.
4. B.M. Add. MS. 52389, ff. 387–8.
5. P.R.O., F.O. 17, 047, ff. 294–6; B.M. Add. MS. 52387, ff. 43–8.
6. B.M. Add. MS. 39109, f. 201.
7. B.M. Add. MS. 52389, f. 393.
8. B.M. Add. MS. 52387, f. 110; Add. MS. 57772E, 17 Feb. 1880.
9. B.M. Add. MS. 52389, ff. 400, 439.

6. THE GRAVESEND COLONEL

Principal Sources

H. W. Gordon, *Events in the Life of Charles George Gordon*, 1886.
More about Gordon, by One who knew him well (Mrs Freese), 1894. Further correspondence between Gordon and Mrs Freese is in the Freese MSS. in St Anthony's College, Oxford, and in the Freese-Pennefather private collection.
W. E. Lilley, *General Gordon at Gravesend*, 1885.
An article by Arthur Stannard in *The Nineteenth Century*, April 1885.
Gordon's *Reflections in Palestine*, 1884, although written some years later, throws some light on the development of his religious ideas during the Gravesend period.

Particular References

1. Note in Gordon's handwriting in Freese-Pennefather MSS.
2. Gordon to Mrs Freese, 12-13 March 1869, in Freese-Pennefather MSS.
3. B.M. Add. MS. 51292, f. 165.
4. Lord Esher in *The Nineteenth Century*, June 1908, p. 934.
5. Information from Ustaz Ahmed Osman Mohed Ibrahim.
6. Gordon to Barnes, 26 Sept. 1883, in Barnes MSS. in Boston Public Library.
7. ibid., 13 Oct. 1883.
8. Information from the Very Revd Dr Isaac Cohen, Chief Rabbi of Ireland.
9. To Sir William Goodenough in Bredin MSS.
10. Nubar Pasha, *Mes Souvenirs* (unpublished), III, ff. 440–43.
11. National Army Museum, 7312-4-1, 3 Nov. 1873 and 7312-4-12, 28 Nov. 1872.

7. THE NEW BROOM

Principal Sources

Gordon's letters to Augusta in B.M. Add. MSS. 51291 and 51292, most of which have been published in General Gordon, *Letters to His Sister*, 1888, and *Colonel Gordon in Central Africa*, edited by C. Birkbeck Hill, 1881.

Gordon's letters to Mrs Freese in St Anthony's College, Oxford, and in private possession, some of which have been published in her anonymous book, *More about Gordon*, by 'One who knew him well'.
Gordon's letters to Colonel Stanton, most of which have been published in *Sudan Notes and Records*, Vol. X, 1927.
Gordon's letters to Watson in B.M. Add. MS. 41340, most of which have been published in S. Lane Poole, *Watson Pasha*, 1919.
Gordon's letters to the Revd H. Waller and to the Anti-Slavery Society in Rhodes House, Oxford.
Gordon's letters to the Khedive Ismail and Khairi Pasha. The originals are in the Abdin Palace Archives, to which I had not access. Some – perhaps all the more important – have been published in Georges Douin, *Règne de Khedive Ismail*, III, III, 1938 and in M. F. Shukry, *Equatoria under Egyptian Rule*, Cairo, 1953.
C. Chaillé-Long, *Central Africa*, 1876. *My Life in Four Continents*, 1912. *The Three Prophets*, 1884.
R. Gessi, *Seven Years in The Sudan*, 1892.
Alan Morehead, *The White Nile*, 1960, especially on the slave-trade.

Particular References

1. *The Academy*, 11 July 1885, p. 20; B.M. Add. MS. 51296, f. 272 (undated).
2. *The Nineteenth Century*, April 1885, pp. 714, 717.
3. F. C. M. Bell, *Khedives and Pashas*, 1884, pp. 5–11.
4. *The Nineteenth Century*, December 1887, pp. 856–7.
5. Nubar Pasha, *Mes Souvenirs* (unpublished), III, p. 513.
6. Church Missionary Society MS. C A6/o 10, f. 31.
7. Lytton Strachey, *Eminent Victorians*, 1918, p. 232.
8. Gordon to Sir W. Goodenough, 18 May 1874, in Bredin MSS.
9. B.M. Add. MS. 51292, ff. 12, 22, 23, 27–9; Museum of the Royal Engineers, GR 47, 17 May 1874.
10. Shukry, op. cit., pp. 179–81; B.M. Add. MS. 51303, undated (approx. Nov. 1874).
11. Douin, op. cit., III, III, pp. 31–46.
12. ibid., pp. 31–4.
13. Gordon's *Khartoum Journal*, pp. 377–8.
14. B.M. Add. MS. 47609, f. 1; Waller MSS., f. 16.

8. FRUSTRATION

Principal Sources

As for Chapter 7, less Alan Morehead, *The White Nile*.

Particular References

1. M. F. Shukry, *Equatoria under Egyptian Rule*, Cairo, 1953, pp. 138–9; B.M. Add. MS. 51303, ff. 4–7.

2. G. Douin, *Règne de Khedive Ismail*, 1938, III, III, p. 53; B.M. Add. MS. 51295, 16 June 1879.
3. B.M. Add. MS. 51294, 11 Nov. 1877; Add. MS. 52388, 12 Nov. 1879.
4. National Army Museum, 7312-4-2, 28 Aug. 1874.
5. B.M. Add. MS. 51392, ff. 60, 66–75.
6. Gordon to the Revd R. Felkin, 27 Aug. 1878, in Gordon Boys School.
7. Shukry, op. cit., p. 312.

9. THE NILE
Principal Sources

As for Chapter 8. Gordon's letters to Augusta are in B.M. Add. MSS. 51292 and 51293.

Particular References

1. G. Douin, *Règne de Khedive Ismail*, 1938, III, III, quoting unpublished notes by Linant.
2. Chaillé-Long, *My Life in Four Continents*, 1912, pp. 122–3.
3. Lytton Strachey, *Eminent Victorians*, 1918, p. 234; Long, *The Three Prophets*, 1884, p. 50.
4. Bernard Allen, *Gordon and the Sudan*, 1931, pp. 82–101; B.M. Add. MS. 51295, 23 Dec. 1881; Add. MS. 51290, 23 Apr. 1879; Add. MS. 43921, f. 186.
5. *The Academy*, 11 July 1885, p. 20.
6. B.M. Add. MS. 51292, f. 181; Add. MS. 51293, 3 Nov. 1875.
7. R. K. Mann, *The Life of Frederick Augustus Burnaby*, 1882, p. 68.
8. Uncatalogued letter to Secretary, Anti-Slavery Society, 9 Mar. 1875 in Rhodes House.
9. Waller MSS., ff. 24, 25.
10. Freese MSS., 29 June 1875; B.M. Add. MS. 51303, undated, f. 125.
11. National Army Museum, 7312-4-4, 15 Sept. 1875.
12. Douin, op. cit., III, III, p. 242; M. F. Shukry, *Equatoria under Egyptian Rule*, Cairo, 1953, pp. 311–12.
13. B.M. Add. MS. 51293, 20 Oct. and 3 Nov. 1875.
14. Sir Ronald Wingate's article, 'Sir Samuel Baker's Papers', in the *Quarterly Review*, No. 305, July 1967.

10. THE GREAT LAKES
Principal Sources

As for Chapter 9. Gordon's letters to Augusta are in B.M. Add. MS. 51293.

Particular References

1. Freese MSS., 1 Nov. and 10 Nov. 1875.

2. Waller MSS. f. 44.
3. B.M. Add. MS. 51292, ff. 174–5; Add. MS. 51293, 4. N. v. 76.
4. B.M. Add. MS. 51293, 11 Sept. 1875.
5. B.M. Add. MS. 51293, 19 May 1876; Museum of the Royal Engineers, GR 47, 31 July 1876.
6. ibid., 25 Nov. 1876; Waller MSS., f. 144; B.M. Add. MS. 51293, 28 July and 19 Oct. 1876.
7. G. Douin, *Règne de Khedive Ismail*, 1938, III, III, pp. 314–16.
8. R. Gessi, *Seven Years in the Sudan*, 1892, p. 139; W. H. Wilkins, *Life of Isobel, Lady Burton*, II, 1897, p. 653.
9. American University of Beirut, Umar Abdin Mustafa, *Thesis on Emin Pasha*.
10. E. de Leon, *The Khedive's Egypt*, 1887, pp. 290–93.
11. Douin, op. cit., III, III, p. 71.
12. B.M. Add. MS. 51293, 20 Oct. 1875.

11. THE GOVERNOR-GENERAL ON A CAMEL

Principal Sources

Gordon's letters to Augusta, as cited for Chapter 7. The originals are in B.M. Add. MSS. 51294 and 51295.
Gordon's letters to Mrs Freese, Waller and the Anti-Slavery Society as cited for Chapter 7.
Sir C. Rivers Wilson, *Chapters From My Official Life*, 1916.
H. W. Gordon, *Events in the Life of Charles George Gordon*, 1886.
Lieut. Col. J. D. H. Stewart's *Report on The Sudan*, in Blue Book, Egypt, No. 11, 1883.

Particular References

1. Nubar Pasha, *Mes Souvenirs* (unpublished), III, pp. 510–11; B.M. Add. MS. 52388, 17 Jan. 1877; Add. MS. 51294, 21 Jan. 1877.
2. B.M. Add. MS. 51294, 11 Nov. 1877; Add. MS. 52388, 12 Nov. 1879.
3. B.M. Add. MS. 51294, 16 May 1877.
4. Stewart's *Report*, p. 8.
5. B.M. Add. MS. 51294, 17 Sept. 1877.
6. Stewart's *Report*, p. 6.

12. THE GOVERNOR-GENERAL IN KHARTOUM

Principal Sources

Gordon's letters to Augusta, as cited for Chapter 7. The originals are in B.M. Add. MS. 51295.
The sources cited for Chapter 11, plus:
P. M. Holt, *The Mahdist State in the Sudan*, 1958.

Richard Hill, *Egypt in the Sudan*, 1959.

R. Gessi, *Seven Years in the Sudan*, 1892.

A. B. Wylde's *Report* on the slave trade, in F.O. Confidential Paper 3780, Nov. 1878.

A long letter from Gordon to Col. Charles Harvey, R.E., describing his abortive mission to King Johannes, in Durham University Library, Oriental Section, SAD 402/5/4.

Particular References

1. B.M. Add. MS. 51295, 23 Sept. 1878; Add. MS. 52388, 17 Jan. 1877.
2. J. D. H. Stewart, *Report on The Sudan*, Blue Book, Egypt, No. 11, p. 21.
3. B.M. Add. MS. 54495, 11 Nov. 1877.
4. B.M. Add. MS. 51295, 25 Aug. 1878; Add. MS. 54495, 26 Aug. 1878.
5. B.M. Add. MS. 51295, 24 Jan. and 27 June 1879; Add. MS. 54495, 5 July 1879.
6. Anti-Slavery Society MSS. in Rhodes House, Secretary to Gordon, June 1877; Waller MSS., ff. 85, 98.
7. James Macaulay, *Gordon Anecdotes*, 1885, p. 138; Church Missionary Society MSS. C A6/o. 11, ff. 1, 13, 15.
8. B.M. Add. MS. 51295, 13 Oct. 1879.
9. B.M. Add. MS. 54495, 23 July and 13 Oct. 1879; Add. MS. 51295, 10 Apr, 24 July, 13 Oct. 1879.
10. Museum of the Royal Engineers, GR 176 17.2176; *The Times* 22 Jan. 1880.
11. Gordon to Giegler, in private collection.
12. Museum of the Royal Engineers, GR 47, 18 May 1879.
13. Naom Chocair, *Jughrafiat wa Tarikh es Sudan*, Beirut, 1967.
14. *The Times*, 22 Feb. 1881; B.M. Add. MS. 51295, 24 Mar. 1879; Sir C. Rivers Wilson, *Chapters From My Official Life*, 1916, p. 196.
15. Gessi to Gordon, 10 May 1880, in Museo dell' Africa Italiana.
16. B.M. Add. MS. 51295, 22 Dec. 1878; Rivers Wilson, op. cit., p. 196; B.M. Add. MS. 54495, 28 Apr. 1879.
17. Rivers Wilson, op. cit., pp. 198–9.
18. Information from Mr Martin Parr, C.B.E.
19. Information from Mr G. R. F. Bredin, C.B.E.

13. THE HERO ON THE SHELF

Principal Sources

H. W. Gordon, *Events in the Life of Charles George Gordon*, 1886.

Gordon's letters to Augusta, in B.M. Add. MS. 51296, some of which have been published in *Letters to His Sister*.

Waller MSS. in Rhodes House.

National Library of Scotland Acc. 4031, 4083, 9814 for Gordon's correspondence with Mackinnon, mainly about the Congo.

Barnes MSS. in Boston Public Library.

Gordon-Harvey correspondence in private possession.
Scott MSS. in private possession.

Particular References

1. B.M. Add. MS. 43921, f. 186.
2. Sir C. Rivers Wilson, *Chapters From My Official Life*, 1916, pp. 199–200.
3. Revd R. Sinker, *Memorials of the Hon. Ion Keith Falconer*, pp. 177–8.
4. B.M. Add. MS. 43626, f. 103.
5. B.M. Add. MS. 52388, 20 Nov. 1880; Add. MS. 51296, 22 Dec. 1880.
6. W. S. Blunt, *Gordon at Khartoum*, 1911, p. 94.
7. B.M. Add. MS. 51296, 28 Mar. 1881.
8. B.M. Add. MS. 51295, 6 Nov. 1878 and 11 May 1879.
9. B.M. Add. MS. 51293, 23 Mar. 1876; Gordon to Charles Harvey, 14 Dec. 1881 and 9 Feb. 1880.
10. B.M. Add. MS. 51296, 20 Jan. 1882.
11. ibid., 17 and 18 May 1881.
12. ibid., 17 Nov. and 25 Dec. 1881; and two undated letters.
13. Museum of the Royal Engineers, GR 150.
14. Gordon's theories on the location of the Garden of Eden are set out mainly in his correspondence with W. Scott, in private possession. There are also references to this in the Waller MSS. in Rhodes House, the Mackinnon MSS. in the National Library of Scotland, and in H. W. Gordon's *Events in the Life of Charles George Gordon*.

14. THE BASUTO PROBLEM

Principal Sources

By far the most important sources are in Cape Government Archives in Cape Town, viz:
Cape Colony Blue Book, G. 6–83, which gives all the official correspondence relating to Gordon's intervention into Basuto affairs.
Unpublished autobiography by Major-General Sir Edward Brabant, Acc. 459.
Unpublished notes by Arthur Garcia, Acc. 250.
Cape Archives, C 3493.
Ena Bradlaw gives an invaluable summary of the papers in an unpublished thesis for an M.A. degree for the University of Cape Town. Copy filed in Cape Archives.

Monica Wilson and Leonard Thompson (eds.), *The Oxford History of South Africa*, 1969.
G. Tylden, *The Rise and Fall of the Basutos*, Cape Town, 1950.
Gordon's letters to Augusta in B.M. Add. MS. 51296, some of which are published in *Letters to His Sister*.
H. W. Gordon, *Events in the Life of Charles George Gordon*, 1886.
J. G. Lockhart and C. M. Woodhouse, *Rhodes*, 1963.

Particular References

1. Blue Book, G. 6–83, pp. 7, 11; Cape Archives, C 3493, p. 72.
2. B.M. Add. MS. 51296, undated, probably late Oct. or early Nov. 1882.
3. B.M. Add. MS. 51296, 6 Oct. 1882.

15. REFLECTIONS IN PALESTINE

Principal Sources

Gordon's letters to Augusta. The originals are in B.M. Add. MSS. 51297 and 51298. Some have been published in *Letters to His Sister*, 1888.
Gordon's letters to the Revd R. H. Barnes, in Boston Public Library. Some have been published in R. H. Barnes and C. E. Brown, *C. G. Gordon, a sketch with facsimile letters*, 1885.
Gordon's letters to Dr W. Scott, in private possession.
Gordon's letters to Sir W. Mackinnon, in National Library of Scotland.
H. W. Gordon, *Events in the Life of Charles George Gordon*, 1886.
Laurence Oliphant, *Haifa*, 1887.
Fortnightly Review, XXXVI, July–Dec. 1884, contains a very full summary of Gordon's researches.

Particular References

1. Lady Ann Blunt's diary for 8 Dec. 1882 in B.M. Add. MS. 53918.
2. Laurence Oliphant, op. cit., p. 274; Valentine Chirol, *Fifty Years in a Changing World*, 1927, pp. 42–3.

16. THE EXPECTED MAHDI

Principal Sources

P. M. Holt, *A Modern History of the Sudan*, 1961; *The Mahdist State in the Sudan*, 1958; Introduction to the *Memoirs of Babikr Bedri*, 1969.
Richard Hill, *Egypt in the Sudan*, 1959.
A. B. Theobald, *The Mahdiya*, 1951.
Cairo Intelligence Report Cairint 3/1/2/1/ Conf. Report No. 167, in library of the University of Durham, Oriental Section.
H. W. Gordon, *Events in the Life of Charles George Gordon*, 1886.
Lieutenant–Colonel J. D. H. Stewart's letters and journals, in the library of the University of Durham, Oriental Section.
'Gordon's Staff Officer', an article in *Blackwood's Magazine*, March 1897.
Blue Book, Egypt, No. 11, 1883.
Blue Book, Egypt, Nos. 1 and 2, 1884.
The Earl of Cromer, *Modern Egypt*, Vol. 1, 1908.
F. Power, *Letters from Khartoum during the Siege*, 1885.
E. S. C. Childers, *Life of the Right Honourable Hugh C. E. Childers*, Vol. II, 1901.

E. G. P. Fitzmaurice, *Life of Earl Granville*, Vol. II, 1905.
J. Morley, *The Life of William Ewart Gladstone*, 1903.
Roy Jenkins, *Sir Charles Dilke*, 1958.
S. L. Gwyn and G. M. Tuckwell, *Sir Charles Dilke*, II, 1917.
B. H. Holland, *Life of Spencer Compton, 8th Duke of Devonshire*, I, 1915.
W. S. Blunt, *Gordon at Khartoum*, 1911.

Particular References

1. Blunt, op. cit., pp. 11, 131, 140; B.M. Add. MS. 51298, 15 Oct. 1883;
   L. Oliphant, *Haifa*, 1887, p. 275.
2. Childers, op. cit., II, pp. 176–7; Fitzmaurice, op. cit., II, p. 381.
3. Blue Book, No. 1, pp. 130–31; Cromer, op. cit., I, pp. 379–82.
4. Gordon Boys' School, MSS.
5. B.M. Add. MS. 52388, 4 Jan. 1884.
6. *Pall Mall Gazette*, 9 Jan. 1884.
7. Blue Book, No. 2, p. 2.
8. Public Record Office, 30/29/134, 8 and 9 Jan. 1884; P.R.O. 30/29/128,
   14 Jan. 1884.
9. *Harper's Magazine*, European Edition, XXXVI, June–Nov. 1898, p. 478.
10. Chatsworth MSS., 340. 1408, Wolseley to Hartington, 4 Feb. 1884; Note
    in Lord Hartington's handwriting, B.M. Add. MS. 44147, ff. 8–14.
11. P.R.O. 30/29/128, 15 Jan. 1884.
12. Cromer, op. cit., I, pp. 426–7.
13. B.M. Add. MS. 43573, f. 89.
14. Wolseley MSS. in Brighton Municipal Library, Gordon to Wolseley,
    16 Jan. 1888; B.M. Add. MS. 51298, 17 Jan. 1884.
15. B.M. Add. MS. 51298, 19 Jan. 1884. R. H. Barnes and C. E. Brown,
    C. G. Gordon, a sketch with facsimile letters, 1885, pp. 102–3.
16. B.M. Add. MS. 43881, f. 153.
17. Blue Book, No. 2, pp. 2–3; Cromer, op. cit., I, p. 443.
18. Cromer, op. cit., I, p. 429.
19. Roy Jenkins, op. cit., p. 180; Gwyn and Tuckwell, op. cit., II, pp. 29–30.
20. Holland, op. cit., I, p. 418; P.R.O. 30/29/128, 18 and 19 Jan. 1884.
21. *Fortnightly Review*, XXXVI, July–Dec. 1884, pp. 516–27.
22. Barnes MSS., 22 Jan. 1884.
23. P.R.O., W.O. 32/6100/7700/346, 19 Sept. 1884.

17. THE ROAD TO KHARTOUM

Principal Sources

As for Chapter 16, less works by Richard Hill and A. B. Theobald.
Blue Book, Egypt, Nos. 2, 7, 12, 16, 1884.
Sir G. Graham, *Last Words with Gordon*, 1887.
In Library of the University of Durham, Oriental Section; Baron de Malortie's
Diary; Wingate MSS.

Particular References

1. B.M. Add. MS. 56451, 12 May 1884.
2. P.R.O. 30/29/162, 19 and 21 Jan. 1884.
3. Wingate MSS., 245/6; B.M. Add. MS. 56451, 22 Jan. 1884.
4. Wingate MSS., 245/3.
5. Blue Book, No. 12, pp. 38–41; P.R.O., F.O. 78/3666, 28 Jan. 1884; P.R.O., F.O. 78/4194, 17 Apr. 1884; P.R.O. 30/29/162, 8 Mar. 1884. A translation of a purported copy of the alleged letter is given in H. W. Gordon, pp. 332–7.
6. P.R.O., F.O. 78/3666, 25 Jan. 1884; B.M. Add. MS. 44629, f. 73; Earl of Cromer, *Modern Egypt*, I, *1908*, pp. 390, 444–6.
7. Wingate MSS. 245/3.
8. Blue Book, No. 2, p. 6; P.R.O. 30/29/162, 28 Jan. 1884.
9. B.M. Add. MS. 43881, ff. 146, 150, 153.
10. B.M. Add. MS. 44147, f. 25. Note dated 9 Feb., unsigned but in Gladstone's handwriting.
11. P.R.O., F.O. 78/3667, 8 Feb. 1884; Blue Book, No. 12, pp. 132–4.
12. Cromer, op. cit., I, p. 482; P.R.O., F.O. 78/3667, 8 Feb. 1884.
13. Stewart's Journal, 12 Feb. 1884.
14. ibid.
15. B. H. Holland, *Life of Spencer Compton, 8th Duke of Devonshire*, 1915, I, p. 425; Chatsworth MSS., 340. 1411 and 1417, Wolseley to Hartington, 8 and 10 Feb. 1884.

18. THE ARRIVAL AT KHARTOUM

Principal Sources

As for Chapter 17, less Sir G. Graham, *Last Words with Gordon*.
Cairo Intelligence Report Cairint 3/1/12/1 Confidential Report No. 171 in the library of the University of Durham, Oriental Section.
F. R. Wingate, 'The Siege and Fall of Khartoum', in *Sudan Notes and Records*, XIII, Part I, 1930.
Blue Book, Egypt, No. 9, 1884.

Particular References

1. Cairint 171, pp. 1–6; Blue Book, No. 9, p. 1; Blue Book, No. 12, pp. 189–90, 192.
2. Blue Book, No. 12, pp. 71–2; P.R.O., F.O. 78/4194, 18 Feb. 1884; Stewart's correspondence, 17 Feb. 1884.
3. Blue Book, No. 12, pp. 72–3; P.R.O., F.O. 78/4194, 18 Feb. 1884; P.R.O., F.O. 30/29/162, 25 Feb. 1884.
4. B.M. Add. MS. 57772D, 26 Feb. 1884.
5. Blue Book, No. 12, p. 115; P.R.O., F.O. 78/3667, 26 Feb. 1884.

6. P.R.O., F.O. 78/3668, 2 Mar. 1884; Blue Book, No. 12, pp. 152–3; Earl of Cromer, *Modern Egypt*, 1908, I, p. 499.
7. P.R.O., F.O. 3668, 3 Mar. 1884; Blue Book, No. 12, p. 156.
8. P.R.O. 30/29/162, 8 and 11 Mar. 1884.
9. B.M. Add. MS. 56451, two unsigned notes in Gladstone's handwriting, one dated 15 Mar. 1884, the other apparently written two or three days later; J. Morley, *The Life of William Ewart Gladstone*, 1903, III, pp. 159–60; S. L. Gwyn and G. M. Tuckwell, *Sir Charles Dilke*, 1917, II, p. 42; P.R.O. 30/29/128, 11 Mar. 1884.
10. Baron de Malortie's Diary, 19 Apr. 1884.
11. Cromer, op. cit., I, pp. 518–19; Blue Book, No. 12, pp. 158, 160–61.

19. THE DEFENCE OF KHARTOUM

Principal Sources

As for Chapter 18.
The Journals of Major-General C. G. Gordon at Khartoum, 1885.
Blue Book, Egypt, Nos. 13, 15, 18, 35, 1884.
G. R. F. Bredin, 'Life Story of Yuzbashi Abdullah Adlam', in *Sudan Notes and Records*, XLII, 1961, pp. 37–52.
Adrian Preston, *In Relief of Gordon; Lord Wolseley's Campaign Journal of the Gordon Relief Expedition*, 1884–5, 1967.

Particular References

1. P. M. Holt, *Mahdist State*, pp. 85, 90; *Mahdi Indharat*, Khartoum, 1964, p. 109; Dr Mohamad Ibrahim Abu Salim, *Al Murshid ila Wathaiq al Mahdi*, Khartoum, 1969, p. 128; Blue Book, No. 13, p. 8 and No. 18, p. 16.
2. F. R. Wingate, 'The Siege and Fall of Khartoum', *Sudan Notes and Records*, pp. 8–9, 12; Information from Mr Martin Parr, C.B.E.
3. Blue Book, No. 12, p. 171; B.M. Add. MS. 34475, f. 4.
4. B.M. Add. MS. 56451, 28 Mar. 1884.
5. P.R.O., F.O. 78/3669, 26 Mar. 1884; P.R.O., F.O. 78/3662, 28 Mar. 1884.
6. P.R.O., F.O. 78/3761, 18 Apr. 1884; Blue Book, No. 15, pp. 1, 3.
7. P.R.O. 30/29/162, 14 Mar. 1884; Baron de Malortie's Diary, 19 Apr. 1884; P.R.O., F.O. 78/4194, 16, 17, 19 Apr. 1884.
8. B.M. Add. MS. 56451, unsigned notes in Gladstone's handwriting, Feb. and Apr. 1885.
9. B.M. Add. MS. 56451, 11 Mar. 1888; P.R.O. 30/29/128, 20 Sep. 1884.
10. P.R.O. 30/29/134, 6 and 7 Feb. 1884.
11. ibid., 15 Mar. 1884.
12. B. H. Holland, *Life of Spencer Compton, 8th Duke of Devonshire*, 1915, I, pp. 441–3; Chatsworth MSS., 340. 1447 and 1449, Wolseley to Hartington, 11 and 13 Apr. 1884.

13. P.R.O. 30/29/134, 16 Apr. 1884.
14. B.M. Add. MS. 56451, note in Gladstone's handwriting dated 19 Apr. 1884; P.R.O. 30/29/128, 23 Apr. 1884; Blue Book, No. 13, p. 15.
15. Blue Book, No. 25, p. 30; P.R.O. 30/29/162, 14 May 1884.
16. B.M. Add. MS. 44147, f. 102; Chatsworth MSS., 390, 1449, Granville to Hartington, 19 Aug. 1884.
17. P.R.O. 30/29/128, 8 May 1884.
18. P.R.O., F.O. 78/3663, 17 May 1884.
19. B.M. Add. MS. 43875, ff. 165, 169, 171.
20. P.R.O. 30/29/163, 27 July and 12 Sep. 1884.
21. *Quarterly Review*, Vol. 305, July 1967, p. 303, quoting Wolseley to Baker, 26 July 1884; P.R.O. 30/29/128, Granville's note to Gladstone, with comment by Gladstone, headed 'Sunday morning', probably 27 July 1884.
22. B.M. Add. MS. 44147, ff. 82–7; P.R.O. 30/29/134, 15 July 1884.
23. B.M. Add. MS. 44147, f. 91; Holland, op. cit., I, p. 472.
24. Chatsworth MSS., 340, 1486, Gladstone to Granville, 1 Aug. 1884.
25. P.R.O. 30/29/128, 12 Aug. 1884; P.R.O., F.O. 14/200, 24 July 1884; B.M. Add. MS. 44147, ff. 106, 148.
26. P.R.O. 30/29/128, 19 and 22 Aug. 1884; Chatsworth MSS., 340. 1500, Hartington to Gladstone, 20 Aug. 1884.
27. P.R.O., F.O. 78/3678, 21 and 29 Sept. 1884; Preston, op. cit., p. 20, quoting Wolseley's Journal of 25 Sept. 1884.
28. Earl of Cromer, *Modern Egypt*, 1908, I, p. 578; Blue Book, No. 5, p. 122.
29. P.R.O., F.O. 141/200, 5 Oct. 1884; P.R.O. 30/29/134, 23 Sept. 1884.
30. G. W. Smalley on *Harper's Magazine*, 1898, European Edition, p. 480; P.R.O., F.O. 78/3678, 20–29 Sept. 1884; Chatsworth MSS, 340, 1535, Gladstone to Hartington, 25 Sept. 1884; and 340. 1546A, Wolseley to Hartington, 9 Oct. 1884.

20. THE DEFENDER OF KHARTOUM

Principal Sources

The Journals of Major-General C. G. Gordon, C.B., at Khartoum, 1885. The originals, in B.M. Add. MSS. 34474 and 34475, contain some very outspoken passages which have been omitted from the published version.
H. W. Gordon, *Events in the Life of Charles George Gordon*, 1886.
F. R. Wingate, 'The Siege and Fall of Khartoum', in *Sudan Notes and Records*, XIII, Part 1, 1930.
C. M. Watson, 'The Campaign of Gordon's River Steamers', in *Sudan Notes and Records*, X, Part 2, 1929.
Adrian Preston, *In Relief of Gordon; Lord Wolseley's Campaign Journal of the Gordon Relief Expedition, 1884–5*, 1967.

Particular References

1. Khartoum Archives, Maymūna Collection, y. 3. 18.
2. B.M. Add. MS. 34474, ff. 38, 55 (partly deleted).
3. ibid., f. 41.
4. B.M. Add. MS. 34475, ff. 4, 32.
5. ibid., f. 35.
6. ibid., f. 37 (partly deleted).
7. *Khartoum Journal*, pp. 206–7, and deductions from p. 271.
8. Bredin MSS., Wolseley to Goodenough, 20 Nov. 1884.
9. Preston, op. cit., pp. XXXII and 18, quoting Wolseley's Journal, 19 and 20 Sept. 1884; G. C. A. Arthur (ed), *The Letters of Lord and Lady Wolseley*, 1922, p. 119.
10. Preston, op. cit., pp. XXXIII–XXXIV.
11. *Khartoum Journal*, pp. 227, 258–9; Bredin MSS., 23 Oct. 1884.
12. Preston, op. cit., pp. XXXIV–XXXV, and p. 57, quoting Wolseley's Journal, 2 Nov. 1884.

21. THE FALL OF KHARTOUM

Principal Sources

As for Chapter 20.
Bordeini Bey's Journal, contained in F. R. Wingate, *The Sudan, Past and Present*, 1892.
Blue Book, Egypt, No. 20, 1884; Nos. 1 and 2, 1885.
Cairo Intelligence Reports, Cairint 3/1/12/1, Nos. 166, 167, 168; and Cairint 1/8/38.
Borelli Bey, *La Chute de Khartoum*, 1893.
Charles Neufeldt, *A Prisoner of the Khalifa*, 1899.
Dr Mohamad Ibrahim Abu Salim, *Al Murshid ila Wathaiq al Mahdi*, Khartoum, 1969.
Ismat Hassan Zulfu, *Karari*, Khartoum U.P., 1973, unpublished translation by Peter Clarke.
Rudolf Slatin Pasha, *Fire and Sword in the Sudan*, 1906.

Particular References

1. Preston, *In Relief of Gordon*, 1967, p. 67, quoting Wolseley's Journal of 17 Nov. 1884; P.R.O., W.O. 32/6112/7700/744, 17 Nov. 1884.
2. *Khartoum Journal*, pp. 270, 301–2, 328, 365–8, 385, 393.
3. P.R.O., F.O. 78/3860, 15 Nov. 1884; Blue Book, No. 1, 1885, p. 97, and No. 2, 1885, p. 1; Preston, op. cit., pp. 67, 102, 104, quoting Wolseley's Journal, 17 Nov. and 31 Dec. 1884, 1 Jan. 1885.
4. ibid., pp. XXXV–XXXVII, 98–100, 104–5, quoting Wolseley's Journal for 24 and 25 Dec. 1884 and 2 Jan. 1885; Blue Book, No. 2, 1885, pp. 1–3.

5. Preston, op. cit., p. XXXVI.
6. Chatsworth MSS., 340. 1612, Wolseley to Hartington, 5 Jan. 1885.
7. Bernard Allen, *Gordon and the Sudan*, 1931, p. 420; Neufeldt, op. cit., p. 301.
8. Cairint 168 and 1/8/38; Wingate, *Siege and Fall of Khartoum*, p. 68; Bordeini Bey, pp. 163–72.
9. Abu Salim, op. cit., pp. 188, 253; *Sudan Notes and Records*, XXIV, 1941, pp. 229–32.
10. Bordeini Bey's Journal, op. cit., p. 171.
11. Cairint 1/8/38.
12. Library of University of Durham, Oriental Section, Box 439/637/2.
13. Zulfu, op. cit., pp. 83–4.

INDEX

Berber—continued
224; and evacuation of Khartoum, 227, 238; telegraph line with Khartoum cut, 239; Graham wishes to push on to, 243; C.G. orders Zebeyr to, 247; Power's despatch telegraphed from, 249; rebels surround, 252; surrenders, 253; C.G.'s plans to capture, 259, 260, 261, 273; Stewart passes, 276; rumours of fall of, 280
Bessarabia, C.G. in, 22
Blue Nile, 239, 240, 241, 243, 258, 259, 260–61, 279
Blunt, Lady Ann, 180, 191
Blunt, Wilfred Scawen, 95, 168, 180, 191, 204–5, 252, 253, 267
Boers, 174, 175, 176, 177
Bogos, 123, 151, 152
Bohndorff, Friedrich, 71, 87, 89
Bombay, C.G. in, 164
Bononi, Don Luigi, 264
Bordeini Bey, 279, 284, 285n, 289, 290
Brett, Reginald, 2nd Viscount Esher, on C.G., 63; and C.G., 198, 206, 248
Britain, and China, 24, 28–9, 31; and Egypt, 187; and Sudan, 294
British Army, in Crimea, 16, 17, 20; theatres of war between 1864 and 1885, 55
Brocklehurst, Captain, 196, 206
Bruce, Sir Frederick, 28–9, 32, 51, 67
Buller, General Sir Redvers Henry, 275
Burdett-Coutts, Angela Georgina, Baroness, 253
Burgevine, Henry, 29, 31, 33, 34, 36, 45, 46
Burnaby, Captain (*later* Colonel) Frederick, 288; on C.G. at Sobat, 97; death of, 287
Burton, Sir Richard, 95, 96, 116, 131, 195
Buzacott, Aaron, 145

Cairo, 69–70, 96, 137, 147, 151, 193, 210–11, 254, 258, 274
Cambridge, Prince George, Duke of, and C.G., 122, 194–5, 206, 248
Campbell, Major William, 71, 81, 87, 88, 121
Cape Colony, 172–3, 174, 175, 179
Capsune, 149, 182, 234
Cardwell, Lady, 230
Cetewayo, Zulu King, C.G. on, 174
Chamberlain, Joseph, 249
Chatham, 23, 25
Childers, Erskine, 195, 205
China, Tz'u-hsi, Empress Dowager of, 24, 29
Chinese, 35, 43, 53
Chinese Imperialist Army, 29, 30, 31, 32, 41, 49
Ching, General, 31, 35, 36, 40, 41, 43, 47, 48–9
Chippendall, Lieutenant H. W., C.G. and, 72, 80, 121, 166; C.G. on, 92; surveyor, 93; unavailable, 97; his carelessness in Nile exploration, 100; strained relations between C.G. and, 100–101; his affection for C.G., 101; on C.G., 119, 120

Christianity, Hung-sen-Tsuen and, 26; C.G.'s conversion to, 38; and transmigration of souls, 128; Christians massacred in Alexandria, 187
Chung Wang (the Faithful King), 27, 28, 31, 45, 46, 47, 53
Chunyi, 41
Coetlogon, Colonel de, 194, 226, 229, 247
Congo, Belgian, 163, 180, 186, 196, 199, 200
Cooksley, Captain, 40
Crimean War, 16, 17, 18, 19, 20–21, 39
Cuzzi, Giuseppe, 224, 245, 254, 264

Daily News, 67
Daily Telegraph, Stanley's letter to, 105
Dara, 127, 128, 131, 132
Darfur, 92, 123, 124, 126, 130, 131, 147, 197 *and* n, 211, 214–15, 217
Davidson, Captain, 45
Debbah, 268, 273, 275, 277, 278, 280
Dervishes, 189, 192, 194, 254, 258, 273–4, 279, 287, 288, 289, 291
Diego Garcia, 170
Dilke, Sir Charles Wentworth, 169, 202, 216, 232, 233, 247, 248–9, 268
Disraeli, Benjamin, 65, 139, 169
Dongola, 136, 250, 255, 257, 258, 262–3, 267, 268, 275, 276, 277
Dongola, Mahmoud el Haj Mohamad, *Mudir* of, 244, 257
Dongolawi, 188, 228, 290
Donnelly, Colonel, 167, 169
Douin, Georges, 78–9
Drew, Captain and Mrs, 15
Dufferin and Ava, Frederick Temple Blackwood, 1st Marquess of, 193
Dufilé, 91, 92, 93, 98, 109, 117
Dykes, Miss, 69

Earle, General William, 271
Egerton, Edwin, 256, 267–9
Egypt (*see also* Cairo), C.G. on extortion by Europeans in, 68–9; growth of public debt, 70; and Tana river, 96; and Uganda, 114; and Abyssinia, 123, 151–3; dependent on Britain and France, 152; C.G. leaves, 155; British occupation of, 187; British public opinion on, 194; change of government in, 196; Zebeyr demands compensation from, 247; British contingent remains in, 293; and Sudan, 294
Egyptian Army, 150, 280n, 293
Egyptians, 84, 105, 106, 112, 157, 272, 278, 290
El Obeid, 128, 134, 149, 190, 192, 243, 264
el Obeid, Sheikh, 224, 238, 279
Elgin, James Bruce, 8th Earl of, 24, 25
Elphinstone, Colonel Sir Howard, 170
Emin Effendi, 113, 117, 118, 155
Enderby, Samuel, 13
Equatoria, extent of province of, 76; fauna of, 76–7, 81, 85, 86, 93, 109; its dependence on Khartoum, 79; climate, 80, 120; C.G.'s

Khartoum, 263; his journals, 263–4, 266, 268, 269, 270, 271, 281, 282, 288; language barrier, 263, 266; allows disaffected troops to join Mahdi, 265; his clerks, 265; his servants, 266; admits to insubordination, 268; in difficulty without cypher-books, 268, 277–8, 280–81; preparations to receive relief force, 270; impossibility of leaving Khartoum with honour, 271; stock-taking of resources, 272–3; advises relief force, 273–4, 283; his detailed programme for relief force, 274; expects relief force in mid-November, 275; in deep distress, 276; battle casualties, 278–9; his contempt for enemy long-range fire, 279–80; declares he will not leave Sudan, 280; message to 'all Confederate Powers', 284; differing accounts of his death, 290–91; public reaction to his death, 293
Gordon, Elizabeth, née Enderby, C.G.'s mother, 13, 36, 63, 66
Gordon, Enderby, C.G.'s brother, 14, 17, 65, 163
Gordon, Frederick, C.G.'s brother, 65
Gordon, Mrs Frederick, 65, 119
Gordon, Henry (*later* Sir Henry), C.G.'s brother, 14, 17, 25, 65, 123, 201, 206, 212, 255
Gordon, Henry William, C.G.'s father, 13, 56
Gordon, Major General Sir William, 60
Graham, Colonel Gerald, 22, 123, 202, 211, 215, 219, 233, 243, 244, 274, 282
Granville, George Leveson-Gower, 2nd Earl, 200; and rebellion in Egypt, 190, 194; C.G. recommended to, 195, 198; on C.G., 199, 216; and C.G.'s proposed mission to Sudan, 202–3, 205; and C.G., 206, 217, 223; his justifiable anxiety, 207; C.G. sends proclamations to, 209; Baring writes to, 210, 212, 230; on the press, 216; and slave-trade, 230, 235; and appointment of Zebeyr, 230, 232, 235; reproves Baring, 236; Baring advises on Graham, 243; proposals over Berber, 244; in state of indecision over C.G. in Khartoum, 245; and recall of C.G., 248; and relief force for Khartoum, 249; Hartington and, 250, 256; complains of non-communication by C.G., 252; and Blunt, 253; Gladstone and, 256, 257; attacked in C.G.'s journal, 269, 270
Great Lakes, glamour attached to, 110

Hadendowa, 189, 193, 210, 216
Hake, Egmont, 212
Halfaya, 240, 242, 265, 282, 289
Hamilton, E. W., 210
Hangchow, 27, 36, 51
Hansal, Martin, 78, 94, 227, 263, 291
Harar, 123, 124, 140
Harcourt, Sir William Vernon, Home Secretary, 249
Haroun al Rashid, 127, 131, 134, 147, 149
Hart, Sir Robert, gives C.G. advice, 51, 53

Hartington, Spencer Compton Cavendish, Marquess of, 216; and C.G., 198, 199; and C.G.'s proposed mission to Sudan, 202, 204, 205; Wolseley advises, 223, 250, 255; and appointment of Zebeyr, 237; Queen telegraphs, 244; and Gladstone, 248; and extrication of C.G. from Khartoum, 248, 249, 250, 256; widely respected, 255; threatens resignation, 256; Gladstone on significance of letter from, 256; believes C.G. unable to send messages, 257; suggests consulting Wolseley, 260; Wolseley warns about C.G., 260, 284; instructions to Wolseley, 284
Hassan Pasha Helmi, 127, 134
Hassan Wassif, Lieutenant, 73, 74
Herbin, M., 227, 266; leaves Khartoum with Stewart, 261; reported killed, 275
Hicks Pasha, William, 193, 194, 272
Hill, Dr Birbeck, 166, 170
Hong Kong, 24
Hope, Admiral Sir James, 28
Hung-sen-Tsuen (Tien Wang, the Heavenly King), 26, 27, 28, 31, 53
Hussein Pasha Khalifa, *Mudir* of Berber, 217, 220, 221, 222, 244, 253, 254
Hussein Pasha Serri, 224, 228

Ibrahim, 110, 111
Ibrahim Abdel Qadir, 264–5
Ibrahim Fauzi, 80, 144, 215, 254
Ibrahim Rushdi, 265
Idris Abtar, 134, 144
India, Ripon Viceroy of, 163; C.G. on, 164; C.G. on Europeans in, 165; safe route to, 170
Indians, C.G. prejudiced against, 163
Ireland, C.G.'s views on, 167–8
Islam, attitude to slavery, 74–5, 129; C.G.'s attitude to, 89–90, 128; and male chastity, 158; Sudanese Moslems, 159; belief in a Mahdi, 188; Zebeyr and, 213; Slatin adopts, 218; Mahdi's prisoners-of-war profess, 242; and conditions of peace settlement, 286
Ismail, Khedive, his gift of persuasion, 70; his extravagance, 70; and C.G., 70, 71, 110, 116, 122, 150, 161; and lack of co-operation between C.G. and Ismail Ayoub, 79; and slave-trade, 80, 92; C.G. shocks, 83; C.G.'s loyalty to, 96, 145; British Government and, 96; and Great Lakes, 112; his troops in Uganda, 114, 115; decorates C.G., 115; his cruelty to Ismail Sadyk, 116; and elephants as transport, 117, 135; makes C.G. Governor-General of Sudan, 123; and Walad al Michael, 123; and Zebeyr, 127, 150; his finances, 137–9, 150; and Raouf Pasha, 140n; and Sudan Railway, 143; C.G. on, 150, 281; deposed, 150
Ismail Pasha Ayoub, 73, 74, 77, 78, 79, 80, 114, 126
Ismail Pasha Sadyk, 116

FINE WORKS OF NON-FICTION
AVAILABLE IN QUALITY
PAPERBACK EDITIONS FROM
CARROLL & GRAF